ON INFORMATION TECHNOLOGY

Video education courses are available on these topics through
National Education Training Group, 1751 West Diehl Road,
Naperville, IL 60563-9099 (tel: 800-526-0452 or 708-369-3000).

Database	Telecommunications	Networks and Data Communications	Society
AN END USER'S GUIDE TO DATABASE	TELECOMMUNICATIONS AND THE COMPUTER (third edition)	PRINCIPLES OF DATA COMMUNICATION	THE COMPUTERIZED SOCIETY
	COMMUNICATIONS SATELLITE SYSTEMS	TELEPROCESSING NETWORK ORGANIZATION	TELEMATIC SOCIETY: A CHALLENGE FOR TOMORROW
COMPUTER DATABASE ORGANIZATION (third edition)	**Distributed Processing**	SYSTEMS ANALYSIS FOR DATA TRANSMISSION	TECHNOLOGY'S CRUCIBLE
MANAGING THE DATABASE ENVIRONMENT (second edition)	COMPUTER NETWORKS AND DISTRIBUTED PROCESSING	DATA COMMUNICATION TECHNOLOGY	VIEWDATA AND THE INFORMATION SOCIETY
DATABASE ANALYSIS AND DESIGN	DESIGN AND STRATEGY FOR DISTRIBUTED DATA PROCESSING	DATA COMMUNICATION DESIGN TECHNIQUES	**SAA**: Systems Application Architecture
VSAM: ACCESS METHOD SERVICES AND PROGRAMMING TECHNIQUES	**Client/Server**	SNA: IBM's NETWORKING SOLUTION	SAA: COMMON USER ACCESS
DB2: CONCEPTS, DESIGN, AND PROGRAMMING	CLIENT/SERVER DATABASES: ENTERPRISE COMPUTING	LOCAL AREA NETWORKS: ARCHITECTURES AND IMPLEMENTATIONS (second edition)	SAA: COMMON COMMUNICATIONS SUPPORT: DISTRIBUTED APPLICATIONS
IDMS/R: CONCEPTS, DESIGN, AND PROGRAMMING	ENTERPRISE NETWORKING: STRATEGIES AND TRANSPORT PROTOCOLS	DATA COMMUNICATION STANDARDS	SAA: COMMON COMMUNICATIONS SUPPORT: NETWORK INFRASTRUCTURE
Security	ENTERPRISE NETWORKING: DATA LINK SUBNETWORKS	COMPUTER NETWORKS AND DISTRIBUTED PROCESSING: SOFTWARE, TECHNIQUES, AND ARCHITECTURE	SAA: COMMON PROGRAMMING INTERFACE
SECURITY, ACCURACY, AND PRIVACY IN COMPUTER SYSTEMS		TCP/IP NETWORKING: ARCHITECTURE, ADMINISTRATION, AND PROGRAMMING	

OBJECT-ORIENTED METHODS
Pragmatic Considerations

A _James Martin_ **BOOK**

THE JAMES MARTIN BOOKS
currently available from Prentice Hall

- Application Development Without Programmers
- Building Expert Systems
- Client/Server Databases: Enterprise Computing
- Communications Satellite Systems
- Computer Data-Base Organization, Second Edition
- Computer Networks and Distributed Processing: Software, Techniques, and Architecture
- Data Communication Technology
- DB2: Concepts, Design, and Programming
- Design and Strategy of Distributed Data Processing
- An End User's Guide to Data Base
- Enterprise Networking: Data Link Subnetworks
- Enterprise Networking: Strategies and Transport Protocols
- Fourth-Generation Languages, Volume I: Principles
- Fourth-Generation Languages, Volume II: Representative 4GLs
- Fourth-Generation Languages, Volume III: 4GLs from IBM
- Future Developments in Telecommunications, Second Edition
- Hyperdocuments and How to Create Them
- IBM Office Systems: Architectures and Implementations
- IDMS/R: Concepts, Design, and Programming
- Information Engineering, Book I: Introduction and Principles
- Information Engineering, Book II: Planning and Analysis
- Information Engineering, Book III: Design and Construction
- An Information Systems Manifesto
- Local Area Networks: Architectures and Implementations, Second Edition
- Managing the Data-Base Environment
- Object-Oriented Analysis and Design
- Object-Oriented Methods: A Foundation
- Object-Oriented Methods: Pragmatic Considerations
- Principles of Data-Base Management
- Principles of Data Communication
- Principles of Object-Oriented Analysis and Design
- Recommended Diagramming Standards for Analysts and Programmers
- SNA: IBM's Networking Solution
- Strategic Information Planning Methodologies, Second Edition
- System Design from Provably Correct Constructs
- Systems Analysis for Data Transmission
- Systems Application Architecture: Common User Access
- Systems Application Architecture: Common Communications Support: Distributed Applications
- Systems Application Architecture: Common Communications Support: Network Infrastructure
- Systems Application Architecture: Common Programming Interface
- TCP/IP Networking: Architecture, Administration, and Programming
- Technology's Crucible
- Telecommunications and the Computer, Third Edition
- Telematic Society: A Challenge for Tomorrow
- VSAM: Access Method Services and Programming Techniques

with Carma McClure

- Action Diagrams: Clearly Structured Specifications, Programs, and Procedures, Second Edition
- Diagramming Techniques for Analysts and Programmers
- Software Maintenance: The Problem and Its Solutions
- Structured Techniques: The Basis for CASE, Revised Edition

OBJECT-ORIENTED METHODS
Pragmatic Considerations

JAMES MARTIN
and
JAMES J. ODELL

PRENTICE HALL P T R
Upper Saddle River, New Jersey 07458

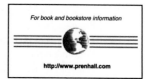

For book and bookstore information

http://www.prenhall.com

Library of Congress Cataloging-in-Publication Data

Martin, James (date)
   Object-oriented methods : pragmatic considerations / James Martin
and James J. Odell.
      p. cm.
   "The James Martin books"—Half t.p.
   ISBN 0-13-630864-3
   1. Object-oriented programming (Computer science) I. Odell,
James J. II. Title.
QA76.64.M3723 1996
005.1'2—dc20   95-38074
                                      CIP

Editorial/production supervision: *Kathryn Gollin Marshak*
Liaison: *Beth Sturla*
Jacket design: *Lundgren Graphics*
Cover design director: *Jerry Votta*
Manufacturing manager: *Alexis Heydt*
Acquisitions editor: *Paul Becker*

Published by Prentice Hall P T R
Prentice-Hall, Inc.
A Simon & Schuster Company
Upper Saddle River, New Jersey 07458

The publisher offers discounts on this book when ordered
in bulk quantities. For more information write:
        Corporate Sales Department, Prentice Hall P T R
        One Lake Street
        Upper Saddle River, New Jersey 07458
        Phone: (800) 382-3419; Fax: (201) 236-7141
        E-mail: corpsales@prenhall.com

Printed in the United States of America

10 9 8 7 6 5 4 3 2 1

ISBN 0-13-630864-3

Prentice-Hall International (UK) Limited, *London*
Prentice-Hall of Australia Pty. Limited, *Sydney*
Prentice-Hall Canada Inc., *Toronto*
Prentice-Hall Hispanoamericana, S.A., *Mexico*
Prentice-Hall of India Private Limited, *New Delhi*
Prentice-Hall of Japan, Inc., *Tokyo*
Simon & Schuster Asia Pte. Ltd., *Singapore*
Editora Prentice-Hall do Brasil, Ltda., *Rio de Janeiro*

TO CORINTHIA
—*JM*

TO HEPHZIBAH TABITHA
—*JO*

Contents

19 Group Facilitation Techniques *267*

20 User Workshop Techniques *281*

21 Interviewing Techniques *291*

22 Domain Experts *299*

23 Prototyping *311*

24 Timebox Development *323*

Preface

The goal of *Object-Oriented Methods: Pragmatic Considerations* is to convey practical methods, techniques, and guidelines for building systems using an OO approach. In doing so, *Pragmatic Considerations* addresses all phases of the system development lifecycle—including those that plan, analyze, design, construct, and transition systems. Furthermore, this book incorporates various technologies into the development lifecycle, such as client/server, business reengineering, rapid application development (RAD), artificial intelligence (AI), relational databases, traditional programming languages, and object-oriented technology. The format of the book is as follows:

- Part I discusses how methodologies should be constructed and used—both now and in the future.
- Part II discusses nine major diagramming techniques currently used to model system requirements. It also provides the step-by-step methods for constructing three of these diagrams.
- Part III describes how OO program code can be generated using design templates (or patterns). It begins with a chapter describing the basics of OO languages. The remaining chapters specify how this code can be generated directly from the models described in Part II.
- Part IV addresses ways to implement OO concepts using non-OO implementations, such as relational databases, COBOL, and non-OO legacy code, in general. Additionally, it presents three approaches using AI and discusses how they can be deployed using OO technology.
- Part V discusses techniques that should be used for individuals as well as teams. These include JAD, JRP, JEM, and RAD workshops, interviewing and facilitation techniques, prototyping, and timebox management.
- Part VI addresses other issues that are important to the system developer. These include the concepts and practice of reusability, standards for object interaction, and the future of software.
- Part VII contains a methodology cookbook that can be used right now for a wide variety of projects. The methodology addresses the complete system development lifecycle and contains methods for developing object-oriented and client/server systems. It also suggests ways in which BPR and AI efforts can be integrated into the system development project.

Pragmatic Considerations is also meant to be a reference book. In particular, Parts II, III, and VIII provide step-by-step guidance for building software systems. These steps provide the developer with general plans as well as detailed methods and techniques for constructing the next generation of automated systems.

The companion volume, *Object-Oriented Methods: A Foundation,* presents the basic, underlying ideas required to specify systems. Just having the building blocks to specify systems, though, is not enough. The system developer also needs to know *how* to specify and construct the system using *Pragmatic Considerations.* Knowing *just* the foundation resembles learning the notes without learning how to compose and play the music. Both the *what* and the *how* are required. One without the other results in cacophony.

This book is the last in the series that replaces *Object-Oriented Analysis and Design.*

James Martin
James J. Odell

ACKNOWLEDGEMENTS

This book includes significant portions of a full lifecycle OO methodology developed by James Martin & Co. It represents the result of many years of experience and intensive development by its staff and management.

I particularly wish to express my appreciation to Brad Kain who generously contributed several chapters. I also wish to acknowledge the important contributions of Curt Hall, Paul Harmon, and Martin Fowler, who also provided chapters for this book. Each brought a different perspective that dramatically expanded its breadth and depth. I am indebted to Kevin Murphy, Sue Rosenberg, Manni Kantipudi, Joy Campbell, and Ben Stivers for the effort each invested in reviewing and commenting on various portions of the manuscript. I would also like to acknowledge John Edwards for his many years of research and development of conceptual schemas and the foundations of paradigms. Finally, I would like to express particular appreciation to Andrea L. Matthies, who had the monumental task of integrating the works of multiple contributors. Not only did she transform our respective texts, she made our different voices blend.

James J. Odell

METHODOLOGY

There is more than one approach to developing systems: there always will be and always should be. Different tasks have different characteristics that require different kinds of approaches. The challenge is in the selection and integration of these approaches. Chapter 1 discusses how methodologies can be engineered. Chapter 2 discusses the effect of object orientation on system-development methodologies. It also addresses the necessary system-development lifecycle (SDLC) phases and scheduling considerations for an OO system-development project.

Method Engineering

INTRODUCTION

A *methodology* is a body of methods employed by a discipline.

A *method* is a procedure for attaining something.

Method engineering is the coordinated and systematic approach to establishing work methods.

Traditional methodologies for information system (I.S.) development are—by nature—general purpose. As such, they contain an ideal set of methods, techniques, and guidelines that in reality can never be followed literally. They must be tuned to the situation at hand. Steps are sometimes omitted, added, or modified. Guidelines are often modified or ignored to fit special circumstances, such as technology, development expertise, the application, and external factors.

To complicate matters further, numerous methodologies exist for I.S. development—each with its own set of tools and techniques. Comparing and selecting an approach from this methodological "jungle" is confusing and difficult. To aid in this selection, various comparison standards have been proposed for object-oriented methodologies, such as those documented by the Object Management Group, or OMG [Hutt, 1994a; 1994b]. Some approaches attempt to harmonize several methodologies—forming yet another rigid methodology [Coleman, 1994]. Other methodologies provide a choice of options, or *paths*, that the user can select depending on the circumstances. In short, an I.S. project can choose from three basic methodologies, as depicted in Fig. 1.1.

METHOD ENGINEERING

Flexibility without control can hardly be considered a methodology, since any systematic and coordinated approach to establishing work methods is absent. For such an approach to be systematic and coordinated requires method engineering.

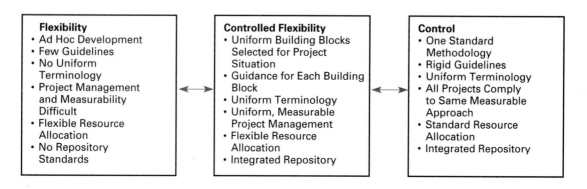

Flexibility
- Ad Hoc Development
- Few Guidelines
- No Uniform Terminology
- Project Management and Measurability Difficult
- Flexible Resource Allocation
- No Repository Standards

Controlled Flexibility
- Uniform Building Blocks Selected for Project Situation
- Guidance for Each Building Block
- Uniform Terminology
- Uniform, Measurable Project Management
- Flexible Resource Allocation
- Integrated Repository

Control
- One Standard Methodology
- Rigid Guidelines
- Uniform Terminology
- All Projects Comply to Same Measurable Approach
- Standard Resource Allocation
- Integrated Repository

Figure 1.1   Methodological approaches fall into three categories (based on Harmsen [Harmsen, 1994]).

Method engineering produces methodologies. For I.S., a methodology is a body of methods employed to develop automated systems. In turn, a method defines the steps needed to automate a system—along with the required techniques and tools and the anticipated products. Adapting a methodology to the needs of a particular project is sometimes called *situational method engineering*. For I.S., situational method engineering designs, constructs, and adapts I.S. development methods.

As indicated in Fig. 1.2, method engineering has various degrees of flexibility. These are:

- *Use of a rigid methodology.* At one extreme, using a rigid methodology permits virtually no flexibility. Such methodologies are based on a single development philosophy and thus adopt fixed standards, procedures, and techniques. Project managers are typically not permitted to modify the methodology.

- *Selection from rigid methodologies.* Instead of permitting only one rigid approach, this option allows each project to choose its methodology from one of several rigid method-

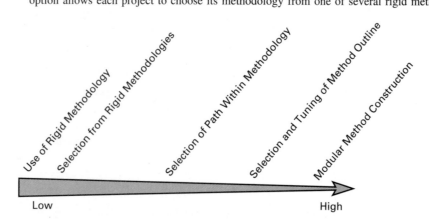

Figure 1.2   Degrees of flexibility for I.S. situational method engineering (based on Harmsen [Harmsen, 1994]).

ologies. This makes possible the selection of an approach that might be more appropriate for the project. However, this is a bit like buying a suit without having it altered. You make the best of what is available, despite the fact that the chosen methodology will probably not fit the project perfectly. Furthermore, each methodology involves additional purchase and training costs.

- *Selection of paths within a methodology.* Many methodologies permit more flexibility by providing a choice of predefined paths within the methodology. Typical development paths include traditional and rapid application development. Some methodologies now include paths that support development aspects, such as package selection, pilot projects, client/server, realtime, knowledge-based systems, and object orientation. A common disadvantage, however, is that it may not be possible to combine some options. For instance, realtime, knowledge-based projects may not be supported.

- *Selection and tuning of a method outline.* This option permits each project to both select methods from different approaches and tune them to the project's needs. Typically, this involves selecting a global method process and data model. These models, then, are further adapted and refined by the project. This option is best supported by an automated tool.

- *Modular method construction.* One of the most flexible options is that of generating a methodology for a given project from predefined building blocks. Each building block is a method fragment that is stored in a method base. Using rules, these building blocks are assembled based on a project's profile. The result is an effective, efficient, complete, and consistent methodology for the project.

An automated tool is recommended for this option. Performing the entire activity manually would require much work and time. Here a project's methodology can be generated automatically and then adapted and further refined by the project manager. Such an option is illustrated in Fig. 1.3.

COMPUTER-AIDED METHOD ENGINEERING

Computer-Aided Software Engineering (CASE) automates automation. In contrast, Computer-Aided Method Engineering (CAME) automates the assembly of methods. A CAME tool should support the following activities [Harmsen, 1994]:

- *Definition and evaluation of contingency rules and factors.* In order to choose the right method fragments for a project, rules and factors for selecting the proper method fragments must be defined. Method engineers are responsible for these definitions. Given the project profile and method base, the CAME tool selects and assembles the appropriate methodology.

- *Storage of method fragments.* Selecting and assembling a methodology from method fragments requires a *method base.* This method base is the repository from which method engineers and the CAME tool can select various method fragments. As new methodologies arise, they can also be incorporated into the method base.

- *Retrieval and composition of method fragments.* Certainly, for a CAME tool to generate a methodology from a method base, retrieval operations must be available for method fragments. However, total automation of methodology generation may never be completely feasible. A more realistic scenario could involve both automatic generation and a method engineer. The method engineer should be able to manipulate and modify method fragments within a methodology.

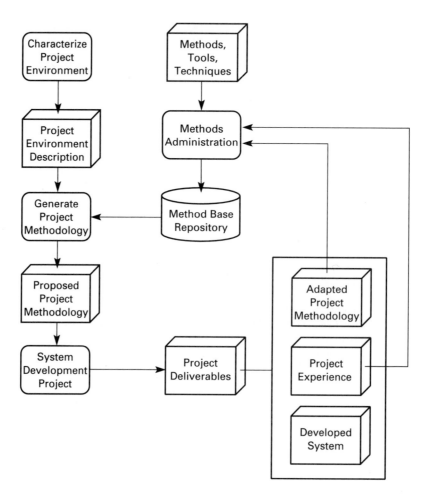

Figure 1.3   An object-flow diagram specifying the process of modular method construction.

- *Validation and verification of the generated methodology.* The CAME tool should not only support selecting and assembling a methodology, but should also check the results. The tool should thus incorporate guidelines to ensure that the correct set of method fragments has been selected. Furthermore, the tool should ensure that the fragments are assembled in a consistent manner. In other words, the CAME tool should ensure, or assist in ensuring, the quality of the generated methodology. (After all, generated methodologies must meet the same standards as standards methodologies.)

- *Adaptation of the generated methodology.* The method base should also accumulate the experience of previous projects and their methodologies. This experience, illustrated in Fig. 1.4, should be used to improve method fragments, along with their contingency rules and factors. In other words, practical experience should be used to adapt future methodologies.

- *Integration with a meta-CASE tool.* CAME and CASE tools should eventually be integrated. When a methodology is generated for a particular project, the appropriate supporting tools should also be integrated. Adapting a CASE tool in this fashion would require configuring the CASE tool to support the resulting methodology. In other words, a meta-CASE tool would be required so that techniques and diagrammatic representations can be defined based on the methodology. Such a tool would be similar in nature to the CAME tool. Within this meta-CASE tool, CASE fragments would have to be defined. Additionally, it would require the ability to retrieve and compose new conceptual fragments.

- *Interface with a method base.* This method base is the repository for the various method fragments from which method engineers and the CAME tool can select.

To support CAME, the I.S. organization requires two additional roles: the *method engineer* and the *method administrator*. The method administrator is responsible for the contents of the method base. The method engineer is responsible for generating the right methodology for each project. Both these positions support and are supported by the CAME tool—and are part of a larger framework called *process management*.

PROCESS MANAGEMENT

To support applications systems, the repository must of course contain information about the *product* of I.S. development. This includes information regarding analysis results, such as structural and behavioral models, business rules, and so on. For design and implementation, the repository would include information such as design templates, application data structures, programs, and interfaces. These kinds of information are indicated by the last three items depicted for the repository in Fig. 1.4.

Additionally, the development repository must also contain *process*-related information, such as intermediate results, human agents, tools involved, process plans, design

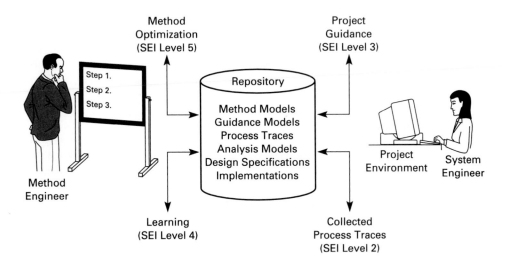

Figure 1.4   An environment for process management.

decisions, and steps taken to execute them. These items are depicted in the top three items for the repository. These include:

- *The method models.* Contain not only the method fragments described earlier, but also a meta-model for handling the process-related information.

- *The guidance models.* Guide the system engineer according to a recommended or enforced way of working. They also give a structure by which process traces should be carried out.

- *The process traces.* Track the various development components as they change during the system development process. The guidance model describes the intended tracing. This portion of the repository contains the tracking instances.

SEI Support

The Software Engineering Institute (SEI) has been influential in the movement toward high-quality products. Its framework proposes five levels of process maturity: initial, repeatable, defined, managed, and optimizing [Paulk, 1993]. This same framework can be applied to process management.

Jarke recommends several kinds of SEI-related actions that should be performed to ensure a high-quality, process-management environment [Jarke, 1994]. These are illustrated in Fig. 1.4. At the *initial* level, an organization does not provide a stable environment. Here, no repository exists. At the *repeatable* level, policies for managing a project and procedures to implement those policies are established. The planning and management of new projects are based on experience with similar projects. This is aided by capturing process traces, as indicated in the lower right of the figure. At the *defined* level, an organization standardizes both its system engineering and management processes. Such an organization exploits effective software-engineering practices when standardizing its processes. Furthermore, an organization's process standards are tailored so that each project can develop its own *defined* processes, as indicated in the upper right of Fig. 1.4. Once this has been established, the organization can introduce procedures for measuring the actual process execution. At this *managed* level, the organization learns to predict trends in processes and product quality. This action is depicted in the lower left of the figure. Finally, at the *optimizing* level, the entire organization is focused on continuous process improvement, seen in the upper left of Fig. 1.4.

Method Models

Figure 1.3 illustrates how a method repository can be used to assemble the method fragments for a given project environment. To do this, the repository must include a method model containing the defined method fragments. If an organization prefers an *activity-driven* approach to defining its project environment, groupings of method fragments are selected to support a given kind of activity. For instance in problem-solving situations, a project methodology could be based on finding and executing a set of *actions* leading to a solution. However, many organizations prefer a *product-driven* approach that defines the deliverables, or *products*, first. The *actions* capable of producing these products are then identified.

Another approach suggested by Jarke is one that is *contextually driven* [Jarke, 1994]. Method engineers in this approach produce a methodology based on the project's situation and utilizing knowledge gained from previous situations. *Contexts*, then, are not only based on *situations*, but on *decisions* made in similar contexts. Additionally, the *arguments* that support or object to a particular context should also be available when generating a project's methodology. The meta-model depicted in Fig. 1.5 illustrates these concepts.

Guidance Models

As discussed earlier, a methodology is a body of methods. It specifies the route a system project will follow to transform the initial requirements into a final product that satisfies the quality criteria. Each of these methods is stored in a repository as a procedural module, called a *method fragment*. A methodology also prescribes the use of certain techniques and tools.

To generate a given project's methodology, a guidance mechanism is needed. The guidance mechanism is a pattern-matching engine which matches products against situations in the repository. Once a match is found, the engine suggests decisions based on method fragment definitions. A guidance model, then, must support the mechanism by

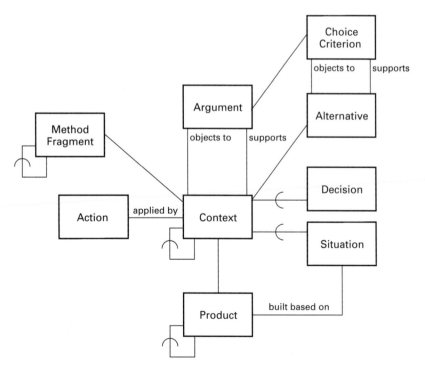

Figure 1.5   A meta-model depicting some of the concepts required for a process-management repository.

aiding the processes of decision making and problem solving and by supporting top-down or bottom-up approaches.

Process Traces

As mentioned earlier, traceability allows us to track the various development components as they change during the system development process. Traceability is important to the development process for many reasons [Ramesh, 1993]: support for product change and reuse; identifying critical requirements and components; recording design rationale; project tracking and cost estimates; responsibility and accountability for fulfilling requirements; interdependencies between documents and components within and across lifecycle stages; and evaluation and improvement of methods.

During the course of a project, process traces are recorded about a variety of things. The most common practice is to trace specification and representation changes. As illustrated in Fig. 1.6, the specification of a project's system often begins when it is little more than a vague idea. As the project progresses, the developers' understanding of the system increases and its requirements are recorded. The goal is to reach an agreement on the system's requirements and to specify these requirements completely. The process traces

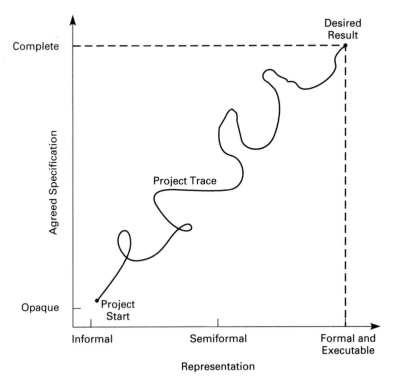

Figure 1.6 Traceability requires tracking the specification and representation path of a project.

should record the various steps in producing the specification. Here, the tracking process should be tied to the methodology and the method fragments generated for the project. Since an agreed-upon specification requires consensus, the team should also track its progress in terms of choices, arguments, positions, issues, decisions, and revised decisions.

Each requirement in a specification will be represented in some manner. This representation can be informal, such as prose or drawings. Or, it can be semiformal using modeling approaches, such as data-flow diagrams, functional decompositions, action diagrams, and entity/relationship diagrams. For any system to function, it must eventually be represented in a formal manner that is executable. This representation can be a programming language. It can also be some other formal representation that can produce an executable system, such as the rules, event diagrams, and object diagrams described by Odell in the previous volume [Martin, 1995]. The tracing process, then, should track these various representations along with their connection to each other and to the agreed-upon specifications. Since many representations require consensus, the team should also track its progress of representation choices, arguments, and so on.

CAME TOOLS

CAME tools are being developed by many organizations around the world. As discussed above, CAME tools automate and control the application development processes, enabling the method engineer to develop fast, fluid, and flexible processes. These tools should increase planning, management, and development efficiency by providing tighter controls over each development project as it evolves. Furthermore, CAME tools ensure that methods are designed to be reusable and can be continually revised and improved through integration of best practices from previous projects.

A CAME tool is typically used for process management in four distinct modes: defining the process, planning the project, delivering the project, and improving the process.

- *Defining the process.* Method components are created based on specific enterprise needs and characteristics. This ensures a successful foundation for a project. New method components can also be added to the library. The focus is on reusability and the intent that the processes will be used by project teams. Figure 1.7 depicts an example of a method components entry screen from Ernst & Young's Automated Methods Environment (AME) tool. This is also the stage where estimating elements are added and individual software tools are linked to method components as possible development mechanisms. Figure 1.8 depicts an example of a task estimation screen from the AME tool.

- *Planning the project.* Project managers are assisted in planning by assembling the necessary methodology for a particular project. Since the method base repository is constantly being improved from many different projects, project managers always have the most successful method components available to them. The methodology is tailored according to constraints of the individual project. For example, Fig. 1.9 depicts a "process filter" screen from James Martin & Company's CAME tool called Architect. This screen helps Architect to select the appropriate method segments based on the objectives selected in the right side of the window. Once the methodology is generated, the project can be estimated and its risk assessed. Figure 1.10 depicts an Architect project metrics screen.

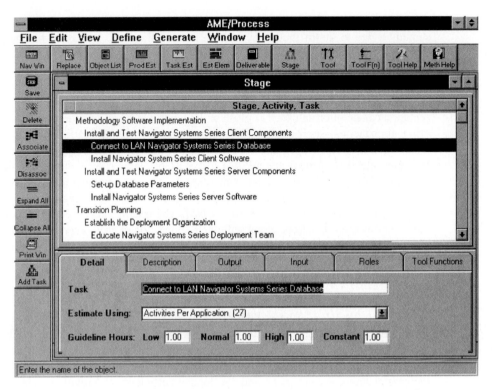

Figure 1.7 A CAME screen showing the structure of a methodology. Information for each method component can be entered, such as estimating details, input and output requirements, role assignments, and automated tool associations (Ernst & Young Automated Methods Environment™, Ernst & Young International, Ltd.).

- *Delivering the project.* System development work assignments can be assigned to individuals and to development tools. CAME tools can then guide the workflow of a project by ensuring that the right task is being completed by the right person, using the right tools.

- *Improving the process.* Continuous improvement is a key factor in process management. Using measurable quantitative feedback from each project, the method components used are reevaluated to determine what worked and what did not. Here method components are modified, added, or deleted to reflect the best practices and lessons from SDLC projects.

REFERENCES

Coleman, Derek, Patrick Arnold, Stephanie Bodoff, Chris Dollin, Helena Gilchrist, Fiona Hayes, and Paul Jeremaes, *Object-Oriented Development: The Fusion Method,* Prentice Hall, Englewood Cliffs, NJ, 1994.

Harmsen, Frank, Sjaak Brinkkember, and Han Oei, "Situational Method Engineering for Information System Project Approaches," *Methods and Associated Tools for the*

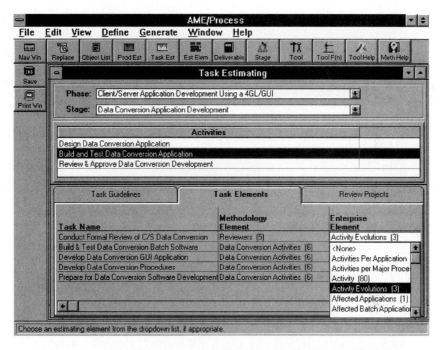

Figure 1.8   A CAME screen that facilitates maintenance of the estimating details for method components (Ernst & Young Automated Methods Environment™, Ernst & Young International, Ltd.).

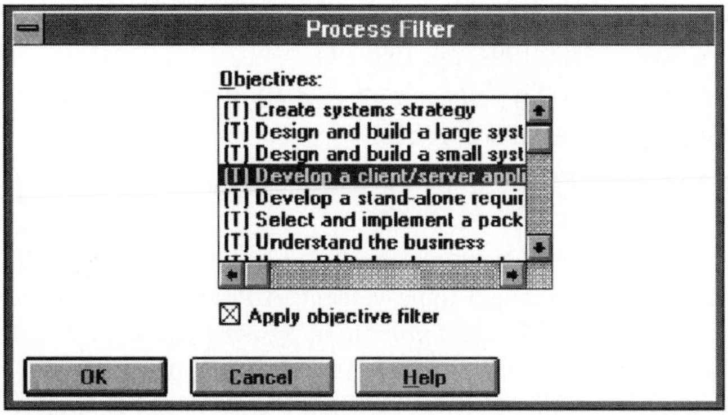

Figure 1.9   A screen that offers a choice of project objectives. Based on these objectives, the CAME tool can generate an appropriate methodology (Architect, courtesy of James Martin & Co.).

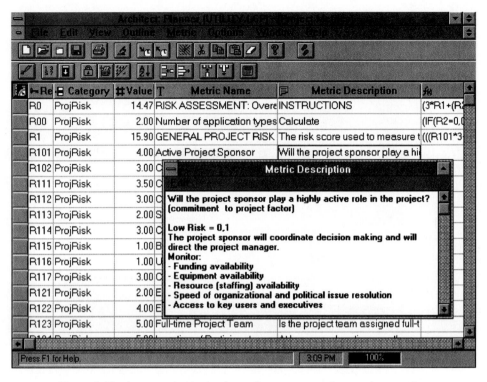

Figure 1.10   A screen that maintains and reports on various project metrics, such as duration and risk (Architect, courtesy of James Martin & Co.).

Information Systems Life Cycle, A. A. Verrijn-Stuart and T. William Olle, eds., Elsevier, Amsterdam, 1994, pp. 169–194.

Hutt, Andrew T. F., ed., *Object-Oriented Analysis and Design: Comparison of Methods,* Wiley-QED, New York, 1994a.

Hutt, Andrew T. F., ed., *Object-Oriented Analysis and Design: Description of Methods,* Wiley-QED, New York, 1994b.

Jarke, Matthias, Klaus Pohl, Colette Roland, and Jean-Roch Schmitt, "Experience-Based Method Evaluation and Improvement: A Process Modeling Approach," *Methods and Associated Tools for the Information Systems Life Cycle,* A. A. Verrijn-Stuart and T. William Olle, eds., Elsevier, Amsterdam, 1994, pp. 1–27.

Paulk, Mark C., Bill Curtis, Mary Beth Chrissis, and Charles V. Webber, "Capability Maturity Model, Version 2.1," *IEEE Software,* 10:4, 1993, pp. 18–27.

Ramesh, B., and M. Edwards, "Issues in the Development of a Requirements Traceability Model," Proc. *IEEE Symp. Requirements Engineering,* San Diego, CA, 1993.

Chapter 2

Object-Oriented Methodologies

OO AND METHODOLOGY

One of the primary differences between traditional and OO methodologies is that traditional approaches were limited to developing conventional data-processing systems. On the other hand, OO methodologies can be used to develop *any* kind of system—whether or not the system is implemented using OO technology.

For many years, object orientation has been associated exclusively with a particular kind of programming language. Today, the notions employed by OO programming languages (OOPLS) are applied as a general philosophy for system development. This does not mean that OO systems development is specified in terms of classes that physically encompass definitions of object variables and coded methods. Nor does this mean that a system is specified in terms of inherited code. While the notions of class structures and inheritance are used to define object orientation, they are in fact just *implementations* of OO. Conceptually, object orientation has come to be interpreted more generally.

Primarily, this broader interpretation means that OO is a way of organizing our thoughts about our world. This organization is based on the types of things—or *object types*—in our world. In this way, we can define the attributes of these object types, operations performed on these object types, rules based on them, machine learning on them, and so on. Instead of one physical unit that contains variables and methods, a more general OO approach provides a way of organizing our knowledge conceptually. Object orientation, then, provides an index for our knowledge—whether that knowledge is expressed in terms of rules, logic, functions, relational languages, neural networks, or something else. Moreover, by extending this idea further, OO can be employed as an approach for organizing and interconnecting many different software technologies including knowledgebase, parallel computing, business reengineering, and rapid application development (Fig. 2.1).

OO Is Not Limited to Information Systems

In many organizations application software development is performed by information systems (I.S.) personnel. Yet, while information is an important product of software systems, it is certainly not all that is involved. Systems for stock transfers, patient monitor-

Figure 2.1 OO can be used as a mechanism that organizes and interconnects many different kinds of systems approaches.

ing, and plant controls are not information systems. Their primary purpose is not the *information* they impart, but the *process* they perform. In fact, providing information is just another process like any other software process. Operations on a Stock object could include create, terminate, transfer, display_current_activity, or print_initial_offer_date. In other words, oo systems developers are not limited to the world of information; they are free to specify *any* kind of process for automation. In addition, they can specify and program the system with a number of approaches (e.g., rules, functions, logic, sql). Perhaps a more descriptive name for this kind of person would be *software-application engineer*. The term *information system*, then, should be limited only to those processes that provide information.

This is not a diatribe on who should be called what, but rather on who should be *doing* what. The point above stresses that software system developers are not exclusively in the business of providing information or even processing data. Their business is developing and implementing software solutions for the organization. Today the best technology available for organizing and interconnecting such development is object orientation. This means employing OO as a development philosophy—not just as a software language.

OO for Systems in General

In addition to going beyond just one kind of programming language, can the OO approach take us beyond software systems in general? Granted, software engineering is a specialty that will survive for many years to come. Software, however, is just one possible mechanism for system implementation. Particularly in this era of business-process reengineering (BPR), the emphasis is on *any* business process—not just those automated by software.

The question is whether an OO approach can be effectively used for business systems in general. Can OO be used to understand and specify nonsoftware-related—as well as software-related—processes? The answer of course is yes. In fact, OO was born from the need for an easier way to simulate systems—not just information systems but *any* kind of system. The founding fathers of Simula determined that managing one big process was not the answer. Rather, the solution consisted of many components that interacted with one another. These components were not based on some ad hoc modularization. Instead they were based on the types, or classes, of things being simulated. The structure and behavior of the system, then, could easily be located and manipulated.

While Simula developed into the first object-oriented programming language, its most important legacy was a philosophical one. Object orientation provides a way to engineer any kind of system—regardless of how the system will be implemented. In addition, this same object-oriented engineering specification can be used to guide many other disciples, whether they involve people, machines, or computers (Fig. 2.2).

OO METHODOLOGY PHASES

System-development methodologies address some or all of the following system-development life cycle (SDLC) phases: planning, analysis, design, construction, and transition. Therefore, OO methodologies must also address these same SDLC phases.

Strategy Planning

Strategy planning produces high level models of a business and, with them, defines a plan to develop a set of interrelated system projects.

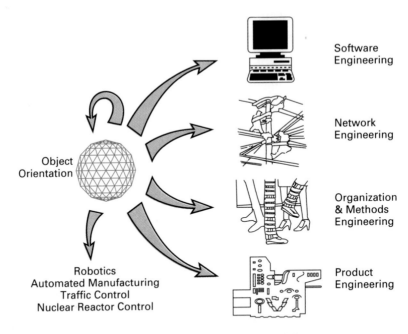

Figure 2.2   OO can support many disciplines.

Strategy planning takes a wide view of the business needs and direction to ensure that short-term decisions fit with long-term aims. The scope may be an area identified in the business plan, or it may be an organizational or functional grouping. It may be identified as a value stream resulting from business reengineering, or it may even be the enterprise as a whole. The common characteristic is the need to build compatible, consistent, and—one hopes—automatable support for the business.

The strategy plan defines a set of interrelated system projects, and it provides a basic description and delivery schedule for each project. The strategy plan does not include a plan for *every* individual project in the future. Instead, it is a high-level map within which detailed projects will be planned at more tactical and operational levels. The map ensures that small iterative projects can be reassembled into cooperating enterprise systems.

System Analysis

> System analysis models a system area based on the domain expert's concepts—deferring any decisions related to implementation.

System analysis is regarded as the first phase of most system projects. It focuses on understanding the business in terms of its activities, rules, locations, and information. When reengineering a business, the analysis goes beyond just looking at information to include *anything* or *anybody* of interest to the business.

The problem with many traditional analysis methods is that they emphasize a complete, detailed, and exhaustive approach which is at best impractical and in many cases impossible. This emphasis on detail gives rise to analysis paralysis. Lengthy analysis projects are incompatible with the goals of system development. The objectives of system analysis are to understand the business so that the systems will support the business, to scope and prioritize the system design areas, and to establish a basis for iterative development.

The analysis identifies object types, event types, and business rules, and employs usage analysis techniques. These are crucial for the correct development of automated—as well as nonautomated—systems. Using objects and events provides a model of the business that is closer to how we humans understand the world. Hence it gives a basis for a design based on real-world concepts. Business rules and usage document the business practice in a way that preserves flexibility for distribution decisions in design.

System Design

> System design develops an implementation model based on the conceptual models developed during system analysis.

System design is not an "extension" to system analysis. It uses the conceptual models developed during system analysis and maps them into implementation models. It involves designing the look and feel of the application and making the technical design decisions, including deciding on data and process distribution. Performance and resource requirements are important considerations here. Usability, however, is the key to a successful application.

For many systems, the design stage is driven by user interface design. As such, this stage should maximize consistency and reusability in the designs. Here, the design approach should use a process of visualizing the user tasks, abstracting to identify common and similar components, and detailing the interface through prototyping. For client/server systems the major decisions in design concern distributing process and data. Before finalizing a system design, the stability and robustness of the design are evaluated and enhanced where needed.

System Construction

> System construction involves building and testing programs, databases, and networks as defined during system design.

The act of construction does not change dramatically for client/server systems. One of the principal differences is that software is built in smaller pieces on multiple platforms. The recommended client/server development approach is first to create a simpler version of the environment for development purposes. For example, code is developed and tested against a workstation-resident database. Then, the application migrates to the true server environment. For client/server systems, unit and integration tasks are both part of constructing code. Systems and acceptance tests are both part of verifying the system operation. This kind of subtle change to the construction task greatly simplifies the task of building client/server applications.

System Transition

> System transition installs the constructed systems.

In system development the job is not over until the system is up and running in the user environment. The last stage in development, then, is system transition. System transition is concerned with getting the system into production. In client/server development, increased attention should be given to establishing support services, software distribution, and continuous training.

System Maintenance

System maintenance is an additional phase that many developers address as part of the system lifecycle. In this phase, the system is enhanced to include such deliverables as bug fixes, performance and usability improvements, and general realignment with business practices. Such enhancements are not usually considered as part of the same development project as the original system development. Typically, such enhancements are scheduled as yet another system-development project that can also include analysis, design, construction, and transition phases. Maintenance, then, becomes an SDLC project, and is scheduled just like any other project. Such scheduling can be defined during the construction phase of the original project or during the planning phase. In this way, system maintenance does not require a separate phase per se. Instead, it can be addressed during the planning through transition phases described above.

TWO MAJOR GOALS

The methodology employs an object-oriented approach to *thinking* about a system. It does not, however, require an OO implementation. An OO way of thinking can be used to develop *any* kind of system—whether or not the system is implemented using OO technology.

Promote Intentional Reuse

Reuse of analysis, design, and implementation components is a powerful facility. It leads to dramatic increases in productivity and quality while at the same time promoting consistency. Many of the tools available today provide object-oriented capabilities that facilitate reuse. However, the availability of such functionality does not in itself *require* reuse.

Reaping the rewards of reuse requires both an understanding of the possible future use of a component and a commitment to build the component for reuse. Building a truly reusable component takes more time and effort. The decision to invest in reuse must be part of the planning process. Any OO methodology must promote intentional reuse, rather than accidental reuse.

Lay the Foundation for Iterative Development

Many development projects employ a *waterfall* approach, illustrated in Fig. 2.3. Such an approach usually delivers too little, too late. While the methodology presented in this book can still be employed in a waterfall manner, a more iterative approach is recommended. This means picking the smallest, most meaningful aspect of the system and delivering the benefit to the business as early as possible. Then, iterate and deliver some more. Furthermore, each iteration can contain components that may be developed concurrently by coordinating multiple—yet interrelated—projects. Here it is possible to use a spiral approach as illustrated in Fig. 2.4.

CONCURRENT ENGINEERING AND THE SDLC

In terms of SDLC, concurrent engineering (CE) is a systematic approach to the integrated, concurrent development of automated systems. First, this means that CE involves making the various components of a system interoperable. For instance, Fig. 2.4 illustrates that a single development spiral can be implemented instead as multiple spirals. In order for these components to communicate within a system, the project teams must also communicate. In a CE environment, direct communication between projects is important. However, if too much communication causes project delays, the number of interrelated projects

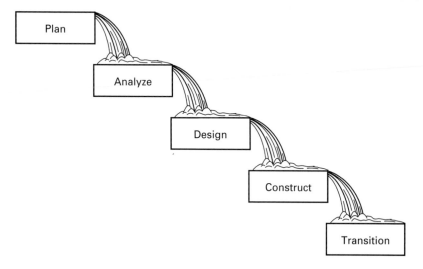

Figure 2.3　A *waterfall* approach to a full SDLC methodology.

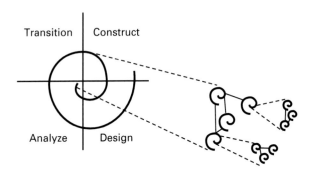

Figure 2.4 A *spiral* approach to development methodology that employs concurrent system development.

must be reduced. In CE, each spiral is expected to be a component in its own right, yet is not developed in its own vacuum.

Another aspect of CE is that it applies *within* each project. In the waterfall and spiral approaches, each phase lays the foundation for the next phase. So, it is important to proceed methodically. In CE, however, these phases can overlap, so that much of the work within a project can proceed concurrently. For example, Fig. 2.5 illustrates the way in which a waterfall approach can be adapted to CE. In this particular example, the development time was limited, or *timeboxed* (see Chapter 24), to be completed in 120 days. Furthermore, this one concurrent waterfall could be one *mini-waterfall* component of a much larger waterfall similar to that depicted in Fig. 2.4.

If a spiral approach to system development is preferred, Fig. 2.6 illustrates how concurrent engineering can be applied to each iteration of a spiral. Furthermore, spirals with overlapping phases can be employed along with the concurrent spiral approach depicted on the right of Fig. 2.4.

REFERENCE

Carter, Donald E., and Barbara Stilwell Baker, *Concurrent Engineering: The Product Development Environment of the 1990s,* Addison-Wesley, Reading, MA, 1992.

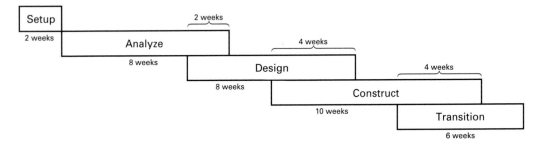

Figure 2.5 A *mini-waterfall* approach using concurrent engineering and a timebox of 120 days.

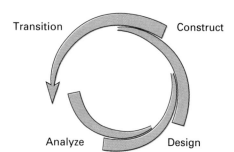

Figure 2.6   Concurrent engineering employed
within a spiral.

PART II

OO DIAGRAMMING TECHNIQUES

Just as there are many different system-development methodologies, there are also many different diagramming techniques that can be employed within the methodologies. No one technique can or should be utilized in every situation. The choice of diagramming technique should be based on both the kind of problem and the way in which the domain experts prefer to express the problem. The closer the modeling "language" is to the user and the problem, the greater the probability of capturing the expert's knowledge. Part II discusses many different OO diagramming techniques. It also describes in more detail three particular diagrams and the techniques for constructing them.

Chapter **3**

Introduction to OO Diagramming Techniques

A technique is a method that defines the way in which technical details are treated. Additionally, a technique is useful in a variety of situations. For example, a technique for constructing object structure models can be used during strategic planning, high-level scoping for a proposed system, and detailed systems analysis. While Part II is concerned with OO diagramming techniques, this chapter provides an initial overview of the predominant techniques.

> A *technique* is a technical method, that is, a specialized method useful in a variety of situations.
>
> An *OO diagramming technique* is a technique for graphically representing OO structure or behavior.

Many kinds of diagrams are used by OO practitioners to model systems. Currently, the principal diagrams employed are:

- Object (structure) diagrams.
- State-transition diagrams.
- Interaction diagrams.
- Event diagrams.
- CRC cards.
- Context diagrams.
- Object-flow diagrams.
- KADS interpretation diagrams.
- Data-flow diagrams.

In the sections that follow, each of these diagrams will be discussed along with various documented techniques for constructing these diagrams.

OBJECT (STRUCTURE) DIAGRAMS

One kind of model employed by virtually all OO approaches is the object diagram. While notations differ, all attempt to represent object structure. All contain the notions of object types, subtypes and supertypes, and associations between object types. For example, Fig. 3.1 depicts one way of representing various library-related structural elements. Many other ideas, such as attributes, composition, and constraints, may also be added to these diagrams. A description of object-diagram components is presented in Chapter 4.

Various techniques have been published that define the process of object modeling. However, they have more similarities than differences. Coad recommends the following basic steps: find class-&-object, identify structure, define attributes [Coad, 1991]. Rumbaugh identifies the following steps: identify objects and object types, identify associations (including composition), identify attributes, organize using inheritance, and verify and refine the model [Rumbaugh, 1991]. Graham employs similar steps and supplements them by identifying business rules [Graham, 1995]. In this book, Chapter 5 presents a technique that is commonly used by object modelers.

STATE-TRANSITION DIAGRAMS

State-transition diagrams are another popular form of diagram. The example, illustrated in Fig. 3.2, expresses the various states of an object type, their permissible transitions, and their associated triggering events and operations. Rumbaugh and Embley provide excellent descriptions of state-transition diagrams [Rumbaugh, 1991; Embley, 1992].

There are several state-transition modeling techniques. However, all begin by identifying the object type for each state-transition diagram. The remaining compo-

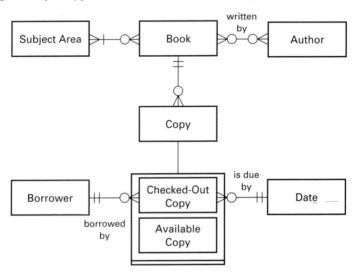

Figure 3.1   An example of an object diagram.

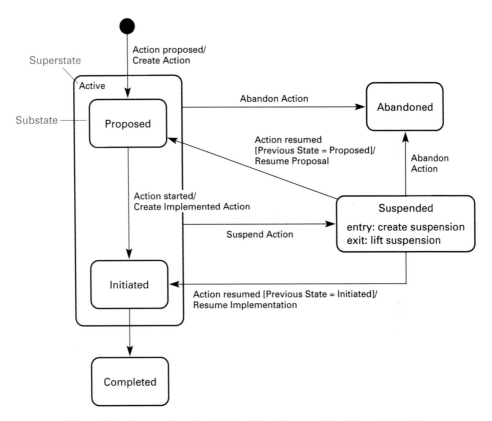

Figure 3.2   An example of a state-transition diagram with states and substates.

nents of the diagram are driven by some aspect of analysis. For instance, Rumbaugh uses an event-driven technique in which events are identified next. Then, for each event, the states, transitions, and operations required to support the event are specified. Coleman's technique, on the other hand, is driven by object lifecycles. Here, the technique begins with identifying the states and permissible transitions that the diagram's particular kind of object may have. From this point, the required operations and events are determined.

Techniques for using state-transition diagrams are published in several other books and will not be repeated here. Instead, a list of books describing these techniques is presented at the end of this chapter.

INTERACTION DIAGRAMS

In a larger context, state-transition diagrams do not define stand-alone "islands" of processing. In other words, a state change in one kind of object can trigger a state change in another. For example, an Order changing to the state of Shipped should trigger the change of a related Invoice object to the state of Transmitted. However, representing all the various state-transition diagrams and their interactions on a single diagram makes it difficult to use. Interaction diagrams, then, can be used to hide some of the overwhelming detail. A common technique involves representing each state-transition diagram by its object type. The associations, then, express processing interactions between the operations performed by these object types. As illustrated in Fig. 3.3, these diagrams can be extended to represent the sequence of interactions. Both Booch and Coad place numbers on them to indicate sequence.

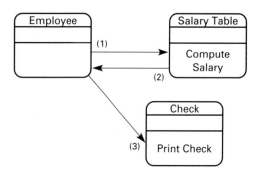

Figure 3.3   An example of a Coad-style interaction diagram.

Sequence of processing, however, does not have to be determined solely by state-transition diagrams. It can be based on workflow descriptions, event diagrams, action diagrams, or pseudocode. Interaction diagrams, then, can be used to express such processing *scenarios* in terms of interactions between objects or object types. Jacobson, Rumbaugh, and Booch all describe techniques that use the interaction diagram to express sequences of interactions between objects that can be read left to right and top to bottom [Jacobson, 1992; Rumbaugh, 1991; Booch, 1994]. A Jacobson-style interaction diagram is illustrated in Fig. 3.4. Since these authors have already written a great deal about interaction diagrams, their step-by-step techniques will not be repeated in this book.

EVENT DIAGRAMS

As mentioned above, diagrams such as Jacobson's interaction diagrams express processing sequence or *scenario*. Another form of scenario diagram is the event diagram. Event diagrams express scenarios in the form of workflows. An example of an event diagram is illustrated in Fig. 3.5. Since workflow representation has become very useful in business reengineering and control flow in general, an object-oriented form would improve reusability and extendibility. Event diagrams, then, are object-oriented workflow diagrams. These diagrams are discussed in Chapter 6, and a technique for constructing them is presented in Chapter 7.

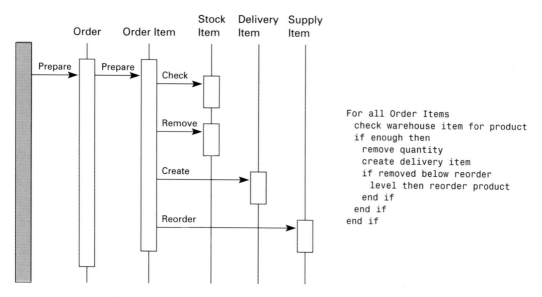

For all Order Items
    check warehouse item for product
    if enough then
        remove quantity
        create delivery item
        if removed below reorder
            level then reorder product
        end if
    end if
end if

Figure 3.4 An example of a Jacobson-style interaction diagram with a pseudocode supplement.

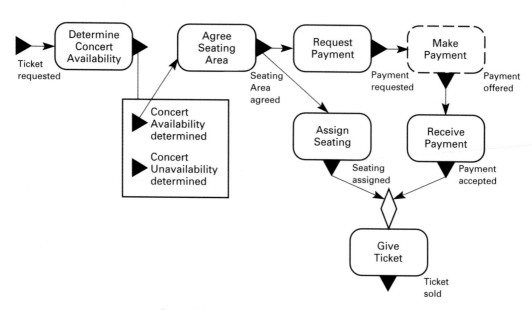

Figure 3.5 An example of an event diagram.

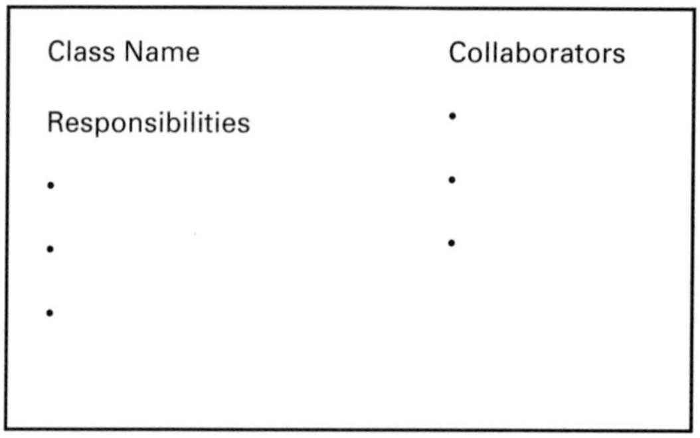

Class Name	Collaborators
Responsibilities	•
•	•
•	•
•	

Figure 3.6   An example of a CRC card format.

CRC CARDS

Ward Cunningham advocates a technique that enhances human interaction in OO design [Beck, 1989]. He uses four-by-six inch index cards called *CRC cards* to represent classes as illustrated in Fig. 3.6. On each class is written:

- The *class* name.
- The *responsibilities* of the class.
- The *collaborators* that the class may use to achieve its responsibilities.

A pile of CRC cards is used to represent all the classes in a design. People sitting around a table use the cards to discuss the classes, responsibilities, and collaborators. Different people may become actors and assume the roles of different classes. A person assuming the role of a class holds the card for that class and thinks about its responsibilities—whether the responsibilities are appropriate and what collaborators must be sent requests. Various situations or problems are discussed, and team members think through how their cards need to interact. Classes may be combined or subtyped and responsibilities moved from one class to another. The CRC-card technique used by most practitioners is already described [Wirfs-Brock, 1990] and will not be repeated here.

CONTEXT DIAGRAMS

A common technique used to define the scope of a system involves using the context diagram. In techniques using this diagram, the system is first represented by a single symbol in the middle of the diagram. The various *actors* and their interactions required for this system are then identified. At this point, the diagram portrays the context of a given system based on external requirements. Given this context, it is then possible to identify the basic functionality required by the proposed system. In this final step, an operation is

specified to support each interaction within the system. Jacobson calls operations specified in this manner *use cases*. An example is illustrated in Fig. 3.7. While many OO
approaches employ the context diagram, Jacobson's work is currently the preferred
source [Jacobson, 1992]. The step-by-step technique for representing context diagrams
can be found there.

OBJECT-FLOW DIAGRAMS

Interaction diagrams are useful for determining the scope of small to medium systems.
However, large systems or systems that should not be defined solely on the basis of external requirements require another technique. Object-flow diagrams are often used to specify such systems. Object-flow diagrams are also employed by organizations wishing to
represent their domain in terms of processes that produce and consume business
resources. It is particularly helpful in BPR efforts that wish to analyze the *value chain*
involved in consuming and producing. An example of an object-flow diagram is illustrated in Fig. 3.8. It is called *object flow* because it models the way business objects are produced by one activity and consumed by another. In other words, it depicts the way these
objects *flow* from one activity to another. Chapter 8 discusses the elements of object-flow
diagrams, and Chapter 9 presents a technique for using them.

Object-flow diagrams are a form of *functional specification*. Functional specifications define processing dependencies based on production/consumption relationships

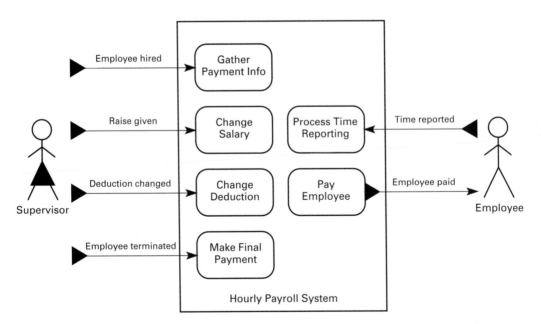

Figure 3.7   An example of a context diagram.

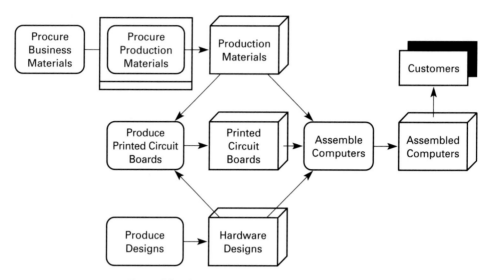

Figure 3.8   An example of an object-flow diagram.

between processes, without regard for algorithmic precision. KADS problem-solving template diagrams (sometimes called interpretation diagrams) and data-flow diagrams are also forms of functional specification.

KADS INTERPRETATION DIAGRAMS

The acronym KADS stands for Knowledge Acquisition and Documentation Structuring. KADS is a cognitive model-driven technique that assists in the high-level definition of systems requirements. Reuse does play a central part. For example, KADS has defined a set of basic operations that provides the processing building blocks for every system. KADS also encourages reusability by providing processing templates. These templates recommend prefabricated models for common forms of processing, such as classification, diagnosis, suitability assessment, monitoring, prediction, modification, planning, and design. For example, the KADS interpretation diagram in Fig. 3.9 is based on the KADS systematic-diagnosis model template. Processing an insurance application would be an adaptation of the suitability-assessment model template. Selecting a drug to treat a particular disease would be based on the modification-model template.

KADS is a cognitive approach, not an OO approach. However, Karen Gardner has combined the elements of KADS and object orientation to create a new approach called KADS Object. When mapping from KADS to an OO approach, she incorporates the use of object diagrams and event diagrams. The technique for creating and using KADS diagrams is already described in detail [Gardner, 1996] and will not be repeated here.

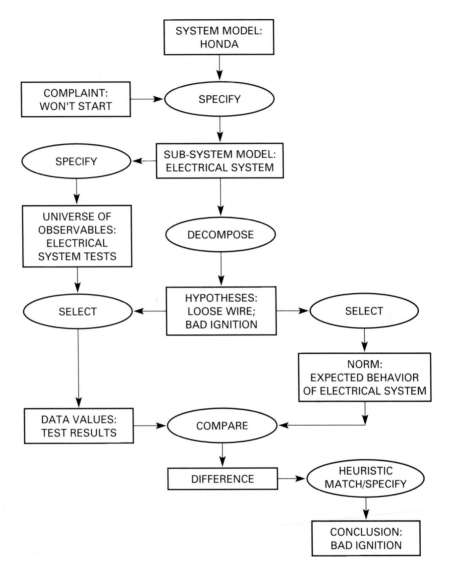

Figure 3.9　An example of a KADS problem-solving template diagram for diagnosing a car (Courtesy of CSC Consulting & Systems Integration, Object Oriented Practice, San Francisco, CA) [Gardner, 1996].

DATA-FLOW DIAGRAMS (DFDs)

Data-flow diagrams (DFDs) are one way of representing functional specification. Though DFDs are not inherently object oriented, they can be modified to incorporate an OO philosophy. Rumbaugh and Shlaer reinterpret the data-store symbol (indicating storage of various types of data) to represent a single object type instead. For instance, Customer in Fig. 3.10 represents the Customer object type—not the storage containing various types of customer-related data.

Furthermore, since the symbol for data stores is reassigned to express object types, the behavior associated with object types can also be expressed. The OO DFD in Fig. 3.10 specifies that four operations are associated with the object type Customer. Create New Customer Record *creates* Customer objects, while the remaining operations *retrieve* Customer-related information. Arrows drawn from Customer indicate retrieval of Customer information. Arrows drawn to Customer indicate modification or creation of Customer objects. The arrowed lines, or data flows, between the operations indicate precedence between the operations. As the name indicates, data flows also transport data in the direction they indicate. However, data flows are not triggers. By definition, DFDs do not specify such dynamics. If such cause-and-effect features are added to DFDs, they become behavioral specifications not unlike event diagrams. The techniques for using DFDs in an OO manner are already described [Rumbaugh, 1991; Shlaer, 1991] and will not be repeated in this book.

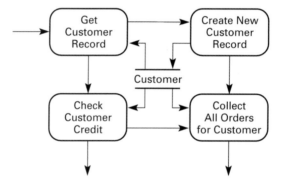

Figure 3.10 An example of a data-flow diagram.

SOURCES OF TECHNIQUES

In the sections above, nine forms of commonly used diagrams are presented, along with a brief discussion of some techniques for constructing them. Below is a list of these same diagrams with a more complete list of technique references.

- Object (structure) diagrams: Chapters 4 and 5 of this book; [Booch, 1994; Coad, 1991; Coleman, 1994; Embley, 1992; Gardner, 1996; Graham, 1995; Henderson-Sellers, 1994; Jacobson, 1992; Rumbaugh, 1991; Shlaer, 1988].

- State-transition diagrams: [Booch, 1994; Coad, 1991; Coleman, 1994; Embley, 1992; Graham, 1995; Henderson-Sellers, 1994; Jacobson, 1992; Rumbaugh, 1991; Shlaer, 1991].

- Interaction diagrams: [Booch, 1994; Coleman, 1994; Jacobson, 1992].

- Event diagrams: Chapters 6 and 7 of this book.

- CRC cards: [Wirfs-Brock, 1990].
- Context diagrams: [Booch, 1994; Coad, 1991; Coleman, 1994; Embley, 1992; Gardner, 1996; Graham, 1995; Henderson-Sellers, 1994; Jacobson, 1992].
- Object-flow diagrams: Chapters 8 and 9 of this book.
- KADS diagrams: [Gardner, 1996].
- Data-flow diagrams: [Rumbaugh, 1991; Shlaer, 1988].

Again, this is not a complete list of diagrams. Many of the references listed above recommend other diagrams and techniques, as well. For instance, Jacobson and Wirfs-Brock present techniques for subsystem diagrams. Coad presents a technique for using his version of a flowchart called a *service chart*.

In addition to graphical representations, there are nondiagrammatic representations of oo structure and behavior. These include such text-based representations as rule tables, business rules, and structured languages [Martin, 1995]. As systems development evolves, so will its representation techniques. The method engineer should be aware of these various techniques and employ them where appropriate.

In the next six chapters, three of the diagrams presented above *will* be described in detail: the object diagram, the event diagram, and the object-flow diagram. In two chapters each, the fundamentals of the diagrams will be presented followed by the techniques for constructing the diagrams.

REFERENCES

Beck, Kent, and Ward Cunningham, "A Laboratory for Teaching Object-Oriented Thinking," *Proceedings of the 1989 OOPSLA—Conference on Object-Oriented Programming Systems, Languages and Applications,* OOPSLA '89 (New Orleans), Norman Meyrowitz, ed., ACM, New York, 1989, pp. 1–6.

Booch, Grady, *Object-Oriented Analysis and Design with Applications* (2nd ed.), Benjamin/Cummings, Redwood City, CA, 1994.

Coad, Peter, and Edward Yourdon, *Object-Oriented Analysis* (2nd ed.), Prentice Hall, Englewood Cliffs, NJ, 1991.

Coleman, Derek, Patrick Arnold, Stephanie Bodoff, Chris Dollin, Helena Gilchrist, Fiona Hayes, and Paul Jeremaes, *Object-Oriented Development: The Fusion Method,* Prentice Hall, Englewood Cliffs, NJ, 1994.

Embley, David W., Barry N. Kurtz, and Scott N. Woodfield, *Object-Oriented Systems Analysis: A Model-Driven Approach,* Prentice Hall, Englewood Cliffs, NJ, 1992.

Gardner, Karen M., *KADS Object,* CSC Consulting course syllabus, San Francisco, 1996.

Graham, Ian, *Migrating to Object Technology,* Addison-Wesley, Reading, MA, 1995.

Henderson-Sellers, Brian, and Julian Edwards, *Book Two of Object-Oriented Knowledge: The Working Object,* Prentice Hall, Sydney, 1994.

Jacobson, Ivar, Magnus Christerson, Partik Jonsson, and Gunnar Övergaard, *Object-Ori-*

ented Software Engineering: A Use Case Driven Approach (rev. ed.), Addison-Wesley, Reading, MA, 1992.

Martin, James, and James J. Odell, *Object-Oriented Methods: A Foundation,* Prentice Hall, Englewood Cliffs, NJ, 1995.

Rumbaugh, James, Michael Blaha, William Premerlani, Frederick Eddy, and William Lorensen, *Object-Oriented Modeling and Design,* Prentice Hall, Englewood Cliffs, NJ, 1991.

Shlaer, Sally, and Stephen J. Mellor, *Object-Oriented Systems Analysis: Modeling the World in Data,* Prentice Hall, Englewood Cliffs, NJ, 1988.

Shlaer, Sally, and Stephen J. Mellor, *Object Life Cycles,* Prentice Hall, Englewood Cliffs, NJ, 1991.

Wirfs-Brock, Rebecca, Brian Wilkerson, and Lauren Wiener, *Designing Object-Oriented Software,* Prentice Hall, Englewood Cliffs, NJ, 1990.

Chapter **4**

Object Diagrams

INTRODUCTION

Object orientation is often described in terms of structure and behavior. The word structure is a visual, spatial metaphor that refers to a static vision of how objects are laid out in space. Structure can specify various object configurations, such as employees, documents, and engineering designs. In contrast, *behavior* refers to how our world changes over time. For example, behavior can hire an employee or tell us that the employee has reached retirement age. In short, it describes the processes that query or modify objects. This chapter summarizes ways of diagramming the structural aspects of objects using *object diagrams*. (An in-depth presentation of the structural elements is presented by Odell [Martin, 1995].)

OBJECT TYPES

We know we possess a concept when we can apply it successfully to the things around us. For example, to say that we have the concept of radish requires only the ability to identify an instance of a radish. Identifying an instance of radish, then, means that we have determined that the concept of radish applies to a particular object in our awareness.

Figure 4.1 depicts several concepts. By applying the tests associated with each concept, we determine which concepts apply to which objects. For instance, Benjamin Franklin passes the conceptual tests of Famous Man, Politician, and Writer. The concept of Perfect Man, however, does not apply. Our reality is based on such tests. In this way, objects can be perceived in many ways, depending on our conceptual tests.

An *object type* is an idea or notion that we apply to the things, or objects, in our awareness. Object type, then, is synonymous with *concept*.

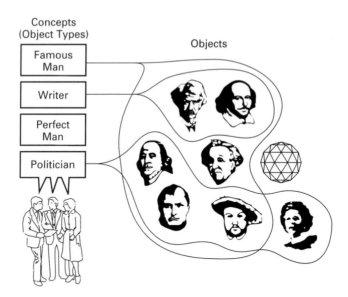

Figure 4.1   People share concepts and apply them to objects, although in OO
the term *object type* is used instead of *concept.*

While the term *concept* is a commonly used English term, *object type* is the term
commonly accepted by OO standards organizations and will be used in this book.

OBJECTS

Our reality consists of those object types (i.e., concepts) that we possess and those *objects*
to which our concepts apply.

> An *object* is anything to which an object type (i.e., concept) applies. It is an instance
> of an object type.

The terms *object* and *instance* can be used synonymously. A simple example of an
object is the plume on your aunt's table—that specific, individual instance of a plume.
Other objects might include the town in which you live, yourself, your occupation, a certain process, a particular event, a point in time, a record in a database, a piece of data, a
sound, an image, an optical signal, the number 42, a magnetic pulse, a document, a vec-
tor, a matrix, or my dog Millicent. Please note that all objects are not data, even though
all data are objects. Object-oriented analysis investigates objects without prejudice
toward what is going to be data or not. In this way, we analyze human understanding
before dealing with bits, bytes, fields, and records.

In this way, *any* thing that we can think of, refer to, describe, discuss, or experience
is an object—as long as we have the concepts to do so. Without the concept of Job, we

would not know how to go to one. Without the concept of Marriage, we could not register them. Objects, therefore, cannot exist in our awareness without at least one concept— or object type—that applies to them.

ASSOCIATIONS

Associations provide a means to link objects of various types in a meaningful way. Figure 4.2 illustrates an example of an association. The two object types Organization and Person are symbolized with rectangular nodes. The line indicates that these two object types are associated.

Nodes, such as the rectangles in Fig. 4.2, are a useful representational device, because they graphically differentiate object types from their associating structures. For example, this figure depicts the object type Person with a set containing the objects John, Jasper, Jane, Susan, and so on. The object type Organization has the instances IBM, NEC, NASA, and so on.

Associations, on the other hand, are represented as lines, because we commonly use lines to connect two or more things. While object types involve *sets* of objects, associations involve connections of objects *between* sets. For example in Fig. 4.2, the connection between IBM and Jane is an instance of an association between Organization and Person sets. This collection of connections between object types forms a special kind of object type called a *relationship type*. Furthermore, using these connections enables us to *map* the objects of one set into objects of another—and back again. Together, relationship types and mappings are two techniques for describing associations between objects.

Relationships

Figure 4.2 contains several Organization and Person objects. During the course of systems analysis, the analyst may wish to refer to associations consisting of Organization-Person pairs. These pairs may be assembled to define employment situations, company representative definitions, lobbyist assignments, or whatever reality the analyst perceives. The important point is that the analyst wishes to refer to each pair of Organization-Person objects as a purposeful unit. For example in Fig. 4.3(a), Jane's IBM Employment refers to the connection between IBM and Jane. The purpose of this unit is to describe an employment relationship between the two. Susan's NEC Employment is a singular collective reference to the employment relationship of NEC and Susan. Jasper's NASA Employment defines an employment relationship between NASA and Jasper, and so on.

Another way of expressing the same four employment occurrences is depicted in Fig. 4.3(b). Each set of parentheses defines a different employment relationship. In this particular situation, the first name in the parenthesis is always the Organization's name; the second, the Person's. By ordering the presentation in a predefined manner, the *type* of object is always understood, and objects named L. L. Bean, Dow Jones, and Smith N. Hawken are never confused. This form of expression is commonly used in relational technology.

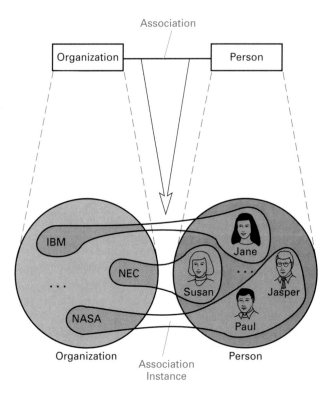

Figure 4.2 An association between two types of objects and the association instances.

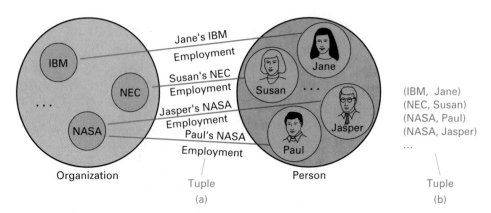

Figure 4.3 Representing relationship instances (or tuples) by illustration and relational notation.

Figure 4.3 depicts these relationships as object *couples*. As mentioned earlier, IBM and Jane form one such employment-related couple. If three objects are related, object *triples* result; four objects result in *quadruples*; and so on. Regardless of the number, these relationship instances are called *n-tuples* or simply *tuples*.

Tuples Can be Treated as Objects

Together, the tuples in Fig. 4.3 comprise a set of relationships whose underlying idea is *employment*. In this way, Jane's IBM Employment can be thought of as an *instance* of an employment contract. Employment Contract, then, is a *type* of object (see Fig. 4.4). Its instances are all employment contract-related tuples. For instance, Jane's IBM Employment relates IBM and Jane, *and* Jane's IBM Employment is an object of the type Employment Contract.

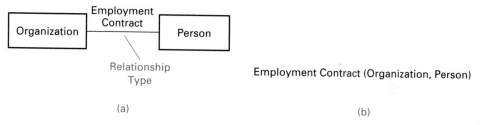

(a)

Employment Contract (Organization, Person)

(b)

Figure 4.4　Expressing a relationship type by graphical and relational notation.

> A *tuple* is an object that relates other objects. Each tuple is a relationship.
>
> A *relationship type* (or *relation*) is an object type whose instances are tuples.

Mappings

Relationships allow us to treat associations as related wholes. Mappings, however, do not look at the whole at once. Instead, they allow us to start from just part of the whole and traverse—or rather *map*—to the other part of that whole. The line in Fig. 4.5(a) is the same as the Employment Contract relationship type depicted in Fig. 4.4. However, this line now has words above and below expressing a directional way of thinking about the association. The word employs, above the line, indicates that each Organization object employs some number of Person objects. For example in Fig. 4.5(b), the IBM Organization object employs the Jane Person object. NASA employs Paul and Jasper, and so on. The inverse indicates that Jane is employed by IBM, Susan by NEC, and so on. In short, employs defines a mapping from the set of Organization objects to the set of Person objects. The employed by defines an inverse mapping from the set of Person objects back to the set of Organization objects.

Relationship type, as a concept and term, is commonly used by systems analysts. The notion of mapping between object types, too, is common. However, most analysts

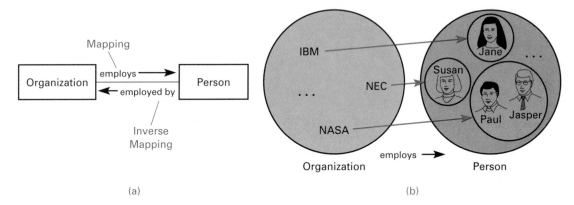

Figure 4.5 The employs mapping assigns Organization objects to Person objects. The inverse employed by mapping assigns Person objects to Organization objects.

have not had a separate name for the word on the relationship line indicating a mapping, except perhaps "the word on the relationship line." Just remember, whenever there is a relationship type, there are two mappings—a mapping and its inverse.

> A *mapping* assigns the objects of one type to objects of another type.

In practical terms, the ability to apply such mappings in the dynamic world of objects requires a process. In OO, a mapping is a process that—given an object—returns an object or a set of objects. A mapping that always returns a single object is called *single-valued*. For example, each Person object maps to a single Woman object that is the person's biological mother. Mappings are *multivalued* when they can return a number of objects. For example, the multivalued employs mapping in Fig. 4.5(b) maps NASA to Jasper *and* Paul.

This book employs a cardinality constraint notation that indicates the minimum and maximum number of objects that must result from a mapping. The word *cardinality* simply indicates that an integer is used to represent the number of objects. A few cardinality constraint notations commonly employed between nodes are illustrated in Fig. 4.6. Alternatively, the analyst may develop another brand of notation. The primary consideration here is that the chosen notation should provide a clear understanding of minimum and maximum cardinality constraints.

GENERALIZATION

When we look in our clothes closet, we recognize—or *classify*—the objects we see as slacks, shirts, coats, shoes, roller blades, and squirting bow ties. Without well developed generalizing capabilities, we might call this storage area, the shoes-slacks-shirts-coats-roller-blades-and-squirting-bow-ties closet. The more kinds of things we have in the closet,

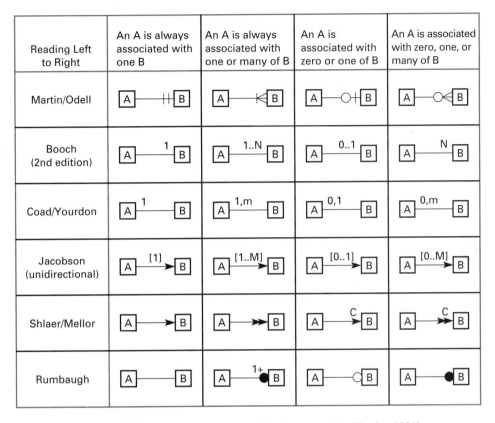

Reading Left to Right	An A is always associated with one B	An A is always associated with one or many of B	An A is associated with zero or one of B	An A is associated with zero, one, or many of B
Martin/Odell	A —‖— B	A —◁ B	A —O‖— B	A —O◁ B
Booch (2nd edition)	A —1— B	A —1..N— B	A —0..1— B	A —N— B
Coad/Yourdon	A 1 — B	A 1,m — B	A 0,1 — B	A 0,m — B
Jacobson (unidirectional)	A [1] → B	A [1..M] → B	A [0..1] → B	A [0..M] → B
Shlaer/Mellor	A → B	A →→ B	A →C B	A →C B
Rumbaugh	A — B	A 1+ ●B	A —O B	A ● B

Figure 4.6   Common notations for cardinality constraints [Fowler, 1994].

the more cumbersome the name becomes. Generalization enables us to examine whether these concepts have anything in common. Does a *more general* concept encompass concepts such as Shoe, Slacks, and Shirt? *In general*, these are known as Clothing. Clothing, in turn, might be encompassed by an even more general category called Merchandise or Household Article—and so on.

> *Generalization* is the act or result of distinguishing a concept (i.e., object type) that completely includes or encompasses another.

Generalization enables us to say that all instances of a specific object type are also instances of a more general object type—but not necessarily the other way around. For example, all Shoe or Shirt objects are also Clothing objects, though not all Clothing objects are Shoe or Shirt objects. Therefore, Clothing is a more general object type than Shoe or Shirt. Whatever makes Shoes different from Shirts is not addressed in the definition of Clothing—only their commonality is recognized.

With generalization, we can define hierarchies of object types, forming more and more general object types. Figure 4.7 shows that a Lifeform is a more general object type (or *supertype*) of Human, and Human is a supertype of Woman.

The opposite of generalization is *specialization*. For example, Human can be *specialized* as Woman or Man; as an Infant, Adolescent, or Adult Human; and as Good, Bad, or Ugly. These specialized object types are *subtypes*. In Fig. 4.7, Woman is a subtype of Human, Human is a subtype of Lifeform, and so on.

One way of thinking about generalization is picturing sets of objects within sets of objects. Figure 4.7 depicts a set of Woman objects, a set of Man objects, and a set of Employee objects. These sets are lodged completely within a set labeled Human—which, in turn, sits completely within the Lifeform set. However, Property Owner is not a subtype of Human, because its set is not *completely* encompassed by the Human set. In other words, the concept of Human is *not* more general than, nor is it a supertype of, Property Owner. The only way Property Owner can be a subtype of Human is to make *every* instance of Property Owner an instance of Human. A representation of the valid hierarchy of supertype relationships, here, is depicted in Fig. 4.8.

Another element that is not a subtype in Fig. 4.7 is the object named Paul. Paul is an *instance* of an object type, not a subtype. Only *types* of objects can be subtypes—hence the "type" in subtype. Part of the confusion comes from the way we verbalize these relationships in everyday language. We say that "Man is a Human" as well as "Paul is a Human." Yet, Man is a *subtype* of Human and Paul is an *instance* of Human. Objects

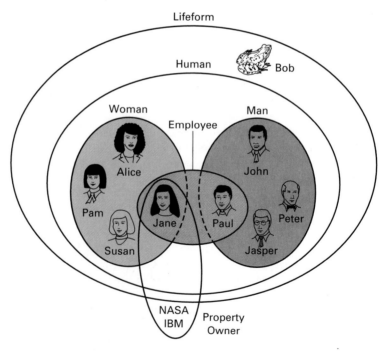

Figure 4.7   Generalization as a set that encompasses other sets.

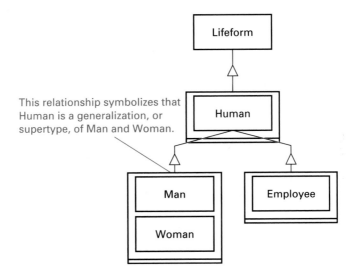

This relationship symbolizes that Human is a generalization, or supertype, of Man and Woman.

Figure 4.8   The generalizations in Fig. 4.7 can be expressed as a hierarchy. (Note: the triangle on the line is an optional symbol.)

are *instances* because they have been *classified*. *Types* of objects are *subtypes* because they have been *specialized*. Classification and generalization/specialization are two different phenomena and, therefore, have different hierarchies.

Type Partitions

Type partitions divide a type into disjoint, or nonoverlapping, subtypes. Type partitioning can be regarded as dividing up an object type's set similar to a pie. For example, one way to partition **Person** is separating it into the subtypes of **Woman**, **Man**, or other disjoint subtypes that occur along the same age/gender lines as **Girl** and **Boy**. A totally different partitioning of **Person** could be based on whether a **Person** is employed or not. In other words every object type can be partitioned in more than one way.

A *type partition* is a division (or partitioning) of an object type into disjoint subtypes.

Figure 4.9(a) illustrates how a set of **Person** objects can be partitioned into disjoint sets. The word *partition* is chosen, because it readily describes dividing a set into nonoverlapping subsets. The object type **Person** (Fig. 4.9(b)), then, is partitioned in two ways: one based on gender and age and the other on employment status. A better notation for representing partitions is shown Fig. 4.10.

As stated above, an object type can be partitioned in more than one way. Sometimes these type partitions (or just *partitions*) have readily identifiable themes. In Fig. 4.10, a **Person** has many such partitions based on employment, gender, age group, creditworthiness, and so on. A **Person** object will be involved in each of its partition cate-

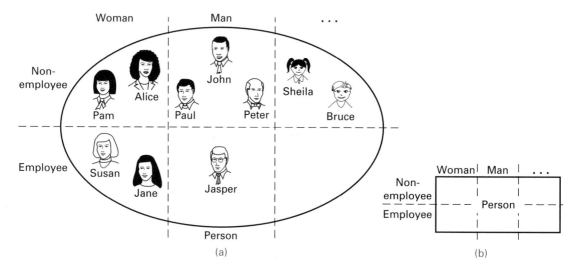

Figure 4.9　Type partitions subdivide object types into disjoint subtypes. With partitioning, an object can clearly be both an Employee and a Man but cannot be both a Woman and a Man.

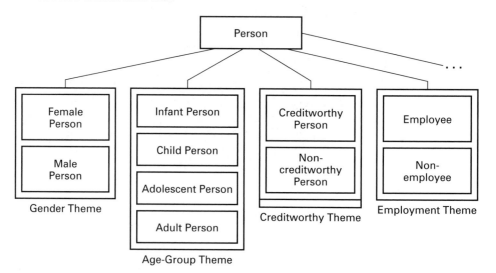

Figure 4.10　Some type partitions of Person.

gories. For instance, a Person object can be a Female Person, an Adult Person, a Creditworthy Person, *and* an Employee object. Multiple partitions, then, allow us to pick one from each column when describing an object. They specify the inclusive, overlapping subtypes that an object type offers.

　　Between partitions, subtypes can overlap. *Within* a partition, however, the subtypes *must* be exclusive and nonoverlapping. For example, a Person can only be an instance of one of the following subtypes: an Infant Person, a Child Person, an Adolescent Person, *or* an Adult Person. In other words, while a Person can be both a Female Person and a Child Person, it cannot be both a Female Person and a Male Person.

Each partition, then, is an exclusive *"or"* statement. This means that within a partition there is the choice of one subset *or* another—but never more than one. The ability to join together several different ideas with an "and" is accomplished by employing multiple partitions. In this way, a Person object can be a Creditworthy Person *and* an Employee, yet cannot be both a Creditworthy Person *and* a Noncreditworthy Person. This provides a neat and orderly way of untangling a potentially incomprehensible mess of "ands" and "ors" among subtypes. When this knowledge is automated, the technique furnishes a well-defined statement of meaning.

Complete Partitions

A *complete* partition is employed when all the subtypes are known for a particular partition. They are particularly beneficial when fixing a partition's contents to a certain list of subtypes and only those subtypes.

> A *complete partition* is a partition with all of its subtypes specified.

Figure 4.11 illustrates some examples of complete partitions. The Fig. 4.11(a) diagram could be read: For any given instance of Employee, it must be either an instance of Male Employee or Female Employee—and not both. It could also indicate: Male Employee and Female Employee are all of the possible [disjoint] subtypes of Employee for this particular partition.

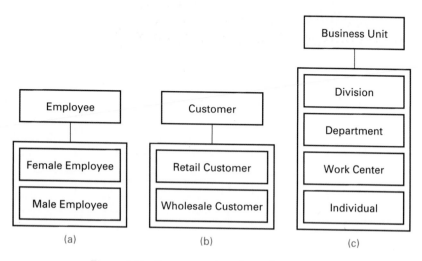

Figure 4.11   Some examples of *complete partitions.*

Complete partitions specify a *mandatory* classification. For example, Fig. 4.11(b) specifies that a Customer must be either a Retail Customer or a Wholesale Customer. In other words, a Customer object cannot exist unless it can be classified as a Retail Customer or a Wholesale Customer.

Incomplete Partitions

Another representation of partitions is the incomplete partition, which is very useful for those situations where a complete list of subtypes is not appropriate.

> An *incomplete partition* is a partition with a partial list of its subtypes specified.

Some examples of incomplete partitions are illustrated in Fig. 4.12. For example, Fig. 4.12(a) could be read: For any one instance of Employee, it must be either an instance of Engineer or Mechanic, or *something else*. It could also indicate: Engineer and Mechanic are *some* of the possible (disjoint) subtypes of Employee.

In the example of Fig. 4.12, a more specialized form of Customer might be an Important Customer—or something else not specified. Why not specify *all* the possible subtypes? What are the appropriate subtypes that belong here? There are probably a few more such as a Somewhat Important Customer or a Totally Unimportant Customer. No one can think of everything at once, *and* no one wants to produce a large, unmanageable diagram. The answer lies in how we obtain expert knowledge. In working with end users, we should analyze the knowledge they hold of their particular function to learn what object types have proven effective. Again, the incomplete partition is useful for representing *only* what is necessary and sufficient for an end user's *domain*.

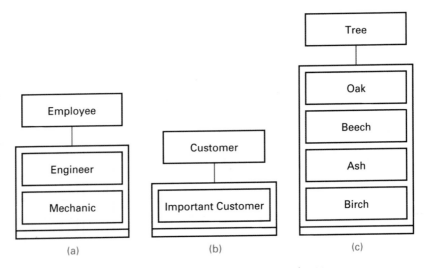

Figure 4.12 Some examples of *incomplete partitions*.

COMPOSITION

Composition (also referred to as *aggregation*) is a mechanism for forming a whole from component parts. For example, composition can configure assembled structures, such as each Sailboat consists of its Hull, Sail, and Engine (Fig. 4.13) or each Hammer consists of its Head and Handle. Other compositions can be more conceptual and subjective in nature, such as a Jury is a collection of Juror members or a Marriage is composed of a Husband and a Wife.

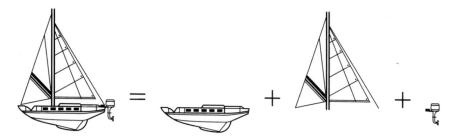

Figure 4.13 Composition can indicate configurations of assembly structures.

Figure 4.14 illustrates one way to model the composed object in Fig. 4.13. This diagram expresses the underlying concepts, or types of objects, depicted in Fig. 4.13. The component parts represented here might, in addition, have their own component parts. Therefore, the Engine in the Sailboat could consist of various Pistons, Rods, Valves, and an Engine Block. In this way, composition can define hierarchies of part-whole configurations.

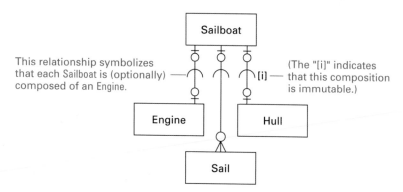

This relationship symbolizes that each Sailboat is (optionally) composed of an Engine.

(The "[i]" indicates that this composition is immutable.)

Figure 4.14 The types of objects composed in Fig. 4.13 (i.e., the underlying concepts) expressed as a hierarchy.

CONCLUSION

This chapter summarizes most of the diagramming elements required to model object structure using the Martin/Odell object diagram. In the previous volume [Martin, 1995],

Odell describes in detail the elements of object structure. The chapter that follows suggests a method for constructing object diagrams.

REFERENCES

Fowler, Martin, "Describing and Comparing Object-Oriented Analysis and Design Methods," *Object-Oriented Development Methods,* Andrew Carmichael, ed., SIGS Books, New York, 1994, pp. 79–110.

Martin, James, and James J. Odell, *Object-Oriented Methods: A Foundation,* Prentice Hall, Englewood Cliffs, NJ, 1995.

Chapter 5

Object Analysis Method

A METHOD FOR OBJECT ANALYSIS USING OBJECT DIAGRAMS

The previous chapter presented elements of object diagrams. This chapter presents a step-by-step method for constructing a structural specification using the object-diagram technique. The method described here (see Fig. 5.1) is independent of any behavioral considerations. As such it describes only part of the requirements for an area being analyzed. In other words, object analysis should also be combined with some form of behavioral analysis to specify an

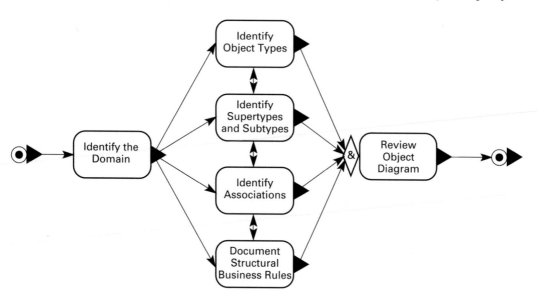

Figure 5.1   An object analysis method.

analysis domain more completely. (Full integration with a behavioral view will be discussed in Chapter 7.)

Identify the Domain

Object-oriented analysis specifies the object structure and behavior relevant to a *domain* of interest. Each domain defines a particular universe of objects, or scope, that we wish to model. It provides a frame of reference. By considering each domain as delineating an area of activity, the analyst and expert will have a manageable area in which they can focus their analysis efforts. While a picture may be worth a thousand words, a picture with a thousand object types is not a good analysis tool. Therefore, each domain must provide a tangible platform for a topic. With it, the analyst is saying "let's discuss a processing specification at this level of detail."

Identify Object Types

Identify concepts (i.e., object types) that are relevant to this domain. Initially, avoid making too many judgments about the validity of each object type—just record its existence.

After listing the possible object types, check the repository to see if they have already been defined and used outside of this domain. For each object type already known, review its existing definition and description to ensure that it correctly reflects the business facts recently discovered. If the identified object type is new, create a definition for it. Define the object type in business terms as thoroughly as possible.

At any point in the process, it may be discovered that an object type is synonymous with another, already identified, object type. When this occurs, consider whether it is exactly the same object type or is, in fact, a subtype or supertype of the existing object type. If it is the same, ensure that the facts about the object type are complete and record the synonym as an alternative name. If it is different, add the new object type to the repository.

Identify Supertypes and Subtypes

For each object type, consider its theoretically possible supertypes. For instance, a possible supertype of House is Residential Building, where the supertype of Residential Building could be Building, and so on. There are two purposes to this step. The first is determining whether the domain is placed at the correct level. For example, if the domain supports a mortgage process, the object type House seems obvious. However people also live in apartments, condominiums, and trailer parks. Here, the object type Residential Building would be more appropriate than House for this domain. The second purpose of this step is to help identify reusable components. For example, a mortgage process for Buildings might have already been defined by the bank—or some vendor of reusable analysis constructs. But if the project team did not recognize that House objects are also Buildings, the possible reuse of Building-related components would also not be recognized.

When new subtypes and a new supertype are identified, use the Identify Object Types step to formalize them.

Identify Associations

As object types are placed on the object diagram, identify associations with other object types. For each association—whether expressed as a relationship or attribute type—specify its cardinality constraints. For relationships, other constraints may also be specified at this time, such as list, tree, invariance, and nontransitive. Nonstandard constraints should be expressed by a business rule.

When a relationship type has its own properties or behavior, it should be expressed as an associative object type (i.e., a symbol that represents the relationship as an object type in its own right).

Relationships, too, can be subtyped and supertyped. For example, a **Message** may be sent to any number of **Persons**. The **sent to** relationship could be subtyped to express the subset of messages **sent privately** to only one person. Often, such relationship types end up being expressed as associative object types.

Composite relationship types can be recognized by their part/whole quality. For instance, **Water** consists of **Hydrogen** and **Oxygen**, and an **Organization** consists of its **Employees**.

Many analysts model associations as model attribute types in addition to relationship types. Use this step when identifying these kinds of associations. Remember that attributes, like any other association, map from one object type to another. Many analysts only document the "from" and not the "to" object type. For example, a **birthdate** attribute type maps from a **Person** object type to a **Date** object type. Omitting either object type could result in an incorrect OO design, thus decreasing the chances of reusability.

If the identified association is new, name it and create a definition for it. Define the association in business terms as thoroughly as possible. Check the repository to see if the association has already been defined and used outside of this project. Check whether the new association is a synonym for an existing one and record the synonym.

Document Structural Rules

As the structural elements are being identified and defined, business rules will be articulated. Ensure that all object types and relationship types expressed in each business rule are also represented on, or with, the object diagram. Also, examine each of the components that are added to the object diagram and question whether appropriate rules, such as derivation or constraint rules, should be specified. If the identified rule is new, create a specification for it. Describe the rule in business terms as well. Check the repository to see if the rule has already been defined and used outside of this project.

Review the Object Model

After incorporating additions and changes to the concept view of the business model, review the integrity of the entire model. Examine the object types for those:

- That are similar in scope and meaning. Consider whether they are the same object type or perhaps participants in a generalization relationship type.

- That have a confusing or imprecise meaning. Try to improve the definition.
- That can be generalized further and made more reusable for the future.

Examine the relationship types for those:

- That have a one-to-one cardinality. Check whether the relationship type is a generalization relationship type.

Examine the subtype/supertypes with:

- Partitions that contain only one object type. Check that the partition is an incomplete partition.
- Partitions that contain multiple object types. Check that the object types in the partition are disjoint.
- Object types which have more than one partition. Check that separate partitions are justified.

Check the object model to ensure that all relevant object types, relationship types, and attribute types are represented. Remove all object types, relationship types, and attribute types that are not used within the domain being analyzed. In other words, the model should contain all that is needed for the domain—and no more. The behavioral view is the determining factor for this. If a component in a domain's object diagram is not accessed or modified by some process, that component has no usefulness in the domain. (See Chapter 7 for a process-driven method that ensures that all the appropriate structure elements are identified and not more.)

Last, in order to be useful as a visual communication device, any diagram must be aesthetically pleasing as well as correct. As such, analysts should judge their diagrams by the following rules:

- If it looks messy, it's probably wrong.
- If it's too complex, it's probably wrong.
- If it's too big, it's probably wrong.
- If people don't like it, it's probably wrong.
- If it doesn't work, it *is* wrong.

Chapter **6**

Event Diagrams

INTRODUCTION

Event diagrams are expressed using four basic process-related notions: operations, events, triggers, and control conditions. Operations are processes that carry out the state change. Event types define state changes that result from operations and invoke other operations via *trigger rules*. *Control conditions* ensure that a certain state exists before a certain operation can be triggered. In the following sections, these core-level notions will be summarized using a graphical notation called the *event diagram*. (An in-depth presentation of these elements is presented by Odell [Martin, 1995].)

An example of event-diagram notation is depicted in Fig. 6.1. Here, each time the operation called Ship Order is invoked, it is expected to result in an Order shipped event. When this event occurs, a trigger invokes the Close Order operation. However, before the actual invocation of the operation, its control condition is checked. In this

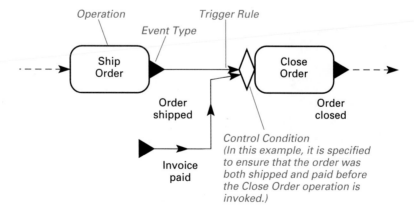

Figure 6.1   An example of an event diagram.

example, the control-condition evaluation ensures that a particular order has been both shipped to and paid for by the customer. Only then can the **Close Order** operation be executed. If no control condition is expressed for the **Close Order** operation, the operation would be executed immediately when triggered by *any* event.

The **Invoice paid** event-type symbol has no associated operation to indicate that such an operation is external to the figure's processing specification. In other words, the way in which an invoice is paid is *outside* the specification's scope. The event type appears here to indicate that it is a stimulus for operations *within* the processing scope.

The event type, **Order shipped**, defines the set of all the events in which a particular order was shipped. The order shipped at 9:23 this morning would be one such event; the one at 11:21 would be another. The operation **Ship Order** is the set of all instances of order-shipping processes. The invoked operation that resulted in the 9:23 A.M. shipment is one such instance; the one that resulted in the 11:21 A.M. order shipment is another. In this way, each event and invoked operation is an object in its own right.

EVENTS VERSUS STATE CHANGES

Our world is full of changes. Uncle Fred arrives unexpectedly. An airline booking is canceled. A machine tool breaks down. A job is completed. Such changes in state are important to us, because they signal a need to acknowledge the change in some way. For instance in Fig. 6.2, the traffic light can change between three basic states. If we are distant from this traffic light, its changes are unknown and, therefore, unimportant to us. However, if we arrive at the intersection when it changes to yellow or red, we should react appropriately. When state changes are important enough for us to acknowledge, they are called *events*.

> An *event* is a noteworthy change in state.
>
> An *event type* is a kind of event.

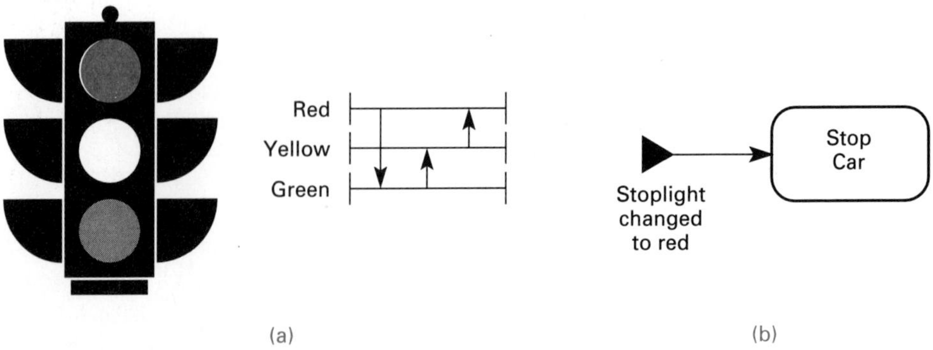

(a)   (b)

Figure 6.2   The traffic light in (a) can change state in three ways. State changes that we should acknowledge are *events*—such as a stoplight changing to red as we approach an intersection (b).

Fundamentally, two kinds of state changes occur: add and remove. An *add* state change brings a new object or relationship into existence. A *remove* state change removes an object or relationship from existence. For example, the person labeled Paul in Fig. 6.3 decided to leave NASA and form his own company called HAL Explorations. Here, a state change is required to remove not NASA or Paul, but to remove Paul's employment relationship with NASA. Another state change is required to add a new **Company** object named HAL Explorations. Yet another state change is required to add a new employment relationship between Paul and HAL Explorations.

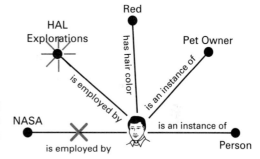

Figure 6.3 State changes result in adding or removing objects. Since relationships can also be treated as objects, state changes can add and remove them as well.

While state changes *fundamentally* add and remove objects, specifying changes in this way is not always user friendly. For instance, when Paul buys his first pet, a state change would add an association between Paul and the **Pet Owner** object type. While such a statement is technically correct, perhaps it would be clearer to say that the state change *classifies* Paul as a **Pet Owner**, instead. However, specifying the addition of **employed by** or **has hair color** associations in this way would not be appropriate. Instead, we could say that the HAL Explorations and Paul objects are *connected* in a new relationship, and the old NASA and Paul relationship is *disconnected*. These and other specifications are addressed with several basic kinds of state changes. In particular, this section discusses how objects can be: created, terminated, classified, declassified, reclassified, connected, disconnected, coalesced, and decoalesced. Every event can be classified as one of these kinds of state changes—even though each fundamentally involves adding or removing objects.

Creation Event

In a *creation* event, an entirely new object appears. For example, the event type **Breakfast started** occurs when an object is created and becomes a member of the **Breakfast** set in Fig. 6.4(a). **Order received** indicates that an object is created as an instance of the object type **Order**. A creation event, then, is the change from not being an object at all to that of being an object of at least one specific type.

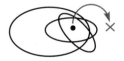

Figure 6.4 Object creation and termination.

(a) Breakfast Started   (b) Breakfast Completed

Termination Event

In a *termination* event, an existing object is removed from our awareness. For example in Fig. 6.4(b), the event type Breakfast completed occurs when a Breakfast object no longer exists.

Classification Event

A *classification* event is the classification of an *existing* object. For example in Fig. 6.5(a), the event type Person classified Employee occurs when a Person object *also* becomes a member of the Employee set. In this state change, an object becomes a member of a set of which it was not previously a member.

Declassification Event

A *declassification* event is the declassification of an existing object. In Fig. 6.5(b), the event type Person declassified Employee occurs when a Person object is removed as a member of the Employee set—after which the object remains a Person but is no longer an Employee. The state change is from being an object of one or more sets to that of being an object of one less set.

     Employee   Employee

    Person   Person

(a)   (b)

Figure 6.5 Object classification and declassification.

Connection Event

A *connection* event adds an entirely new association between two objects. For example in Fig. 6.6(a), the event type Person employed occurs when a Person object is associated with an Organization via an is employed by/employs relationship. Such an event appears to be the same as a *create* event, because a new relationship is created. While this is true, some developers prefer the metaphor of connecting objects an easier one to understand. Connection events, then, are creation events for relationships. The state change is the change from not being a relationship at all to that of being a relationship

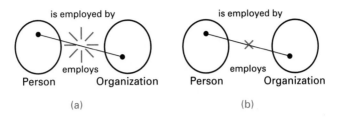

Figure 6.6　Object connection and disconnection.

of some particular type. (The connection event is also used to describe changes in attributes.)

Disconnection Event

A *disconnection* event removes an existing relationship between two objects. For example in Fig. 6.6(b), the event type **Person unemployed** occurs when an **is employed by/employs** relationship is removed between a **Person** object and an **Organization** object. Disconnection events, then, are termination events for relationships. The state change is from being a relationship of some type to being a relationship that no longer exists.

Compound Events

Create, terminate, classify, declassify, connect, and disconnect are the kinds of events that either add or remove an object from a set. However, some events are more transactional, because they require simultaneous adds and removes. This is particularly true of reclassification and reconnection events.

Reclassification Event

Object reclassification is a compound event, because it consists of an object-declassification event and an object-classification event. It is useful when these two events cannot occur separately. For example, in Fig. 6.7(a) a **Person** object must either be married or unmarried. Declassifying an **Unmarried Person** object without *simultaneously* classifying it as a **Married Person** would create an illogical void. Object reclassification eliminates the difficulties of this by classifying and declassifying at the same time.

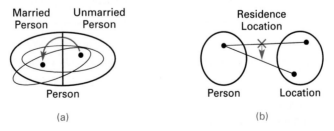

Figure 6.7　Reclassification and reconnection events.

Reconnection Event

A *reconnection* event is the simultaneous termination of one relationship and creation of another of the same type—while keeping one of its related objects the same throughout. For example, in Fig 6.7(b) each relationship in a **Residence Location** relationship associates a **Person** object and a **Location** object. Here, the **Residence Location** relationship type requires that each **Person** object relate to *exactly* one **Location** object at all times. To remove a relationship—even for a moment—violates the **Residence Location** cardinality constraint. Such a situation makes changing a person's residence impossible unless **Residence Location** relationships can be terminated and created simultaneously. The reconnection event eliminates the difficulties of this by connecting and disconnecting at the same time.

Coalesce and Decoalesce Events

In a *coalesce* event, a set of objects—previously recognized as distinct—becomes the same object. For example, many mystery stories have one **Murderer** object and one **Chauffeur** object. Following the event called **The Chauffeur Did It**, these two objects are perceived as one and the same object. As indicated in Fig. 6.8(a), all object types that applied to each object separately now apply to the coalesced object. The previous two objects are henceforth recognized as the same thing. The *object decoalesce* in Fig 6.8(b) has the opposite effect.

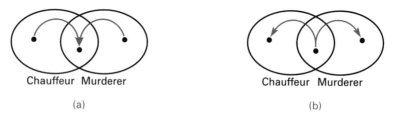

Chauffeur Murderer   Chauffeur Murderer

(a)   (b)

Figure 6.8   Object coalesce and decoalesce.

Event Prestates and Poststates

As indicated earlier, each event is a change in the state of one object. This change implies that each event has a specified prestate and a specified poststate.

> An *event prestate* is a state that *must* apply to an object *before* the event occurs.
>
> An *event poststate* is a state that *must* apply to an object *after* the event occurs.

Figure 6.9(a) specifies the prestates and poststates required for each of the eight most common kinds of events. In addition, Fig. 6.9(b) provides examples of each of these events.

Event Type	Event Prestate	Event Poststate
X created	not Object	X
X terminated	X	not Object
X classified C	X, but not C	X and C
X declassified C	X and C	X, but not C
R connected	No R between C1 and C2 objects	R between C1 and C2 objects
R disconnected	R between C1 and C2 objects	No R between C1 and C2 objects
X reclassified from C1 to C2	X and C1, but not C2	X and C2 but not C1
R reconnected from C1 to C2	R1 but no R2 between C1 and C2 objects	R2 but no R1 between C1 and C2 objects

(a)

Event Example	Event Prestate	Event Poststate
Breakfast created	not Object	Breakfast
Breakfast terminated	Breakfast	not Object
Person classified Employee	Person, but not Employee	Person and Employee
Person declassified Employee	Person and Employee	Person, but not Employee
Person employed	Organization and Person not related	Organization and Person related
Person unemployed	Organization and Person related	Organization and Person not related
Person married	Unmarried Person	Married Person
Residence changed	Residence	Residence (different tuple)

(b)

Figure 6.9 Examples of event prestates and poststates for the eight most common kinds of events.

Internal, External, and Temporal Events

Events are not spontaneously generated. They are caused by some process that makes the state change occur. Events, then, result from the completion of an operation.

Events can also be regarded as being internally, externally, or temporally caused. An *internal event* occurs as a result of an operation that is within the analyst's domain. For example, the event depicted in Fig. 6.10(a) specifies a Book transferred event that occurs as a result of a Transfer Book operation. The word *internal* is usually omitted when referring to events of this kind.

An *external event* is the result of an operation external to the analyst's domain. Even though the operation is considered external, external events are identified when they have an impact on the analyst's system. For example, the external event in Fig. 6.10(b) indicates that requests to check out library books occur. For the book borrower with a term paper to write, the event would actually be internal, because requesting books is something that borrowers do. For a library, however, the event is external because the

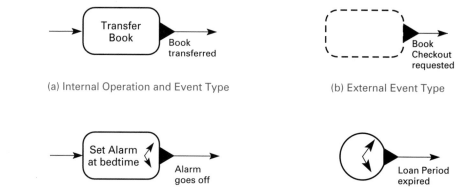

Figure 6.10   Expressing internal, external, and temporal events.

processes leading up to the event belong to the borrower—not the library. Yet, even though the actual operation is external to the library, **Book Checkout requested** is an event to which a library must respond. Therefore, to the library, the event depicted in Fig. 6.10(b) is externally *caused*. Since the causing operation is external to the library, the operation symbol may be omitted entirely. (Some analysts prefer to use a dashed-operation symbol as depicted in the figure. However, such a symbol is just a visual aid and should not be associated with any particular external operation, because it is external. Furthermore, an external event type may result from one of several different external events. For instance, a **Person washed** event could result from **Bathe Person**, **Shower Person**, or **Hose Down Person**. If the operation is external, it is outside of the analyst's scope. Only the external *event* is in the analyst's scope.)

Temporal events are the results of clock operations which are operations that emit a specified pattern of clock-tick events. For example, a temporal event could be **End-of-year is reached**, **April 15th has occurred**, or **My Birthday has arrived**. Since the actual clock operation can be internal and external to the analyst's domain, temporal events can be represented in two ways. Figures 6.10(c) and (d) depict internal and external clock event types.

Event Partitions

As discussed in Chapter 4, object types can have subtypes and supertypes. Event types are no exception, because they too are object types. The example in Fig. 6.11(a) depicts a **Gas Usage determined** event type. Its partition contains two mutually exclusive event types: **Gas Usage from Meter determined** and **Gas Usage estimated**. In other words, every instance of **Gas Usage from Meter determined** event *or* a **Gas Usage estimated** event *is* a **Gas Usage determined** event. This figure indicates that if *either* event subtype occurs, a **Gas Usage determined** event also occurs. **Gas Usage determined** is *implied*—not caused—by **Gas Usage from Meter determined** or **Gas Usage estimated**.

Figure 6.11(b) expresses the **Light Switch turned** event type as a form of decision-branching mechanism. Here, depending on what occurs during a **Turn Light Switch** oper-

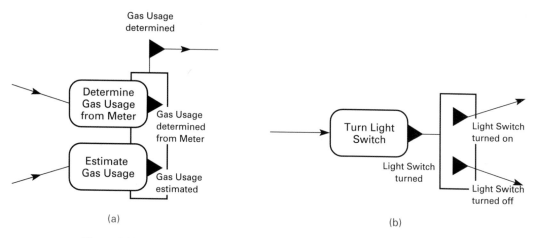

Figure 6.11   Approaching an event partition from its subtypes or its supertype.
One converges processing, the other acts as a decision branch.

ation, a Light becomes either turned on or off. In other words, an occurrence of a Light
Switch turned event might also be an occurrence of a Light Switch turned on or a Light
Switch turned off event—each triggering different processes.

OPERATIONS

While events are noteworthy changes in state, operations are the processing units that
make the change.

> An *operation* is a process that can be requested as a unit.

In Fig. 6.12, for example, each Person employed event is a change resulting from the
Employ Person operation. When invoked, this operation changes the state of an object
from an Unemployed Person to an Employed Person. In other words, the invoked operation is a process that employs a Person according to a specified method. Its event is the
completed operation.

Because operations and event types differ in meaning, they are represented by two
separate symbols. They are paired to acknowledge that, in principle, they are two different views of the same thing. The oo analyst focusing on the mechanism for change uses
the operation view. When focusing on its effect, the analyst uses the event-type view. In
this way, operations and event types may be defined together.*

---

*Operations are not *required* to end with events. For example, a Perform Finances operation
may have no ending point. Instead, once invoked, it could continue as long as a company is in business. Such operations are present in object-flow diagrams (see Chapter 17). Only those operations
that conclude with a noteworthy state change are specified with events.

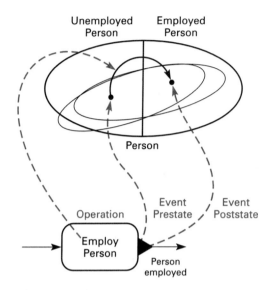

Figure 6.12 Events are change, and operations are agents of change.

Operation Input Variables

Each operation requires objects on which to operate. For example, the **Wash Person** operation requires a **Person** object to wash. Without an object to wash, the operation has no purpose. The operation resulting in an **Employee classified Manager** event requires an **Employee** object to classify. All operations then require objects as variables.

A major benefit of the OO approach is that it provides a way of organizing our knowledge. With OO, knowledge is organized around *types* of things. Prior to OO, knowledge of data and process was modeled in ad hoc ways—by programmer, subsystem, disk drive, and so on. With the advent of data modeling, knowledge of *data* was modeled by types—called entity types. However, knowledge of processes remained ad hoc.

With OO, *processing* is also organized by types. For example, an object type such as **Person** could be a point of organization, or *index*, for those structural and behavioral aspects of people. This would include structural properties, such as the person's name and address, date of high school graduation, and so on. This would also include those operations required to access and maintain **Person** objects, such as **Change Person Name, Change Person Address,** and **Get Person High School Graduation Date.** In this way the analyst could ask, Where could I find an operation that gets a person's age? Since the operation queries the state of a **Person** object as the input variable, the **Person** object type would be a place to find the **Get Person's Age** operation. The **Change Order Status** and **Delete Order** operations would probably be associated with the **Order** object type. The **Create Order** operation cannot begin with an object, because the **Order** cannot exist until the operation is completed. In these situations, the operation is traditionally associated with the object type that is *to be* created. The **Create Order** operation, therefore, would be associated with the

Order object type. In this way, locating an operation (especially for modification or reuse) is greatly simplified.

The input variables of operations (or the output variable of an object-creation operation) serve as indexes that organize our knowledge of the operations. As such, they should be documented carefully. Figure 6.13 indicates three ways of graphically documenting the type to which an operation is associated. In Fig. 6.13(a), the type of input is specified above the operation symbol. In Fig. 6.13(b), the type of input is represented with a rectangular symbol and is associated with the operation symbol. In Fig. 6.13(c), the type of input is specified in parenthesis below the name of the operation. Figure 6.13 indicates just a few ways the analyst can document that operations have been assigned to types. Because some analysts prefer not to clutter their diagrams, they document these properties on separate sheets of paper or by double-clicking on the operation symbol in a CASE environment to bring up a separate screen.

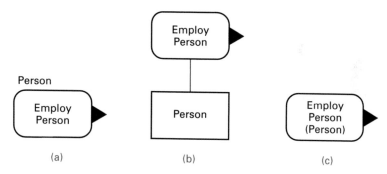

Figure 6.13   Three ways (among many) for associating operations and the types of objects they require as input. In OO analysis, this provides a mechanism for organizing operations. In OO design, it indicates the class to which the operation should be attached.

Handling More than One Input Variable

Operations such as Employ Person and Terminate Order could have single variables as input. However, changing the telephone number associated with a person would require at least two objects: a Person object and a Telephone Number object. Attach Wing to Plane requires both Wing and Plane objects. As above, operations are indexed by the types of objects that are required as input. Therefore, the Change Person's Telephone Number would be indexed by Person and Telephone Number—which is appropriate during OO analysis. However, in OO design this can pose a problem, because most OO implementations permit operations to be associated with only *one* type, or *class*. Therefore, in Smalltalk or C++ the Change Person's Telephone Number operation must be *either* part of the Person class *or* the Telephone Number class. A customer service agent would probably choose to attach the operation to the Person class. A telephone switching technician would probably attach the operation to the **Telephone Number** class.[*]

However, such implementation-related choices are not made during analysis. The analyst should index those operations having multiple input variables with multiple object types and should defer implementation-related decisions until OO design. There-fore, operations such as **Change Person's Telephone Number** could be represented in the same manner as Fig. 6.13, except that it should be associated with multiple types: **Person** and **Telephone Number**. These same diagrams, then, could be used during tradi-tional OO design. Here, the designer could annotate the analysis diagram with numbers indicating the *sequence* of input variables—where the *first* variable would indicate the class to which the operation is attached.

Operation Output Variables

The input variables of an operation receive a lot of attention, because of their role as indexes both in OO analysis and in class encapsulation in OO design. However, the output must also be defined for each operation. In OO, an operation is a function that, given input, returns a result. If the input is the right kind and the process is correctly specified, the correct result should be produced. The result can yield objects of various kinds. Out-put variables, then, are required to specify just what kinds of objects will come out of the operation. For instance, **Employ Person** would take a **Person** object and return an object that is both a **Person** and an **Employee**.

Operation Preconditions and Postconditions

To ensure that an operation performs correctly, constraints specify those conditions that must hold before and after the operation. Such constraints are vital to the execution of an operation and are completely independent of the context under which the operation is invoked. Bertrand Meyer states that the presence of these constraints should be viewed as a contract that binds an operation and its requestors. Here, the operation says "if you call me with the precondition satisfied, I promise to deliver a final state in which the postcon-dition is satisfied" [Meyer, 1988 and 1992].

A *precondition* specifies the constraints under which an operation will perform cor-rectly.

A *postcondition* specifies those conditions that must result when an operation com-pletes.

---

[*]The same operation *could* be placed in both classes. However, this would result in code redundancy that could easily get out of hand unless carefully controlled. With languages like CLOS and implementations like the Object Request Broker, such decisions may not be required, as they are with traditional OO languages.

In a correct system, the operation cannot go ahead unless its preconditions are met. Examples of preconditions are:

```
Promote Staff Employee to Manager
    ONLY IF this Employee is not a Manager.
Marry Couple
    ONLY IF both Persons are not married.
```

In contrast, *postconditions* guarantee the results. This kind of constraint says that when an operation is executed, a certain state must result—*provided* the operation was invoked with the precondition satisfied. Examples of postconditions are:

```
Promote Staff Employee to Manager IS CORRECTLY COMPLETED
    ONLY IF this Employee is a Manager.
Marry Couple IS CORRECTLY COMPLETED
    ONLY IF both persons are married to each other.
```

METHODS

In OO, operations can be thought of as transactions. Transactions are processes or series of processes acting as units to change the state of objects [Tsichritzis, 1982]. When considered in this way, operations are expected to complete their processing—even if it takes seconds, days, or years. The specification for carrying such operations is called the *method*.

A *method* is a processing specification for an operation.

In most OO programming languages, the method is specified by lines of code. In OO analysis, various techniques can be used. For example, Fig. 6.14 depicts just two ways of representing a method. A so-called pseudocode approach is used in Fig. 6.14(a), where the method is specified in a line-by-line form. The graphic approach of an event diagram is used in Fig. 6.14(b). The first technique is familiar to most programmers because of its format and linear nature. The second supports both sequential and concurrent specification techniques. Both, however, invoke other operations to carry out their purpose. Several other approaches can be used to represent behavior, such as SQL, production rule, fuzzy logic statements, and neural networks.

Operations Can Consist of Other Operations

In Fig. 6.14, the method of an operation can invoke other operations to achieve its end. This means that—in addition to sequence, concurrence, and control-condition specifications—an operation can consist of other operations. In this way, operations can be treated

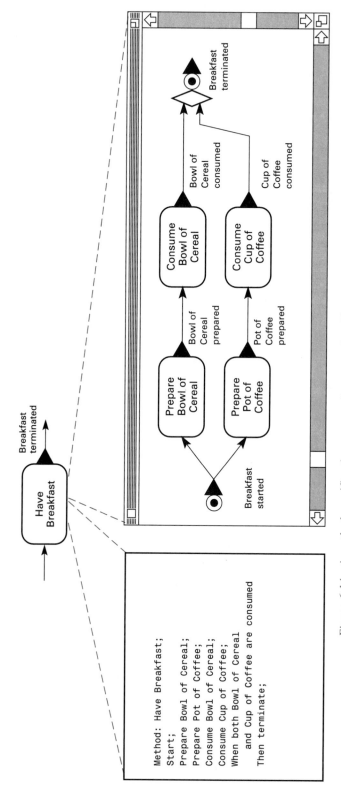

Method: Have Breakfast;
Start;
Prepare Bowl of Cereal;
Prepare Pot of Coffee;
Consume Bowl of Cereal;
Consume Cup of Coffee;
When both Bowl of Cereal
    and Cup of Coffee are consumed
Then terminate;

Figure 6.14 A method specifies the process of an operation. Here, two methods for the Have Breakfast operation are expressed using pseudocode and an event diagram.

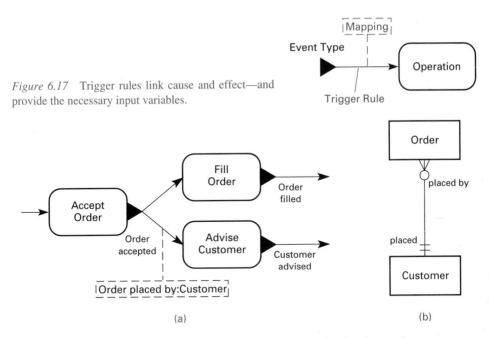

Figure 6.17 Trigger rules link cause and effect—and provide the necessary input variables.

Figure 6.18 Example of a *trivial* and a *named* mapping by trigger rules.

```
WHEN     Order accepted with Order object,
THEN     DO Fill Order operation with the Order object.
```

Trigger Rules with Named Mappings

However, an event often occurs with a different object from that required by a triggered operation. For example, the Advise Customer operation in Fig. 6.18(a) requires a Customer object. Yet the preceding Accept Order operation results in an Order object. Somehow the trigger must resolve the difference between the output of one operation and the required input of another operation. This is accomplished by using the placed by mapping, depicted in Fig. 6.18(b), that assigns each Order to the Customer that placed the Order. Therefore, to be the cause-and-effect link between Order accepted and Advise Customer, the trigger must use a *named* mapping. In Fig. 6.18(a), the trigger uses the placed by:Customer mapping to obtain the Customer object associated with the given Order object.

Trigger Rules That Involve More Than One Object

Operations are not restricted to requiring only one object as an input variable. Figure 6.19(a) illustrates one such example. The output variable from Obtain Marriage License is a Marriage License object. However, the operation that performs the marriage ceremony requires two variables: a bride and a groom. In Fig. 6.19(b), a given Marriage License

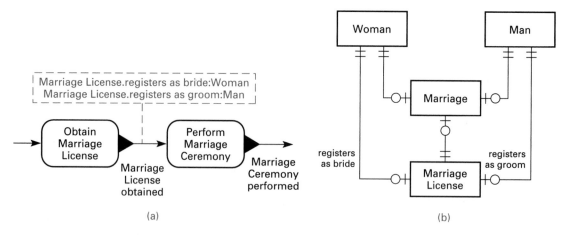

Figure 6.19   An operation that has multiple input variables and its object diagram.

object has an association with both a bride and groom object via the **registers as bride** and **registers as groom** mappings. The trigger rule in Fig. 6.19(a) uses these mappings to obtain the two objects required by the **Perform Marriage Ceremony** operation. Instead of the graphic representation in Fig. 6.19(a), the following rule could be used:

    WHEN   Marriage License obtained
              with Marriage License object,

    THEN   Do Perform Marriage Ceremony
              with registers as bride:Woman
              and registers as groom:Man.

In the example above, the **Perform Marriage Ceremony** operation is defined requiring bride and groom objects as input. Instead, the operation could be defined as only requiring a marriage license object. Once invoked, the operation could determine the bride and groom from the marriage license—minimizing the coupling between operations. Here, the invoking trigger would involve only a trivial mapping from **Obtain Marriage License** to **Perform Marriage Ceremony**. However, reusing such a **Perform Marriage Ceremony** operation would not be possible in other contexts that do not *require* a marriage license. For example, ship captains conducting ceremonies on the high seas may not require a license. Common-law marriages, by definition, do not require licenses. Therefore, while striving to minimize coupling, the analyst should also consider reusability.

CONTROL CONDITIONS

In the section above on operations, *preconditions* specify those constraints under which an operation will perform correctly. An operation cannot go ahead unless its preconditions have been met. Such constraints are vital to the execution of an operation and must always be true whenever the operation is invoked. Control conditions are also constraints that must be checked before an operation can begin execution. However, these constraints can differ based on processing context.

A *control condition* is a mechanism that when triggered permits its associated operation to begin only when its constraints are met.

For instance, the precondition for the **Close Order** operation in Fig. 6.20 is that the **Order** object supplied as input cannot be a closed order. This condition must hold whenever the **Close Order** operation is invoked. In addition to this precondition, two control conditions define additional constraints. The control condition on the left of the **Close Order** operation is invoked whenever an **Order shipped** or a **Payment received** event occurs. It specifies that before the **Close Order** operation can begin, its order must have been shipped *and* its payment received. The control condition on the top of the operation is invoked whenever an external **Order Cancellation received** event occurs. It specifies that the **Close Order** operation can begin only if its order has not already been shipped.

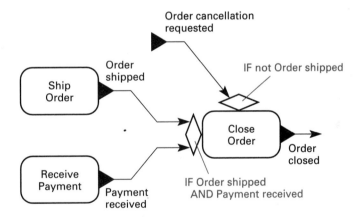

Figure 6.20 When triggered, a Close Order control condition is evaluated. Only when the condition is true can the operation begin. In addition to the precondition, multiple control conditions are also possible.

An operation's precondition can be thought of as part of the operation, because its constraint must be met whenever the operation is invoked. The control condition should not be regarded as part of the operation, because the control condition need not always be true. It must be true only when invoked by a particular trigger (or triggers). Therefore, on event diagrams the diamond-shaped, control-condition symbol is attached to the *outside* of the operation. Thus, it is graphically apparent that control conditions are not part of an operation—but are trigger dependent.

In summary, a precondition must always be true when the operation is invoked. However, an operation's control conditions can differ based on context. Taken all together, the preconditions, trigger rules, and control conditions of an operation can be thought of as the *complete* precondition of an operation.

Specifying Control Conditions

Control conditions can be expressed in an "if. . . then. . ." form. When invoked, they determine if certain conditions are true. The statements of condition can be simple or can consist of a very complex set of "ands" and "ors." For example, a conditional statement could read: If (A or B) and (C) and (not D or E) and so on. Such conditions are called Boolean because they result in either a true or a false condition.

Figure 6.21 depicts another example of a control condition. Its conditional statement is defined as follows:

```
IF a product has been dispensed,
    and the correct change has been given,
THEN begin Complete Sale operation.
```

In this example, at least the **Product dispensed** event must occur to fulfill the conditional statement. If a customer inserts 75¢ and a 75¢ item is dispensed, no **Give Change** is required. In this scenario, the control condition is satisfied and the sale can be completed.[*] However, if a customer inserts 75¢ and a 60¢ item is dispensed, 15¢ in change is due. Therefore, the sale is not completed when the **Product dispensed** event occurs, because the "correct change has been given" condition in the conditional statement has yet to be fulfilled. At this point, no further condition checking occurs until the control condition is again triggered. (In other words, the control condition does not continuously check if the condition is true. Such an approach would cripple processing if there were many control conditions.) When the **Change given** event finally does occur, the control condition will be retriggered and the entire condition will be reevaluated—this

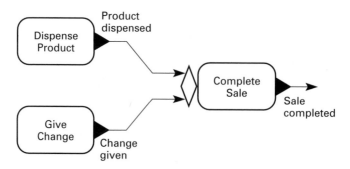

Figure 6.21   A vending machine sale can be completed if its control condition is true. This control condition does not always require both events to occur.

[*]In another approach to this, the **Change given** must still occur—even if the amount given is 0.

time resulting in a **Sale completed** event. If the event never occurs, the control condition will never be reevaluated and the operation will never be invoked.

Control Conditions Provide Synchronization

The primary purpose of control conditions is to synchronize a series of operations. For example, the control condition in Fig. 6.21 synchronizes completing a sale only after its product is dispensed and change is given. In Fig. 6.22, the control condition synchronizes sending a **Job Bill** only after all of the **Tasks** for a particular **Job** are complete. In this example, each instance of the **Perform Task** operation on the left completes one **Task**. After each **Task** is completed, the **Send Job Bill** control condition is evaluated. The control condition determines whether any **Tasks** remain uncompleted for the **Job**. If *any* of the associated **Tasks** has not been completed, the **Send Job Bill** operation cannot begin. In this example, various **Tasks** run to completion (either in serial or in parallel fashion). The control condition for **Send Job Bill** synchronizes its billing application by not allowing any subsequent processing to occur until all **Tasks** are completed.

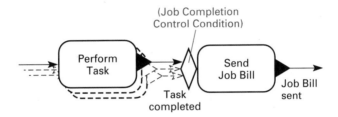

Figure 6.22 A control condition synchronizes processing by ensuring that all tasks are completed before the Send Job Bill operation can begin.

Common Control Condition Shorthand

Two common types of control conditions are so simple that they can be expressed with special symbols instead of words. For example, sometimes the control condition is simply an "and" condition of the events triggering it and nothing else. In Fig. 6.23(a), the control condition for **Cancel Sale** is true when **Change given** and **Cancellation requested** events occur—and nothing else. The *simple-and* (or *conjunction*) control condition is expressed with an "&" in the diamond. (This notation is used extensively in Part VII.) Another control condition could be true when no more processing is pending for an event diagram at some point. The *when-all-is-quiet* control condition is expressed with a "z" in the diamond and is illustrated in Fig. 6.23(b).

Figure 6.23 Expressing *simple-and* and *when-all-is-quiet* control conditions.

(a)   (b)

CONCLUSION

This chapter summarizes most of the diagramming elements required to model object behavior using the Martin/Odell object diagram. The following chapter suggests methods for constructing event diagrams.

REFERENCES

Martin, James, and James J. Odell, *Object-Oriented Methods: A Foundation,* Prentice Hall, Englewood Cliffs, NJ, 1995.

Meyer, Bertrand, *Object-Oriented Software Construction,* Prentice Hall, New York, 1988.

Meyer, Bertrand, "Applying 'Design' by Contract," IEEE Computer, 25:10, 1992, pp. 40–51.

Tsichritzis, Dionysios C., and Frederick H. Lochovsky, *Data Models,* Prentice Hall, Englewood Cliffs, NJ, 1982.

Chapter **7**

Event Analysis

A METHOD FOR GOAL-DIRECTED EVENT ANALYSIS

The previous chapter presented elements of event diagrams. Event diagrams can be constructed in two general ways: goal-directed or event-directed. Additionally, such diagrams can be constructed employing process-driven steps. These will all be discussed later in this chapter. A step-by-step method for constructing goal-directed event diagrams is discussed in this section and summarized in Fig. 7.1.

Define Analysis Focus

When constructing an event diagram, the analyst must begin by examining what to model—and what not to model. In short, the analyst and domain expert must define the focus of the diagram.

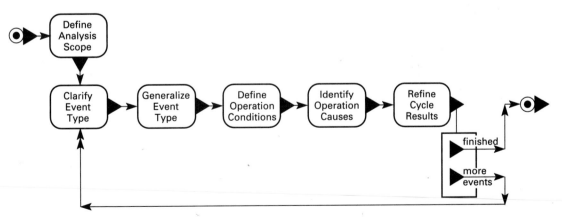

Figure 7.1   An event-analysis method that is object-oriented, process-oriented, and goal-directed.

Identify the Domain

As discussed in Chapter 5, OO analysis specifies the object structure and behavior that is relevant to a *domain* of interest. Each domain defines a particular universe of objects, or scope, that the analyst wishes to model. It provides a frame of reference. (Other methodologies refer to domains as realms, universes, and spaces.) Since event analysis is a technique for specifying process, each domain defines a specific processing scope. In this way, management payroll, product manufacturing, or vending-machine operation could each be domains for which its method is defined. By considering each domain, then, as delineating a method for a given operation, the analyst and expert will have a manageable area in which they can focus their analysis. Each domain must provide a tangible platform for a topic. With it, the analyst is saying "let's discuss a processing specification at this level of detail."

Identify the Target Event Type

Once the domain has been identified, its purpose or *target* must be expressed. This target identifies the desired endpoint of the domain's processing. For example, some domains and their target event types might be:

Domain	Target Event Types
Recruitment	Employee added
Accounts Payable	Payment created
Order Administration	Order terminated
Vending-Machine Operation	Sale completed
Battle Management	Threat removed

Identifying the target event types is crucial to the method. Without a target, or goal, the selected domain has no clearly understandable purpose. (Either object-flow diagrams or use-case diagrams can help in such situations. See Chapter 8 for object-flow diagrams.)

The starting event type is also important (see Fig. 7.2). Identifying when a domain begins its processing provides another analysis boundary. By knowing the start and end of a domain, the analyst and end user can identify the borders of the specification and can "bracket" their work.

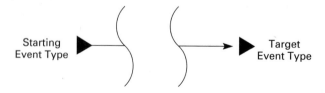

Figure 7.2   While the target event type is mandatory, the starting event type is also important.

Since this method is goal directed, the target event type is selected as the starting point for the next step.

Clarify Event Type

This step enables the analyst to define the underlying meaning of the chosen event type and provide its label.

Formalize Event Type

As discussed in the previous chapter, several basic kinds of events are: create, terminate, classify, declassify, reclassify, tuple substitution, and so on. In this step, the analyst identifies the kind of event to which the chosen event type conforms.

Associated with each basic kind of event are event prestate and poststate object types. The event prestate is an object type that applies to the underlying object before the event takes place. The event poststate is an object type that applies to the underlying object after the event takes place. In addition to indicating the basic kind of event, this step also identifies its associated event prestates and poststates. Examples of these are illustrated in Fig. 7.3.

The purpose of this step is to formalize the meaning of the event type. The event-type name (defined in the next step) provides us with a way of referencing the event type. Names are just meaningful labels—not meaningful definitions. Therefore by explicitly stating the kind of state change and the actual object types that must apply before and after an event, the meaning of the event is rigorously expressed.

Name the Event Type

An event-type name must be brief and readable, since it is meant to be a label for human communication. As such, these names should not be expected to convey everything defined in the previous step. However, the name should be short enough to be used as a label while still conveying enough of the event's meaning.

Event-type names convey meaning effectively if they incorporate two characteristics. First, the name should express one or both of the prestate and poststate object-type names. For example, **Account opened** indicates an operation on the object type **Account**. **Staff Employee promoted Manager** indicates a reclassification from **Staff Employee** to **Manager**. **Account reclassified from Major to Key** refers to three object types: **Account**, **Major Account**, and **Key Account**. Second, the name should convey some indication of the process it represents. Since an event is the successful completion of an operation, naming the event type in the past tense is appropriate. The process of changing one's residence might be successfully completed with a **Residence changed** event.

Some deviations to this are allowed for the sake of clarity. For example, consuming a **Dinner** results in its termination. Placing this in the past tense yields **Dinner terminated**. However, the name **Dinner completed** may be more user friendly. In another example, the **Pay Employee** operation may have an event type named **Employee paid**. However, this event's underlying object type may not be **Employee**; it may be **Employee Payment**. Here, the event name would be **Employee Payment created**—if stan-

Naming event types provides understanding when reading event schemas.

Event Type	Example Event	Event Prestate	Event Poststate
Create	**Breakfast started**	not Object	Breakfast
Terminate	**Breakfast completed**	Breakfast	not Object
Classify	**Person classified Employee**	Person, but not Employee	Person and Employee
Declassify	**Person declassified Employee**	Person and Employee	Person, but not Employee
Reclassify	**Person married**	Unmarried Person	Married Person
Tuple substitution	**Residence changed**	Residence	Residence (different tuple)

Formalizing the event type's actual state change provides exactness.

Figure 7.3   Examples of event prestates and poststates for various kinds of events.

dards were strictly enforced. In short, names need not be precisely standardized, although the underlying meaning should be. This is why the Formalize Event Type step, above, is vital.

Generalize Event Type

Once the underlying meaning is clarified, the chosen event type should be examined for more general event types. The purpose here is twofold. First, it helps the analyst determine whether the analysis is being performed at the appropriate level of abstraction or scope. Second, it encourages integration with other, more general, analysis efforts.

Generalize Event Type and Choose Level

Generalizing an event requires the analyst to rise above the immediate details of a system and momentarily explore a broader scope. For instance, an analyst may be specifying a management payroll system. A key event in that system will be **Manager paid**. As depicted in Fig. 7.4(a), a more general form of this is **Employee paid**. By considering **Payment** creations in a yet more general form, the **Payment made** event type may describe the next level of abstraction. The ultimate generality however is **Object created**.

Once the possible levels of abstraction have been explored, the analyst should choose which level is appropriate for the system at hand—and change the chosen event type, if necessary. For example, the **Employee paid** abstraction is perhaps a better level than **Manager paid**. In this situation, the scope of the system may change to a more general payroll system. Without the generalization step, the analyst may never have considered the possibility.

A useful technique for identifying possible generalizations is illustrated in Fig. 7.4(b). Here, the event type is expressed along with its prestates and poststates. By generalizing these, the event type is also generalized. As indicated, prestate and poststate can be generalized separately. For example, since a **Library Item** is a more general form of **Book, Audio Tape, Disk-based Work**, and so on, the poststate of checking out an **Available Book** is also a **Checked-Out Library Item**. Additionally, the **Available Book** object type can itself be generalized to **Available Library Item**, resulting in a more general **Library Item checked out** event. Abstractions such as these encourage the analyst to ponder more general systems—in this case a library system that administers more than just collections of books.

Integrate the Event Type

The results of generalization also aid system integration. After generalizing the event type, check if it has already been specified. If so, the generalized event may already be part of a system that is in progress or one that is already completed. In this case, an integration point has been identified and can be administered accordingly.

Define Operation Conditions

By this point, the event type should be well understood. Now, the operation and its triggering conditions need to be considered.

Identify the Operation

In order to produce the change in state specified in Clarify the Event Type, above, an operation is required. This step identifies the operation that, when applied, will result in the specified type of event. For example, an **Order shipped** event occurs as a result of a **Ship Order** operation. Events **Part stored in Bin** and **Bin Contents increased** may both have the same operation: **Store Part in Bin**.

In addition to naming the operation, the analyst should also indicate whether the operation is internal or external. Here, the analyst chooses one of the forms illustrated in

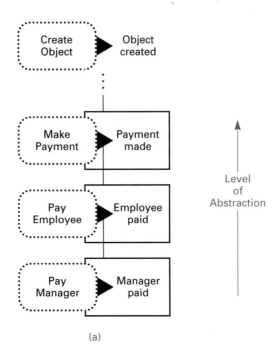

(a)

Event Type Name	Event Prestate	Event Poststate
Object Reclassified	Object Type	Object Type
⋮		
Item checked out	Available Item	Checked-Out Item
Library Item checked out	Available Library Item	Checked-Out Library Item
Book checked out	Available Book	Checked-Out Book

Level of Abstraction

(b)

Figure 7.4   Generalizing event types.

Fig. 7.5. An *internal operation* is an operation whose processing occurs within the domain (as defined in Identify the Domain). In addition, since its process is internal, its method can be expressed as another event diagram.

An *external operation* is an operation whose processing occurs outside the domain being analyzed. Since its processing method is not addressed with this diagram, no further analysis is required for this operation. To indicate this, a different symbol is used as illustrated in Fig. 7.5(b). (Some analysts prefer to omit the symbol altogether, leaving the event triangle as a stand-alone symbol.)

(a) Internal Operation   (b) External Operation

Figure 7.5   Symbolizing internal and external operations.

Specify Conditions, Parameters, and Establish Reusability

In this step, the analyst defines the contract that binds the operation and its invokers. For an operation to execute correctly requires specific preconditions to be satisfied. If an operation is invoked with these preconditions met, it should yield a result that satisfies the postcondition. The contract can be paraphrased as "If you promise to call an operation with its precondition satisfied, the operation promises to deliver a final state in which the postcondition is satisfied," [Meyer, 1988].

In addition to the contractual conditions, input and output parameters for each operation must be specified. An example of these specifications is depicted in Fig. 7.6. To reduce clutter on the event diagram, such information should probably not be recorded on the diagram itself. Instead, it should be recorded on a separate piece of paper or in a repository.

Once the operation's name, parameters, and conditions have been specified, the analyst should determine whether the operation is already recorded in the repository. Instead of looking through a list containing every operation to find a match on the operation name, narrow the search. Look for the object type that is associated with, or *hosts*, this operation. The input parameters determine the host object type to which the operation is associated. (In most—not all—oo languages, the operation may only be associated with the first parameter. In analysis, there is no such restriction.) At this point, the analyst can scan the other operations hosted by the object types to determine whether the operation identified in this step has already been defined. No match on the name could mean

Input Parameter: Accepted Order
Output Parameter: Assembled Order

Precondition: The Order must be an Accepted Order but not an Assembled Order.

Postcondition: The Order must be both an Accepted Order and an Assembled Order.

Input Parameters: Bride, Groom
Output Parameter: Marriage

Precondition: The Bride and Groom must not be married.

Postcondition: The Bride and Groom must be married to each other.

(a)   (b)

Figure 7.6   Examples of specifying the parameters and contractual conditions for an operation.

that the operation has a different name. For example, the **Assemble Order** operation could already be associated with the **Accepted Order** object type, but its name could be **Perform Order Assembly** or **Put the Order together**.

Another technique for locating a match is examining those operations with the same parameters and conditions. In fact, this is a more accurate technique than matching names, because two operations could have the same name, yet have different conditions and parameters. For instance, the **Perform Marriage** operation may already exist, but have a different precondition. In Islamic countries, only the bride must be unmarried, and in Tibet, only the groom must be unmarried. The marriage operation, then, is different in the U.S.A., Saudi Arabia, and Tibet. In other words, marriage has really three distinct methods of operation—or three different operations. So, before deciding whether an operation already exists and can be reused, it must have the same parameters and conditions. If an operation is reusable, no further analysis on that operation is required.

If the operation does not already exist in the repository, the team can determine if the operation should be reusable. If so, the operation should be added to the repository along with its parameter and condition specifications. Eventually, the method definition should be added to the operation specification. This can be done using another event diagram.

Identify Control Conditions

An operation may be invoked by one or more triggers. However, certain preexisting conditions, called *control conditions*, may be necessary before an operation can actually begin its process (see Fig. 7.7). Take, for example, the **Terminate Order** operation. The analyst must first ask the user expert, "Under what conditions is the **Terminate Order** operation permitted to begin?"

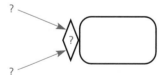

Figure 7.7   Determining control conditions.

The expert should then respond with the required conditions. A control condition that proves "true" implies that the proper circumstances exist for the operation to begin. A "false" condition makes no such implication.

An expert's response to the question of "Under what conditions . . . ?" will be an expert's statement in an expert's own language. For example, the question "Under what conditions is the **Complete Sale** operation in a vending machine permitted to begin?" may lead to an answer like this:

> Well, let me see. Ummm. The machine can definitely complete a sale when the product the person selected is dispensed. Oh, and also when the machine has given the correct change. And that's it, I think. No, there's one other situation: when the customer hits the "cancel" button. When that button is hit, all the money is returned and the sale is considered "complete" even though it was canceled.

Expert statements in the expert's own language, such as the one above, should be encouraged. The analyst needs to glean as much expert knowledge as possible. Therefore the user should be allowed to speak in an unrestricted manner using familiar terms. The user should be encouraged (and even prompted) to provide as much detail as necessary. This will increase the probability that the knowledge transfer will be complete and accurate.

Normalize Control Conditions

While expert statements of the control condition are vital to systems analysis, they need to be transformed into a simple and standard arrangement of conditional statements. One way of expressing these is called the *disjunctive normal form (DNF)*. DNF is often a convenient form in which to write Boolean expressions for switching circuits or conditions for something to happen. In DNF, the conditions that must all occur at the same time are grouped and tested separately. If any *one* group is true, the entire *conditional clause* is true—justifying the change in state. If *none* of the condition groups in the clause holds true, the state change is not justified.

For example in Fig. 7.8, condition-1, *and* condition-2, *and* condition-3 must be true for the entire condition group to be true. If the condition group is true, the change in state can proceed as specified. If one condition group is not true, other groups may be. This is why each group is connected by the word "or." In the example, this means the state change can also be warranted if condition-3 is true and condition-4 is not true. Additionally, if condition-5 is true, the state change can proceed as specified.

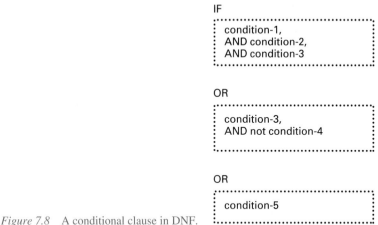

IF

> condition-1,
> AND condition-2,
> AND condition-3

OR

> condition-3,
> AND not condition-4

OR

> condition-5

Figure 7.8   A conditional clause in DNF.

Figure 7.9 illustrates taking the expert knowledge from the above question "Under what conditions is the Complete Sale operation in a vending machine permitted to begin?" and transforming it to DNF. The conditional statements assume that all values relate to a particular Sale that is in progress. If this were not the case, the terms in the conditions would require qualification as to which Sale the terms relate. At the bottom of the example, the initial DNF expression is refined even further.

"Well, let me see. Ummmm. The machine can definitely complete a sale when
the product the person selected is dispensed. Oh, and also when the
machine has given the correct change. And that's it, I think. No, there's
one other situation, and that's when the customer hits the 'cancel' button.
When that button is hit, all the money is returned and the sale is considered
'complete' even though it was canceled."

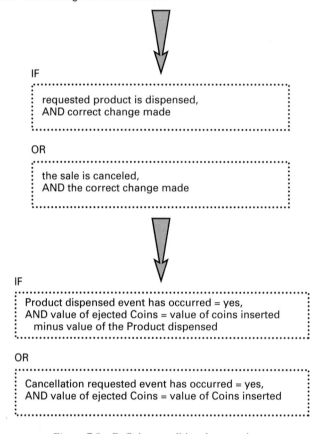

IF

> requested product is dispensed,
> AND correct change made

OR

> the sale is canceled,
> AND the correct change made

IF

> Product dispensed event has occurred = yes,
> AND value of ejected Coins = value of coins inserted
>   minus value of the Product dispensed

OR

> Cancellation requested event has occurred = yes,
> AND value of ejected Coins = value of Coins inserted

Figure 7.9   Refining conditional expressions.

Identify Operation Causes

In the previous step, the control conditions for processing were defined. Now, the analyst
should determine *when* a control condition should be evaluated, so that the associated
change in state can occur. In other words, the analyst should establish what events must
occur for one or more of the conditions to be true—so that another event can occur. The
analyst should also establish the nature of their triggers.

Identify Triggering Event Types

Often the condition for processing is simple. For example, in Fig. 7.10 the Consume Bowl of Cereal operation requires only one condition that must be true: a Bowl of

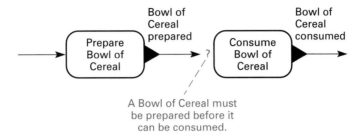

Figure 7.10　A simple conditional clause and its triggering event type.

Cereal object has been created to be consumed. In order to make this condition true, a Bowl of Cereal object must be created. Therefore, a preceding Bowl of Cereal prepared event must occur to satisfy the processing preconditions of the Consume Bowl of Cereal operation.

When the conditional clause is more complex, several events may be required for a control condition to be evaluated as "true." The example in Fig. 7.11 requires five event types. Notice that each condition and each term within a condition needs to be examined. For the "Product dispensed event" for this Sale to be equal to yes, a Product dispensed event must occur. (Yes, events *are* objects.) To compute the "value of ejected Coins," Coin objects must be ejected. To compute the "value of Coins inserted," Coin objects must be inserted. To examine the "value of Product dispensed," the price of a Product must have been changed.

All of these events can change the vending machine so that the control condition might evaluate as "true." However, not all of them should trigger a Complete Sale operation. For instance, a Product dispensed event must occur before a sale can be completed. Each time Product dispensed occurs, the Complete Sale's control condition should be checked to see if it proves true. The same rule applies to Coin ejected and Cancellation

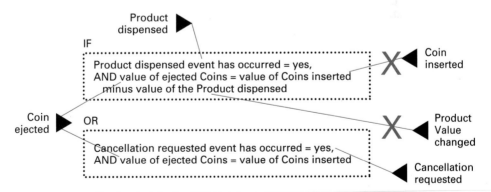

Figure 7.11　Control conditions should not be constantly reevaluated to determine if they are true. They should be reevaluated only when an event occurs that might cause the entire condition to be true. Here, candidate event types have been identified for the depicted condition.

requested event types. Any time they occur, the control condition should be checked. However, a Product Value changed event should *not* be an immediate cause for checking the condition, because a change in Product Value should not trigger a vending-machine to complete a sale in progress. The expert could also decide that the same is true for Coin inserted events. Just because more money is inserted into a vending machine, this is no cause to evaluate whether the Complete Sale operation should be invoked.

In summary, this step first asks which events must occur to cause a control condition to evaluate as "true." Then it determines which of these events *should actually* trigger the operation.

Indicate Complex Control Conditions

Often, a control condition is limited to requiring only that one event or another must occur before a process can begin. For instance, a Consume Bowl of Cereal operation should begin whenever a Bowl of Cereal prepared event has occurred. In another example, a Determine Gas Usage From Meter operation can begin whenever either a Closing Gas Bill Request or a Gas Bill Cycle Request event occurs. When diagramming situations such as these, the control-condition diamond should not be displayed. The diamond is reserved for those operations that may *not* begin immediately when triggered. The diamond indicates that the operation must *first* evaluate its control condition. In Fig. 7.12, both operations begin whenever they are triggered by *any* event. In other words, the control conditions are when a Bowl of Cereal prepared event has occurred or when a Closing Gas Bill Request *or* a Gas Bill Cycle Request event occurs, respectively.

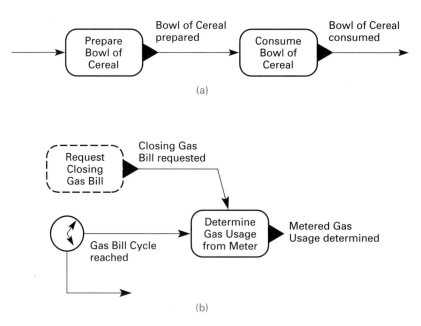

Figure 7.12 Triggering without depicting a control condition.

However the condition clause specified in Fig. 7.11 requires more than simple WHEN conditions in order for it to begin. Instead, a complex IF. . . AND. . . OR requirement exists. Since a **Complete Sale** operation has such a requirement, a control-condition diamond is required. The resulting event diagram is depicted in Fig. 7.13.

Normalize Triggering Event Types

In Step 3d, above, conditions were grouped so that if any one group is true, the entire condition clause is true. This approach to grouping is called disjunctive normal form (DNF). The diagram in Fig. 7.13 depicts a control condition whose condition clause is expressed in DNF. If every event in this figure required evaluation of the entire control condition, Fig. 7.13 would remain as illustrated. However, as indicated in Fig. 7.11, the first condition group should be evaluated only when three types of events occur; the second, only when two types of events occur. For example, the **Product dispensed** event relates to the first condition group and not the second. Therefore the control condition should be expressed as two control conditions—each with a different condition group (see Fig. 7.14). In this way, each control condition is triggered only by those events appropriate to the condition group.

Some analysts, however, find that each of the control conditions in Fig. 7.14 implies different types of events. One way to accommodate this is by representing each control condition with its own operation (Fig. 7.15). Expressed in this way, each new operation would result in an event that occurs only when its control condition is true. In other words, the event is simply an explicit indication that a "true" evaluation had occurred. For example, a successful evaluation of the control condition at the top of the figure results in a state change named **Sale successfully completed**. The state change

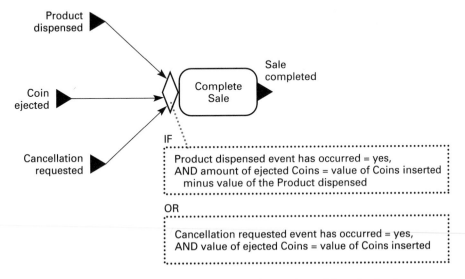

Figure 7.13 The triggering event types and control conditions for the Complete Sale operation.

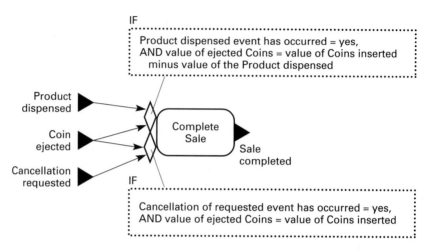

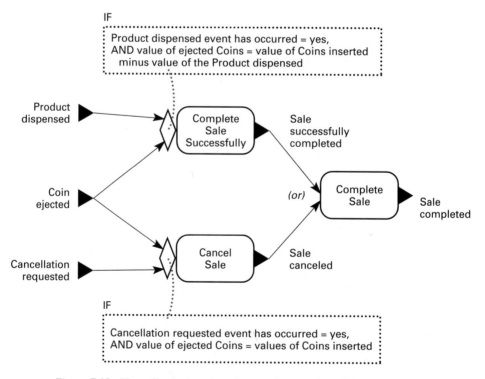

Figure 7.14 Normalized triggering using multiple control-condition diamonds on an operation.

Figure 7.15 Normalized triggering where each control condition has its own specialized operation.

might classify a Sale object as a Completed Sale object or terminate it altogether. Or, the evaluation result itself could be classified as True. In either case, the Complete Sale operation is triggered.

Some analysts would argue that using operations solely to indicate control-condition results is too artificial. After all, the event is actually the direct result of the control condition, nothing else. Therefore, they believe that in this kind of situation, the operation symbol is not really necessary—or should at least be minimized. To maintain a consistent use of symbols, this book also provides two alternative notations, illustrated in Fig. 7.16. In Fig. 7.16(a), the operations are still agents for events, but their role is minimal. Representing the operation in reduced form means that its method is limited to causing a state change only when its control condition results in a "true" evaluation. In Fig 7.16(b), the control conditions are treated as operations in their own right, having their own events. (The latter approach will be used in Part VII of this book.)

In summary, to be in DNF, trigger rules may need regrouping, because certain events apply only to certain condition groups. When this occurs, the original control condition needs to be divided accordingly. The division can be represented as multiple control-condition diamonds on the same operation as illustrated in Fig. 7.14. Or, each control condition can be expressed with its own specialized operation whose event triggers the original operation.

Specify Trigger Rules

Now that normalized triggering events are in place, the analyst needs to complete the specification of operational causes by identifying exactly what objects are needed to invoke the operation. In other words, the analyst must determine which arguments are needed to trigger the operation and what mappings are required to do the appropriate assignment.

For instance, the argument needed for a sale completion operation is a Sale object. Since this is the same underlying object resulting from the Sale successfully completed or Sale canceled events, the mapping is a *trivial* mapping. However, the trigger rules required for the operations in Fig. 7.17 involve a little more thought. In order to perform a wedding, two objects are necessary. The trigger rule in Fig. 7.17(a), then, consists of two mappings.

The coin-ejection operation in Fig. 7.17(b) requires a currency value to eject the appropriate coins. The amount of Coins to make change mapping computes the amount of required change by subtracting the value of the selected product from the amount of money inserted into the machine. The result of the mapping is a currency value—a value from which the coin-ejection operation can determine which coins will be ejected. The all Coins mapping simply computes the value of all the money put into the machine during this sale and passes it to the coin-ejection operation.

Refine Cycle Results

The previous steps guide the analyst in working with a given event, formalizing it, and determining what leads up to it. Basically, this cycle is now complete. However, before proceeding through the next cycle, a few refinements are useful.

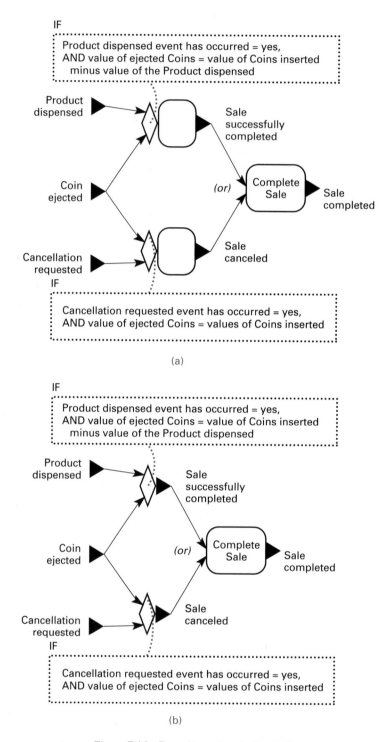

Figure 7.16   Two alternatives to Fig. 7.15.

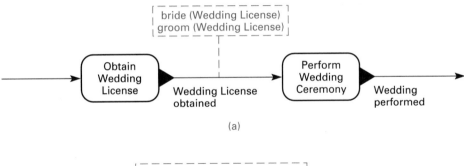

(a)

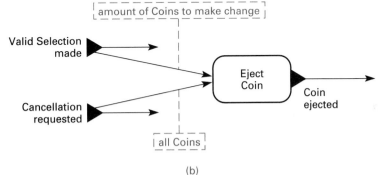

(b)

Figure 7.17   Defining the mappings on trigger rules.

Generalize Triggering Event Type

Triggering event types can often be defined in terms of a more general event type. For example, Fig. 7.18(a) depicts three events triggering the target event A. Examining B, C, and D more closely, the analyst can determine that B and D are really special cases of one general event, E. This means that whenever B and D occur, it is also an occurrence of E. The event type E, therefore, has two event subtypes.

In the example of Fig. 7.15, two of the triggering event types can be generalized, Sale successfully completed and Sale canceled. In Fig. 7.19, the event supertype is named Sale finalized. This is another way of saying that a Sale finalized event is a mutually exclusive

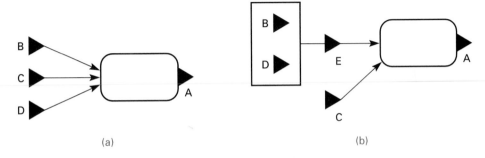

(a)   (b)

Figure 7.18   Generalizing triggering event types.

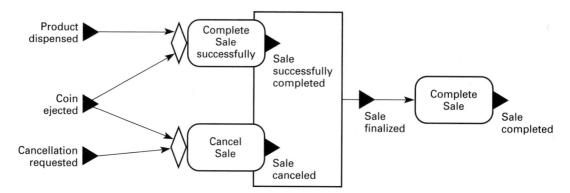

Figure 7.19   Two triggering event types from Fig. 7.15 generalized.

occurrence of either a **Sale successfully completed** or a **Sale canceled**. Generality provides the convenience of homogeneity. Simplifications of this sort clarify thought processes.

Specialize Target Event Type

In contrast to the step above, operations are sometimes specified too abstractly. For example in Fig. 7.20(a), the target event **A** is triggered by three events. Perhaps the **B**, **C**, and **D** events trigger specialized applications within the operation resulting in **A**. If this is the case, the specialization can be expressed as event subtypes of **A**. In Fig. 7.20(b), **A'** and **A"** are the specializations of **A**, triggered by **B**, **C**, and **D**.

Figure 7.21 illustrates an example of how a target event might be specialized. In the example, the target event type **Coin ejected** may be applied in two ways. First, a currency value is supplied by the trigger from the events **Valid Selection made** and **Cancellation requested**. Here, the coin-ejection operation determines which coins must be ejected, based on their value. Second, specific **Coin** objects must be ejected. In this scenario, when an improper coin is inserted by a customer or a coin is inserted into a busy vending machine, that *same* coin must be rejected. The notion of value does not apply to these coins at all. Therefore, the object passed by the trigger is not a currency value, but a

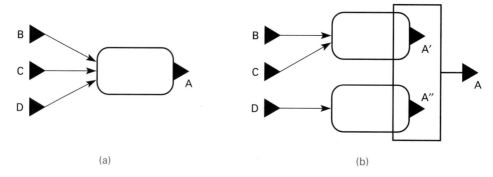

Figure 7.20   Specializing target event types.

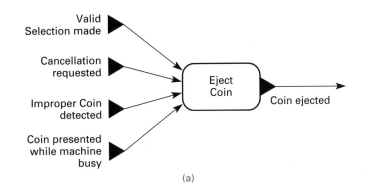

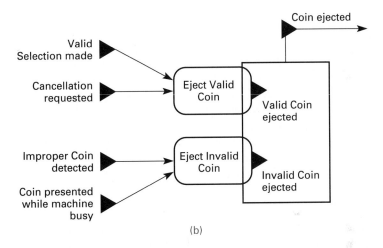

Figure 7.21   An example of specializing a target event type.

coin. In this way, Coin ejected can be specialized as two different methods of it: Valid Coin ejected and Invalid Coin ejected.

Specializing target event types often clarifies the meaning, though it is not always necessary. For example, if Coin ejected was not expressed as two event subtypes, the method selection mechanism would need to be defined *within the method* of the Eject Coin operation. One way or another, then, the specialization will be expressed. The choice of level is determined by the analyst and expert.

Check for Duplicate Events

Another situation to look for is a triggering event type that is either the same as, or a subclassification of, the target event type. For instance in Fig. 7.22(a), the expert may determine that event type B and A are really the same event type, except that they have two different names. In other words, the occurrence of B is no different from the occurrence of A. B does not trigger A to do anything different from what B has already

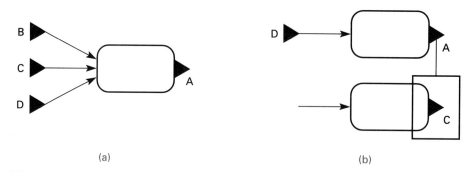

Figure 7.22   Removing duplicate event types.

done. B and A should, therefore, be combined. This is why **B** no longer appears in Fig. 7.22(b).

Event type **C**, on the other hand, is not *exactly* the same as event type **A**. It is, however, a specialized form of **A**. In this way, **C** does not trigger an operation resulting in **A**. An occurrence of **C** is *already* an occurrence of **A**. There is no intervening operation, because every instance of a **C** event *is* an **A** event.

As a result of this step, the event diagram in Fig. 7.19 is modified as indicated in Fig. 7.23. The reason for removing the **Sale finalized** event type is that its occurrence is exactly the same as **Sale completed**. Therefore, a **Sale finalized** does not trigger an operation to complete a sale: it *is* a **Sale completed**. Similarly, every instance of a **Sale canceled** event is an instance of a **Sale completed** event.

Next Step

Starting with a target event, the method described above guides the analyst in formalizing the event, specifying its causes, and making refinements to the resulting diagram. The analyst can now take each newly identified triggering event type, and—treating each as a target event type—continue again with the Clarify Event Type step. As long as internal

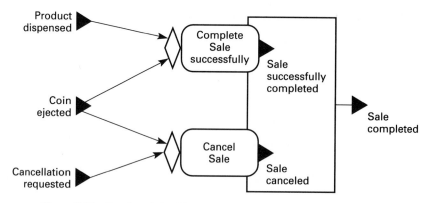

Figure 7.23   Results of checking for duplicate event types from Fig. 7.19.

events exist, this "spin-until-dry" cycle continues. It stops when only external operations remain and the starting event type has been reached. For example, in Figs. 7.19 and 7.23 the event types Product dispensed, Coin taken, and Coin ejected should each be treated as target event types and input to the Clarify Event Type step. Cancellation requested, however, does not become a target event. Its operation is defined by the customer—not the machine—and is therefore outside the focus of the diagramming domain.

LEVELING THE RESULTS

What happens when the event diagram is completed? Is the analysis complete, or should it be taken to the next level of detail? The answer depends on the nature of each event diagram operation, the scope of the analysis project, and the expertise available:

- For those operations that are at the elementary level, no next level of modeling detail exists. This applies to those operations where the only task is to create, terminate, classify, declassify, reclassify, and so on.

- However, when an operation is not at the elementary level, it can be specified at the next level of detail. For instance the operation resulting in a Coin ejected is one such operation that could be expressed in more detail. This more detailed specification is called the *method* specification, as illustrated in Fig. 7.24.

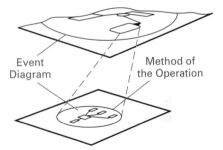

Event
Diagram

Method of
the Operation

Figure 7.24   Leveling event diagrams.

- The choice to express operations at the next level of detail belongs to the analyst, the expert, and the manager. The manager may determine that pursuing more detail in a particular area is outside the project's current scope. The analyst may determine that the next level cannot be diagrammed without making implementation decisions. In this situation, further work will be continued by a design team. On the other hand, the expert and analyst may decide that the extra detail is required to clarify their modeling effort. Either way, if it is to be automated, someone will eventually define the method.

The bulleted items above provide a rationale for decomposing operations in a top-down fashion. However, the event diagram produced with the steps above also defines a subdomain for a higher level event diagram. In other words, the event diagram can be used for bottom-up analysis as well. An approach of this kind is very practical at the beginning of an analysis project when a high level of understanding is lacking. Analysis should always begin at the level of the expert's ability. Rising above the expert's level of competency jeopardizes the accuracy of the analysis project. Practicing top-down analysis in a top-down manner is not the *only* way to analyze a process. In fact it is usually a dangerous way of conducting an analysis effort.

PROCESS-DRIVEN ANALYSIS

Object-oriented specification is often divided into structural and behavioral approaches. The structural approach is a visual, spatial metaphor that provides a static vision of how things are laid out in space. In contrast, the behavioral approach describes what a thing does. While this dichotomy is a handy slogan, it can cause the OO analyst to miss the point. The important distinction concerns who defines the process. The structures of the structural approach are primarily defined by and for the builders of databases. Processes, however, are defined by application developers and are intended to be universal. The structures defined by the processes then are real and important ones. Therefore, a useful OO analysis method should rest on a behavioral foundation [Kent, 1990]. The diagram in Fig. 7.25 illustrates a process-driven method that intimately incorporates structural definitions.

The diagram in the center depicts the major components of object diagrams. By using the event analysis steps described in the beginning of this chapter, the analyst is presented with a very good way of finding and identifying the object types. In fact, by using this method, *all* the necessary object types will be identified—and not more.

Below are the steps indicated in Fig. 7.25. The description of each step is specified in detail within this chapter. They are reiterated here to add the structural portion of this method. Any structural elements identified within these steps must be defined for the domain. Any structural elements *not* identified should *not* be defined for the domain.

Clarify Event Type

Within this step, the event prestates and poststates are specified in terms of object types. For example, a Person classified Employee event identifies two object types that must be present in the object diagram: Person and Employee. In other words, if the object types Person and Employee have not been identified for the domain, they should now be added.

Generalize Event Type

If a more general event type is identified to become part of this event diagram, new event prestates and poststates must be identified as in the step above—yielding more general object types. These object types may replace or supplement already defined object types for the domain. For example, if the object type Bank Item is chosen as a more appropriate level of abstraction than Mortgage, the Mortgage object type should be removed from the domain (unless it is being used by another event or operation within the domain).

Define Operation Conditions

The conditions defined in this step contain terms. Each term requires a valid object type that must be expressed in the object diagram. For example, the condition that a Plate of

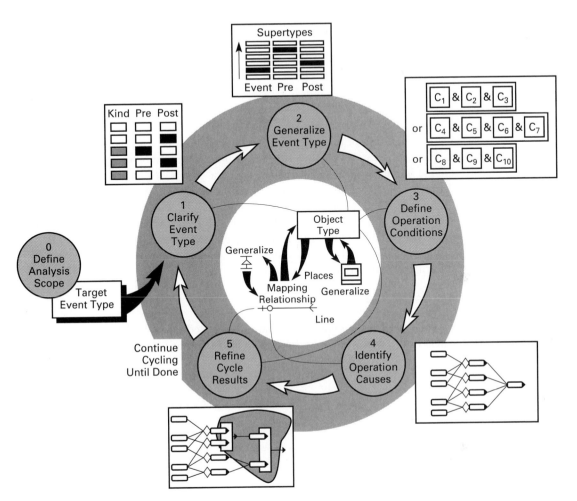

Figure 7.25   Using event analysis to identify and refine structural elements.

Paté object must be available for consumption requires a Plate of Paté object type in order to execute the condition check. If the Plate of Paté object type is not already defined for the domain, it should now be added.

Identify Operation Causes

Within this step, the trigger rules are specified for the event diagram. Each contains at least one mapping. For instance, to trigger a wedding operation, a mapping assigns a given Wedding License object to bride and groom objects. In this way, the Wedding object type and its bride and groom mappings must also be present in the object diagram.

Refine Cycle Results

During the refinement, both object types and mappings can be generalized, specialized, or even removed. These changes, too, must be reflected in the object diagram.

A METHOD FOR EVENT-DIRECTED EVENT ANALYSIS

As stated at the beginning of this chapter, event diagrams can be constructed in two general ways: goal directed and event directed. The goal-directed method was presented first. This technique is very useful for analyzing behavior that is not well understood. By defining the objectives of a process, a way to reach these objectives should be sought, which, in turn, become new objectives. In other words, the technique ensures that the analysis is always focused. For those situations driven by the responsiveness of the business or where the behavior is reasonably well understood, an event-directed analysis is useful. A step-by-step method for constructing goal-directed event diagrams is discussed in this section and is summarized in Fig. 7.26.

Define Analysis Focus

This step is performed in the same way as the goal-directed method. The only difference is that the next step begins with the *starting event* instead of the target event.

Clarify Event Type

This step is performed in the same way as the goal-directed method.

Generalize Event Type

This step is performed in the same way as the goal-directed method.

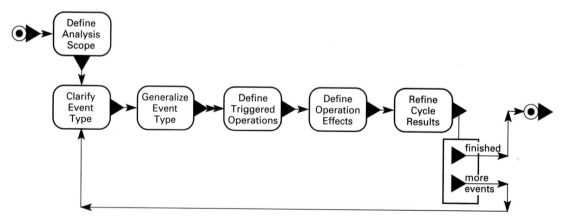

Figure 7.26   An event-analysis method that is object oriented, process driven, and *event directed.*

Define Triggered Operations

This step is similar to the Define Operation Conditions step in the goal-directed method. In the goal-directed method, the operation being defined was the one that *caused* the given event. Here, one or more operations are defined, where each is identified based on being *triggered* by the given event. Once this is established, the remaining Define Operation Conditions procedure can be used as described above.

Identify Operational Effects

This step is similar to the Identify Operation Causes step in the goal-directed method. In the goal-directed method, the triggering events were identified. Here, the event type resulting from the operation is identified (although many analysts still examine the triggering events to ensure completeness). Once this is established, the remaining Identify Operation Causes procedure can be used as described above.

Refine Cycle Results

This step is performed in the same way as the goal-directed method. However, the choice to continue the analysis loop is based on whether or not the target event has been reached or not.

SUMMARY

This chapter attempts to impart some science to the process of object-oriented behavior analysis. It does so by describing two step-by-step event analysis techniques for constructing event diagrams: goal-directed and event-directed methods.

The division between the object diagram and event diagram corresponds to the dichotomy of the structural and behavioral approaches. While this dichotomy is popular, it can cause the OO analyst to miss the point. Instead, a useful OO analysis method should rest on a behavioral foundation that incorporates the structural. This chapter intimately integrates object analysis techniques with object behavior analysis techniques.

REFERENCES

Kent, William, *A Framework for Object Concepts,* Hewlett-Packard, Report HPL-90-30, April 1990.

Meyer, Bertrand, *Object-Oriented Software Construction,* Prentice Hall, New York, 1988.

Chapter 8

Object-Flow Diagrams

Behavioral modeling methods, like event analysis, are appropriate for describing processes in terms of triggers, events, control conditions, and operations. However, for complicated processes like companies and large organizations, specifying the dynamics of events, triggers, and control conditions is not always possible or appropriate. Under these circumstances, a different representation method should be employed.

This chapter presents a strategic-level approach to modeling processes. In particular, it describes an approach compatible with both event diagramming and strategic planning. The models built with this approach are called *object-flow diagrams*.

A HIGH-LEVEL FUNCTIONAL VIEW

A method that clarifies complicated processes is very important. An approach producing a coherent overview of a process landscape is preferable to an ad hoc approach which produces isolated islands of information. Specifically, this high-level perspective is very useful in the following scenarios:

- When an organization is analyzed, the problem domain is often too vast or intricate to understand using behavioral techniques (at least initially). Dividing complicated processes into manageable chunks is critical for understanding complex situations.

- The high-level understanding gained above is immediately helpful to the knowledge administrator. Those object types and processes identified form the beginnings of an enterprise model that will provide the standards for further analysis work. In this way, these reusable components support a cut-and-paste environment in which domain experts can evolve their diagrams. Additionally, the simplifications inherent in this high-level orientation often provide insights into more generally useful components than originally recognized. Just how much depends on the level of abstraction. Scheduling, Allocation, and Transaction Accounting are examples of high-level processes, because they apply to many types of enterprise objects: people, money, goods, and so on. Reusability is actually amplified through abstractions like these.

- Existing process diagrams can be expressed in terms of more general processing notions. By eliminating the details of event/trigger/condition dynamics, the analyst can concentrate on representing activity-control flows and protocols. Identification of more generally useful components is now possible as described above.

- Strategic planning requires a general view of how an organization functions. Without this perspective, planning and plan execution lack coherence. For strategic-level models, the dynamics of a behavioral model are neither necessary nor helpful. Here a firm's collection of activities and their interactions are the important focus. The series of corporate functions define a baseline business model.

The Function of a Process

As already stated, the OO analyst requires a method for analyzing complicated processes, such as companies and large organizations, in terms of the way they function. Here, an enterprise *function* refers to the purpose of a process. This function or purpose, then, determines the essential activities that manage the operations and resources of an organization. As such, strategic-level models do not specify dynamics. They do not indicate when activities will be started, nor whether they will terminate on their own. Strategic-level models describe interactions among processes. The activities depicted can exist in parallel, can occur at different places, and are not synchronized with one another [Harel, 1988].

Data-Flow Diagrams

One way of modeling at the strategic level is with data-flow diagrams (DFDs), as illustrated in Fig. 8.1. DFDs readily depict the strategic-level model's sense of decomposition and information flow. For example, the data can flow without necessarily defining whether or when it will flow, how often it will flow, and whether the flow will be initiated by the former activity or requested by the latter.

In other words, the strategic-level approach describes the possible flow of information and the decomposition of activities. However, it indicates nothing about how these activities and their inputs and outputs are controlled [Harel, 1988].

Object-Flow Diagrams

Instead of being limited just to data that flow, OO strategic-level models indicate *any* kind of object that flows between activities.* This characteristic is relevant to the object-oriented analysis. The strategic-level model presented in this book is called an object-flow diagram. Object-flow diagrams employ a strategic-level approach that is object-oriented. Additionally, they represent processing requirements in a way that business planners can understand and apply to strategic planning projects—not just I.S. projects.

---

*Object-flow diagrams can cause the hair on the neck of many OO purists to stand up. These are not warmed-over data-flow diagrams. They may have similarities to data-flow diagrams, but they are not data-flow diagrams. Object-flow diagrams use OO underpinnings to understand and specify a strategic-level view of an enterprise.

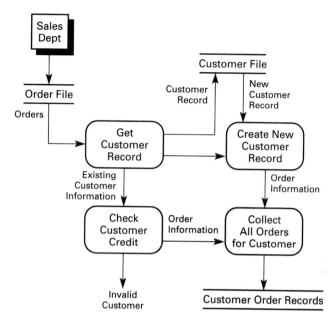

Figure 8.1   An example of a data-flow diagram.

> *Object-flow diagrams* represent key enterprise activities linked by the products that activities produce and exchange.

As illustrated in Fig. 8.2(a), object-flow diagrams have two primary elements—*activities* and *products*. An activity will *produce* a product, and its product is *consumed* by one or more activities. For example, in Fig. 8.2(b), the **Produce Printed-Circuit Board** activity produces its product, **Printed-Circuit Boards**. This product is, in turn, consumed by the **Assemble Computers** activity (along with two other products) to produce yet another product, **Assembled Computers**. Products are considered *consumed*, because they become an integral part of the end product in some way. For instance, the **Production Materials** and **Printed-Circuit Boards** become actual components in the **Assembled Computers**. The **Hardware Designs** knowledge is also an essential part of the final product—even though the knowledge is not used up in the process as are physical components. All three of these products are considered consumed, because they are present in some form within the end product.

PRODUCTS

Products reflect the purpose of the activities that the analyst expects to understand and model. Linking back to the purpose is a sound technique in business modeling. Products are the manifestation of that purpose. When seeking productivity improvements or cost

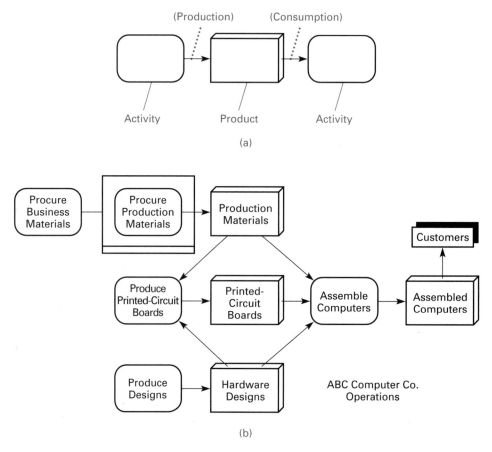

Figure 8.2   Object-flow diagram elements and example.

reductions, the business analyst should first identify the products. Products justify process. When designing data-processing systems, these products will guide the database structure.

> A *product* is the end result that fulfills the purpose of an activity.

Correct product identification is vital to company direction. For example, one national railway company defined its product as Running Railways, when in fact their real product was Transportation. Lacking this knowledge, they failed to realize that they were competing with other transportation vendors, such as airlines and buses. Consequently the railway company's business and system planning went down the wrong track.

Products, therefore, should satisfy two criteria: they should be salable and have a measurable quantity and quality.

Product Salability

An activity can have many *outputs* such as sweat and paperwork. However, by ensuring that products are actually or potentially salable, the modeling effort acquires a business-driven perspective.

While every product is not necessarily for sale, it should at least be potentially salable. For example in Fig. 8.2(b), Assembled Computers is obviously a product, because external Customers are purchasing them. While Printed-Circuit Boards, Hardware Designs, and Production Materials are not currently being sold by ABC Computers, they could be sold to external customers. Additionally, if the three producing activities were external to the company, or a strict accounting existed between departments, the Assemble Computers activity would be the paying customer.

While value is an important criteria for products, ownership is also important. For instance, the presence of Disneyland in Southern California dramatically boosted land values in parts of Orange County. However, Higher Land Value was not a product as far as the amusement park was concerned. Since Disneyland did not own the surrounding land, it could not sell it. Only landowners could claim this product.

Product Measurability

In addition to its value, a product should be quantifiable and its quality measurable. Unless the product can be counted and graded, the reason for producing and consuming it is questionable. For example, if a marketing firm promises to bring a company potential customers, the company should want to know how many, of what kind or quality, and when. If the marketing firm cannot provide answers, there is no way of knowing whether or not they have a product.

Worthless Products

Rigidly requiring that a product be salable is not always appropriate. While a worthy goal of any activity, it is not always practical. For example, the Time Reports and Invoices produced by accounting and billing functions are not products that can be *sold* to accounts-payable activities. Nevertheless, they are consumed in the paying process—along with Available Money—and Payments are produced. Can this be considered value-added? Certainly the end product of the payable function is better and more useful to some consuming activity. Otherwise, the payables process would not be needed.

The point is that not every product can be sold. However, every product must be, at least, a *useful* commodity. It must be valuable enough to be consumed by another activity—one that produces something more important and useful out of something that is less so. Therefore, object-flow diagrams do not *always* represent measurable, salable products. They do, however, model how new, more complex and subtle qualities are created at every step in an enterprise.

Products and Goals

Products and goals are often confused because both are produced by an activity. For example, in response to the analyst's question, "What is the product of this organization?" a familiar answer is, "Good profit." However, companies do not sell **Good Profit.** While a good profit is an important selling point, it is not a product. It is, however, a goal. In short, activities *produce* products and *support* goals. The solid, arrowed line leaving an activity represents production; the rectangle, its product. A different technique would have to be devised for representing goal support (such as presented in Fig. 8.3).

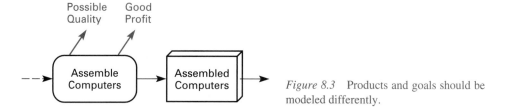

Figure 8.3   Products and goals should be modeled differently.

Another common mistake is including goal statements as part of the product name. One such example states that the product of **Assemble Computers** is "The Best Possible Quality of Assembled Computers at a Good Profit." Again, this name confuses *what* is produced with *why* it is produced. Products determine what business the activity is in; goals determine why the activity is in business. While both are immensely important for strategic planning, both have different meanings and uses. Products and goals therefore require separate representation.

Producer/Consumer Relationships

Each product is produced with the assumption of having at least one consumer. (Otherwise, the product has no real purpose.) Each product exchanged between a producer activity and a consumer activity establishes a relationship. Such a relationship occurs only when two activities come to an agreement on an exchanged product. Products, then, are what producers and consumers discuss.

For example, Fig. 8.4 depicts a relationship between the activity of **Telephone Operations** and the external activity of **Telephone Customers.** This relationship is based on the **Communications Channel.** The agreement is a strictly defined dialing sequence that is understood and adhered to by both parties. In this way, the caller does not need to know about the internal operations of the telephone company as long as it responds correctly to a dialing sequence. The telephone company does not need to know what is being communicated, as long as the caller initiates a call with the correct sequence of pulses or tones. Moreover, either party is free to reengineer the internals of its activities, as long as the interface is unaffected. If the interface is changed, it must do so with the agreement of both parties.

Figure 8.4   A telephone producer/consumer relationship.

Two producer/consumer relationships are depicted at the top of Fig. 8.5. (These are extracted from the ABC Computer Co. Operations diagram presented earlier.) The single shared subject between Produce Printed-Circuit Boards and Assemble Computers is Printed-Circuit Boards. Between Assemble Computers and Customers, it is Assembled Computers. These products might actually involve orders placed by the consumer, responses to these orders, product specifications, exception problems, product returns, and so on. A language should be used to express products in a clear and formal fashion. In Fig. 8.5, the Assembled Computers product is expressed with an object diagram.

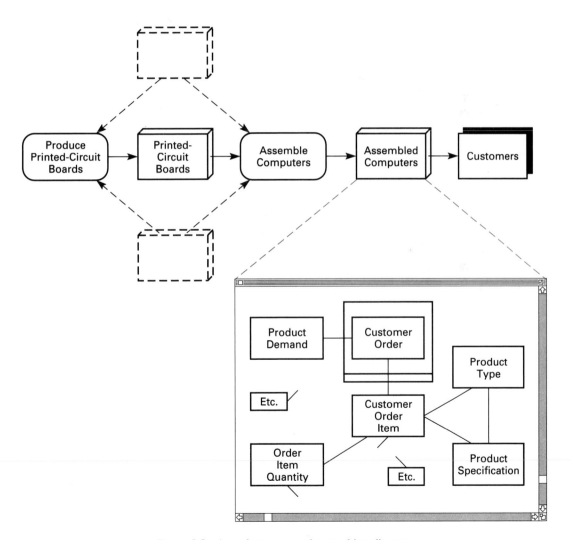

Figure 8.5   A product expressed as an object diagram.

Handoff Versus Final Product

Sometimes an activity's product is used by another activity to produce another product. Products passed from one activity to another are called *handoffs*. Products passed to external consumers are called *final products*. In either case, a product is being produced by one activity and *bought* by another. For handoffs, the *buy-in* is internal to the analysis; for final products it is external. Qualifying products in this manner may (or may not) improve communications between analysts and experts but in no way restricts a product's usage. In other words a product may be a handoff, a final product, or both. For example, in Fig. 8.6 Printed-Circuit Boards is a handoff from Produce Printed-Circuit Boards and Assemble Computers. However, if the ABC Computer Co. decided to sell its PC boards to Customers as well, Printed-Circuit Boards would also be a final product.

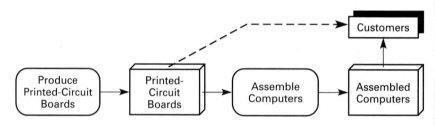

Figure 8.6   Handoffs and final products.

Products Can be Subtyped

Products can be partitioned. In Fig. 8.7(a), Hardware Sales, Software Sales, and Customer Services are subtypes of the Computer Store Sales product. Another example involves a video display company. In Fig. 8.7(b), its product is indicated as Video Displays. However, in order for the company executives to illustrate the type of business

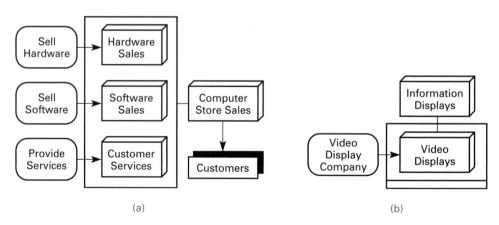

(a)   (b)

Figure 8.7   Products can be subtyped and supertyped.

they were in, a product supertype is depicted. Information Displays, then, is a more general business segment into which the video display company fits.

ACTIVITIES

Each activity fulfills a function, namely, to produce a certain product. In the process of creating its products, an activity usually consumes products created by other activities.

> An *activity* is a process whose production and consumption are specified.

In other words, activities are just processes whose dynamics are not specified. If the dynamics of events, triggers, and control conditions are known and useful, the process can be represented using an event diagram.

Activity Persistence

Due to their high-level nature, activities are typically regarded as continuous processes. Because of this, each activity can be viewed as a small business in its own right. It maintains its own internal *black box* world with no indication of when it is activated and when it is terminated. We only know that each activity consumes and emits a product.

For example, Fig. 8.8 illustrates a Flower Sales activity. In the process, it consumes two products, Available Flower Stock and Flower Requests, and emits Delivered Flowers. Apparently, when Flower Sales receives an instance of Flower Requests, the

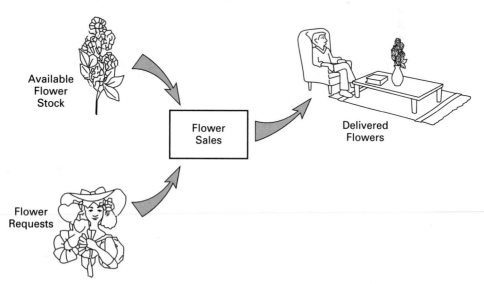

Available
Flower
Stock

Flower
Sales

Delivered
Flowers

Flower
Requests

Figure 8.8 Activities are typically continuous processes in a black box.

activity is activated. However this would probably not be true unless business was incredibly slow or a new shop had just received its first order. While the activity is usually not activated by flower requests, it does react to them. Additionally, the product is not necessarily emitted immediately—perhaps stock of the requested flowers has to be ordered from a supplier. Once the flower stock has arrived and been packaged for the customer, the product may then be emitted. At that point, the activity is not necessarily terminated, because other orders may also be in the works. In fact, there may be standing orders to deliver fresh bouquets periodically to various locations. In this way, activities can be processing continuously, while the external world knows nothing of how the processing occurs. While activities must react and emit, their processes are unknown—thus the term *black box*. Such process boxes remain opaque unless an analyst *chooses* to examine their contents.

Activities Add Value

In most data-processing methods, activities transform data. An activity takes data produced by other activities and increases its value by transforming it. The transformed data then becomes a product used by other activities. In object-oriented analysis, this transformation can occur on any enterprise object—not just data objects. As indicated in Fig. 8.8, the Flower Sales activity takes two externally provided products of some value. The activity transforms these products in a way that adds value, since a new product must be more valuable than its components in order to be marketable.

Value Chains

These value-added transformations form *value chains*. Value chains both help analysts to think about process analysis and are a useful technique for business planning. Value-chain analysis, as illustrated in Fig. 8.9, examines the value of the products consumed, the cost of their transformation, and the value of the produced product.

In particular, each activity can be analyzed to obtain the cost of carrying out the activity and the value of assets that will be tied up. Additionally, both the value of its

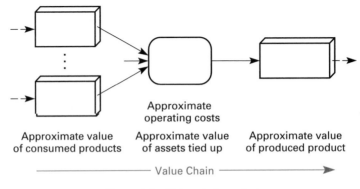

Approximate
operating costs

Approximate value   Approximate value   Approximate value
of consumed products   of assets tied up   of produced product

———————————— Value Chain ————————————➤

Figure 8.9   Value-chain analysis.

product and the products it consumes can also be determined. In this way value-chain analysis offers a sound financial basis for further business planning [Porter, 1985].

Activity-Product Pairs

As stated earlier, each product results from some purpose, and one activity fulfills that purpose. In short, each activity produces exactly one product, and each product is produced by exactly one activity. This keeps object-flow diagrams product oriented and encourages clear and direct business modeling. In addition, this product orientation leads to object orientation, because each product is a *clump* of object types. (In information engineering, these were called *subject areas.)*

The activity in Fig. 8.10(a) creates two products, Access to Buying Public and Magazine. To clarify the underlying complexity, breaking down such activities into two or more activities is helpful. Each activity will produce just one discrete product. Figure 8.10(b) depicts one solution to decomposing the activity in Fig. 8.10(a).

Figure 8.11(a) illustrates a different situation where one product results from more than one activity. Here, the extent to which Magazine Products is produced separately by each activity is unclear. An accurate value-chain analysis is not possible.

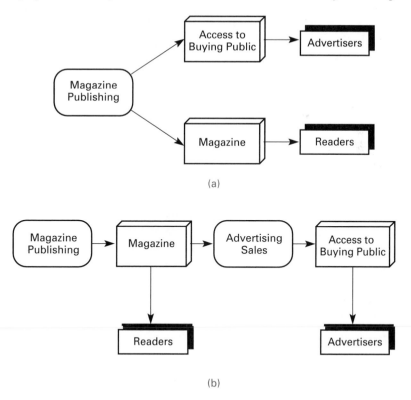

(a)

(b)

Figure 8.10 Splitting the activity to express one product for one activity.

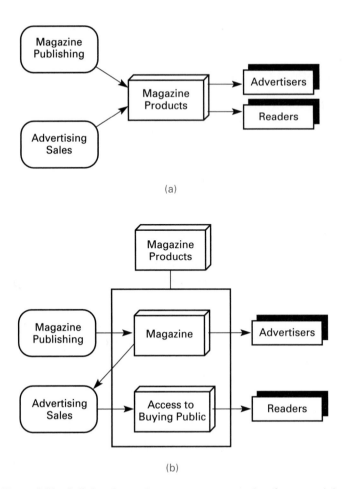

Figure 8.11   Splitting the product to express one product for one activity.

Additionally, the portion of the consolidated end product going to **Advertisers** and the part going to **Readers** is unknowable. Without a precise idea of who produces what for whom, the analysis result will be at best fuzzy. Figure 8.11(b) provides greater clarity. Each activity has one product, while both products can be represented as sub-products of a more encompassing **Magazine Products**. Both production and consumption lines are now clear and understandable; the notion of **Magazine Products** is preserved.

Products and By-products

Associating one activity with one product is a sound analysis guideline. The only exception is when the product is a natural by-product. *By-products* emerge as an inherent addition to an activity's primary product. By-products are often produced by an indivisible process within an activity. For example, when metal is melted, dross appears on the surface. Figure 8.12 depicts the product and a by-product of the Car Servicing activity. The by-product, Scrap Metal, is indicated with a dashed line.

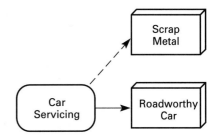

Figure 8.12   Activity product and by-product.

Consumed Products

Object-flow diagrams depict only those items that are consumed to add value—not just any kind of object flowing into an activity. This approach to object-flow representation is not so much restrictive as it is more appropriately focused. In this way, flow is addressed at its relevant level of abstraction—not earlier or later than is useful. For example, Fig. 8.13(a) represents only two valid products for Flower Sales consumption. The remaining products are not appropriate at this level of abstraction. Resources, such as Working Capital and Order Filling Personnel, are important to any organization. Yet, they are not consumed in order to increase value. Their consumption does not produce Delivered Flowers. Instead, they may be consumed by other activities such as those that are *internal* to Flower Sales.

Activity Leveling

Until now, activities have been presented as black boxes. This method furnishes a tangible approach, while it promotes reusable, modular thinking. At some point, however, the analyst may wish to examine the inner workings of an activity. As illustrated in Fig. 8.13(b) and Fig. 8.14, activities are composed of process clusters. By *leveling down,* an activity can be functionally decomposed into its appropriate process components. In contrast, by *leveling up,* a group of interrelated processes can be defined as a higher level activity.

Each level in a hierarchy establishes its own separate process space or *domain.* Each process domain is subject to its own object diagram, with its own nested behavior. An activity's process domain is not visible to its higher level domain until a product is emitted or consumed products are injected. This modularity greatly simplifies large processes. Some objects may be known only within a domain, while others may be known externally as well. As long as the external products have been agreed on, each process domain can have an internal reality that is quite different from any of the others.

Figure 8.15 illustrates an example of activity leveling. On the left, a Primary Enterprise Activity produces an Enterprise Product. (Nonprimary or *supporting activities* are presented following this subsection.) *Primary activities* involve product creation, its sale and distribution, and any subsequent servicing. These activities are diagrammed within

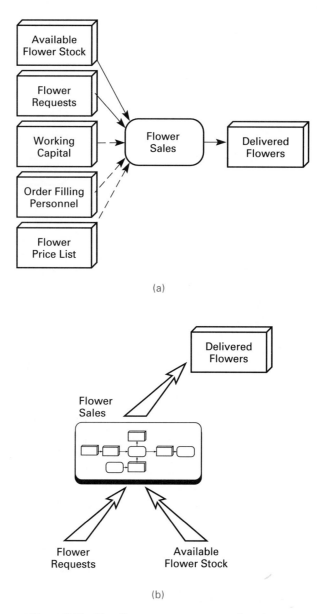

(a)

(b)

Figure 8.13   Not all resources are consumed products.

the shaded domain. While each of them has its own specialized purpose, together they fulfill the function specified for the **Primary Enterprise Activity**.

These five activities are generic to most organizations. Each activity is decomposable into even more distinct activities depending on the particular industry. **Inbound Logistics** involves materials handling, storage, inventory control, and returns to suppliers.

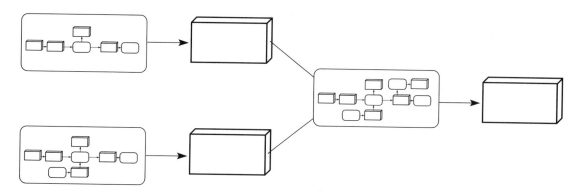

Figure 8.14   Each domain is a nested activity space.

If it were tied to another general enterprise activity, Inbound Logistics would be declared a subtype of Procurement. Operations includes such activities as machining, assembly, testing, packaging, and facility operations. Outbound Logistics is associated with warehousing finished goods, material handling, and delivery operations. Marketing and Sales includes everything from advertising and promotion to pricing and order processing. Finally, a Service activity provides the service to enhance or maintain the value of a product, such as installation, training, and repair [Porter, 1985].

The Primary Enterprise Activity, described above, is one example of activity leveling. When doing top-down leveling, activity analysis is not completely accurate, because not enough is known about the detail it comprises. However, even having a high-level strategic view that is approximately correct gives a vantage point for planning and coordinating the enterprise process.

Object-Flow and Event Diagram Leveling

The object-flow diagrams in Fig. 8.16 are depicted as decomposing to further levels of object-flow diagrams. However, since activities represent processes, each can also be decomposed into an event diagram. In top-down analysis, object-flow diagrams are commonly decomposed to object-flow diagrams until enough is known to represent a process as an event diagram. However, this is not necessarily the case. Object-flow diagrams are one way of describing processes; event diagrams are another. Therefore, an object-flow diagram can be decomposed into either or both descriptions, depending on the analyst's need.

Additionally, object-flow diagrams are not just used for top-down analysis but also for bottom-up analysis. In many cases, an analyst may wish to do both. For example, one analysis approach might begin with a top-down approach followed by a bottom-up refinement once the details are better understood.

Activities Can be Subtyped

Like the product, activities can also be partitioned. For example, Fig. 8.17(b) represents Establish Material Costs partitioned into two more specific activities. In this case, an

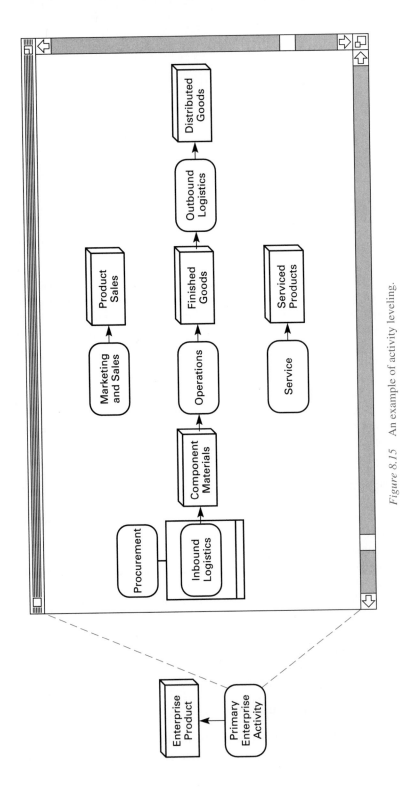

Figure 8.15 An example of activity leveling.

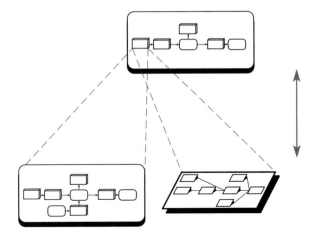

Figure 8.16 Leveling with object-flow diagrams and/or event diagrams.

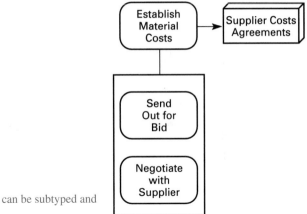

Figure 8.17 Activities can be subtyped and supertyped.

execution of either Send Out for Bid or Negotiate with Supplier activities is also an execution of Establish Material Costs.

Figure 8.18 depicts an example of partitioned activities at the highest level of modeling. As with the example in Fig 8.15, these activities are generic examples of those found in any competing industry. Government services and nonprofit organizations may differ, but only slightly. The Enterprise Activity is initially partitioned into two activities, a Primary Enterprise Activity (presented earlier) and a Supporting Enterprise Activity. Support activities are separated, because they service the primary activities and each other through various companywide functions.

The Supporting Enterprise Activity is further partitioned into four more activities. Enterprise Infrastructure Management consists of activities including general management, planning, finance, accounting, legal, government affairs, and so on. Human Resource Management entails all personnel issues from recruiting, hiring,

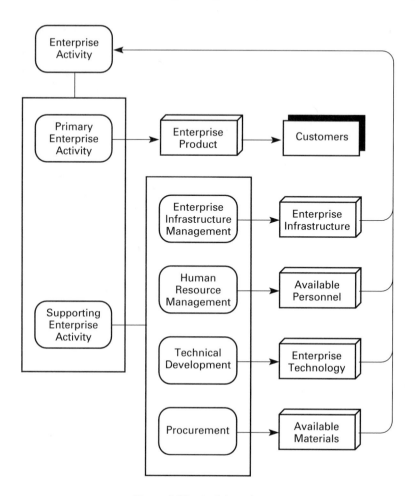

Figure 8.18 Activity subtypes.

and contracting through training, development, and compensation. **Technical Development** is involved in improving the product and the process and takes many forms. It embodies the know-how and procedures for product design, product servicing, and equipment design as well as all supporting services. Last, **Procurement** refers to the function of purchasing products to be consumed by all of the firm's activities. It deals with suppliers, orders, and goods and tracks them to their final distribution point [Porter, 1985].

Activity subtypes, then, provide a hierarchy of activity subtypes and supertypes that can be reused during activity analysis. In Fig. 8.15, every instance of **Inbound Logistics** is an instance of **Procurement**. With Fig. 8.17, this same instance is also an instance of **Supporting Enterprise Activity**, which is also an instance of **Enterprise Activity**.

CONCLUSION

Object-flow diagrams provide an architecture of self-contained components and strictly defined interfaces. By dividing complicated processes into manageable chunks, they enable an understanding that is critical in complex situations.

Object-flow diagrams represent the *function* or purpose of a process instead of the dynamics of its triggers, events, and control conditions. They describe interactions among processes, yet do not indicate when or how processes will be activated or terminated. Their processes can exist in parallel, can occur at different places, and are not synchronized with one another. Object-flow diagrams employ a strategic-level approach in an OO manner. Additionally, they represent processing requirements in a way that business planners can understand and apply to strategic planning exercises.

Each *activity* is a process performed to achieve a specific purpose. A *product* is the end result of that purpose. Each product is potentially salable. Activities consume these salable objects, add value to the objects, and produce a new product.

Object-flow diagrams indicate chains of producer/consumer relationships, by depicting them as a series of activities and exchanged products. Such a relationship occurs only when two activities come to an agreement on an exchanged product. The product, then, is the subject matter of their communications.

Object-flow diagrams offer additional benefits in the following areas of systems construction:

- *Concurrent engineering.* Object-flow diagrams clearly show those sets of activities that exhibit sequence independence. They are therefore considered to be acting in parallel. For example in Fig. 8.18, Technical Development and Procurement, though they may interface in some manner, they operate in parallel. In this way, object-flow diagrams can support the concurrent engineering of application systems as well as develop distributed processing or parallel computing applications.

- *Systems integration.* The history of systems development has taught us that independent development of component activities is no great trick. The real skill is ensuring that independently developed activities are integrated. This can be achieved by locking down their interfaces. Object-flow diagrams aid integration by precisely defining the products exchanged and the communications specification for this exchange. Once these are defined, the analyst can evolve the implementation rules for interface communication.

REFERENCES

Harel, D. et al., "Statemate: A Working Environment for the Development of Complex Reactive Systems," *IEEE 10th Conference on Software Engineering,* 1988.

Porter, Michael E., *Competitive Advantage,* The Free Press, New York, 1985.

Tsichritzis, Dionysios C., and Frederick H. Lochovsky, *Data Models,* Prentice Hall, Englewood Cliffs, NJ, 1982.

Chapter 9

Object-Flow Analysis Method

A METHOD FOR GOAL-DIRECTED OBJECT-FLOW ANALYSIS

The previous chapter presented the elements of object-flow diagrams. Object-flow diagrams are typically constructed in two ways: goal-directed or activity-directed. These resemble the goal and event-directed methods of event analysis (see Chapter 7). Goal-directed event analysis identifies the ending event first, then identifies the causes of the event. In goal-directed object-flow analysis, the *product* is identified first, followed by the activity that generates the product. A step-by-step method for constructing goal-directed object-flow diagrams is discussed in this section and summarized in Fig. 9.1. (An activity-directed method is discussed at the end of this chapter.)

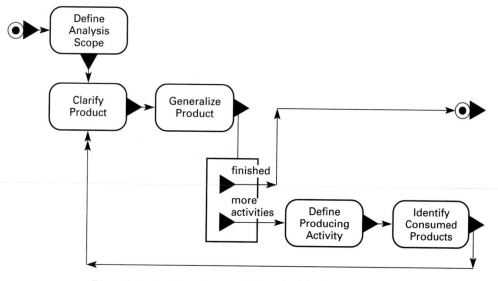

Figure 9.1   An object-flow analysis method that is goal-directed.

Define Analysis Scope

As with the analysis methods presented earlier, object-flow analysis must also begin by examining what to model—and what not to model. In other words, the analyst and domain expert must define a *domain* of interest. Once the domain has been identified, its purpose or *target* must be expressed. This target identifies the desired product of the domain's processing. For example, some domains and their target products might be:

Domain	Target Products
Sales Organization	Signed Order
Advertising Firm	Product Awareness
Consulting Firm	Discharged Contract
Commercial TV Company	Audience Access

The starting products are also important (see Fig. 9.2). Here, the analyst and expert identify those resources that a domain uses as ingredients to its value-adding processing. By knowing the starting and ending products of a domain, the object-flow specification can be given borders.

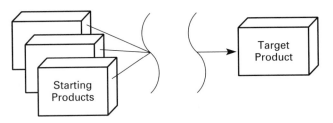

Figure 9.2   While the target product is mandatory, the starting products are also important.

Clarify Product

To ensure that the product is understood, its underlying concepts should be identified. For instance, a product called Goods Order could be produced by a Product Sales domain. However, the name Goods Order alone is not sufficiently explanatory. The product must also be defined in some manner. Figure 8.5 illustrates one technique for doing this—using an object diagram. An object diagram expresses our concepts and their associations and can be constructed using the object-analysis method described in Chapter 5.

Generalize Product

Generalizing a product requires the analyst to rise above the immediate details of a system and momentarily explore a broader scope. For instance an analyst may be specifying a product-sales system. The target product in that system will be Goods Order. As illustrated in Fig. 9.3, a more general form of Goods Order could be Order. After exploring the possible levels of abstraction, the analyst should choose the appropriate level for the

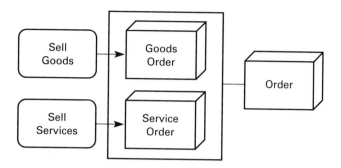

Figure 9.3   Products may be generalized or specialized.

system at hand and change the chosen product, if necessary. For example, the product Order may be a more appropriate generalization than Goods Order. In this situation, the scope of the system may move to a more general sales system. Such a consideration may or may not change the domain and its product. Without the generalization step, however, the analyst may never have considered the possibility.

The results of generalization also aid system integration. After generalizing the product, the analyst should look to see if it has already been specified. If so, the generalized product may already be part of a system that is in progress or one that is already completed. In this case, an integration point has been identified and can be administered accordingly.

Define Producing Activity

In order to create the product specified in the previous step, an activity is required. If the only products on the diagram are *starting* products, the analysis is complete. If the diagram contains products that are not starting products, the activities that create these products must now be identified. For example, if the diagram contains the Goods Order and Service Order products, the activities that produce each of these must be defined. In Fig. 9.3, these activities are Sell Goods and Sell Services, respectively.

Identify Consumed Products

An activity is a process that creates a product by adding value to those products it consumes. With each activity identified in the previous step, identify the resources to which it adds value. For example, the Sell Goods activity requires Available Stock and Potential Customers. Each of these products becomes input to the next step in the analysis method: Clarify Product.

A METHOD FOR ACTIVITY-DIRECTED OBJECT-FLOW ANALYSIS

In activity-directed object-flow analysis, the steps described above can be used in a different sequence. Instead of a target product being identified first, a starting activity is identified. The analysis continues by identifying the product that is created by the activity, which is in turn consumed by another activity that yields yet another product. This whole procedure concludes when the target product is reached. As with event analysis, goal-directed object-flow analysis is useful for processes that are not well understood or are goal driven by their nature. Activity-directed object-flow analysis is useful for processes that are reasonably well understood or are driven by the responsiveness of the business.

OO DESIGN

Design is defined as the mapping from the conceptual world to a chosen, target implementation world. In this book, the conceptual world is expressed in terms of models defined during the system analysis phase, such as event diagrams, object diagrams, and state-transition diagrams. This part of the book discusses how to take these analysis models and map them into object-oriented implementations. It begins by first describing the target implementation world of OO programming languages. This is followed by a description of various techniques for mapping object and event diagrams into an OO implementation.

Chapter 10

OO Programming Languages

THE GENESIS OF OO TECHNOLOGY

The genesis of the technology now called *object-oriented* dates back to the early 1960s. It arose from the need to describe and simulate a variety of phenomena such as nerve networks, communications systems, traffic flow, production systems, administrative systems, and even social systems. In the spring of 1961, Kristen Nygaard originated the ideas for a language that would serve the dual purpose of system description and simulation programming. Together with Ole-Johan Dahl, Nygaard developed the simulation language now known as Simula I. The first Simula-based application package was implemented for the simulation of logic circuits. However, operations research applications were the most popular usage. For example, in 1965 a large and complex job shop simulation was programmed in less than four weeks—with an execution efficiency at least four times higher than that of available technology.

Simula was intended to be a system description and simulation programming language. However, its users quickly discovered that Simula also provided new and powerful facilities when used for purposes *other than* simulation, such as prototyping and application development. In September 1965, the possibilities of a "new, improved Simula" as a general purpose language were being planned. By December 1966, the necessary foundation for the new, general programming language, called Simula 67, was defined.

In the late 1960s, another development of OO technology was under way, guided by research at the University of Utah and by the central ideas of Simula. Alan Kay envisioned that by the 1980s

> Both adults and children will be able to have as a personal possession a computer about the size of a notebook with the power to handle virtually all their information-related needs. . . . Ideally the personal computer will be designed in such a way that all ages and walks of life can mold and channel its power to their own needs [Kay, 1977].

Early in the 1970s, Alan Kay went to Xerox and formed the Learning Research Group (LRG). Xerox was responsible for producing the interim model for the personal computer, called Dynabook. The LRG was engaged to produce the software, called Smalltalk. After observing the project, they quickly realized that one of the major design problems of such a PC involved expressive communication, particularly when children were seriously considered as users. For this reason, the LRG invited some 250 children (aged six to fifteen) and 50 adults to try versions of Smalltalk and suggest ways of improving it. In order to test the usability of Smalltalk, they started with simple situations that embodied a concept and gradually increased the complexity of the examples. A major goal of Smalltalk was to provide a single name (or symbol) for a complex collection of ideas. Later, these ideas could be invoked and manipulated through the name. They found that children were able to do this by the age of six.

While the Dynabook project did not realize its goal, the concept remains a kind of Holy Grail for computer manufacturers. However the Smalltalk language is alive and well today. Alan Kay foresaw the need to characterize and communicate application concepts in developing computer programs. Smalltalk provides the means to write programs in a style that brings our concepts to life. Alan Kay expected the personal computer to be a human medium of communication. The actual term *object-oriented* originated during the development of Smalltalk.

The Evolution from Untyped to Typed Languages

The so-called object-oriented approach introduced by Simula and Smalltalk was not a totally new idea, but resulted from an evolutionary momentum. Object orientation grew out of the need to organize the kinds, or *types*, of data on which a program could operate. Initially, only one data type described the universe of bit strings in a computer memory: the data type Word. Words are bit strings of fixed size that can be used as units of information.

However when developers design their systems, they organize their universe of data in different ways for different purposes. The need for data types arises whenever data must be categorized for a particular usage. As early as 1954, FORTRAN distinguished between Integer and Floating-point types of data. Later, ALGOL 60 incorporated data types for Integer, Real, and Boolean. Still later, languages included additional data types, such as the Character, String, Bit, Byte, Array, Pointer, Record, File, and Procedure.

A *data type* describes a certain kind of data—its representation and the set of valid operations that access and maintain that data. In this way, each data type is a known commodity, protected from unintended use. For example, the data type Character describes the kind of data that is displayable by a program. Furthermore, a set of operations is provided for creating, destroying, examining, and manipulating Character data. Since arithmetic operations such as add and subtract are not defined for Character data, computational requests are not permitted.

User-Defined Types (UDTs)

Prior to the early 1970s, a programmer could reference only those data types built into a programming language compiler. As a result, even often-used types like Month, Date, Time, Coefficient, Tree, and Stack were not explicitly accessible. These ideas had to be implicitly embedded somewhere in the programmer's code. Another limiting characteristic of built-in types was that they defined the way that data was physically stored. They had little useful relationship to the real-world objects that the application was trying to implement. Programmers spent more time thinking about whether or not a number should be an Integer than about Customer Orders and Part Requisitions.

Eventually, the computer industry felt pressured to provide programmers with a facility for expressing their own typing needs. The first languages to offer *user-defined types (UDTs)* were Pascal and ALGOL 68. In Pascal, for example, a programmer could write

type month = (January, February, March, April, May, June, July, August, September, October, November, December);

This expression would then define the UDT Month as being the set of twelve literals. At this point, the developer could define relational operations to compare two given Month variables for less than, equal to, and so on. Other operations could include computing the preceding or succeeding month when supplied with a Month variable.

The *types* of Pascal and the *nodes* of ALGOL 68 were an important step forward. They permitted the programmer to go from manufacturer-imposed types to user-imposed types. UDTs raised the expressive power of programming languages. More importantly, they encouraged systems developers to translate the real-world object types of the system application into coded data types.

Abstract Data Types (ADTs)

The *abstract data type (ADT)* extends the notion of the user-defined type (UDT) by adding encapsulation. Each ADT contains the specifications and the operations of its data type. The *encapsulation* feature of the ADT not only hides the data type's implementation, but also provides a protective wall that shields its objects from improper use. All interface occurs through named *operations* defined within the ADT. The operations, then, provide a well-defined means for accessing the objects of a data type. In short, ADTs give objects a public *interface*. An ADT's interface, then, consists of all of the operations (and their associated parameter requirements) that may be requested outside of the ADT. However, the data specification and programming code (or *method*) for each operation are hidden from outside view.

The ADT facility first appeared in Simula 67. Its implementation is called a *class*. Modula refers to its ADT implementation as a *module*, while Ada uses the word *package*. In all cases, the ADT provides a way for the systems developer to identify real-world data types and package them in a more convenient and compact form. In this way, ADTs can be defined for things like Dates, Screen Panels, Customer Orders, and Part Requisitions. Once defined, the developer can address the ADTs directly in future operations.

THE BASICS OF OO PROGRAMMING LANGUAGES

Classes

Since ADTS are called classes in OO programming languages, and this part of the book is dealing with OO program design, the word *class* will be used. Figure 10.1 illustrates an example of the class named Employee. At its heart, the class is defined by its data structure specification. For Employee, this includes data about exemptions, position, salary amount, phone extension, and so on. The class is also defined by a set of permissible operations. These operations, such as hire, promote, and change phone extension, provide an interface to access and maintain Employee-related data.

> Each declared operation has a name, a set of objects it takes as parameters, and a set of objects it returns when the operation is completed. This is known as the operation's *signature.*
>
> The set of all signatures for a class is called the *interface* for that class.

In other words, a class's interface is the complete set of requests that can be sent to the class and its objects.[*]

Additionally, each procedure, or *method,* employed to carry out an operation, is hidden from its users. What the user must provide is an appropriate object to invoke, or *request,* the operation along with any applicable supporting parameters. For example, Fig. 10.2 depicts three instances, or *objects,* of Employee. In order to give Bob a promotion, the request must provide the Bob object, the promote operation, and the salary grade of his promotion. In its abbreviated form, this request could be thought of in the following manner: Bob, promote, director.

Objects as Encapsulations

Figure 10.2 depicts three Employee objects as miniature representations of the Employee class.

> An object can be regarded as any instance of a class—each encapsulating its own private data and its own permissible operations.

Each object can be considered as a thing in its own right, with its own behavior. In other words, any request that matches a signature within the object's interface may be sent to that object.

[*]Some OO languages differentiate between *private, public,* and *protected* operations. A private operation may only be invoked by the class which contains it. A protected operation may only be invoked by the class that contains it or its subtypes. A public operation has no restrictions. C++ also uses these classifications for structural elements as well.

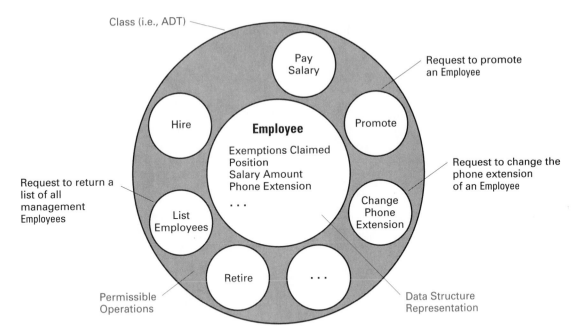

Figure 10.1   Requests to access and maintain Employee-related data are made through the operations defined on the Employee class.

While each object should encapsulate a physical record of its own data, encapsulating a physical copy of each operational method is unnecessary and wasteful. Since the same coding is contained within each class, a class's operations need only be *virtually* available to an object. In other words, all operations that apply to a particular class also apply to the instances of that class.* As illustrated in Fig. 10.3, since Bob is an instance of the Employee class, all Employee operations (such as promote) also apply to Bob, without the object having to contain them physically. When an instance of a class is created, this linkage is established. Object-oriented languages usually accomplish this with a physical pointer or some other *reference* mechanism.

Objects and Requests

With encapsulation, the programmer need only know *what* operations can be requested of an object, because operations are the interface for all objects. All the specifics of *how* its structure is stored and *how* its operations are coded are tucked neatly out of sight. This not only protects each object, it simplifies the interactions between them. Most OO languages call these interactions *messages*. For instance, a Customer object can send a message to an Order object to add a product to its already existing line items. The Order

---

*Most OO languages differentiate between *instance operations* and *class operations*. Instance operations apply to class instances. Class operations, on the other hand, apply to the class as a whole—not to its instances.

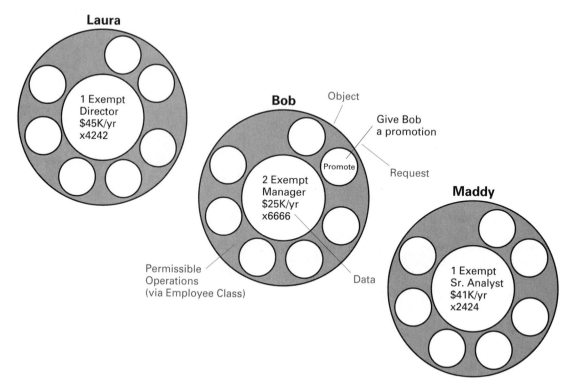

Figure 10.2   An object's permissible operations are defined by its class.

object, in turn, may send a message to a **Customer Account** object with a request to update the amount due for the customer.

While the word message is a useful metaphor in some contexts, the idea of inanimate objects sending messages to one another can cause conceptual difficulties. (An example is the interaction of **Orders** and **Customer Accounts**.) Figure 10.4 depicts several objects sending messages. To say that object A is sending a message to object B means that one of the encapsulated operations of object A has been invoked. This operation of A requires—and therefore *requests*—the invocation of an operation permitted on object B. For clarity, then, the standard term emerging for a message is the *request*.

Object Identification

While a class's operations act as a gateway for object access, its data structure describes the data attributes that each object possesses. This structure allows objects to be considered as records. Their *fields* may contain values or references to other objects. For example, Fig. 10.5(a) depicts two **Musical Composition** objects. Each contains a musical catalog identifier, a composition name, and a reference to a **Composer** object. The **Composer** object's structure contains: the name of the composer, the year of the composer's birth, and the year of the composer's death.

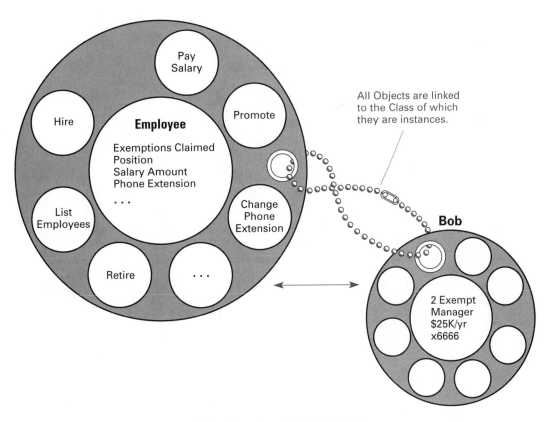

Figure 10.3　Every class is linked to its instances.

As Fig. 10.5(b) suggests, objects of various types can contain various kinds of data and can reference and be referenced by other objects. However, in order to reference an object, every object must be uniquely identifiable.

Each object is created by an explicit action. Therefore, it is distinct from those objects created previously or those to be created in the future. It has a unique identity. Even if two objects have identical characteristics, they are not the same object, just as identical twins are not the same person. In order for an OOPL to provide this knowledge, a good object-identification mechanism is required. These are typically implemented using memory references, user-supplied names, and identifier keys.

Inheritance

Inheritance is an important feature of OO programming languages. While different OOPLs have different inheritance mechanisms, we can think about them in the following way. When a request for an operation goes to a subclass, that class's list of permissible operations is checked. For instance, if a move operation is requested for a square, the Square class is checked first for the move operation. If the operation is found on the list, it is

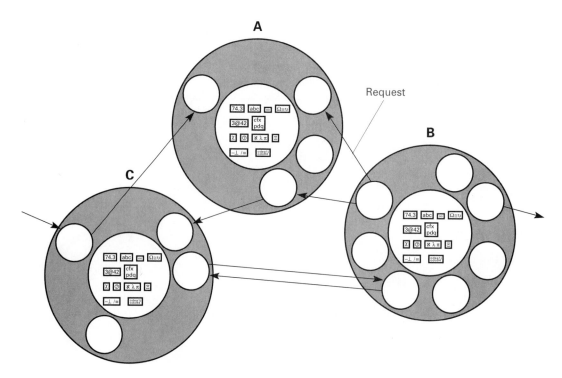

Figure 10.4   The operation of one object *requests* the operation of another.

invoked; if not, the parent classes are examined to locate the operation (as illustrated in Fig. 10.6). In this example, the move operation is actually located in the **Polygon** class. (Smalltalk performs this inheritance search at run time; C++ binds it at compile time.)

Polymorphism

An important feature of inheritance is the ability of a class to *override* inherited features. Here, the processing algorithm, or *method*, of an inherited operation can be redefined at the subtype level. The example in Fig. 10.6 illustrates three classes. The most general, **Polygon**, contains the data structure and permissible operations for polygons. Because every instance of a **Rectangle** is also an instance of a **Polygon**, the **Rectangle** subtype need not repeat those features it inherits from **Polygon**. However, while all **Polygon** operations apply to subtypes, the *method* of operation may be different. For example, the method for computing perimeters may differ. The perimeter of a **Polygon** is the sum of all its sides; the perimeter of a **Rectangle** is the sum of two of its adjacent sides multiplied by two. The **Square** perimeter differs again as the product of multiplying four times the length of any one side.

Whenever a request is made for an operation on an object, the method selected depends on whether or not the inheritance hierarchy has been overridden. The method for moving a **Square** three centimeters to the right is selected from **Polygon**. However, even

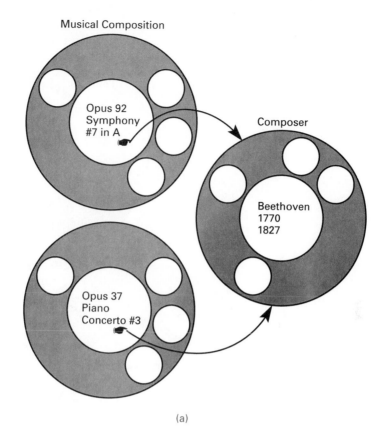

(a)

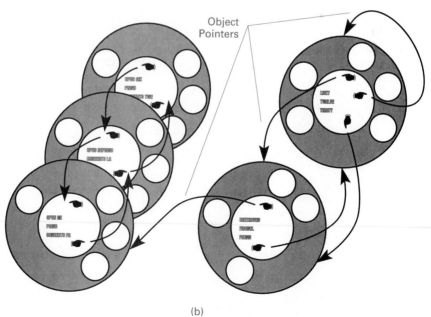

(b)

Figure 10.5 Object pointers, or references, require object identification.

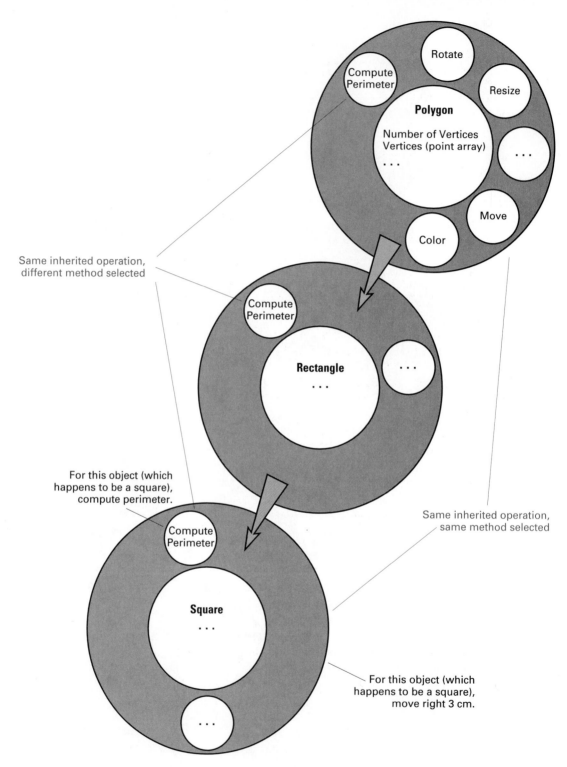

Figure 10.6 Inheritance searches can be overridden—resulting in polymorphism.

though the *operation* for compute perimeter is inherited from the Polygon, the *method* selected for a Square is located in the Square class. This phenomenon is known as *polymorphism* and is an important reason for preserving the difference between operations and methods.

An *operation* is the kind of process being requested.

A *method* is the procedure for how the operation is carried out.

Polymorphism is the ability of an operation to support multiple types of objects—via different methods.

Canceling Inherited Features

Some expert systems in AI allow some inherited features to be canceled. For example, one of the features of Birds includes flying. However, this same feature does not apply to Penguins and Ostriches. Therefore, this feature can be canceled. The arbitrary overriding and canceling of inherited features is a questionable practice. Logically it is incorrect, because, by definition, all features of a type apply to its subtypes. Therefore, to rectify the problem of Birds flying and Penguins not, the subtyping hierarchy needs to be changed. To solve this, Bird can be specialized into two subtypes: Flying Bird and Nonflying Bird. Following this, all the data structures and operations relating to flying should be shifted from Bird to Flying Bird. Types such as Penguin and Ostrich should then be realigned as subtypes of Nonflying Bird. This would correct the logical inconsistency. However, *physically* it might create an intolerable system overhead. For this reason, some languages allow the programmer to deviate from what is logically correct for the sake of performance.

Multiple Inheritance

Allowing a class to inherit from more than one immediate supertype is called *multiple inheritance*.

For example, the type Working Student has the supertypes Employee and Student. A Great Panda is a Bear, a Herbivore, and an Endangered Animal. In Fig. 10.7, the example defines Sales Manager as a subtype of Manager and Salesperson. This means that the features of both Manager *and* Salesperson apply to Sales Manager. Since every instance of a Sales Manager is also an instance of Manager and Salesperson, both sets of data structures and permissible operations are reusable for a Sales Manager object.

Unfortunately, combining the features of supertypes is not straightforward. A conflict arises when data items or operations from different supertypes have the *same name* but have *different meanings*. For instance in Fig. 10.7, Manager and Salesperson both have a feature named "skill." In one case, skill reflects the ability to manage people; in the other, the ability to sell. The same situation applies to the two supertype operations

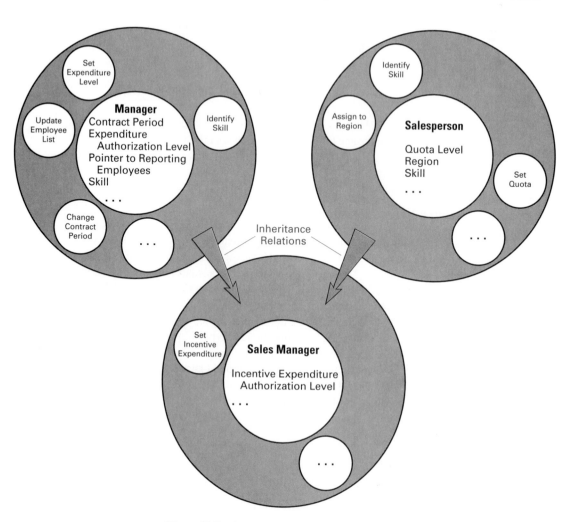

Figure 10.7   An example of multiple inheritance.

named "identify skill"—same name but totally unrelated meanings. What, then, are the ramifications when a subtype inherits both? On the one hand, all the features of a type are inherited by its subtype. On the other, the ability to request just one of the available operations based on its name presents a problem. Which operation is chosen when requested to "identify skill?" Several strategies exist for resolving conflicts of unrelated features. In one strategy, an algorithm is defined to choose a feature based on placement in the supertype hierarchy. While this hides the conflict resolution from the user, it does not always produce the desired results. Another strategy forbids such conflicts and renames the offending features, thus removing the problem entirely. Typically, the programmer overrides the method to specify the correct code to be executed. In any case, the benefits of multiple inheritance must be weighed against such drawbacks.

OBJECT-ORIENTED AND OBJECT-BASED IMPLEMENTATIONS

In the preceding sections, two important programming language characteristics were presented. A language is *object-oriented* if, and only if, it satisfies the following requirements.

- *It Supports Classes.* Classes are ADTs. Therefore every class has an interface and every object is encapsulated.
- *Class Inheritance Is Supported.* With class inheritance, systems are extended and refined using existing class components.[*] Class inheritance allows systems to be constructed from existing type hierarchies. It provides mechanisms for both construction and reuse of software. In this way, we do not have to reinvent the wheel—only the portion of it that is different.
- *Method Selection Is Supported.* With method selection, the user need only request that the operation should be applied to an object. The system will then choose the method appropriate for the specified parameters. In other words, the user only needs to specify what is to be done, and the method selector determines how it is to be applied. Polymorphism is one of the most common applications of method selection.

Much debate has focused on which languages are more object-oriented. The requirements for an object-oriented implementation can be summarized in the following way:

OOPL implementation = classes + class inheritance + method selection[†]

If the language does not satisfy these requirements, it is not object oriented. However, a few programming languages, including Modula and Ada, do satisfy the first of the three requirements. These languages are called *object-based*.

REFERENCES

Budd, Timothy, *A Little Smalltalk,* Addison-Wesley, Reading, MA, 1987.

Cardelli, Luca, and Peter Wegner, "On Understanding Types, Data Abstraction, and Polymorphism," *ACM Computing Surveys,* 17:4, 1985, pp. 471–522.

Cox, Brad J., and Andrew J. Novobilski, *Object-Oriented Programming: An Evolutionary Approach* (2nd ed.), Addison-Wesley, Reading, MA, 1991.

Dahl, Ole-Johan, and Kristan Nygaard, "SIMULA - An Algol-based Simulation Language," *Communications of the ACM,* 9:9, 1966, pp. 671–678.

Goldberg, Adele, and David Robson, *Smalltalk-80: The Language and its Implementation,* Addison-Wesley, Reading, MA, 1983.

---

[*]The term *class inheritance* is used because there are several forms of inheritance. See Glossary in [Martin, 1995].

[†]Some refer to this as encapsulation, inheritance, and polymorphism, instead. However there is more to method selection than polymorphism. There is also the notion of handling requests.

Horowitz, Ellis, *Fundamentals of Programming Languages* (2nd ed.), W. H. Freeman, New York, 1984.

Kay, Alan C., "Microelectronics and the Personal Computer," *Scientific American,* September 1977, pp. 231–244.

Kent, William, "A Rigorous Model of Object Reference, Identity, and Existence," *Journal of Object-Oriented Programming,* 4:3, 1991, pp. 28–36.

Khoshafian, Setrag, and Razmik Abnous, *Object Orientation: Concepts, Languages, Databases, User Interfaces,* John Wiley & Sons, New York, 1990.

Liskov, Barbara, and John Guttag, *Abstraction and Specification in Program Development,* MIT Press, Cambridge, MA, 1986.

Martin, James, and James J. Odell, *Object-Oriented Methods: A Foundation,* Prentice Hall, Englewood Cliffs, NJ, 1995.

Nygaard, Kristen, and Ole-Johan Dahl, "The Development of the Simula Language," *History of Programming Languages,* ACM SIGPLAN History of Programming Languages Conference (Los Angeles), Richard L. Wexelblat, ed., Academic Press, New York, 1981, pp. 439-493.

Soley, Richard Mark, ed., *Object Management Architecture Guide,* Object Management Group, Document 92.11.1, September 1, 1992, Framingham, MA.

Taylor, David A., *A Manager's Guide to Object-Oriented Technology,* Addison-Wesley, Reading, MA, 1990.

Chapter **11**

Moving from Analysis into Design*

QUALITY AND SOFTWARE PROCESS MATURITY

In recent years, the movement toward developing formal procedures to increase product quality has grown. The work has been inspired by W. Edwards Deming, who was sent to Japan after World War II to help rebuild their industry. His ideas on quality management, widely ignored in the United States, were taken up enthusiastically in Japan. Many consider this a key reason why Americans have lost so much economic and technical ground to the Japanese.

This movement toward high-quality products, often led by defense agencies, has influenced software engineering. In particular, the work of the Software Engineering Institute (SEI) has proven deeply influential [Humphrey, 1989]. Its framework proposes five levels of process maturity: initial, repeatable, defined, managed, and optimizing.

The two lowest levels are the *initial* level (often referred to cynically as the chaotic level) and the *repeatable* level. While success in level 1 depends on the heroics and competence of individuals, project developers in level 2 can rely on established management policies and implementation procedures. These are based on the results of previous projects and the demands of the current project. Developers meet schedules and budgets. Basic project standards are defined and followed. SEI studies have shown that the vast majority of organizations are at these bottom levels of process maturity.

This chapter provides an approach that will support organizations wishing to take a further step—up to the *defined* level. At the defined level, an organization standardizes both its system engineering and management activities. Such an organization exploits effective software-engineering practices when standardizing its activities. Furthermore, an organization's activity standards are tailored for each project to develop its own *defined* activities [Paulk, 1993]. One technique that supports defined-level organizations is *template-driven* design.

*This chapter is based on material contributed by Martin Fowler.

TEMPLATE-DRIVEN DESIGN

In this approach, design activity focuses on forming a set of design templates that can implement the analysis model (see Fig. 11.1). These design templates (also referred to as *patterns*) are formulated using a definition of both the analysis method and the implementation environment. In theory, the design templates are applied to the analysis model, and a fully working system can be produced. This system then will accurately reflect the analysis model, though the system may not be the most efficient.

The analysis model should *define the interface* of the software components. When used in conjunction with the analysis model, design templates suggest the *implementation* of those components. As a result, a programmer—new to the domain, but familiar with the templates—should recognize the interface of all the components simply by looking at the analysis model. While each template is a suggested implementation, its interface is dictated by the analysis model. (In practice, achieving this goal completely may not be possible but the aim is to get as close as possible.)

This approach enables both *consistency* and *traceability*. If a single set of design templates is used to develop code from the model, the resulting code will have a consistent style—a boon to maintenance and extension later on. This consistency comes from both naming the variables and operations and using the same mechanisms to implement bidirectional associations and subtyping. The link's directness eases tracing back from the code to the analysis model. Traceability is always useful and a key element for quality standards [ISO, 1987 and 1991].

SPECIFYING DESIGN TEMPLATES

The design templates can be specified in two ways. The first, and easiest, approach uses the design templates' document that has been adopted as a standard by a project or an organization. This document describes how to implement an analysis-level model for a particular implementation environment. Since the design templates are dependent on both the analysis approach and the implementation environment, each combination of the two should have a design-template document.

The second approach encodes the design templates in a computer program. (This approach is currently very limited, but is becoming more important.) Of course, this encoding is exactly what compilers and code generators do. A compiler merely uses a set of design templates to transform each kind of high-level language statement into binary code. Program-language compilers are not new. However, the technology to automate design templates is still very immature, although being developed rapidly. Code generators do exist that can take these models and produce much of the system code using templates.

This approach naturally has practical limits. While experience in formulating templates is growing, the idea of using design templates in this way is still fairly new. Furthermore, while design templates can be provided to cover most cases, they cannot be applied to some special cases. Another practical limit is that the choice of design templates is not always well defined. Design-template documents may indicate preferred

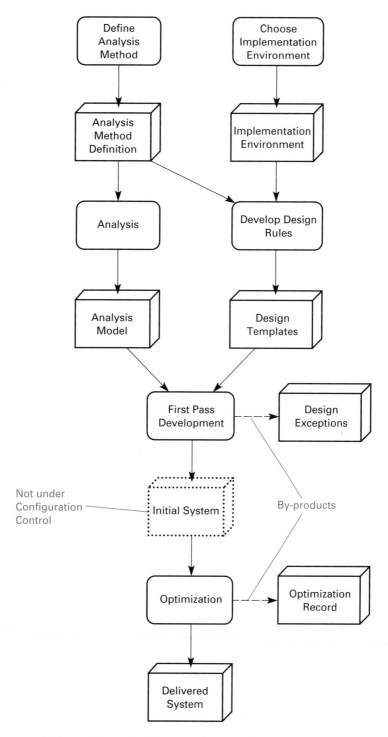

Figure 11.1 An object-flow diagram which describes the process of template-driven designs.

implementation options, while leaving the choice to the implementer on a case-by-case basis.

The template-driven approach can be accomplished using documented design standards coupled with a formal review to ensure the quality of the results. In fact, the entire process can be done so that it complies with ISO-9000. Some organizations, however, have little or no formal approach at all. For example, at a large British bank the templates adopted were gleaned from internal memos and word of mouth. The alternative produced no OO systems until formal procedures were developed and approved. Certainly, sound and consistent procedures are important. Yet, the bank found that they still delivered a system of acceptable quality—rather than none at all. (The bank did, however, consider preserving traceability of all choices of options and variations from the templates to be vitally important.)

OPTIMIZATION

The result of this development is an initial system which should be fully functional. However, it may not necessarily be compact or fast enough to run effectively. If this is the case, optimization will be necessary. It is important to stress the fact that optimization should come *after* the system is developed. In particular, design variations carried out earlier should *not* be done to improve performance. Any ad hoc changes to the system to improve performance should only be carried out *after* the initial system is running. This use of post-implementation tuning to improve system performance is based on the following principles:

- 90 percent of a system's time is spent in 10 percent of the code.
- Programmers are not good at finding that 10 percent.

The effort required to optimize a system needs to be concentrated in the critical 10 percent of the code—where the biggest payoffs apply. A single procedure should be used for optimization:

- Find the biggest bottleneck.
- Remove or reduce the bottleneck.
- Repeat until the situation is acceptable.

Finding the bottlenecks is a task that is almost impossible to do by eye. Key to discovering these are performance monitors which watch the software as it runs and give information on where the system is spending its time. Developers are always surprised by which parts of the system consume the most time. This is why optimization should be done *after* the initial implementation, because performance tuners only work on a running system. Optimization, guided by performance monitors, can provide dramatic increases in speed without sacrificing the integrity of the design. Indeed, this post-implementation approach is often regarded as producing faster systems than those approaches where performance hacks have been applied early.[*] This is particularly true in environments with flexible architectures. In another large British company, serious performance problems were solved because the architecture allowed processing to be moved easily between processors in a client/server architecture. In this case, optimizing after the design helped the organization with its performance problems. Again, to maintain traceability, a log of optimizations needs to be recorded and kept under change control.

A key part of the final documentation for an OO system is the class catalog. This list of all the classes in the system and their interfaces is the essence of the documentation of the delivered code. This information should be produced *automatically* from the delivered code and should be the basis against which unit testing is carried out. It can be produced automatically from the delivered code by a text processor that extracts class header information and comments from the source code.

REFERENCES

Humphrey, W. S., *Managing the Software Process,* Addison-Wesley, Reading, MA, 1989.

ISO, *ISO 9001 Quality Systems—Model for quality assurance in design/development, production, installation and servicing,* International Organization for Standardization, Report ISO 9001–1987, 1987.

ISO, *ISO 9000-3 Quality management and quality assurance standards—Part 3: Guidelines for the application of ISO 9001 to the development, supply and maintenance of software,* International Organization for Standardization, Report ISO 9000–3:1991, 1991.

Paulk, Mark C., Bill Curtis, Mary Beth Chrissis, and Charles V. Webber, "Capability Maturity Model, Version 1.1," *IEEE Software,* 10:4, 1993, pp. 18–27.

---

[*] There are always some exceptions. Some architectural design decisions cannot be easily optimized in this manner. Such bottlenecks need to be considered in advance, and designs developed to ease them. Early performance prototypes are valuable here.

Chapter 12

OO Design with Object Diagrams[*]

INTRODUCTION

Design templates have several goals:

- To ensure that the software is structured in the same way as the analysis models, as far as is practically possible.
- To provide a consistency within the software.
- To provide guidelines on constructing software so that knowledge is effectively propagated around the organization.

As suggested in the previous chapter, the analysis model should *define the interface* of the software components and design templates *suggest the implementation* of those components. Additionally, programmers may either choose the template from a suggested list or produce an alternative. In other words, the class implementer may change the implementation but may not alter the interface. The user of the class should not need to know, or care, which implementation is chosen.

Since design templates are employed using analysis information, the analysis model performs two roles. It is both a conceptual picture of the enterprise and a specification of its software components. Since these roles are very different, the analysis model cannot fully satisfy them both. Thus, some "impurities" will appear. However, the alternative is keeping separate models, which is costly and difficult because of the overhead of updating multiple models.

This chapter takes a number of analysis constructs and describes possible templates for each. The description is provided in terms of both interface and suggested implementation. These general considerations and the sample template should provide readers with enough guidance to develop templates for their own environments.

[*]This chapter is based on material contributed by Martin Fowler.

TEMPLATES FOR ASSOCIATIONS

Associations—that is, relationship types and their mappings—specify how object types associate with one another. A number of OO practitioners are uncomfortable using associations in OO analysis, because they see associations as "violating encapsulation." Encapsulation dictates that the data structure of a class is hidden behind an interface of operations. For some, the presence of associations breaks this by making the data structure public. However, associations describe the responsibilities that objects must fulfill in their relationships with other objects.

For example, Fig. 12.1 specifies that each Employee object must be able to both know and change its employer. Conversely, each Organization must know its employees and be able to change them. In most OOPLs, this responsibility is implemented by retrieval and modification operations. Data structure may be present, and, in most cases, will be. However, data structure is a design consideration and is not specified by the analysis model.

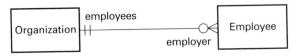

Figure 12.1 Analysis models do not specify data structure. Here, each Organization has a mapping to some number of Employee objects. The employees mapping, then, is a property of Organization. To support this mapping, operations must certainly be implemented by the Organization class. However, a data structure may or may not be used to implement the mapping.

Interface for Association Templates

For each association, the OOPL interface consists of a set of operations that access and update the association. The exact terms and structure of these operations depend on the cardinalities of the relevant mappings.

In general, a single-valued mapping requires two operations: an *accessor* and a *modifier*. The accessor operation returns the object to which a given object is mapped. The modifier operation changes the mapping for a given object by reassigning the mapping reference from one object to another. Access requests require no input parameters. However, modification requests require an input parameter that specifies the object to which the mapping must now point. Thus, for Fig. 12.1, the Employee class would have two operations. In C++, no standard naming convention exists. Thus, many programmers use get or set somewhere in the name. For example, the names getEmployer[*] and setEmployer (Organization org) could be used to access and modify the employer mapping. The names getEmployer and setEmployer are the most natural. However, some prefer employerSet and employerGet, because both operations will appear together in an

---

[*]Many names in this chapter will not include spaces as separators.

alphabetically sorted browser. In Smalltalk, both operations are conventionally given the mapping name. Here, modifiers are distinguished from accessors by the presence of a parameter. Therefore, the Employee class would have get and set operations named employer and employer: anOrganization.

Multivalued mappings require three operations—again, with one accessor. Single-valued accessors return just one object. Multivalued accessors, however, return a set of objects. (All multivalued mappings are assumed to be sets unless otherwise indicated. The interface for non-sets will be different and is beyond the scope of this book.) Multivalued modifiers require two operations: one to add an object to a set, the other to remove an object. The accessor will usually be named in the same way that a single-valued mapping is named. However, a plural form is recommended to reinforce its multivalued nature—for example, employees or get-Employees. Modifiers would take the form of addEmployee (Employee emp), removeEmployee (Employee emp), or employeeAdd: anEmployee, employee-Remove: anEmployee.

Modifiers, whether single-valued or multivalued, should also ensure that the constraints are met. For example, the setEmployer operation should ensure that the employer mapping of Employee is not set to null. In other words, the modifier should ensure that both minimum and maximum cardinality constraints are met. Any other constraints, such as invariant, tree, and user-defined constraints, should also be enforced at this time.

Type checking should also be performed. For example, if a setEmployer: anOrganization operation is requested, the object supplied via the anOrganization parameter must always be an Organization object. If type checking is not built into the programming language, extra code can be added to the modifier operations to ensure type integrity.

Association Template Option 1: Using References in both Directions

In this option, mappings are implemented by references from both participating classes. If a mapping is single valued, there is a single reference from one object to another. For example in Fig. 12.2, each Employee has a single reference to his employer. If a mapping is multivalued, the object will have a set of references to the other objects. In Fig. 12.2, NASA points to a set of references which in turn contains references to Peter, Jasper, and Paul. For languages that support *containment,* an object may hold its set of mapping references internally rather than point to an external collection. Containment, therefore, has implications for space requirements. Since reference sets can dramatically increase in size, an object's size can swell. Single-valued mappings can also use containment. Here, the actual object will be stored internally, instead of a reference to that object. Typically, single-valued containment is limited to storing fundamental objects internally, such as Integer or Date objects. (Fundamental objects will be discussed later in option 6.)

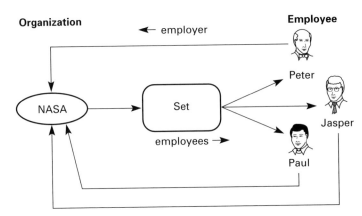

Figure 12.2 Associations may be implemented using references in both directions.

In option 1, the accessor operations are relatively straightforward. For a single-valued mapping, the accessor merely returns a reference to the mapped object.[*] For a multivalued mapping, the accessor returns a set of references. However, it should not return *the* set of references. If it did return the set, the set's user could change the set's membership—thereby violating encapsulation. The encapsulation boundary should include all sets implementing multivalued mappings. One solution is returning a copy of the set. Thus, if any alterations are made, they do not affect the actual mapping. However, this may incur a significant time overhead for large sets. An alternative is to use a *masking class*. A masking class is a simple class that has a single field containing the set. Only those operations that are permitted on the contained set are defined in the masking class. This way modifications can be blocked. Another alternative, particularly for C++ implementations, uses *iterators* as described by Gamma [Gamma, 1995]. Iterators provide a highly flexible way to access the elements of a multivalued mapping without exposing underlying representation.

Since two references implement each relationship, modifiers should maintain a two-way, or referential, integrity. Thus a modifier called to change Peter's employer to IBM must not just change Peter's reference to IBM. It must also delete the inverse reference to Peter in NASA's employees' set and create one in IBM's employees' set.[†]

---

[*]In C++, the issue about what should be returned by accessors is important. Should the object or a pointer to the object be returned? The choice should be made explicit by the design templates. A common convention is returning the value for all built-in data types such as String or Integer, the object for all fundamental classes such as Date and Currency, and a pointer for all other classes. In Smalltalk, this does not apply since it always *appears* to work with objects rather than pointers. This article will always refer to returning references. For C++ and other languages that are pointer explicit, the actual templates should make clear exactly what is being returned.

[†]Of course, care must be taken not to enter into an endless loop. Such as example would be where removeEmployee requests removeEmployer, which requests removeEmployee, and so on. In C++, this is a typical situation that requires a *friend* construct. In Smalltalk, a friend-like operation must be created—but marked private (which does not, of course, stop Employee from using it). In these cases, having only one modifier do the actual work is useful. The other modifier should then call just that one modifier. This will ensure that only one copy of the update code exits.

This template option has both benefits and drawbacks. Its accessor navigation is fast in both directions. However, ensuring referential integrity requires extra processing time. So, while this option provides fast access, modification requires extra time. Additionally, the technique to ensure referential integrity is not trivial. However, once a solution has been chosen, replication is easy. Another disadvantage lies in the space required for this option. Not only are references required in both directions, but multivalued mappings can require large sets.

Association Template Option 2: Using References in One Direction

Another option for association templates is using references in *one* direction only. In Fig. 12.3 for example, the **Employee** objects point to their employer **Organizations**. However, the inverse mappings are not implemented. Therefore, if all the employees for NASA are requested, a different method from option 1, above, is required. A common technique would be to read all instances of **Employee**, selecting only those whose **employer** is NASA. The containment approach described in option 1 can also be used here.

Without implemented references, accessors require more logic than the preceding template option. However, modifiers require less logic, because only the class with the reference changes the reference. The class without the reference requests just the modifier operation in the other class. Referential integrity will not be violated when multiple references get out of step. This option requires less space than option 1, since it stores only one reference per association. However, it will be slow when accessing objects to which there are no mapping references. So, compared to option 1, this option provides the same access time in one direction, but slower access in the other direction. Furthermore, this option requires less modification time and less reference storage.

Association Template Option 3: Using Association Objects

Association objects are objects with two references that are simply used to link two associated objects, as illustrated in Fig. 12.4. Typically, a table of such objects is provided for

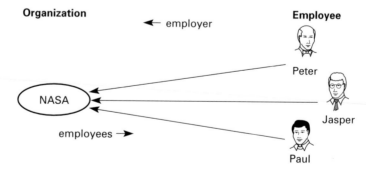

Figure 12.3 Associations may be implemented using references in only one direction.

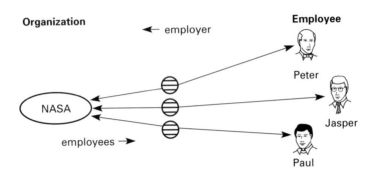

Figure 12.4   Associations may be implemented with association objects.

each association. Accessors work by retrieving all objects within that table, selecting those objects that point to the source, and then following each reference to the mapped objects. Modification operations are simple. They merely create or delete the association object, thereby ensuring referential integrity without the two-way processing required in option 1. To support associations of this kind, special association classes can be built. Additionally, dictionary classes using hash-table lookups may be used to implement them.

Space is used only when associations are needed. This can be a benefit or drawback. When the objects of two classes are rarely related, few associations and less space are required. When the objects of two classes are usually related, more space is required. Furthermore, association objects provide slower access than previous options. Indexing them (by using a dictionary) can improve speed. One benefit of associations, however, is that referential integrity will not be violated. In addition, no modifications are required to the data structure of the two associated classes. In this way, any number of association classes can be established or removed without having a structural impact on the associated classes.

Association Template Option 4: Derived Associations

Associations can be supported without any immediate data structure. For example in Fig. 12.5, the mother and father mappings will probably be implemented with two fields that store the references to the Person's mother and father. However, the parents mapping does not require a data structure because it can be derived using the mother and father mappings. Mappings, such as parents, are usually derived in one of two ways—*eager* or *lazy*.

A lazy derivation produces its result only when a specific request is made. For instance, if the ancestors mapping were lazy, it would evaluate the ancestors only when a getAncestors request was issued. Therefore, implementing a data structure for a lazy association such as ancestors is not necessary. To ensure that a derivation is immediately available and accurate, eager associations are used. An eager association derives its result whenever a change in one of its component mappings occurs.

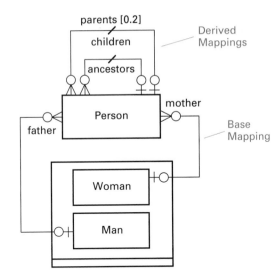

Figure 12.5   An example of derived and base (i.e., underived) mappings.

For instance, if the parents mapping were eager, it would calculate the parents in the unlikely event that the mother or father of a Person were changed. The product of eager derivations is typically stored in the object. Otherwise, the results of the derivation could be lost. In this situation, implementing a parents data structure is useful.

In this template option, the lazy accessor method involves more than following a reference. It involves a method that eventually derives the reference. The eager accessor, however, follows a reference derived earlier by a modifier. Either way, the interface remains the same. The requester does not know whether the getAncestors operation follows a reference or performs a derivation. The requester only needs to know that requesting the getAncestors operation returns a set of Person objects that are the ancestors of a given Person.

Since the mapping is derived, modifier operations should not be available.[*] For instance, the ancestors mapping should not be modified directly. Any modification should be made to the mother and father mappings. If the ancestors mapping were lazy, any subsequent getAncestors operations would obtain the updated set of ancestors. If the ancestors mapping were eager, a modifier operation would have to be written to recompute and store the set of ancestors whenever mother and father mappings changed. Such a modifier should be invoked only from the setMother and setFather operations—and unavailable publicly.

---

[*]An exception to this is *hybrid* mappings. Here, a mapping instance can be asserted or derived. For instance, a person's grandparents may be expressed explicitly, yet the great grandparents be derived from the grandparents. This is particularly useful in those situations where the mother or father are unknown. Hybrid mappings, then, would require an appropriate data structure and modifier operation.

Association Template Option 5: Hybrid Associations

Up to this point, associations have been implemented either as base or derived. Some applications may require that an association accommodate both modes. For instance, a particular ancestor of a Person may be known and explicitly asserted by an application, yet the remaining ancestors may still require derivation. In both cases, the ancestors mapping is a mapping from a given Person to the Person's ancestors. However, different methods are selected to access them. Here, the template option can involve a combination of option 4 and a preceding option.

Associations for Fundamental Types

Some object types are fairly simple and prevalent throughout all parts of a model. As such, they require slightly different treatment from most object types, particularly with respect to associations. Examples of such object types are the so-called *built-in* data types of programming environments, such as Integer, Real, String, and Date. Additionally, good OO analysis will uncover other examples of commonly used object types, such as Quantity, Money, Time Period, and Currency. The built-in data types, together with other commonly used types, comprise the *fundamental types.*

Fundamental types, then, are commonly used types and have a certain internal simplicity. Because of their common use, they will have many associations with other types. Mappings *to* a fundamental type are not a big concern. Mappings *from* a fundamental type require a large amount of pointer space and significant effort in maintaining referential integrity. This situation would also suggest a large number of accessors to support the queries indicated for these mappings. To avoid the possibility of highly bloated interfaces, the mappings of fundamental types to nonfundamental types are typically not implemented.

Fundamental types should be declared in some way. One method marks the object type as fundamental in the glossary. For many modelers, associations with fundamental types are also referred to as *attribute types*. Declaring a mapping to be an attribute type would be a good indication to the designer that the inverse mapping should not be implemented. (This is the same structure described in option 2 but with a different interface.)

IMPLEMENTING GENERALIZATION

One of the most noticeable differences between OO and conventional modeling practices is the prominent use of generalization. While generalization has long been a part of many data modeling approaches, it has been often seen as an advanced or specialized technique. The close relationship between generalization and the class inheritance of OO programming languages ensures a central place for it in OO analysis.

Many OO analysis approaches use *generalization* as an equivalent to *inheritance*. However, generalization can be implemented in several ways—inheritance being only one of them. Other implementation forms are also required, particularly for those situations in which objects may change their object type or be an instance of multiple object types. For instance, if a particular Employee object is changed from being a subtype of Staff to a subtype of Manager, this is known as *dynamic classification*. Or, if a particular object is both an instance of Property Owner and Employee (where neither Property Owner nor Employee is required to be a subtype of the other), this is known as *multiple classification* [Martin, 1995]. These require more thought since conventional OO languages support only single, static classification. The approaches to implementing multiple and dynamic classification can also be used to reorganize inheritance structures and to implement generalization in environments that do not support inheritance.

(Interface for generalization will be discussed at the end of this section.)

Generalization Template Option 1: Inheritance

In most OO approaches, the notions of *subtype* and *subclass* are synonymous. In other words, inheritance is the chosen method of implementing generalization. This provides the best form of implementation when such an implementation is possible. The interfaces for each object type are placed on corresponding classes, and method selection is supported directly by the OO programming language. Thus, this approach is usually preferred, if possible. Its disadvantages are that it does not support multiple or dynamic classification.

Generalization Template Option 2: Creating a Replacement Object

One way to handle changes in object type is to employ inheritance as described in option 1. However, when an object changes in type, remove the old object and replace it with a new one of the appropriate class. For example in Fig. 12.6, if a Customer object becomes a Priority Customer object, the old Customer is deleted and a new Priority Customer is created. This allows the programmer to retain the advantages of inheritance and method selection while still providing dynamic classification. The full procedure for carrying this out is to:

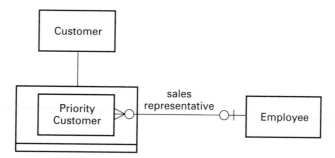

Figure 12.6   In most OOPLs, to change a Priority Customer requires creating a Customer object, moving everything from the old Priority Customer object to the new Customer object, and deleting the old Priority Customer object.

- Create the object in the new class.
- Copy over all common information from the old object to the new.
- Change all the references pointing to the old object to point to the new one.
- Delete the old object.

In many environments, the biggest problem is finding all the references to the old object and moving them to the new one. Without memory management this may be nearly impossible. Any references that are not caught will be invalid *dangling* pointers and lead to a crash that is difficult to debug. Thus, this approach is not recommended for C++. Languages with memory management will make this easier. Languages like Smalltalk make it even easier by supporting this option using the become method.

Providing all references can be found and changed, this approach is plausible. Its remaining disadvantage is the time required to copy common information and to find and change the references. These will vary considerably between environments. The amount of time required will determine the approach's suitability.

Generalization Template Option 3: Flags

If a programmer who had never heard of inheritance was asked how she would implement Customer records to indicate whether they are priority or not she would probably answer: "With a status flag." This old-fashioned scheme is still effective as well for OOPLs, because it supports both multiple and dynamic classification. Flags are easily changed and one flag field can be defined for each subtype partition.

The principal difficulty with this approach is that it does not use inheritance. All operations and fields required to support subtypes, then, need to be moved to the supertype class. Thus, the Customer class in Fig. 12.6 implements both the Customer and the Priority Customer object types, resulting in an implementation such as that depicted in Fig. 12.7. In other words, generalization is not being implemented using inheritance.

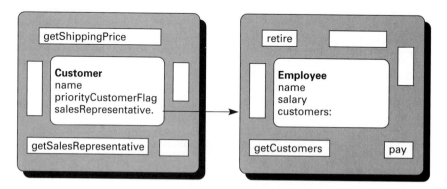

Figure 12.7   When inheritance is not used to implement the Priority Customer class, one option is to add a flag field and any Priority Customer-related data structure to the Customer class.

Instead, it is being implemented using a flag field. In the case of Customer, the priority-CustomerFlag is a field in the Customer class.

One of the problems that occurs when inheritance is lost involves making sure that the proper operations are invoked. For example, it is clearly not appropriate to get or set the salesRepresentative field for a nonPriority Customer. If inheritance were used, such a request would cause an error (a runtime error in Smalltalk, probably caught at compile time in C++). Without inheritance, this template option must ensure that all operations originally defined on a subtype are guarded against incorrect usage. This is accomplished by checking the appropriate status flag to ensure that the correct kind of object is being accessed. For example, the getSalesRepresentative operation must guarantee that the status flag indicates that the Customer object is a Priority Customer. If that check fails, the routine exits yielding some sign of the problem—usually an exception. One drawback of this approach is that this kind of error cannot be caught until runtime.

Since inheritance is lost, its partner polymorphism is also only a memory. For instance, if a getShippingPrice operation is polymorphic for Customer and Priority Customer, selection of the appropriate method needs to be implemented by a programmer. This is typically accomplished by using a CASE statement inside the Customer class. A single getShippingPrice operation is provided as part of Customer's interface. In the method for that operation, there must be a logical test based on the status flag of Customer, with possible calls to internal private methods. Providing the CASE statement is kept within the class and a single operation is published to the outside world, all the advantages of polymorphism remain. Thus the soul remains even if the body is absent.

The final disadvantage of this implementation is that the class must now allocate space for all the data structures defined for its usurped subclass. In the example above, this means that the data requirements for a Priority Customer must be supported within the Customer class. Thus, all Customer objects that are not Priority Customers effectively waste this space. If the subtype has many data structures—and few instances of the subtype—this is very wasteful indeed.

Generalization Template Option 4:
Combination Subclasses

Object types with multiple subtype partitions, such as depicted in Fig. 12.8(a), usually indicate the need for multiple classification. For instance, a given object may be both a Corporate Customer *and* a Priority Customer. One template option to support multiple classification is using *combination* subclasses. This would involve creating classes for Priority Corporate Customer and Priority Personal Customer. By using multiple inheritance, the classes can neatly capture all the required interfaces and let the programming system deal with method selection in the usual way. This approach is depicted in Fig. 12.8(b).

There are two principal disadvantages to this approach. The first is that an object type with many partitions could cause an unwieldy set of combination classes. For exam-

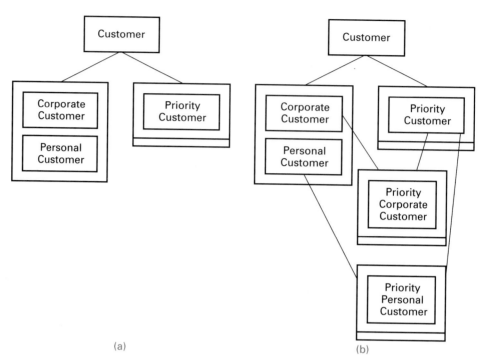

Figure 12.8 Multiple subtype partitions (a) suggest multiple classification. One option to implement this uses combination classes (b).

ple, Customer could also be subtyped as Large Customer, Medium Customer, and Small Customer in one partition and Government Sector Customer and Private-Sector Customer in another. Including the partitions in Fig. 12.8(a), this would involve at least 24 more classes to express all the possible combinations. The other disadvantage is that this approach only supports static classification.

Some C++ authorities advocate care in using multiple inheritance. In particular, one convention does not allow common root classes in a multiple inheritance lattice. The diagram in Fig. 12.8(b) is one such example. Here, Customer is the superclass of Priority Corporate Customer through both Priority Customer and Corporate Customer superclasses. The alternative is to inherit only from Customer for one partition and to use the other partition as a *mixin*. A mixin is designed as an abstract class that is mixed into another class to form a subclass with multiple inheritance. In this example, Corporate Customer could be defined as a subclass of Customer but have Priority Customer as a mixin. Priority Customer would not be a subclass of Customer. Priority Corporate Customer would then be a subclass of Corporate Customer and Priority Customer but would no longer inherit Customer from two different directions. Note that this is an implementation technique only. In analysis, it is perfectly acceptable for the Priority Corporate Customer type to be a subtype of Customer type via two supertypes.

Generalization Template Option 5:
Delegation to a Hidden Class

This template option uses *delegation* to handle the subtyping. Here, a class is defined for the subtype but is hidden from all except its superclass. A field must be provided in the superclass for a reference to the subclass (which can double as a status flag). As with flags, all the operations of the subtype must be moved to the superclass's interface. However, the actual methods and data structure for the subtype remain in the hidden subclass. In this way, all requests are received by the superclass. Those requests that involve a hidden subclass are then passed to the hidden subclass for the actual processing.

For example in Fig. 12.9, an executive employee would have two objects: one Employee object and one Executive object. The Executive object, and indeed its class, would not be seen by any class other than the Employee class. (In C++, all its members would be *private* and Employee its *friend.*) The giveStock operation, defined only for Executive object, would be placed in the Employee class. When giveStock is sent to an Employee object with an associated Executive, the method in Employee for giveStock would merely call the giveStock method in the Executive class. The Executive class would then return any result. In this way, no other part of the system would know how the subtype is implemented.

Note that this delegation is *hidden.* A common delegation approach is to make both classes public. In this situation, copying the operation definitions from Executive to Employee is not necessary. The user of the classes is responsible for knowing that certain operations exist on the Executive rather than Employee. (This is often referred to as giving Employee the role of Executive.) This approach would not satisfy our requirement in this section that all the options share the same interface.

Method selection for polymorphic operations can be handled in a number of ways. One approach resembles that used with flags. Here, Employee would include a condition to check if the executive field is null. If the field is null, Employee uses its usual imple-

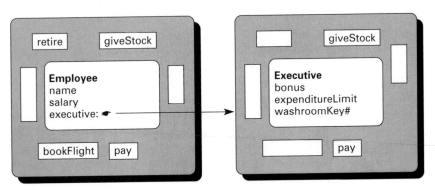

Figure 12.9   The Employee class with the Executive subtype implementation delegated to a hidden class.

mentation. If not, it delegates the call to Executive. If Employee does not have the operation, Employee raises an exception.

A different approach provides a separate hierarchy to handle the dynamic polymorphism. As illustrated in Fig. 12.10, the executive field (now renamed grading) refers to an abstract EmployeeGrading class, which is subclassed into concrete DefaultGrading and ExecutiveGrading classes. An employee who is not an executive would have this reference set to a DefaultGrading, while an executive would point to an ExecutiveGrading. The usual default implementation would be written into DefaultGrading and Employee would always delegate the call to the class in the grading field. No condition tests are required. This structure is rather more complicated than the one described in the previous paragraph. However, its advantage is that new gradings can be added without changing Employee. (This approach is described in more detail as the *state* pattern in Gamma [Gamma, 1995].)

The principal advantage of this option is increased modularity, which is particularly valuable if many classes are hidden and the state pattern is used. In addition, this approach does not waste space for those objects that do not need the extended data structure.

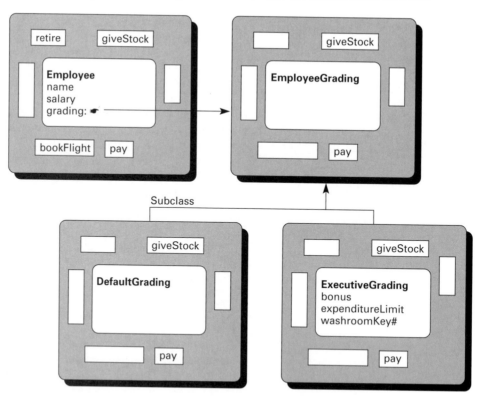

Figure 12.10   The Employee class with the Executive subtype implementation delegated to a hidden class.

Generalization Template Option 6: Object Slicing

This template option is a more general form of the delegation option described above. In order to support the dynamic and multiple classification requirements of a system, one recommended technique is called *object slicing*. In object slicing, an object with multiple classifications can be thought of as being sliced into multiple pieces. Each piece is then distributed to one of the object's various classes. For example, an object named Sigourney might be an instance of the Employed Person and Property Owner classes. To record these two facts in a single classification, one piece of the Sigourney object must become an instance of Employed Person and the other an instance of Property Owner.

Obviously, objects cannot be "sliced" and made into instances of classes: It is a metaphor. These slices, however, can be implemented by surrogate objects. Each surrogate becomes an instance of a hidden class, as described in option 5. In addition, an unsliced version of the object must also be recorded to serve—physically and conceptually—as a unification point for its surrogates. Each original (unsliced) version of the object becomes an instance of some unhidden superclass called, for example, Conceptual Object. The instances of the other classes, such as Property Owner and Employed Person, are the object slices, where each is an instance of a different—but hidden—subclass. The instances of Conceptual Object are the unsliced objects, where each maintains references to its various slices, as described in option 5.

An example of how object slicing can be applied is illustrated in Fig. 12.11. In this figure, the unsliced Sigourney object is represented as an instance of the Conceptual Object class. This one object representing Sigourney as a whole points to multiple Sigourney object slices. The instances in the Property Owner and Employed Person classes are slices of the Sigourney object. In other words, object slices of the whole Sigourney object are also Sigourney objects. However, the slices comply with the conventional OOPL requirement that each is an instance of only one class.

Changes in state can be accomplished by adding or removing the surrogates and the references to them. For instance, when Sigourney was classified as Unemployed Person, there was a reference from the Conceptual Object Sigourney to the Unemployed Person Sigourney surrogate. When Sigourney became employed, the surrogate Unemployed Person object and its reference were removed and replaced by a surrogate Employed Person Sigourney object and its reference.

As each object is added or removed from the various classes, the Construct and Destruct operations would still apply. However, the object-slicing mechanism must add to these class-level operations by ensuring that objects do not have conflicting multiple states. For instance, an object can simultaneously be an instance of the Property Owner and Employed Person classes. However, it cannot simultaneously be an instance of both the Unemployed Person and Employed Person classes: it must be an instance of one or the other. In other words, an object cannot be classified as an Employed Person without first removing the object from the Unemployed Person class.

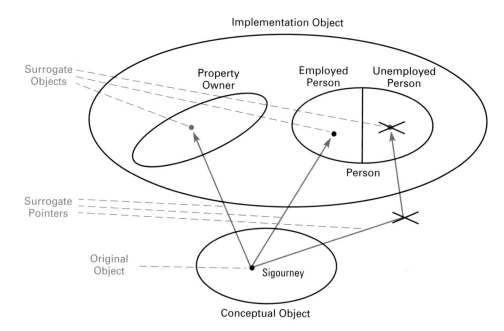

Figure 12.11   Object slicing supports dynamic and multiple classification.

Object slicing is a reasonably elegant solution to a problem not yet well supported by OOPLs. However, in addition to the programming overhead mentioned above, object slicing also requires extra logic to support polymorphism and supplement the OOPL's method-selection mechanism. This extra requirement is not used for those subtyping partitions declared as static. When a partition is static, the normal polymorphic support of the OOPL can be used. In this way, object slicing can be selectively applied. The developer must choose according to the application's requirements.

Interface for Generalization Templates

Generalization also has its accessors and modifiers. Accessors return an object's classification, and modifiers change the classification.

A controversial question in OO programming is whether an operation *should* return an object's classification. It turns out that such an operation is often important. Without it, for example, how can a process take a set of **Person** objects and filter it leaving only the **Women** objects? Such an operation, however, also presents a danger: that programmers will use it within a CASE statement in a way that subverts polymorphism. There seems little that can be done within the structure of OO programming to eliminate this dilemma. An operation that returns an object's classification is often necessary and thus should be provided. Good programming style, however, dictates that such an operation should not be used *instead* of polymorphism. As a general guideline, classification information should only be requested as a part of pure information gathering within a query or for interface display.

Some conventions currently exist for determining the classification of an object. Both Smalltalk and C++ programmers use operations named isStateName to determine whether an object is in a certain state. Smalltalk has a message isKindOf: aClass to determine class membership. C++ does not hold class information at runtime. However, operations that effectively give this information are sometimes provided when needed.

Two broad type-testing schemes can be used to test whether an object is a particular type or not. The first uses the naming form isTypeName. For example, to check whether an object is an instance of the type Person, an isPerson operation is employed. The disadvantage of this more conventional approach is that adding a subclass to the model forces a change in the superclass to provide the new isTypeName operation. Adding an Employee class, then, would require an isEmployee operation to be added to the Person class. In this way, if a method were passed, a set of Person objects, the Person class, could test which objects were Employee objects.

The second type-testing scheme provides a parametric operation such as hasType (TypeName). Here, the Person test would be expressed as hasType (Person). The hasType convention is more extensible since subclasses can be added without a change to the superclass. (This is described more fully in the next subsection.)

No naming standard exists for type changes. Names such as makeTypeName or classifyAsTypeName are reasonable. A general convention is that such operations are responsible for declassifying from any disjoint types. Thus, a complete partition need only have as many modifiers as there are types in the partition. Incomplete partitions need some way to get to the incomplete state. This can either be done by providing declassifyAsTypeName methods for each object type in the partition or by providing a single declassifyInPartitionName operation. Note that those partitions whose object types are invariant will not have these modifiers.

When these modifiers are used, associations imply similar issues to those discussed under creation and deletion. Thus, mandatory mappings require arguments in a classification routine, and a declassification routine might lead to choices akin to single and multiple deletion.

Implementing the hasType Operation

Each class in the system will need a hasType operation. The method will check the argument against all the types implemented by the class. If flags have been used, the method checks the object's type based on its flag values. Even if no flags are present, the class will almost certainly implement a particular type and that type must be checked. If any of these tests are true, a value indicating "true" is returned. However, if none of the class's types match, the method on the superclass must be invoked and the result of that returned. If no supertype exists, "false" is returned. Thus, in practice a message sent to the bottom of a hierarchy will slowly bubble up through the hierarchy until it hits a match or runs out at the top and comes back false. This mechanism makes it easy to extend the type hierarchy, because only the class that implements the type needs to check for that type.

TEMPLATES FOR COMPOSITION

Composition is just another kind of association. Therefore, the association templates described earlier can be used—with extension. Since operations may be propagated from a whole to its parts, the designer must ensure that the right operations are propagated. For instance, requesting a rotate operation on a Car object would also imply that the rotate operation applies to all parts of the Car. The owner field in the Car class could very well propagate to all of the parts, as well. However, requesting a paint operation on a Car object would not imply that the paint operation applies to all of the parts of the Car— only to the exterior parts. Furthermore, an exterior color field in the Car class would not apply to all its parts.

Since propagation is not yet directly supported by OO programming languages, a template is required to ensure that the proper code is in place. For those operations that are propagated, methods must be supplied for all of the appropriate parts. Furthermore, the method for the whole must ensure that the methods for the parts are also invoked. The methods for the parts, however, might not be invoked unless the method for the whole is also invoked. For example, the move operation on a Car object would also imply that the move operation applies to all of the parts of the Car. Yet, you would probably not move the frame if you did not also move the Car. In other words, the move operation is not inherited, it is propagated, only.

In contrast, propagated fields do not have to be replicated to the parts. However, the part classes must have a method to access propagated fields, even if they are only contained in the whole class. In this sense, propagated fields can be thought of as being derived (as described above in association option 4).

TEMPLATES FOR CREATING OBJECTS

Mechanisms are required to create new objects. This applies both to those objects implemented directly by a class and to those implemented indirectly.

Interface

Each class must have a way of creating instances of the types it implements. Creation does not imply merely forming a new object. The various constraints that exist for the object must also be satisfied so that it is a "legal" object. All mandatory associations must be filled during the creation operation. This implies that the creation operation must have arguments for each mandatory mapping. Similarly, any subtypes in complete partitions implemented by the class must be chosen through arguments or the naming of the creation method. Additionally, invariant associations and object types should also be chosen through arguments.

Optional and changeable features *may* also be included in the creation arguments. However, it is usually better to create the object first and then send it the necessary messages to set up these features. This reduces the size of the interface for the class. While usually carried out by the class, object creation is not always done by the class. There are other ways to organize object creation. See the creational patterns in Gamma [Gamma, 1995].

Template

All object-oriented languages have their own conventions for creating new objects. Typically, these provide for allocating the storage of an object and its fields. However the initialization routine is not always an appropriate place for setting up the mandatory features passed via arguments.

In Smalltalk, the usual idiom is to have each class support a creation message (often called new) which may take arguments. During creation it is often arranged for the new object to be sent an initialize message that takes no arguments. This initialize is useful for setting the instance variables of multivalued mappings to a new set, but it can not support initializing associations since it takes no arguments. Such work is best done in the new method.

C++ provides a constructor for initialization. Much may be done here but some compilers do make life difficult by not allowing this (or self in Smalltalk) to be used in an assignment within the constructor. Such a reference is necessary for associations implemented with references in both directions. In this case, a two-step creation is needed, using the constructor to allocate storage and a create routine to set up a legal object.

TEMPLATES FOR DELETING OBJECTS

Objects that can be created may also be destroyed.[*] The biggest problem in destroying objects is living with the consequences. Deleting an instance of Order, depicted in Fig. 12.12, would cause a problem if there were any Order Lines connected to it. As specified by the mandatory association, every Order Line must have an Order. So, if the Order were simply deleted, the associated Order Lines would violate cardinality constraints.

Two approaches can be taken to this problem. The first is the *single* destruction—the kinder, gentler approach. Here, if an object's deletion would cause any constraints to be violated, the destruction is not permitted to occur. The second approach is the *multiple* delete. In this approach, if an object is deleted, any objects that require it are also deleted. For instance, if an Order were deleted, its Order Lines would also be deleted—causing a ripple effect throughout the database.

In practice, delete templates will vary from mapping to mapping, not from object type to object type. So, one mandatory mapping may only permit single deletes while another only permits multiple deletes—even though both mappings might associate the same object types. As long as the destruction is all or nothing, integrity is preserved.

---

[*]Not all objects should be destroyed. Some objects, such as medical records, must live forever. Here, one alternative to destruction is archiving the object.

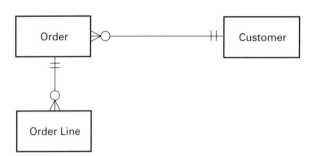

Figure 12.12   Order objects may not be deleted when they have Order Item objects. Customer objects may not be deleted when they have Order objects.

Interface

Different object-oriented environments have their own approaches to destruction. All objects that may be destroyed should have a single-destruction operation. Technically, this is all a programmer needs. However, this places a burden on the user of the class to destroy things in the correct order. For example, to delete a Customer object, the programmer must also know that all Order objects for that Customer must first be destroyed. Furthermore, to delete all these Order objects, the Order Lines must first be destroyed.

Together with a single destroy, some multiple deletes may also be provided. It must be clear, however, which mappings permit multiple deletes and which do not.

Template

During destruction, memory management is a very important issue. While it makes little difference to the destruction method itself, it does affect the consequences of error. The object being destroyed must have all its links broken with associated objects *in both directions*. Additionally, all constraints must be checked for violation. Any violations that have already occurred due to the destruction operation must be rolled back. With a non-memory-managed system, the final step is to deallocate the storage. With a memory-managed system, no explicit deallocation is made. Here, once all its links are removed, the object dies of loneliness and gets "garbage collected."

TEMPLATES FOR DERIVING OBJECTS

Returning a set of objects for a particular class is reasonably straightforward. However, the instances of some classes can be derived. For example, the Person object type in Fig. 12.13 has both derived and base (i.e., nonderived) subtypes. Employee is derived from those Person objects that are employed by an Organization. In contrast, Retired Person objects are not derived but must be explicitly classified as Retired Persons.

Derived classes are similar in nature to derived associations, discussed above in Association Template Option 4. They can be lazy or eager. Such classes provide only accessor operations. For lazy classes, construct and destruct operations are not permitted,

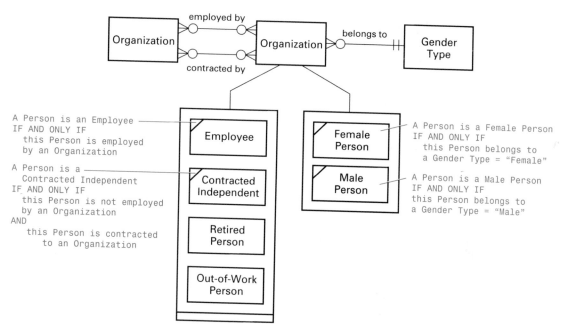

Figure 12.13 An example of some base and derived subtypes of Person.

because derived objects are determined by criteria external to the class. Eager classes will have constructors and destructors. However, these operations should not be available as part of the public interface—only to those operations that implement derivation rules.

TEMPLATES FOR ENTRY POINTS

At this point, a well designed structure exists of objects that are usefully connected together. From any kind of object, using the object diagram to decide how to navigate to any other kind of object is easy. However, one important question remains. How do you get into the object structure in the first place? This may seem odd to those who use traditional and, in particular, relational databases, because the entry point to these databases is via their record types. Getting hold of the data involves starting at the record type and selecting individual records. Starting from a list of all instances of a type is not always the most appropriate approach. Object-oriented systems, in particular, can provide different forms of access which can be more efficient and provide other useful abilities.

The first way in which this can be done is not to provide lists of all instances for all types of object. Consider the example in Fig. 12.12. Since all instances of **Order Line** are connected to an instance of **Order**, there is no need to hold a reference from the type **Order Line** to all its instances. If it is considered that it would be rare for anyone to ask for all **Order Lines**, regardless of **Order** or **Product**, the reference can be neglected. In the unlikely occurrence that someone would want a list of all **Order Lines**, this could be provided by getting a list of all instances of Order and navigating across the mapping to Order Line. Thus, the storage required to hold all the references to all instances of Order Line can be saved at the cost of one level of indirection should all instances of Order Line ever be required. This is a purely implementation trade-off. In a relational database, the trade-off is irrelevant since the database uses fixed tables.

The same argument can be extended to Order. Here it might be considered that all instances of Order are required if a person wishes to select an Order by typing in an order number. Since the order number would typically be a String, references from string to Order would not usually be held. Certainly if an application required it, access to Order could be provided by way of an order number index. However, it might be argued that Orders were, in reality, always accessed once the Customer was found. In other words, references to Order could be obtained via the Customer object. Again, it is an implementation question as to whether to hold the references or not.

This argument cannot be extended to Customer since Customer lacks any mandatory relationships. Thus, a Customer can exist that is not related to any other object. A list of all instances of Customer is then necessary to ensure that such a Customer is found—making Customer a useful entry point.

Note that the decision of which object types should be entry points is purely a conceptual issue, not just an application requirements issue. Object types with no mandatory relationships must be entry points. Those with mandatory relationships may hold a list of instances, but that in itself does not make them conceptual entry points.

Interface

It is useful for all objects to have an operation that returns all instances of the type. This is essential for references in one direction to work when navigating against the grain.

Providing some operation to find an instance according to some criteria can often be useful. An example might be findCustomer (customerNumber). While offering general rules is difficult, the most natural way is using navigation. Thus, rather than asking to find all orders whose customer is ABC, asking customer ABC for all its orders is conceptually easier. Optimization problems may occur due to the navigational expression of the query, but these can often be resolved within Customer's accessor.

When access occurs using fundamental types, this option does not apply and a general find routine is more useful. Even then, it should be done in as general a way as possible. The easiest approach is to ask for all instances of a class and then use the built-in select operation on the returned collection. This will not work very well for classes with many instances. The next move is to provide a select operation which will take any Boolean operation as argument. This allows maximum flexibility with only one operation on the class's interface. However, it is much harder to do in some languages than in others.* Only when these approaches are exhausted should a find with specific arguments be

---

*It is easy in Smalltalk since the select operation can be invoked with an arbitrary block of code as an argument. In C++, a function has to be written which makes the whole thing a lot less elegant. One alternative is for each class to provide a general purpose find function which can be used to select instances. This can be called whenever collections of that class are needed.

used. However, this should be done only when it is too expensive to do it in a more generic way. Care should always be taken not to bloat a class's interface.[*] Another reason for using a find operation is the presence of a relational database. Here, there may be strong optimization reasons to provide a find operation that corresponds to an SQL select.

Note that these instance-finding operations would be as valid for non-entry points as they are for entry points. Indeed the instance accessors should fit the same pattern.

Entry points need an additional operation to make an object fit within the structure. Merely creating an object may not place it within the structure, particularly if it is not related to any other object within the structure. Thus entry point objects need an operation to insert them within the structure.

The above comments on interface are true for in-memory systems. Slightly different characteristics occur when using databases. Different data-management systems (either OODBMSs or relational interfaces) have their own conventions. Those conventions should be used with the proviso that interfaces be as free as possible of data-management system specifics.

Implementation

The usual way of implementing an entry point is through some collection class. This collection can be a static field for the class. Asking an object for its instances means that the objects of the collection are returned. As with multivalued associations, it is important that the collection cannot be changed except through the entry point's interface. Another way is to have a manager class which looks after holding instances of entry point classes. This class is usually a singleton class. A nonentry point will typically also have an operation to return all instances. This can be done by navigating from an entry point. Selects and finds would work in a similar way.

REFERENCES

Gamma, Erich, Richard Helm, Ralph Johnson, and John Vlissides, *Design Patterns: Elements of Reusable Object-Oriented Software*, Addison-Wesley, Reading, MA, 1995.

Martin, James, and James J. Odell, *Object-Oriented Methods: A Foundation*, Prentice Hall, Englewood Cliffs, NJ, 1995.

[*]In C++, a common approach is to provide an external iterator and let the user of the class loop through the selection manually. Although this is much more awkward than using Smalltalk's internal iterators, it is often better than using C++'s internal iterators [Gamma, 1995].

Chapter 13

OO Design Using Event Diagrams*

*This chapter is based on material contributed by Martin Fowler.

INTRODUCTION

The previous chapter on object-oriented design stressed that much of the OO system's processing code can be defined using the structural specifications expressed in object diagrams. This code is concerned with updating and reporting on the state of the object base. It also embodies the various constraints and ensures the integrity of its objects. In other words, even though object diagrams express object structure, this structure must be realized and supported with what many people think of as object behavior, that is, processing code.

Operations and event diagrams are concerned more directly with processing behavior. In particular, they address complex—often scripted—manipulations of the object base and the presence of cause-and-effect object behavior. This leads to a more complicated processing code that relies on the underlying object diagram. Two elements are involved in mapping to an implementation: the mapping of individual operations and the mapping of an event diagram.

MAPPING OPERATIONS

An operation in an event diagram corresponds directly to the definition of an OOPL operation. The object diagram defines the fundamental accessor and modifier operations that a class needs to support the structural model. Operations that appear in the behavioral model may also be simple accessors or modifiers, or they may be more complex. If they are simple accessors or modifiers, they are already generated via the structural model templates and require no more work.

Complex operations are also mapped into OOPL operations. Their specification should provide all the information required for implementation. An operation takes the inputs with a state that satisfies the precondition and produces the outputs that satisfy the postcondition. Any problems that cause it to fail should raise an exception. The implementer may have a suggested method that may be ignored, or a required method that must be implemented as defined.

Host Classes

In most OO languages, every operation must be "bound" to one class. Such a class can be called the *host* of the operation. Identifying the host of each operation is a fundamental notion of OO. In most cases, this is fairly straightforward since many operations will have a single input. This input defines the host. In the example of the operation, Get Employee Salary, an Employee object is required as input. Therefore, the host of the Get Employee Salary operation would be the Employee class. A particular exception occurs in the case of creation operations. Here, the convention makes the operation's host the output class. This happens because the object did not exist before the operation, making the assignment of a host based just on input an exception to the case. For example, the host of the Create Order operation would be the Order class.

Multipolymorphism

Having more than one input may increase the difficulty of assigning the host class. For example, in Attach Engine to Train (Engine, Train), is the host the Engine or the Train class? Except for languages like CLOS, there is no clear answer which is a conceptual limitation of the OO paradigm. In practical terms, it presents some problems but not insurmountable barriers. One template could arbitrarily assign one host class for the operation. Another template could place copies of the operation in each class, so that all input classes can be hosts. Since this template creates redundant code, another template option would be to place the actual method in one class only. The remaining classes hosting the operation would know where the actual method is and invoke it when the operation is requested. In this way, the programmer is not required to know which class is *the* host class. Languages like CLOS determine the method based on all of the input parameters. This technique is sometimes referred to as *multimethods*. However, the term *multipolymorphic* may be more accurate.

Operation Synonyms

Two or more operations on an event diagram may represent the same operation. A banking event diagram may have operations Debit Customer Account and Credit Customer Account which make perfect sense in the context of the event diagram. These may both be implemented by a Create Account Transaction operation. In this case, invoking these event diagram operations is identical to invoking Create Account Transaction with different arguments.

Condition Checking and Exceptions

The inputs for an operation are defined as a set of arguments, each with its types defined. These translate readily into an operation with typed arguments in strongly typed languages. A weakly typed language, like Smalltalk, may require runtime type checking at the beginning of the method. Similarly, any outputs (typically a return value) should be type checked. The presence of multiple outputs will require arguments that are allowed to change. Most operations generate a single return value.

Checking preconditions and postconditions is another concern. Eiffel has the advantage of direct support for precondition and postcondition checking. Sadly, this is an almost unique feature. Precondition checks can be made at the beginning of the operation's method and postcondition checks at the end. These may well have to be removed for production delivery but are invaluable during testing. In C++, the preprocessor can be used to compile precondition and postcondition checks.

Exceptions are increasingly part of modern languages. They are supported by the latest version of C++ and are being added to many Smalltalk environments. Exception processing can be supported in other environments. In any case, some mechanism for handling errors needs to be defined as part of the design rules. Ideally, the system should work so that the signaling of errors could be changed to throwing exceptions without a change in the method code.

In all cases, the implementation of an operation should completely ignore all the control conditions and trigger rules defined on any event diagram. This separation of the operation from its causes and effects is necessary to allow its reuse and to preserve the operation's modularity.

CENTRALIZED AND DECENTRALIZED PROCESSING

Currently, the I.S. community is concerned about two approaches: centralized and decentralized processing. The distinction is best illustrated with an example. Consider the payroll system with an object diagram in Fig. 13.1. In this diagram, an Employee has a number of Employee Payments over time. Each Employee Payment consists of a number of Entitlements. Each Entitlement would be associated with a particular kind of pay as defined by an Entitlement Category. Instances of Entitlement Category would include basic pay, overtime, vacation, and so on. Instances of Entitlement would include a particular employee's overtime worked on the first day of 1994 or her vacation taken at the end of June 1993.

Various processes would be needed to report on information in this kind of structure. To begin with, consider a process which would report the total amount of pay an employee has received in a given year. In the traditional procedural approach, a subroutine would be written to calculate this (in pseudocode):

```
Employee: Annual Pay (theYear: Year)
   Total = 0
   For all Employee Payments (P)
     If P.date in theYear
     then
       For all Entitlements (e)
         Total = total + e.money
       endFor
```

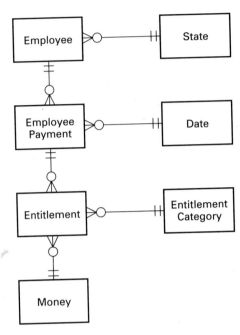

Figure 13.1   An example of an object diagram for payroll.

```
        endIf
      endFor
Return total
```

Many object-oriented developers would disapprove of this approach due to its very procedural quality. The objects are merely passive elements under the subroutine's control. (Such a subroutine is often referred to as a *controller*.) Even assuming the objects are properly encapsulated and data is only extracted using accessor routines, the behavior is too centralized in one place. A better, more object-oriented, approach is to move the behavior to the object classes. In this context, the Annual Pay would request operations withinYear (theYear:Year) and total pay(). In other words, the annual pay processing would now be split between the Employee and Employee Payment classes.

```
Employee: Annual Pay (theYear: Year)
    Total = 0
    For all Employee Payments (P)
      If P.within Year(theYear)
      then
         total = total + P.total pay
      endIf
    endFor

EmployeePayment: totalPay()
    total = 0
    For all entitlements (e)
      total = total + entitlement.money
```

```
      endFor
      return total
EmployeePayment: withinYear(theYear)
      If date in theYear
        then
           return true
        else
           return false
```

The most immediate advantage of this approach is that some of the algorithm's complexity has been factored out. The totalPay operation on Employee Payment would also be reusable in different circumstances. The decentralized approach also reduces the coupling between the classes. In the first example, Employee needs to send requests to both Employee Payment and Entitlement. In the second example, the need to send messages to Entitlement is eliminated, removing the coupling between Employee and Entitlement. This principle is often referred to as the *Law of Demeter*. Essentially, this law says that an object should only send messages to one of the following:

- Objects to which it is directly related in the object diagram.
- Parameters of the operation which is executing.
- Objects created locally within the operation.

Use of this law reduces coupling. A study by a group at Boeing concluded that using a decentralized approach to implementing behavior reduced coupling by a factor of 2 [Sharble, 1992]. (It also resulted in improvements to other quality metrics.) Controllers tended to be highly coupled to all the objects in the system. The use of a decentralized design increased the coupling on the noncontroller objects, but the total amount of coupling was reduced.

The advantages of decentralized design begin to diminish as the system concerned becomes larger. As more and more complex behaviors are introduced for specific cases, the classes have to absorb more and more specialized methods that are only used in certain cases. Furthermore, the definitions of these procedures are scattered across all the participating classes, making it harder to work out what to change when changes are needed. In these cases the argument for centralized controllers strengthens. Each controller can encapsulate a particular special case need. All the requirements of the special case are contained within the controller. The general domain classes can handle general requirements, while the controllers handle specific cases. This approach is formalized in Objectory where each *use case,* or scenario of usage, is given a controller to implement it [Jacobson, 1992]. Here, the scenario-specific behavior is separated from the general behavior. Objects are separated into entity objects (which correspond to objects in the object diagram) and controllers. Controllers are highly coupled to the entity objects, but the coupling is only one way (from controller to entity object) and thus easier to control. It also removes the common complaint that object-oriented systems are harder to understand, because the control is spread out so much among the objects.

There is no general answer to the question of how much to centralize processes. Each case has to be considered on its individual merits. Excessive decentralization leads to complex objects with large interfaces of operations that are only used in a few circumstances. Decentralizing tends to lead to overly passive objects with missed opportunities for reuse.

Event diagrams provide a way of visualizing complex processes. Event diagrams may be implemented in either a centralized or decentralized manner. The event diagram centralizes the description which helps people to understand the whole process. The choice of centralized or decentralized design is left to the implementer.

CENTRALIZED IMPLEMENTATION

The centralized approach uses a controller object to implement the triggering on an event diagram. This has the advantage of putting all the triggering in a single place, which makes it easier to control and modify. This controller will be coupled to all the classes which are used in both operation definitions and other elements which are needed to implement the event diagram.

Few programming environments provide the necessary features to support the constructs of event diagrams directly. Most languages follow a procedural approach to behavior and do not support an event-driven approach very well. Faced with implementing an event diagram, a designer can either choose to transform the diagram into a procedural code or to build the support for an event-driven approach into the language. This is often already present but may not be available to the programmer. Graphical user interfaces (GUIS) use event-driven behavior to control the complex interface. (A GUI is inherently a reactive system.) Similarly, operating systems and job schedulers have used an event-driven approach for a long time.

Turning Event Diagrams into Sequential Code

Turning an event diagram into sequential code is not as difficult as it may seem initially. The first thing to remember is that parallel behavior in an event diagram indicates that there is no sequence to the parallel operations. Thus, they can be carried out in any order.

As an example, consider the event diagram in Fig. 13.2. In the first pass, turn all multiple triggers into loops and make arbitrary choices for parallel trigger rules. Since the routine begins with the receipt of an Order received external event, the method would yield the following sequential pseudocode:

```
ReceiveOrder (anOrder)
    For all items in order
        If CheckStockForItem (item) = satisfied
        then
          AssignStocktoDelivery (item)
          If DispatchDeliveryCondition (anOrder)
          then
            DispatchDelivery (anOrder)
          endIf
        else
```

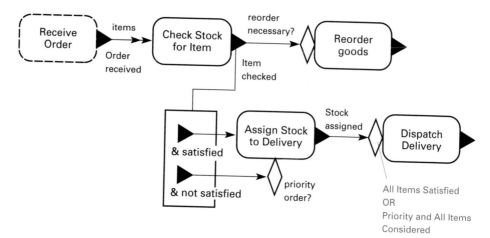

Figure 13.2   An example of an event diagram.

```
If AssignStockToDeliveryCondition (item)
then
  AssignStockToDelivery (item)
  If DispatchDeliveryCondition (anOrder)
  then
   DispatchDelivery (anOrder)
  endIf
 endIf
endIf
If ReorderGoodsCondition (item.product)
then
   ReorderGoods (item.product)
endIf
endFor
```

This implementation ignores the fact that the control condition on Dispatch Delivery is dependent on all the items being processed. With this knowledge, the code can be arranged to:

```
ReceiveOrder (anOrder)
   For all items in order
    If CheckStockForItem (item) = satisfied
    then
      AssignStocktoDelivery (item)
    else
     If AssignStockToDeliveryCondition (item)
     then
       AssignStockToDelivery (item)
     endIf
    endIf
    If ReorderGoodsCondition (item.product)
    then
      ReorderGoods (item.product)
```

```
    endIf
  endFor
  If DispatchDeliveryCondition (anOrder)
  then
      DispatchDelivery (anOrder)
  endIf
```

Other simplifications may be made. The important thing to check is that the sequential code is consistent with the event diagram. Many sequential algorithms may be consistent with a single event diagram and one should be chosen which has the right combination of clarity and efficiency.

Note how the arguments in the subroutine calls reflect the mapping associated with the trigger rules. In this case, a purely procedural algorithm is suggested. An object-oriented one would work by sending requests, or messages, to objects. Such an algorithm would look like this (in OO pseudocode).

```
Order::ReceiveOrder
    self items
    Do
       If eachItem checkStock == satisfied
       then
         eachItem assignStocktoDelivery
       else
         If eachItem assignStockToDeliveryCondition
         then
            eachItem assignStockToDelivery
         endIf
       endIf
       If eachItem product reorderGoodsCondition
       then
          eachItem product reorderGoods
       endIf
    endDo
    If self dispatchDeliveryCondition
    then
       self dispatchDelivery
    endIf
```

Note that the effective change is to turn the first argument of each subroutine (i.e., the first input of each operation) into the receiver of the message. The overall message is, then, itself part of a message on Order.

Such an approach can work well for simple event diagrams with a single point of entry. As more complex event diagrams are developed, with multiple points of entry, this approach becomes more complicated. The approach still works with a sequential operation defined for each point of entry (external event). Each one can be considered as a separate process and turned sequential in each case. If more than one external event converges on the same sequence of events, that sequence can be turned into a single operation and called by the other procedures. In this way, even a complex event diagram can be described in terms of a number of sequential processes.

Using a Scheduler for Event Diagrams

As event diagrams become more complex, turning them into sequential processes becomes harder and the results less elegant. To deal with this, another more direct approach can be used: a queue-based scheduler. An example of such a scheduler is illustrated in Fig. 13.3.

1. An operation is taken from the operation queue and invoked. In environments that permit concurrent processing, such as parallel computers or client/server architectures, multiple operations can be taken from the queue for processing at the same time. Once an operation's execution is completed, its event occurs.

2. All triggers that are induced by the event are identified. These involve triggers directly induced by the event, its supertypes, and any applicable subtypes.

3. For each induced trigger, the operation it invokes is identified. Arguments required by the operation for its eventual execution are filled. If the resulting arguments require multiple invocations of an operation, several instances of the operation should be scheduled for the operation queue. (Multiple invocations on triggers are discussed in more detail by Odell [Martin, 1995].)

4. Each of these operations is now considered separately. If the operation is triggered without control conditions, the operation is pushed onto the operation queue. If a control-condition evaluation is required and found to be true, the operation is pushed onto the

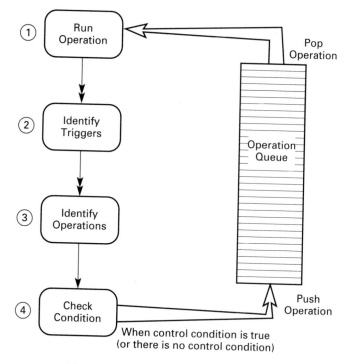

Figure 13.3   A queue-based event scheduler.

operation queue. If control-condition evaluation is found to be false, the operation is discarded.

Consider applying such an event scheduler to the example in Fig. 13.2. Here, the processing begins with an Order received event which has one trigger. However, this is a multiple trigger, so it will invoke the Check Stock for Item operation for all the items attached to the order. Each of these operations is placed on the queue in any order. They are then individually popped off the queue. For the first one, the operation is executed and the resulting event generated, which for example is satisfied. This has two triggers that will be fired: one from the Item checked event to Reorder Goods, and the other from the Item check & satisfied event subtype to the Assign Stock to Delivery operation. Each operation is created with the necessary argument. The condition on Reorder Goods is checked and, if true, placed on the queue and, if not, discarded. In any case, the Assign Stock to Delivery operation is placed on the queue, since it lacks a trigger. Then the next operation is popped from the queue, which will be the second Check Stock for Item operation. When this is executed, assume that it returns Item check & not satisfied event. Again two triggers are identified, but this time the one to Assign Stock to Delivery is also conditional. If both return false, no operation would be added to the queue. In this way, operations are continually popped and pushed onto the queue until the queue becomes empty.

Implementing this structure is quite straightforward. The queue is implemented as a class with operations for push and pop. Each operation becomes a class, because we must refer to instances of operations as they are manipulated via the queue. All the operations are placed as subclasses of an abstract Operation class. The operations for run and buildTriggers are defined on this class. The run operation executes the operation with each operation class providing its own method as appropriate. The buildTriggers operation carries steps 2–4 above and produces a set of operations as its output. Again each operation can contain code for determining the triggered operations, or the event diagram can be encoded into a table and a general buildTriggers operation defined. The whole process is then controlled by a simple loop (in oo pseudocode).

```
While theQueue notEmpty
    currentOperation := theQueue pop
    currentOperation run
    currentOperation buildTriggers
    Do
    eachOperation pop
    endDo
endWhile
```

This loop can be placed in the queue class. A less oo version of the pseudocode would be:

```
While theQueue is empty
    currentOperation := pop (theQueue)
    currentOperation run
    For all applicable events
```

```
    For all fired triggers
      For all invoked operations
        If control condition is true or not present
        then
          add invoked operation to theQueue
        endIf
      endFor
    endFor
  endFor
endWhile
```

This approach is not new. Indeed, it is the basic principle underlying both GUIs and operating systems. The scheduler presented here is very simple. More sophisticated ones could involve queues employing scheduling priorities. In addition, multiple processors can easily be brought into this approach by simply allowing each processor to take an operation off the queue as soon as the processor is free. Scaling up from a single processor to a multiprocessor approach is quite straightforward, although concurrency raises a number of locking problems when multiple processors are employed.

While many proponents have cited GUIs as an example of how OO can simplify a complex problem, they have not noticed that event-based behavior is another essential part of taming a GUI's complexity. GUIs are an equally strong argument for using event-based programming to handle complex behavior.

Decentralized Implementation

A decentralized implementation seeks to make each operation responsible for immediate subsequent behavior. Using the example in Fig. 13.2, this means that the Receive Order operation would finish by providing calls to Check Stock for Item. Similarly, Check Stock for Item would do its processing and then finish by calling Reorder Goods and Assign Stock to Delivery. In this way, the Receive Order operation only knows about its immediate successors and knows nothing about Reorder Goods. To an extent, this reduces the potential coupling between classes by partitioning out behavior on a need-to-know basis. The code might look like this:

```
Order::Receive Order
    self items
    Do
      eachItem checkStock
    endDo

Item::CheckStock
    processing...
    If satisfied
    then
      self assignStockToDelivery
    else
      If self assignStockToDeliveryCondition
      then
        self assignStockToDelivery
```

```
      endIf
   endIf
   If self product reorderGoodsCondition
   then
      self product reorderGoods
   endIf
```

Item::AssignStockToDelivery
processing...
```
   If DispatchDeliveryCondition
   then
      DispatchDelivery
      OrderItem::CheckStockforItem
   endIf
```

This would work well if OO languages really operated by asynchronous message passing. However, message passing is an illusion. A message in reality is a subroutine call. Under these circumstances, implementing a process in this way might well lead to an unnecessarily long stack. To reduce this effect, it is worth looking for synchronization points later in the diagram. In this case, the control condition on Dispatch Delivery is synchronizing across the multiple triggers coming from Receive Order. The behavior can then be reorganized so that the Receive Order method issues the message to check the control condition on Dispatch Delivery. Such a method might look like this:

Order::Receive Order
```
   self items Do
      eachItem checkStock
   If DispatchDeliveryCondition
   then
      DispatchDelivery
   endIf
```

Item::CheckStock
processing...
```
   If satisfied
   then
      self assignStockToDelivery
   else
      If self assignStockToDeliveryCondition
      then
         self assignStockToDelivery
      endIf
   endIf
   If self product reorderGoodsCondition
   then
      self product reorderGoods
   endIf
```

Clearly, with such a short example, the approach is very similar to the centralized example above. The important difference is that Check Stock for Item is responsible for calling Reorder Goods. The general controller is not. Thus, there is no coupling between Receive Order and Reorder Goods.

Object-oriented methods often stress the importance of thinking carefully about how decisions are made about hosting operations. It is a substantial part of the design phase of mature methods such as Objectory [Jacobson, 1992] and Fusion [Coleman, 1994]. This aids the designer in determining how much decentralization is required, particularly with synchronous environments. Techniques such as interaction diagrams are very useful in these circumstances, since they allow the reader to see the message flows between objects [Jacobson, 1992].

REFERENCES

Coleman, Derek, Patrick Arnold, Stephanie Bodoff, Chris Dollin, Helena Gilchrist, Fiona Hayes, and Paul Jeremaes, *Object-Oriented Development: The Fusion Method*, Prentice Hall, Englewood Cliffs, NJ, 1994.

Jacobson, Ivar, Magnus Christerson, Partik Jonsson, and Gunnar Övergaard, *Object-Oriented Software Engineering: A Use Case Driven Approach*, Addison-Wesley, Reading, MA, 1992.

Martin, James, and James J. Odell, *Object-Oriented Methods: A Foundation*, Prentice Hall, Englewood Cliffs, NJ, 1995.

Sharble, R. C., S. S. Cohen, M. A. Armstrong, A. Yaghoobi, M. J. Ogino, I. B. Mayo, and H. A. MacLean, *The Object-Oriented Brewery: A Comparison of Two Object-Oriented Development Methods*, Boeing, Document No. BCS-G4-59, October 19, 1992.

NON-OO DESIGN

As discussed in the previous part, design activities map from the conceptual world to a selected implementation world. Part IV discusses how to take these analysis models and map them into non-OO implementations. Chapter 14 begins by first describing how the design process for typical non-OO languages, such as COBOL or FORTRAN, might be used to create an OO implementation and concludes by discussing strategies for migrating from non-OO implementations to OO.

Often, code will be implemented in languages other than those that are object oriented. This is particularly true when the non-OO code provides a better implementation solution. In Chapters 15–17, three alternate implementation solutions are described in detail: neural networks, fuzzy logic, and genetic algorithms. While many other solutions exist, these are fast becoming popular and useful ways of handling problems that traditional languages cannot readily support.

Chapter 14

OO Design for Non-OO Programming Languages

INTRODUCTION

Object orientation is an approach, not just a form of programming language. OO provides us with a way of organizing our data and procedures around types of things in our world. Object-oriented designs then do not require an object-oriented programming language to implement them. As stated in Chapter 10, the required elements for an object-oriented implementation can be summarized in the following way:

OBJECT-ORIENTED IMPLEMENTATION =
CLASSES + CLASS INHERITANCE + METHOD SELECTION.

OO MAPPINGS FOR IMPERATIVE PROGRAMMING LANGUAGES

While OOP languages make it easier to implement OO designs, *imperative* languages such as FORTRAN, COBOL, and PL/I can be coded in an OO manner. This section gives an outline of how to do this with event diagrams and object diagrams. Those interested in more detailed aspects should consult Rumbaugh [Rumbaugh, 1991].

Classes

Non-OO program modules can be formed based on classes. In other words, the program modules can implement classes such as Employee, Paycheck, and Salary Table, instead of a program that implements a process called Payroll. Classes are based on kinds, or types, of data. Therefore, each object type can be mapped to class record structure in the same way as it is mapped to a class in OO programming languages. In addition, each class protects its data from improper use by offering a number of permissible operations. A set of procedural sections or subroutines should then be defined in the same way that operations are defined for classes in Chapters 12 and 13. In OO programming languages, these operations provide a protective wall that shields objects from improper use. The notion of encapsulation, however, is not enforced in non-oo languages. Under these conditions, data access is at the mercy of programmers' sense of honesty and fair play.

Class Inheritance

Class inheritance provides code and data reuse through generalization hierarchies. Conventional imperative languages, however, have no notion of subtypes and supertypes whatsoever. What is automatically built into the oo environment now requires an explicit programmer code. Some ways for implementing inheritance include:

- Physically copying the code from supertype modules. This can be accomplished by copying and pasting the code or by using COPYLIB statements. While this results in redundant code, it can be controlled with proper maintenance procedures.

- CALLing the routine in supertype modules. Instead of copying code, the operations could be CALLed from a module to its supertype module. For example, the change-phone-extension section in a Manager COBOL program may not contain the code or data to change a phone extension. Instead, the section would CALL the Employee program that has the change-phone-extension code and data. In this way, a manager object could still be handled by the Manager program, yet *inherit* the code from the Employee program. This approach will work as long as the programs are kept up-to-date with what they are supposed to inherit. As with the previous approach, proper maintenance procedures are important.

- Build an inheritance support system. Instead of building the reuse into individual program modules, construct an inheritance mechanism that is external to the programs. This mechanism would route requests to their appropriate modules based on object diagram and event diagram information. In this way, a change-phone-extension request for a Manager object could be automatically routed to the Employee module, as long as the Manager subtype does not have its own overriding routine. Since it would be unnecessary to build inheritance-related logic into the programs, the modules are much more stable. In addition, since the inheritance support system is based on event diagrams and object diagrams, it is model-driven instead of hard-coded.

Method Selection

With method selection, the user need only specify which operation should be applied to one or more objects. The system will then choose the method appropriate for the specified parameters. However, non-oo languages do not recognize operation requests and polymorphism. Two ways to implement method selection are:

- Hard-code the selection logic within the requesting routine. This approach will work as long as the programs are kept up-to-date with all of the request and selection criteria (a monumental task).

- Build a method-selection support system. This mechanism would first enable modules to make requests for operations without knowing where the appropriate code, or method, is located. It would be driven by a table that matched selection criteria to the physical location of the code. Additionally, the selection mechanism would be integrated with the inheritance support system described above thus taking advantage of the event diagram and object diagram information.

The Event Scheduler, Revisited

An event-scheduler mechanism was described in the previous chapter. This mechanism could be expanded to include the support for inheritance and method selection described above. Such a system would create a true object-oriented environment: an environment that would support OO and non-OO languages. This hybrid approach would bridge the gap between past, present, and future development.

OO MAPPINGS FOR RELATIONAL DATABASES

Relational databases (RDBS) are a common form of implementation that presents some additional issues for implementing an OO model. These issues involve database design, the use of triggers within the conceptual model, and the interface to application code.

The database design is of course driven by the object diagram. At the very least, each object type can be implemented as a table, with each mapping implemented as an attribute within the table. As with OOPLs, attributes are either references to other tables or to internally stored data values. Using the object diagram in Fig. 14.1 as an example, the Employee table could be expressed as

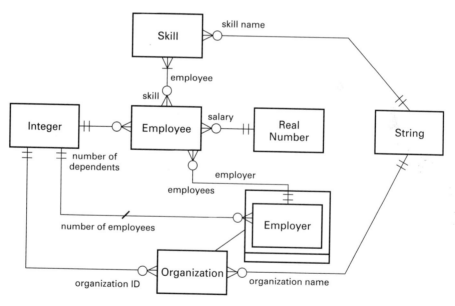

Employee (employee_OID, salary, no_of_dependents, employer.organization_OID)
Organization (organization_OID, organization_id, organization_name)
Employer (organization_OID, no_of_employees)
Employee Skill (skilled_employee.employee_OID, skill.skill_OID)
Skill (skill_OID, skill_name)

Figure 14.1   An object diagram and a translation to a relational structure.

> Employee (<u>...</u>, salary, no_of_dependents, employer)

Since salary and no_of_dependents[*] map to fundamental data types provided by relational databases, they could be implemented as internally stored data values. (The double underline indicates the primary key.)

The employer attribute is a different situation. If you do not want to embed the Organization information in the Employee table, this attribute serves as a pointer. Pointers in RDBs are typically implemented as *foreign keys*. In other words, they contain the unique identifier of the table to which it points. So the next step for an RDB designer is defining the unique identifier, or primary key, for each table. For Organization, the natural choice would be organization id. The Organization table could then be expressed as

> Organization (<u>organization_id</u>, organization_name)

The Employee table could then be expressed as

> Employee (<u>...</u>, salary, no_of_dependents, employer.organization_id)

Instead of choosing a primary key from a table's attributes, another technique is that of assigning a single unique identification attribute to every table, called the *object identifier (OID)*. The OID value for each table record would be system generated and unchangeable. If the record is deleted, the OID could never be reissued to any other record. Some RDBs already have a facility to assign *surrogate keys*. While these correspond to the notion of OIDs, surrogate keys are not accessible to programming languages. With an OID mechanism, the Employee and Organization tables can be expressed as

> Employee (<u>employee_OID</u>, salary, no_of_dependents, employer.organization_OID)

and

> Organization (<u>organization_OID</u>, organization_id, organization_name)

While every table has a primary key, other attributes may also serve as secondary unique identifiers. For instance, in the Organization table, the organization_id can serve as an alternate key via the indexing mechanism offered in most RDBs. The OID, however, helps to alleviate the immense problem of referential integrity inherent in RDBs.

1:M and M:M Situations

Tables in relational databases can only contain single values, not sets of values called *repeating groups*. This affects the storing of multivalued mappings. Many-to-many relationships, such as that between Skill and Employee, require an additional table to maintain the linkage. This Employee Skill table could be expressed as

> Employee Skill (<u>employee.employee_OID</u>, <u>skill.skill_OID</u>)

[*]For clarity, nouns will be used for mapping names here.

However, one-to-many relationships, such as that between Organization and Employee, do not require an additional table to maintain the linkage. In this situation, the Employee table will contain a reference to Organization, but the Organization table will not contain a reference to Employee. While a separate Employment table could be defined to handle the two way linkage, one way references are all that are needed. Relational databases can still retrieve all of an Organization's employees by choosing all Employee records for a given Organization.

Generalization Hierarchies

Generalization hierarchies are not currently supported by RDBs. Instead, the designer can implement the subtype relations as separate tables. Or, the subtype attributes can be incorporated into their subtype table along with *flag* fields indicating the subtypes that applied. In the end, though, the RDBs will not provide any inheritance capability.

Implementing generalization hierarchies requires a similar approach to implementing dynamic classification in a static classification language (described in the previous chapter). The same approaches can be used: flags and guards, *private* objects, and object slicing.

Compromises and Normalization

Other RDB design issues are resolved similarly to that of non-OO programming languages. However, special design attention must be given to the high overhead involved in joins. Supporting joins means that following an object reference from one table to another can be cumbersome and slow, especially if the mapping is multivalued. This alters the performance and integrity trade-off—making it more desirable to collapse what would be separate classes into single tables. Performance tuning is particularly important for databases and should be done to test the design at an early stage.

In discussing relational databases, the issue of normalization is worth mentioning. The basic principal of normalization—that data should only be stored in a stable, nonredundant fashion—is as valid for OO implementation as any other. However, if the *first cut* database is defined by mapping an object diagram's object types and mappings to relations and attributes, as described above, the design is already normalized. Therefore, any deviations from the *first cut* database mapping should be examined in light of the performance and integrity trade-offs. Such deviations typically dictate the need for additional code to control any ensuing redundancies.

Integrity

Relational databases store data and do not store the operations that permit access to the data. Ideally, operations should be placed in the database so that whenever an application wishes to alter the database, the appropriate operations can be invoked. Since RDBs do not yet support imbedded operations, the application code must ensure the integrity of the data. In fact, one major breakthrough of OO data management is moving application logic out of the programs and into the database.

Interface Between Program and Database

As demonstrated above, relational database designs can be generated directly from an object diagram using the following method:

1. Every object type becomes a table, except built-in object types such as String and Number.
2. Every (nonderived) 1:1 mapping becomes an attribute.
3. Every M:M mapping becomes a new table.
4. Every 1:M mapping optionally becomes a new table.
5. Identify the primary key for each table.
6. Define the storage data type for each attribute. Attributes that mapped to such types as String and Number become fundamental data types of the same kind. All other attributes become foreign key pointers to the associated table's OID.

While this approach will create a database design that conforms to conceptual specifications, it will most likely not perform very efficiently. Performance tuning is the next step in RDB implementation, resulting in a design that differs from that specified in analysis. Over time, this design will change many times, based on considerations of performance and storage. Therefore, having a set of classes that handles only database manipulations would be wise. In this way, the conceptually designed classes would be insulated from any database change as only the DB *server* classes would change. The conceptually designed classes should only change when the conceptual model changes. (Further detail on this approach can be found in Booch [Booch, 1991].)

With relational databases, server classes have another benefit. In the example depicted in Fig. 14.1, each Employee object is related to an Organization object. To determine the organization_name of an Employee's employer, the Employee class would send a request to the Organization class. The Organization class would then obtain the related employer object and return its organization_name.

However, when data-related requests are made from one class directly to another class, the call is essentially hidden from the database performance analyzer. Consequently, the performance analyzer will be unable to consider that call when planning the access—possibly resulting in poor performance. A preferable approach is that of implementing a *virtual column* that relates the required data through an SQL view. This will enable the optimizer to plan for the access and insulate the application from database changes. Views, then, can be considered *virtual object* classes defined at the query language level [Stonebraker, 1991a and 1991b].

USING NON-OO CODE IN AN OO ENVIRONMENT

Not every piece of code can or will be rewritten in an object-oriented language. Yet, when non-OO code must execute within an OO environment, the code must be adapted. This section describes several strategies for adapting non-OO code.

Wrap Non-OO Code

One reason not to rewrite code is if you do not expect to convert the code into an OO language—at least not in the near future. This could include code that has accumulated over the lifetime of an organization. Converting such *legacy* code could take years. Yet, this same code, with all its non-OO blemishes, must *continue* to support the organization in the meantime. Furthermore, some applications might *never* be rewritten in an OO language. For example, this could include such situations as:

- Only the object code exists.

- The environment does not support OO.

- A software package was purchased and a change in code would violate the agreement or warranty.

- No expertise exists that can understand and rewrite the existing code, yet the code's performance is acceptable.

- The application is best supported by a non-OO language. In particular, this is true where traditional solutions would take too long or not represent the problem well. For example, artificial intelligence (AI) is a common solution for many kinds of application problems. Here, bond rating and credit-card approval applications are now commonly supported by neural net software.

When using an architecture like the Object Request Broker (ORB), rewriting non-OO code is not required. Instead, a program can be "wrapped" with a small amount of code to appear object-oriented to an OO environment. Essentially, the program either becomes a class in its own right or becomes associated with a more encompassing class. For example, a non-OO program named Calculate-Salary, could be wrapped as a Calculate Salary class containing a single Calculate-Salary method. Or, the Calculate-Salary method could be wrapped and included in a more encompassing Payroll application class. On the other hand, many analysts would probably decide that the Calculate-Salary method is a process performed on employee objects and would, therefore, be a method in the Employee class.

When adapted in this way, the services provided by these wrapped modules can be requested in the same manner as any other OO method. For instance, a C++ program may request a Calculate Salary operation from the ORB. The ORB would then determine the appropriate code that supports this request and invoke it. As illustrated in Fig. 14.2, the language actually supporting the request is not important to the requesting program—only that the request be fulfilled. The code could be written in C, COBOL, FORTRAN, or any other imperative language. The code could be an AI application, such as a neural net, fuzzy logic, or a genetic algorithm. In this way, the original non-OO code may remain as non-OO code, be modified, or be replaced by other code at some future time without changing the requesting programs. In other words, a method (OO or non-OO) can be designed in such a way that its implementation is transparent to the requester. (The Object Request Broker is discussed further in Chapter 27.)

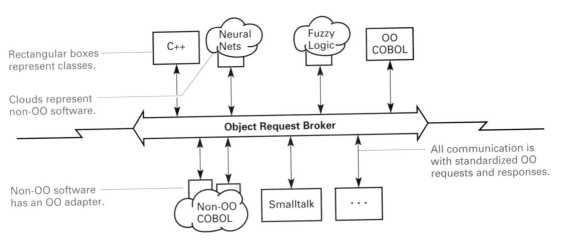

Figure 14.2 The Object Request Broker (ORB) supports both OO and non-OO implementations. Client/server environments using the ORB are known as *distributed object* environments.

Wrap Stable Code

Another reason not to rewrite legacy code—at least not in the near future—is if the code has been stable for quite some time. For example, if an Autocoder program has been working for 20 years without modification, why rewrite it now? If an I.S. department has many other priorities, this Autocoder program could probably go unwritten for another 20 years. The same goes for other less arcane languages. If a COBOL or FORTRAN program has not required change for some time and there are many other more pressing matters to attend to, rewriting it can be difficult to justify.

Convert Stable Code to Use OO I/O

The strategy of wrapping stable code is considered sound, at least in the short term. Eventually, however, the programmer will want this code to become more of a citizen within the OO environment. For example, a common migration strategy is to remove all I/O statements from within the stable code and replace them with ORB requests to I/O method in OO classes. This provides three benefits. First, the stable code becomes more stable. Changes in I/O can be made to an external method, rather than changing the stable code. Second, it capitalizes on reusability. If a change affects more than one program, such changes usually require modifying only a single class method, rather than changing multiple wrapped programs. Finally, isolating I/O processing from an application means that the code can now request *what* its data requirements are without having to know *how* the requirements are fulfilled.[*]

Multiple I/O conversion projects can be scheduled over a period of years, if necessary. The number and importance of new system-development projects is a major consideration in scheduling I/O migration projects.

---

[*]This phenomenon used to be referred to as *data independence*.

Convert Common Processes Within Stable Code to OO

I/O conversion is just one strategy for migrating into an OO environment. Other prevalent strategies include converting date and time processing, standard calculation procedures, and the handling of money (particularly international currency). In other words, multiple projects can also be set up to migrate very common processes into OO classes. The benefits are the same as I/O conversion above: stability and reusability.

Migrate When Code is Being Modified

Short of a massive, legacy-code conversion, another strategy is to convert the legacy code when it is being modified, such as during maintenance or application redesign. In other words, since the code is going to be modified anyway, why not convert it partially or completely to be OO? This may, however, add time to the modification effort. Therefore the maintenance team must decide whether there is a sufficient return on investment that justifies the extra work. In other words, will the benefits of stability and reusability outweigh the effort required? This strategy also requires enough of the right kind of resources, such as OO programmers and OO development environments.

Migration Strategy Summary

As discussed above, one or more strategies can be adopted when migrating to OO. These strategies can be summarized as follows:

- Legacy code that must be accessed in an OO environment should be wrapped. This includes code that cannot be converted in the short term, yet is required to operate in an OO system. It also includes code that will not be converted in the near term, or ever, such as code that is unlikely to be modified, AI applications, object code, and so on.

- Where possible, remove common processing routines from wrapped legacy code and place them in appropriate OO classes. The legacy code, then, will place a request through an ORB if such common processing is required. I/O routines are the most common for migrating to classes. Date and monetary-related procedures are also candidates for migration, along with any other common organization-related routines.

- A good opportunity for converting code is when it is being modified. Depending on the size of the modification, return on investment, and its availability, any or all of a legacy program can be converted to an OO format.

AI IMPLEMENTATIONS

As suggested above, code can be implemented in languages other than those that are object oriented. This is particularly true when the non-OO code provides a better implementation solution. In the three chapters that follow, three alternate implementation solutions are described in detail: neural networks, fuzzy logic, and genetic algorithms. While many other solutions exist, these are fast becoming popular and useful ways of handling problems that traditional languages cannot readily support.

REFERENCES

Booch, Grady, *Object-Oriented Design with Applications,* Benjamin/Cummings, Redwood City, CA, 1991.

Rumbaugh, James, et al., *Object-Oriented Modeling and Design,* Prentice Hall, Englewood Cliffs, NJ, 1991.

Stonebraker, Michael, "An Interview with Michael Stonebraker: Part I," *Data Base Newsletter,* 19:1, Jan/Feb 1991, 1991a, pp. 1, 12–16.

Stonebraker, Michael, "An Interview with Michael Stonebraker: Part II," *Data Base Newsletter,* 19:3, May/June 1991, 1991b, pp. 1, 13–19.

Chapter **15**

Neural Networks[*]

INTRODUCTION

Neural network technology has received a lot of attention since 1988, when the Defense Advanced Research Projects Agency (DARPA) decided to begin spending millions of dollars to encourage neural network research. Until 1991, however, commercial applications were scarce. Since then, a number of interesting commercial applications have been marketed (see Box 15.1). Some highly visible applications include handprinted, character-recognition systems for the new pen computers, process-control products, "database mining" systems, and intelligent, character-recognition packages for entry systems using automated forms. Several hybrid products are also being sold that combine the processing capabilities of expert systems with those of neural networks.

The technology has now moved out of the labs and into corporate I.S. departments. Moreover, applications are no longer confined to small systems running solely on PCs or systems running specialized hardware. Neural networks can now be found operating on mainframes to assist with such tasks as detecting credit card and bankcard fraud.

From a vendor's standpoint, deploying technology to supplement a number of otherwise unintelligent information systems—such as fax machines for inbound fax routing and for fax-based data entry and pen computers—is even more important. Indeed, the arrival of pen computers has not only created what is basically a new market for handwriting character recognition, but what may be the opportunity for a highly useful application of the technology—a cursive handwriting-recognition system.

Whether deployed as off-the-shelf applications or as systems developed in-house, neural networks are beginning to solve otherwise unsolvable problems. They are also providing a way to enhance the performance of more traditional, data-processing systems.

[*]This chapter was contributed by Curtis Hall, Editor, Intelligent Software Strategies Newsletter, published by Cutter Information, Inc., Arlington, MA. Copyright © 1994 by Harmon Associates. All rights reserved.

BOX 15.1 Possible applications for neural networks [Nelson and Illingworth, 1990].

Biological

- Learning more about the brain and other systems.
- Modeling retina, cochlea.

Business

- Identifying corporate candidates for specific positions.
- Mining corporate databases.
- Optimizing airline seating and fee schedules.
- Recognizing handwritten characters, such as Kanji.

Environmental

- Analyzing trends and patterns.
- Forecasting weather.

Financial

- Assessing credit risk.
- Identifying forgeries.
- Interpreting handwritten forms.
- Rating investments and analyzing portfolios.

Manufacturing

- Automating robots and control systems (with machine vision and sensors for such factors as pressure, temperature, and gas).
- Controlling production line processes.
- Inspecting for quality.
- Selecting parts on an assembly line.

Medical

- Analyzing speech in hearing aids for the profoundly deaf.
- Diagnosing/prescribing treatments from symptoms.
- Monitoring surgery.
- Predicting adverse drug reactions.
- Reading X-rays.
- Understanding cause of epileptic seizures.

Military

- Classifying radar signals.
- Creating smart weapons.
- Reconnaissance.
- Optimizing use of scarce resources.
- Recognizing and tracking targets.

This chapter will examine the latest developments in the commercial use of neural networks. Our primary focus will be on commercial development and use and will largely steer clear of research issues and arguments.

A BRIEF HISTORY OF NEURAL COMPUTING

An overview of the history and development of neural computing can be divided into roughly four periods (see Fig. 15.1):

1. Theories, early interest, and research.
2. Increased interest, research, and excessive hype.
3. Declining research and funding.
4. Renewed interest and commercial development.

Early influences on the theory and development of neural computing can be traced back as far as 1890 to the American psychologist William James and his insights into brain functions and activities. Other influences often cited include Alan Turing's research into the brain as a model of computing and Warren McCulloch and Walter Pitts's publication of their highly influential paper, "A Logical Calculus of Ideas Immanent in Ner-

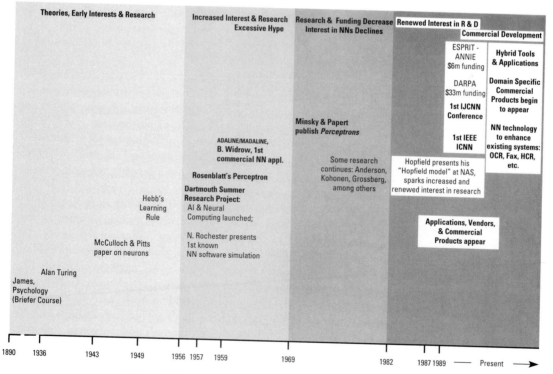

Figure 15.1　A history and development of neural computing.

vous Activity." Donald Hebb's *The Organization of Human Behavior,* often referred to as Hebb's Learning Rule, was significant for positing that neural pathways grow stronger with each use.

The field of neural computing really came into being at the same time as AI, at the 1956 Dartmouth Summer Research Project conducted by Marvin Minsky, John McCarthy, Nathanial Rochester, and Claude Shannon. Researchers gathered here to discuss the possibilities of higher computing, and John McCarthy coined the term *artificial intelligence.* Nathanial Rochester from IBM Research also presented what is usually considered the first known software simulation of a neural network.

In 1958, Frank Rosenblatt published the first major research project on neural computing. His Perceptron—originally developed solely in hardware—was basically a pattern-classification system that could identify both abstract and geometric patterns. Rosenblatt's influence on the field of neural computing cannot be overstated. He sparked a period of immense research, as well as excessive hype, into the capabilities of the Perceptron and neural computing in general.

In reply to such exaggerated claims, Marvin Minsky and Seymour Papert wrote a book, *Perceptrons,* which criticized Rosenblatt's approach. They concluded that the neural network approach had serious conceptual flaws, stating in effect that the Perceptron was basically unable to solve any real or useful problems, though it was interesting in itself. The influence of Minsky and Papert's critique was dramatic, leading to a reduced interest in the neural computing approach and a subsequent reduction in funding. Neural network research appeared to dry up, and traditional AI researchers were resented by the neural networkers, who largely considered this period as the "Dark Age" for their field.

Knowledge-based AI researchers were also inclined to dismiss neural network research. AI was divided into two camps. The more traditional AI researchers were primarily interested in knowledge-based systems. In contrast were those still intent on pursuing research in neural computing, though at a much reduced level. Researchers interested in the knowledge-based approach worked primarily with explicitly stated facts and rules. Neural network researchers, however, were more interested in using powerful algorithms to identify the decision-making knowledge that could be used to solve problems without human intervention.

Neural network research regained respectability in 1982, when John Hopfield of CalTech presented a paper at the National Academy of Sciences that analyzed neural processing in a garden slug. Hopfield maintained that the problem with Rosenblatt's approach had been the linear nature of his Perceptron. Hopfield demonstrated that nonlinearity could be introduced by providing feedback within the network. Basically, he showed that a neural network is an interconnected set of processing elements that seek an energy minimum. Most importantly, the power of the neural network lies in the computational abilities of the network *as a whole*—not in the state of any one processing element. It is largely through research inspired by his work that the most popular neural network, back propagation, was developed.

Chiefly due to Hopfield's work, research and funding for neural computing once again took off. Groups such as the International Neural Network Society (INNS) and the

IEEE chapter on Neural Networks were formed. Initially each hosted its own conference, but the groups soon combined their efforts, culminating in 1989 with the First International Joint Conference on Neural Networks (IJCNN). This remains the largest and most respected conference on the subject, attracting researchers and vendors from around the world. At this time, vendors began to appear along with soon-to-be-released commercial products in the form of neural-network development systems, hardware, and a few applications largely attributed to research.

WHAT ARE NEURAL NETWORKS?

In order to understand the technology and its applications, we need to look at the basic functionality of a neural net. The first step is to compare neural nets to conventional processing and expert systems.

Neural network computing is referred to by the following terms: parallel processing, connectionist machines, adaptive systems, self-organizing systems, artificial neural systems, and statistically based mapping systems. Neural networks differ from both conventional processing methods and expert systems in several ways—including type of input, processing method, and output (see Fig. 15.2).

Conventional processing applies explicit procedures or steps to numerical data in order to arrive at an output, for example the transaction processing of bank account data. Expert systems, on the other hand, use logical facts as input and employ an inference engine to apply knowledge. This knowledge must be explicitly specified as rules in a knowledge base, in order to arrive at a decision or recommendation, for example to recommend equipment repair.

Neural networks, on the other hand, use no explicitly specified knowledge or procedure to analyze new data. Instead, they seek pre-existing patterns or examples from statistically based data. The knowledge or expertise used in their pattern-matching techniques is not maintained in a knowledge base. Rather, it is created automatically by the network in a process known as *learning* which takes place when a network is exposed to new data. This problem-solving knowledge is captured in the many interconnections that make up a neural network. In effect, neural networks are statistically based systems that seek to extract and identify existing patterns in data as they are presented.

An example is a handwriting program to recognize printed characters. A neural network may never have encountered a particular user's writing style before. But once exposed to a number of the user's printed samples, it can soon learn to recognize letters and numbers with an acceptable degree of accuracy.

The main reason to use a neural network instead of some other more conventional processing system is increased accuracy. In some situations, neural networks can provide added capabilities with regard to both the kind of problems you can solve and the degree of accuracy you can attain in forecasting, prediction, and classification. For some applications, such as a loan approval application, even a slight increase in accuracy can result in significant savings over a period of time. In contrast to conventional computing and expert systems, neural networks are extremely fault tolerant—allowing them to process incomplete, missing, or fuzzy data without crashing.

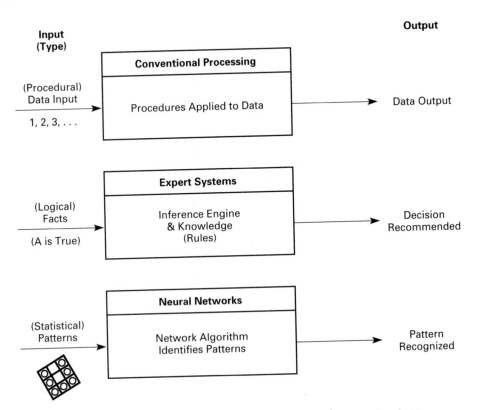

Figure 15.2   A comparison between conventional processing, expert systems, and neural networks.

At this time, most people—including even the most diehard neural networkers—have concluded that neural computing is not the paradigm to end all others. Like their expert-systems counterparts, neural networks are most effective when integrated with more conventional computing techniques. Neural networks can supplement traditional numerical processing systems, such as statistical modeling, and pattern recognition and classification. Also included are forecasting and process-control applications involving nonlinear situations. Likewise, they are useful in situations where large amounts of information reside in databases. This information can be used as training data for a network, which can extract the expertise. This is proving particularly true in the process control industry, where neural networks model plant operations using ever increasing amounts of historical plant data. Some contend that neural nets provide an edge compared to other technologies, because you can *train* them on available data without necessarily having an in-depth understanding of neural networks.

The reason that neural networks have not been widely deployed is that they have some serious shortcomings. These include a steep learning curve, no real development methodologies, demanding preprocessing requirements, and integration issues. They also have a limited ability to explain their basis of reasoning—an argument put forth particularly by proponents of the expert systems approach.

PROCESSING ELEMENTS: THE OBJECTS
OF A NETWORK

The fundamental building block of a neural network is the *processing element (PE)* and its interconnections. Therefore, the basic nature of a PE and its interconnections should be studied in order to understand how they work and what makes neural networks useful for a number of different tasks.

Figure 15.3 shows a single PE, consisting of its inputs and outputs, connection weights, as well as summation and transfer functions. PEs can receive any number of inputs. The inputs can come from either other programs (spreadsheets, DBS, ASCII format) or other PEs. The connection weights determine the intensity of an input and can be compared (very loosely) to the synaptic junction in a biological nerve cell.

Processing takes place in the following manner. Inputs coming into the PE (all simultaneously) are first multiplied by a stored connection weight. The weighted inputs are then summed by the summation function. The sum of the weighted inputs then becomes the input to the transfer function, where it is compared to a threshold value. If the sum of the inputs is greater than the threshold value, the PE *fires* or generates a signal. If the sum is less than the threshold value, no signal is generated (or in some instances, some form of *negative,* or inhibited, signal is generated). In other words, the transfer function compares the weighted sum of the input value to a predetermined value before passing the signal on as output.[*]

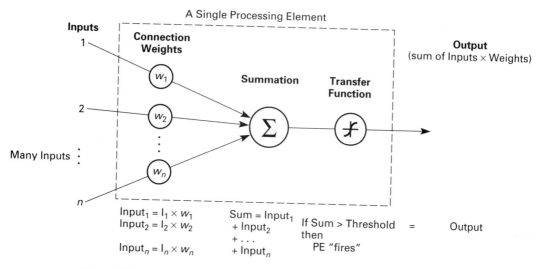

Figure 15.3 A single processing element (PE) showing inputs, connection weights, summation, transfer function, and output.

[*]Transfer functions are typically nonlinear in nature, in that there are a number of varying types, all differing in their processing capabilities. For our purpose, however, it is not necessary to go into them.

Just as inputs can come from other programs or other PEs, outputs can be passed to other programs or other PEs. Thus, PEs can be combined to form a layer, each of which can again receive any number of inputs. Figure 15.4 shows three PEs combined to form a layer. Note that inputs may be distributed among PEs and that each PE produces an output. (In this simplified example, not all the connection weights are shown.)

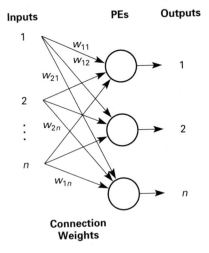

Figure 15.4 Multiple PEs combined to form a layer. (Note: only some connection weights are shown.)

This ability to combine PEs is significant because—as Hopfield determined—the real power of a neural network lies in the overall processing capabilities of many PEs working together in a parallel structure. Like their biological counterparts, PEs can be organized into multiple layers and are then said to form a network. Figure 15.5 shows a multilayer network composed of 14 PEs arranged in an input layer, 2 hidden layers, and an output layer. Inputs are shown feeding into PEs in the first layer, each of which is connected to PEs in subsequent layers. The final layer is called the output layer. Hidden layers are so termed because their outputs are used only internally by the network.

This simple network has weighted connections going from the input PEs in the input layer to three PEs in the first hidden layer. Likewise, weighted connections from the first hidden layer go to PEs in the second hidden layer, which, in turn, has weighted connections leading to the output layer. In other words, each output from a PE in a preceding layer becomes the input for a PE in a subsequent layer, and so on. (Theoretically, any number of PEs may be arranged in any number of layers, the limitations being actual computing power and functionality of the net.)

There are two basic types of neural networks: feedforward and feedbackward. In our example, because the output of each PE is fed to PEs in a following layer, the network is said to be a feedforward network. In a feedbackward network, the output from the PEs is fed back to itself, to other PEs in the same layer, or to PEs in a previous layer. Both networks are useful in solving certain kinds of problems. However, the most popular

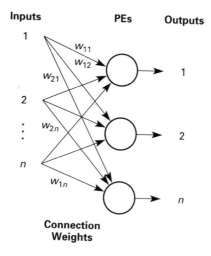

Inputs   PEs   Outputs

**Connection
Weights**

Figure 15.5 A multilayer neural network consisting of many interconnected PEs. (Note: there are more connections than PEs.)

network in use today is a specific type of feedforward net called the back-propagation network.

USE AND IMPLEMENTATION

Neural networks have proven useful in applications that have posed problems for other computing techniques, including expert systems. These include some types of pattern recognition, realtime control systems, classification, and optimization problems.

Neural networks can be regarded as a collection of different algorithms, each particularly suited (but not restricted) to a different application domain. In neural network terminology, the terms *algorithm* and *network* are often used interchangeably. The term network can be used in a generic way, that is, not referring to any specific type of network, or it can be used to refer to a specific algorithm (or learning rule), such as the back propagation network. Table 15.1 contains some well known algorithms, the person or persons responsible for their creation, some application domains, and comments on their use. MADALINE (and its predecessor ADALINE), developed by Bernard Widrow, is particularly interesting. This algorithm was the first used in the commercial application of neural network technology. It is still being used to reduce echoes on long-distance phone lines and to reduce transmission errors with modems. In honor of his work, Widrow was awarded the Alexander Graham Bell Award.

The most important neural network from a commercial perspective is the widely used back propagation (or back prop) algorithm. Back prop gets its name from the fact that, during training, the output error is propagated backward to the connections in the previous layers. In this way, it is used to update the connection weights in order to achieve a (more) desired or correct output. This has the effect of distributing the blame for the network's erroneous output among all PEs comprising the net.

Table 15.1 Some well known neural-network algorithms.

Network	Developer (Year)	Application Areas	Comments
Adaptive Resonance Theory (ART)	Gail Carpenter, Stephen Grossberg (1978–86)	Real-time pattern recognition and classification	Very sophisticated algorithm; uses unsupervised learning.
Back Propagation (Back prop)	David Rumelhart, David Parker, Paul Werbos, Jeffrey Hinton, R.D. Williams (1974–85)	Signal processing, noise filtering, prediction, pattern classification	Most popular net with wide-range of application areas. Most software vendors support some form of BP. Training can be lengthy requiring large training sets of data; supervised training only.
Bidirectional Associative Memory (BAM)	Bart Kosko (1985)	Pattern association for image recognition	Development intended for optical computers.
Boltzman & Cauchy Machines	Jeffrey Hinton, Terry Sejnowsky, Harold Szu (1985–86)	Pattern recognition for images	Applicable to combinatorial optimization tasks featuring many choices and constraints—such as placing chips on circuit boards, etc.
Brain State in a Box (BSB)	James Anderson (1977)	Realtime classification	Studied as a model for human cognition. Used for hierarchical recall in "bird" classification database; also medical diagnosis of disease and prescribed treatment.
Counter Propagation	Robert Hecht-Nielsen (1986)	Pattern classification	Three-layer network. Supports many PEs and connections.
Hopfield	John Hopfield (1982)	Analog and optical implementation	Developed from neuro-physiology research on garden slugs. Much interest shown for use in chip implementations for optical pattern recognition systems, both military and civilian.
Learning Vector Quantization (LVQ)	Originally suggested by Teuvo Kohonen (1988)	Classification problems	Classification net that assigns vectors to one of several classes.
MADALINE	Bernard Widrow (1960–62)	Adaptive noise cancellation	Performs adaptive noise cancellation in telecommunications; reduces echoes on phone lines and transmission errors on modems. In commercial use for more than 20 years.
Necognitron	Kunihiko Fukushima (1978–84)	Visual pattern recognition	Multistage pattern recognizer and feature extractor that simulates the way visual information feeds forward in the human brain.
Perceptron	Frank Rosenblatt (1957)	Classification and character recognition, vision systems	Earliest net paradigm; computational model of the retina designed to explain the pattern recognition capabilities of the visual system; implemented in hardware; slammed by Minsky and Papert in *Perceptrons.*
Self Organizing Map (SOM)	Teuvo Kohonen (1980)	Categorization and optimization, realtime applications, aerodynamic modeling	Sorts items into appropriate categories of similar objects by creating a two-dimensional feature map of the input data in such a manner that order is maintained.

Back prop is overwhelmingly the most popular algorithm for neural net applications and is used probably 95 percent of the time. There are at least three reasons for this. First, it is relatively easy to develop a back prop net. Second, the back prop is suitable for a wide range of applications—from signal processing to stock market and weather prediction. Finally, most neural-net development tools on the market support back prop and/or some of its many variations.

In addition to back prop and the other algorithms listed, many researchers, as well as companies and vendors, develop their own proprietary, neural-net algorithms.

DEVELOPMENT AND DEPLOYMENT

To develop and deploy a commercial neural network system, the basic steps include the following (see Fig. 15.6).

1. *Determine the need, including preprocessing and integration requirements.* Neural networks can only process numerical data. Data must be put into some format that the network can interpret. In almost all applications, some preprocessing of input data is required. Preprocessing could be as simple as converting loan or insurance information to a suitable format or as complex as converting video pictures or speech. Preprocessing of input data can be one of the most trying aspects of developing an application.

2. *Determine the algorithm(s) best suited to the domain.* Some applications are more efficient using several networks. Back propagation is used probably 95 percent of the time. Still, there is no widely agreed upon methodology for examining problems and then systematically selecting transfer functions and network algorithms that are best suited for those specific problems.

3. *Develop and train the network.* Here it is important to use a hand-picked or precise data set for training, so that the trained net will provide the desired output. Depending on the application, training can consume much time and effort.

4. *Test the network.* Testing the network's performance requires the use of a different set of data from the data sets used for training. If test cases are representative of the data the network will see in the real world, the tester will have a better idea of how well the network will perform its desired task when in actual use. An additional problem involved in network development involves selecting data sets for training and testing to assure that the system will respond correctly when faced with a wide variety of real-world examples.

5. *Deploy the network as either a stand-alone or embedded system.* This depends on the particular needs of the end user(s). Because the very nature of neural nets enables them to handle large inputs of data, neural net applications must usually be integrated into or

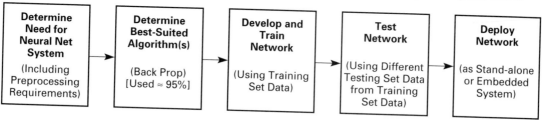

Figure 15.6   The steps involved in developing a neural network application.

alongside other systems. For instance, in a process-modeling application, an engineer would find it impossible (not to mention inappropriate) to enter all the necessary data. Even a small application for stock market predicting should ideally be able to download information from one of the financial wire services to a spreadsheet for the net to use. Most neural networks work best when they are integrated or embedded.

LEARNING: THE INTELLIGENT ASPECT OF NEURAL NETWORKS

Neural networks are said to be intelligent because of their ability to "learn" in response to input data by adjusting the connection weights of multiple PEs throughout the network.

There are primarily two types of learning: *supervised* and *unsupervised.* In supervised learning, the net is presented with a set of data elements represented by inputs and corresponding desired outputs. The goal of the network is to learn the association between the inputs and the desired outputs. Unsupervised learning occurs when a network is presented with a set of inputs but without any corresponding desired outputs. In unsupervised learning, the network adapts itself (makes adjustments to its connection weights) according to the statistical associations in the input patterns. At present, unsupervised learning is a complicated process and is primarily associated with research. Supervised learning, on the other hand, produces good results and is the more commonly used form of learning.

Learning takes place during a training period in which the network is presented with a chosen set of data representative of the type it will process when actually deployed. The learning process is illustrated in Fig. 15.7, which shows a hypothetical network designed to evaluate an insurance applicant in order to determine the person's risk as a potential policyholder. In such an application (which would be considerably more complex than the one represented), an insurance provider would use a neural network to learn how different factors, such as previous medical history, age, occupation, and lifestyle habits affect an applicant's risks. These factors would be gleaned from previous policyholder information (ideally anonymously) and would be used as inputs to the network. Depending on the type of insurance being provided, other factors (e.g., corresponding health-care payments and frequency of automobile accidents or work-related injuries) would be used to form the desired outputs. Hence, this network is said to use supervised learning. The system would be used to correctly associate the relationship between risk factors (inputs) and the likelihood of an event that would result in an expenditure for the insurance company.

Training consists of presenting input data to the network that contain a corresponding desired output. Before training, however, the connection weights for each PE are given a random value (i.e., no connection is favored over another). As soon as training starts, the network begins comparing its actual outputs to the desired outputs, and any error is used to correct the network. The network corrects itself by adjusting the set of connection weights of each PE. After what can sometimes take a considerable amount of time, the connections leading to the correct answer (desired output) are strengthened (or are said to be *adjusted*). Similarly, the incorrect connections are weakened. Figure 15.8 shows the strengthened and weakened connections.

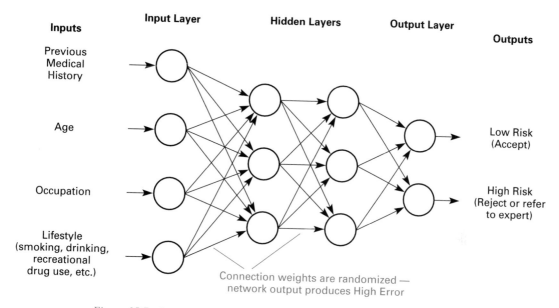

Inputs

Previous
Medical
History

Age

Occupation

Lifestyle
(smoking, drinking,
recreational
drug use, etc.)

Input Layer

Hidden Layers

Output Layer

Outputs

Low Risk
(Accept)

High Risk
(Reject or refer
to expert)

Connection weights are randomized —
network output produces High Error

Figure 15.7 Insurance evaluation network before training. (Note that connection weights are randomized.)

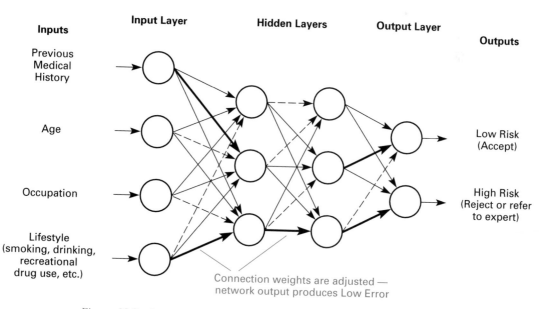

Inputs

Previous
Medical
History

Age

Occupation

Lifestyle
(smoking, drinking,
recreational
drug use, etc.)

Input Layer

Hidden Layers

Output Layer

Outputs

Low Risk
(Accept)

High Risk
(Reject or refer
to expert)

Connection weights are adjusted —
network output produces Low Error

Figure 15.8 Insurance evaluation network after training. (Note: connection weights are adjusted, with bold lines indicating strengthened connections and dashed lines indicating weakened connections.)

Training is considered complete when the network produces the correct output for each set of inputs (it is then said to converge). Then, depending on the type of network or application, the weights are "frozen" at their trained state. It is important to note that for each step—training and testing—separate sets of data are required. For training, an optimum data set should be used that has been pruned of any extreme deviations.

Once training is completed, new input data—without the corresponding desired output—is presented to the network. By generalizing, the network determines the appropriate output. In our insurance-evaluation network shown in Fig. 15.7, the network would determine whether a prospective applicant should be insured or presents too high a risk. It should be noted that neural networks do not provide an absolutely correct answer. Rather, they provide an optimum or best answer.

At this point, the effectiveness or accuracy of the network should be tested. There are two key differences between the training and testing stages. The major difference is that during testing, the network's connection weights remain fixed at the levels to which they were adjusted during training. In other words, they are not allowed to undergo further adjustment in response to any new inputs. The other key difference is that testing requires different sets of data. Test data that closely match real-world data will more accurately indicate how well the network will perform its desired task, (i.e., produce the desired output).

Neural networks are regarded as "intelligent," because they correctly adjust the connection weights of multiple PEs in response to input data. They identify and classify data by learning to associate input patterns (ideally with desired output) and adapt by adjusting their connection weights. This makes them useful for a number of applications that depend on such association and pattern matching capabilities. Examples of these include machine vision systems for product inspection and sorting, optical character and handwriting character recognition, prediction, as well as voice and signal analysis.

SUMMARY

Neural networks are statistically-based mapping systems that seek to extract and identify patterns in data as they are presented. They are proving to be useful in applications that have posed problems for other computing techniques. The real power of a neural network lies in the overall processing capabilities of many PEs working together in a parallel structure. In effect, the problem-solving knowledge or expertise responsible for their pattern-matching techniques is not maintained in a knowledge base or any central location. Rather, it is distributed throughout the many interconnections that make up the network.

Neural networks differ from conventional processing methods and expert systems in both the type of data they process and the manner in which they do so. In addition, they are extremely fault tolerant, allowing them to process incomplete, missing, or fuzzy data without crashing.

Problems associated with neural networks include a steep learning curve, lack of real development methodologies, demanding preprocessing requirements, and integration issues. In addition, their basis for reasoning is still somewhat unclear. However, integrated effectively, they can supplement a number of traditional, numerical processing systems.

OO IMPLEMENTATIONS

As stated above, the fundamental building block of a neural network is the processing element (PE) and its interconnections. The PE, in turn, is composed of connection weights, a summation method, and a transfer function. These same building blocks, together with their inputs, outputs, and processes, can be implemented as classes in an OO language directly. If the neural net is not written in OO code, it can also be wrapped and requested within an ORB environment.

REFERENCES

Hebb, Donald, *The Organization of Human Behavior,* Wiley, New York, 1949.

Hopfield, John J., "Neural Networks and Physical Systems with Emergent Collective Computational Abilities," *Proceedings of the Academy of Sciences,* 79, 1982, pp. 2554–2558.

McCulloch, Warren, and Warren Pitts, "A Logical Calculus of Ideas Immanent in Nervous Activity," *Bulletin of Biological Physics,* 5, 1943, pp. 115–133.

Minsky, M. L., and S. Papert, *Perceptrons: An Introduction to Computational Geometry* (2nd ed.), MIT Press, Cambridge, MA, 1988.

Nelson, Marilyn, and Bill Illingworth, *A Practical Guide to Neural Nets,* Addison-Wesley, Reading, MA, 1990.

Rosenblatt, Frank, "Perceptron: A Probabilistic Model for Information Storage and Organization in the Brain," *Psychological Review,* 65, 1958, pp. 386–408.

Chapter **16**

Fuzzy Logic[*]

INTRODUCTION

If Jim's height is 7 feet, is he tall? Most people would say yes. What about Bill, who is an even 6 feet? Or Paul who is 5 feet 11 3/4 inches? Are these people considered tall? Again, most people would say that yes, they can all be considered representative of a group of tall men. Many would go even further and categorize members of this group of tall men by adding adverbs such as "very" and "rather": Jim is *very* tall, Bill is tall, and Paul is *rather* tall.

What about Milo, though, who is 5 feet 10 inches? How would you categorize his height in regard to our group of tall men? He is neither very tall nor very short. Many people would categorize Milo's height as average. But if Milo came from a short family, they might regard Milo as somewhat tall. In effect, many people would say that, to a varying degree, Jim, Bill, Paul, and Milo could all be considered as members of a group of tall men. (Actually, as we will see, Milo could be included in both of our groups of either tall or average men.)

The basic principles are equally applicable to groups of women, inanimate objects, or concepts. Moreover, they can be applied using different variables such as old, new, bright, dark, warm, large, and so on. Now, consider a group of new cars (for the sake of argument we will define our group of new cars as those ranging from 1993 to 1996 models) you can definitely say that a 1996 model is new. A 1995 model is rather new and a 1994 may be considered somewhat new. However, a 1991 model would not be included in our group of new cars. Rather, it would fall in a category of old cars or possibly older cars.

In the real world, there are situations where the membership of objects or concepts within a given group is not a yes-or-no, black-or-white absolute. Rather, inclusion in such

[*]This chapter was contributed by Curtis Hall, Editor, Intelligent Software Strategies Newsletter, published by Cutter Information, Inc., Arlington, MA. Copyright © 1994 by Harmon Associates. All rights reserved.

groups is determined by varying degrees of membership. In addition, the boundaries between groups of objects or concepts can also be ill-defined, and membership of such groups of objects or concepts may not be limited to a single group, depending on the context of a given situation. In other words, groups or sets of objects or concepts may have blurred boundaries which can sometimes overlap.

In effect, objects are allowed to have *partial membership*—to a varying degree—in one or more groups. This is the basic tenet of fuzzy logic—that all things *are* to a degree. Here, we provide an overview of fuzzy logic—focusing on some of the underlying theory of fuzzy logic, its commercial implementation, and some fuzzy-systems applications.

A LITTLE BACKGROUND AND HISTORY

Fuzzy logic is now receiving a lot of attention in the popular press. Although not widely embraced in the West—with only moderate interest being shown in Europe and even less in North America—fuzzy logic has received considerable attention in Japan. Here, fuzzy systems are appearing in everything from automatic car transmissions and subway-train braking systems to consumer appliances and electronics, such as washing machines and video recorders. Indeed, the Japanese have embraced fuzzy logic to such an extent that the term fuzzy has become a marketing buzzword in Japan, and it commonly appears in advertising literature for a whole range of consumer products.

Encouraged by the accelerating interest in Japan, and to a lesser degree in Europe, companies and academic institutions in North America are beginning to step up their research into the commercial application of fuzzy logic technology. Since 1993, the number of conferences focusing on fuzzy logic has increased greatly in the United States and elsewhere.

The real impetus to fuzzy logic is mostly attributed to Lofti A. Zadeh, a professor at the University of California at Berkeley, who published a paper on the subject in 1965. (Zadeh is considered by fuzzy gurus to be the founding father of fuzzy logic.) Basically, Zadeh proposed a new methodology to deal linguistically, rather than mathematically, with complex systems. He formally introduced a new set theory, known as *fuzzy sets*. Fuzzy sets include membership functions that allow us to determine the degree to which an element is or is not a member of a set.

Fuzzy set theory provides a formal mathematical method in which imprecise, vague, or otherwise abstract phenomena can be modeled using concepts and linguistic variables. It allows programming to be done more along the lines of the way people think and speak when describing concepts or complex systems. Simply put, fuzzy logic describes vagueness more precisely.

Although often described as *fuzzy logic technology,* fuzzy logic is really more of a technique for defining and handling data. It can be implemented using fuzzy rule-based systems, neural nets, or embedded in hardware (such as accelerator boards and microcontrollers). Fuzzy techniques are also being implemented in hybrid systems that combine several different computing methods.

Suitable areas for applying fuzzy systems are very similar to expert-systems application domains. In one area, human judgment, evaluation, and decision making are important. In another area, the ability to use traditional, linear-programming techniques is prohibited due to the highly complex nature of the system (too complex to model mathematically) or is unsuitable because of time-to-market and other development considerations.

To date, the most popular use of fuzzy logic has been in fuzzy controllers for process-control applications and as controllers for consumer appliances and electronics. Many of these fuzzy controller systems are embedded in low-cost, microcontroller hardware devices and are designed to perform mundane yet crucial tasks, such as evaluating load and wash settings in washing machines and dishwashers.

Fuzzy logic has also been applied to information systems, although not to the degree that it has been applied in fuzzy control:

- Financial forecasting.
- Stock selection.
- Manufacturing scheduling.
- Product pricing.
- Law enforcement (for suspect identification).

The technology is still very young and no standard development methodologies exist. For the most part, advanced corporate computing groups are just beginning to investigate fuzzy technology and how it might be practically applied to I.S.

From a core of fuzzy gurus devoted to spreading the "fuzzy word" and to easing the task of developing fuzzy systems, several vendors have appeared that are currently selling a wide range of fuzzy-systems development tools. These vary considerably in price and performance, and more vendors and products are continually appearing. Most of the vendors have to date focused on providing fuzzy development tools targeted at creating fuzzy control systems (currently the most successful application area).

Fuzzy set theory provides the foundation for fuzzy logic. Therefore, without getting too hung up on the mathematics involved, some clarification of how fuzzy set theory compares to the conventional set theory associated with traditional (Boolean) logic must be provided.

FUZZY SET THEORY

Traditional logic is based on either/or propositions. Statements are either true or false. Likewise, traditional set logic imposes rigid membership requirements upon the elements within a set. In order to get a better picture of the significant difference between traditional set theory and fuzzy set theory, let us return to our earlier discussion of tall men. Our original set of tall men included the following:

- Jim, who is 7 feet tall.
- Bill, who is an even 6 feet.
- Paul, who is 5 feet, 11 3/4 inches.
- Milo, who is 5 feet, 10 inches.

Traditional set logic requires a single, sharply defined evaluation for what constitutes the concept Tall. Moreover, traditional set logic does not allow for any varying degree of membership for elements included within a set. Therefore, Tall, as defined in traditional set logic to include everyone ranging in height from 5 feet 10 inches to 7 feet, would appear as shown in Fig. 16.1. In other words, the degree of membership between the elements Jim, Bill, Paul, and Milo is exactly the same: 1 (as indicated by the degree of membership rule running along the left side of the figure ranging from 0 to 1). Simply put, in traditional set logic you are either completely tall or you are not tall.

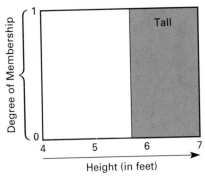

Figure 16.1   The degree of membership in a traditional set for Tall.

Fuzzy sets, on the other hand, allow for what is termed *gradual* or *partial membership* in a set. Even more importantly, they provide a means of expressing degrees of membership by assigning a precise numerical value to the elements of a set. In effect, fuzzy set theory introduces a second dimension or axis. Compare our set of Tall men shown in Fig. 16.1 to the same set indicated in Fig. 16.2 using fuzzy set theory.

The degree of membership in a fuzzy set (described as membership function) is expressed using values defined between 0 and 1. 1 indicates complete membership and 0 indicates no membership. Everything in between can be said to have partial membership. Notice in Fig. 16.2 that only Jim can be said to have complete membership in the fuzzy set Tall and returns a numeric value of 1 (sometimes referred to as a *truth value.*) Whereas Bill, Paul, and Milo all have varying degrees of membership as indicated by their corresponding truth values: 0.70, 0.50, and 0.37, respectively. In the traditional set shown in Fig. 16.1, each of these people receives an equal degree of membership—with a value of 1. In other words, according to traditional set logic, Milo (5 feet 10 inches) is equally as tall as Jim (7 feet).

The difference between the concept of membership in a traditional set and membership in a fuzzy set can be visualized through an analogy provided by Earl Cox of Metus Systems. (Metus Systems is a development/consulting group for fuzzy systems and other advanced-computing technologies.) A traditional set resembles an on/off light switch. An element is either a complete member or it is not a member at all. In contrast, a fuzzy set works like a dimmer switch that provides varying degrees of light. An element may be a complete member or a partial member to a varying degree.

Truth values as defined by membership functions in a fuzzy system are sometimes confused with or inappropriately compared to confidence factors sometimes used in con-

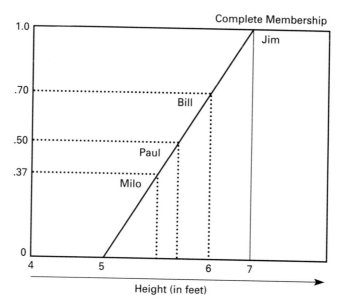

Figure 16.2   The degree of membership in a fuzzy set for Tall.

ventional expert systems. Confidence factors differ from fuzzy truth values in that they say nothing about the membership of a set. For example, a fuzzy truth value of 0.9 for the fuzzy set Tall would mean (depending on the shape of the membership function) that a person is 90 percent tall. Whereas an expert systems confidence factor of 0.9 means that you believe the person to be 100 percent tall—with 90 percent certainty. In fact, confidence factors do not really involve a percentage but supply a number indicating how confident the human expert is.

Fuzzy logic is sometimes confused or likened to probability because degrees of membership in both fuzzy sets and probabilities are numbers from 0 to 1. The difference between the two is that probability deals with the uncertainty of occurrence of well-defined events, while fuzzy logic deals with the degrees of occurrence of ill-defined events.

Overlapping Fuzzy Sets

Fuzzy sets provide for a gradual transition from membership to nonmembership. This allows for overlap—the degree to which the domain of one fuzzy set overlaps with that of another. In effect, this allows for elements of one set to belong to another set. Again, referring to our set of tall men, we can demonstrate overlap. Remember Milo, who at 5 feet 10 inches was said to be not very tall. Neither was he very short. Most likely, he could be categorized as Average in height. Also remember how he could be considered as somewhat tall.

Figure 16.3 shows how Milo could have membership in two fuzzy sets: one denoting Average, the other, Tall. (Incidentally, membership functions can take on various shapes.)

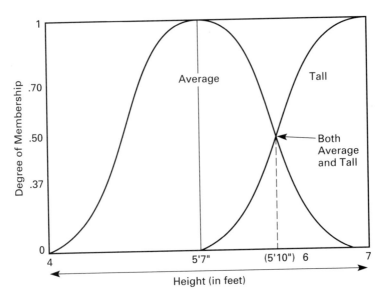

Figure 16.3   Overlapping fuzzy sets for Average and Tall.

In the Average height set shown at the left, 5 feet 7 inches indicates complete membership (or a truth value of 1). However, as a person continues to get taller (moving to the right), his membership value or truth value for Average decreases until he is no longer considered average in height. Instead, he is beginning to become Tall (again as indicated as the truth value for tall begins to increase steadily as he becomes taller). In effect, fuzzy set theory allows Milo to be both Average and Tall at the same time, as shown in Fig. 16.3.

Figure 16.4 shows how poorly traditional set logic models this ambiguity of the concepts Average and Tall. Notice that there is no degree of membership between the two sets Average and Tall. Fuzzy-logic set theory, on the other hand, provides a means to define vague and sometimes abstract terms, such as tall, short, average, and so on. They are

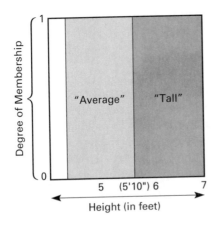

Figure 16.4   Degree of membership in the traditional sets for Average and Tall.

defined mathematically so that their degrees of membership can be precisely indicated as truth values. The ability for fuzzy sets to overlap is a very important aspect of fuzzy logic. It allows fuzzy systems to be designed to handle problems requiring "continuous" logic-processing capabilities, such as process-control systems and complex modeling applications.

Fuzzy Hedges

Before looking at how a fuzzy system operates, another important aspect of fuzzy set theory (and fuzzy system development)—fuzzy hedges—must be examined. Fuzzy hedges are adjectives and adverbs, such as very, somewhat, and rather. They are used as a means for creating new fuzzy membership functions from already existing ones. Fuzzy hedges not only resemble adjectives and adverbs used in a sentence but, when incorporated into fuzzy system rules, they behave like adjectives and adverbs by changing the membership functions of a fuzzy set. Depending on the type used, fuzzy hedges either dilute or intensify the membership functions in a fuzzy set. For example, in the fuzzy rule:

```
(IF person_1 is Very Tall AND. . . )
```

the fuzzy hedge Very intensifies the fuzzy set Tall by skewing its membership functions forward. This has the effect of reducing the number of possible members that could become part of that set. Let us take our original fuzzy set Tall and see how the fuzzy hedge Very affects it. Figure 16.5 shows the fuzzy set Tall modified by the fuzzy hedge Very—in effect, producing the new fuzzy set Very Tall.

On the other hand, fuzzy hedges such as Somewhat and Rather have just the opposite effect on a fuzzy set as do hedges like Very. Figure 16.6 shows how the fuzzy hedge

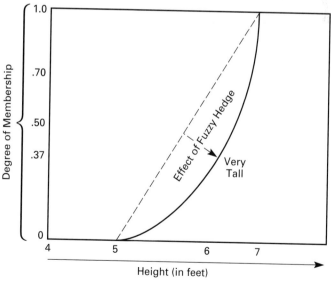

Figure 16.5   Very Tall = the fuzzy set Tall modified by the fuzzy hedge Very.

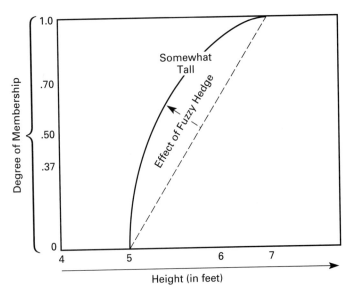

Figure 16.6   Somewhat Tall = the fuzzy set Tall modified by the fuzzy hedge Somewhat.

Somewhat dilutes the membership functions for our fuzzy set Tall. By skewing the membership function backwards, the fuzzy hedge Somewhat allows a larger number of elements to become potential members of that set. By changing the shape of membership functions, fuzzy hedges can bring greater precision to a fuzzy system.

FUZZY SYSTEMS OVERVIEW

An overview of the fuzzy-system development process helps to provide an outline and to clarify how a fuzzy system operates. The steps involved in developing a fuzzy system are as follows:

1. Analysis and design—developing understanding of overall system.
2. Definition of input/output variables by creating fuzzy sets and their associated membership functions.
3. Writing of rules to create a conceptual model of the system.
4. Generation of appropriate system code.
5. Testing and refining of system through simulation and test deployment.

Fuzzy-system development is no different from expert systems development, or for that matter, any programming effort. A thorough understanding and analysis of the task at hand is required—preferably by someone intimately familiar with the problem. The system analysis task varies depending on the fuzzy development tool used. Some tools, like Togai InfraLogic's TILshell, operate much like a standard CASE tool, whereby the developer draws the various system components and then compiles the necessary code. Others provide a shell environment where fuzzy sets and membership functions are defined in tables and charts.

A large part of the fuzzy-system development effort is spent on defining input/output variables and creating fuzzy sets and their associated membership functions. Figure 16.7 shows the input and output variables and their respective membership functions (fuzzy sets) for a fuzzy washing-machine controller (used to evaluate load settings based on the degree of dirtiness of the wash water). This process is closely associated with the development of a conceptual model of the system, which is accomplished by writing English-like rules. Although fuzzy rules resemble free-form natural language, a developer is actually constrained to a very limited set of linguistic terms and strict syntax. These rules (which very much resemble expert systems rules) describe the action to be taken on each combination of variables. For a fuzzy washing-machine controller application, rules might resemble the following, with inputs being supplied by sensors:

```
IF dirtiness is moderate AND type_of_dirt is greasy
THEN wash_time is long.
```

In these rules, it is important to remember that dirtiness, type_of_dirt, and wash_time are variables, and that Clear, Oily, and Greasy are actually fuzzy sets, for those input variables represented in Fig. 16.7.

For a fuzzy marketing system, rules could resemble the following, with inputs being supplied by a marketing representative or obtained from an appropriate database:

```
IF Market is large AND Vendors are many
THEN Margins are tight.
```

Once the fuzzy system is developed, code may be generated for it. The type of code generated depends largely on the application and, of course, the tool. If the fuzzy application will be implemented mainly in software, then C or C++ is commonly used. If the application will be embedded in a microcontroller or other hardware device, some form of Assembly language or possibly FORTRAN (or another high-level language) is required.

Test and refine the system through simulation and beta deployment. (Again, depending on the functionality provided by the fuzzy development system used, simulation and testing may precede deployment and debugging.) One of the major benefits associated with fuzzy development techniques, often touted by fuzzy proponents, is a significant savings in time by alleviating all or some of the overhead associated with developing and refining a complex mathematical model of a process. With fuzzy system development, modeling, creating, and refining the system can be largely done by editing rules and membership functions.

Obviously, this is a very simplified look at the process of developing a fuzzy system application. However, it does provide a general high-level overview of what is involved.

Fuzzy Processing

Fuzzy rules resemble conventional expert systems rules in that they have a premise consisting of one or more antecedents (i.e., Market is small), and a conclusion consisting of one or more

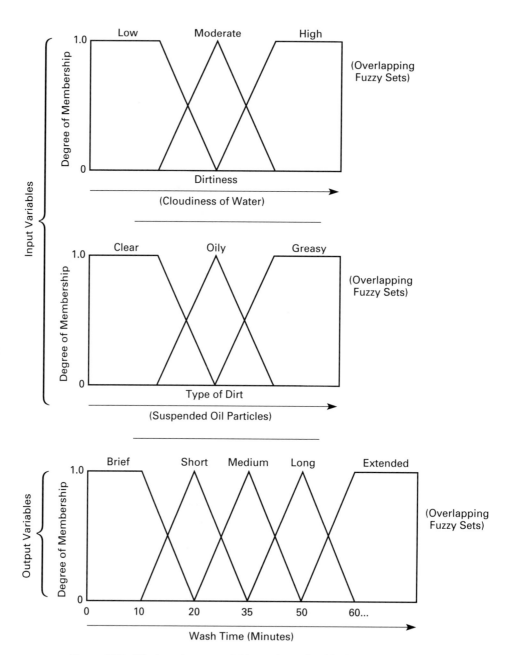

Figure 16.7 The input/output variables and membership functions (fuzzy set) for a fuzzy washing-machine controller.

consequences. The fuzzy operators AND, OR, and NOT allow one to combine antecedents into premises. The similarities between fuzzy and expert systems rules can be confusing. Fuzzy logic uses many of the constructs similar to rule-based systems, but assigns them very different meanings. Figure 16.8 defines the fuzzy logic operators AND, OR, and NOT.

A **AND** B	Take the value of the *smallest* variable.
A **OR** B	Take the value of the *larger* variable.
NOT A	Take the largest possible value for A *minus* the current value of A.

Figure 16.8   The fuzzy logic operators AND, OR, and NOT.

The fuzzy operator AND means take the minimum truth value returned by the membership function. For example, in the expression (IF Height is Tall AND Weight is Average), if Tall returned a truth value of 1 for the membership function Height, and Average returned a truth value of 0.3 for the membership function Weight, the minimum (0.3) would be the outcome of that rule.

OR means take the maximum truth value returned by the membership function. For example, in the expression (IF Height is Tall OR Weight is Average), if Tall returned a truth value of 1 for the membership function Height, and Average returned a truth value of 0.3 for the membership function Weight, the maximum truth value (1) would be the outcome of that rule.

NOT means take the truth value expressed for the degree of membership and subtract it from 1 (the maximum truth value that can be expressed by the membership function for a fuzzy set). For example, if the truth value returned for the expression (NOT Tall) is 0.8, then the outcome would be 0.2, or 1 minus 0.8.

Fuzzy Reasoning

Fuzzy reasoning or fuzzy inferencing is the process of applying the degree of membership computed for a production rule's premise to the rule's conclusion to determine the actions to be performed. Figure 16.9 provides an overview of fuzzy reasoning.

In a fuzzy system, rules fire to different degrees, according to the truth value defined by a fuzzy set's membership function. (This contrasts with an expert system, where the rule fires completely or not at all.) All rules that have any degree of truth in their premises (with a truth value of greater than 0) will fire and produce truth values. These are then combined using fuzzy operators to contribute to the final solution's output fuzzy set, or fuzzy output set. (A fuzzy output set is a temporary-output fuzzy set created by the fuzzy system during inferencing.) When all the rules have fired, the solution fuzzy set is defuzzified into the actual solution variable. (In a control system, the final variable might be the one that represents a wash-cycle time or fan motor speed. In a fuzzy decision system, the final variable might be the one that determines a price for a product or determines that a certain market is not viable.)

In an actual production fuzzy system, the result of rule evaluation may in fact mean that a number of rules have contributed their outputs to the final solution's output fuzzy set. As we mentioned, all fuzzy rules having a truth value of greater than 0 will fire and

1 Fuzzy reasoning is the process of making logical inferences based on fuzzy sets, rules, and operators.

2. In fuzzy-reasoning systems, the rules run in parallel.

3. The fuzzy system creates a temporary fuzzy set that corresponds to each consequent in a rule.

4. Each rule contributes to the final shape of a solution set, depending on the level of truth determined from associated membership functions (fuzzy sets).

5. Defuzzification extracts the expected value of a fuzzy set and produces a "crisp" numeric value.

Figure 16.9   An overview of fuzzy reasoning.

contribute to the outcome. Several methods can be used to combine the results of two or more rules into a single outcome. In the most popular methods, the fuzzy output sets are summed (or unioned) together to produce a combined fuzzy output set.

The final step in the inferencing process is defuzzification, whereby the combined fuzzy output is converted into a single numerical value. There are several methods of defuzzification. However, the most popular is the centroid or center of gravity method (supported by most fuzzy development systems). This method is mathematically complex and will not be addressed in this book. Basically, the easiest way to think of the centroid method is to imagine the fuzzy set as a tangible object balancing on a point, like a teeter-totter. The point at which the set balances is the center of gravity or middle value—the numerical value that best represents the final fuzzy output set.

Figure 16.10 shows the fuzzy rule evaluation process being applied to our hypothetical fuzzy washing-machine controller. In this example, two rules are being evaluated:

Rule 1

```
IF dirtiness is Moderate
AND type_of_dirt is Greasy
THEN wash_time is Long.
```

Rule 2

```
IF dirtiness is Low
AND type_of_dirt is Greasy
THEN wash_time is Medium.
```

The first rule causes the long wash time to be copied into the (currently empty) temporary output fuzzy set **Wash Time**. Before doing this, its height is truncated at the truth of the rule's premise—0.48 (the minimum of the truth values 0.68 and 0.48)—as shown. When the second rule fires, the medium **Wash Time** fuzzy set is also truncated at the truth of its premise—0.22 (the minimum of 0.22 and 0.48). It is then copied into the temporary output fuzzy set **Wash Time**. However, since this temporary output set is not empty, this modified fuzzy set is combined with the **Long Wash Time** fuzzy set (contributed by the output of rule one) by taking the maximum

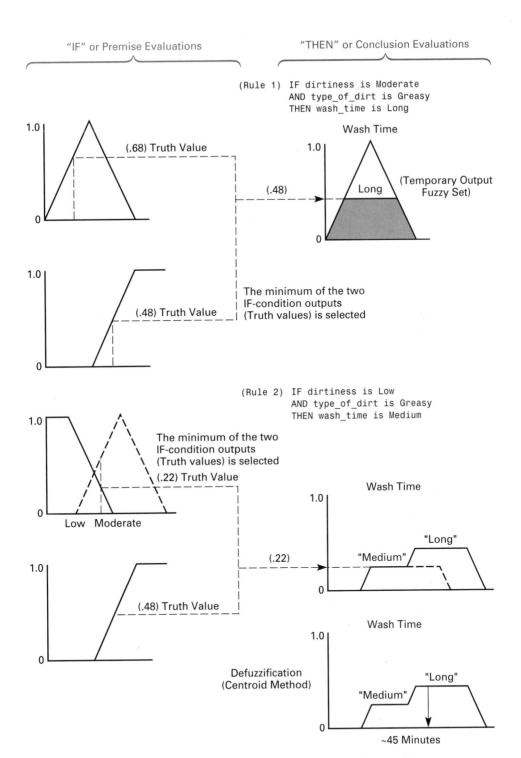

Figure 16.10 The fuzzy rule evaluation in a fuzzy washing-machine controller.

of their respective membership grades. Finally, from this combined set, we apply the Centroid defuzzification process to produce the value for the expected wash time of 45 minutes.

Fuzzy systems can be executed in both software and hardware. Implemented in software, fuzzy systems work at relatively high speeds. Implemented in hardware, they perform fuzzy inferencing at extremely high speeds. Today, fuzzy systems are proving useful for a number of applications.

One way to think about fuzzy logic systems is to compare them to other advanced computing methods, such as expert systems and neural networks as in Fig. 16.11. Both expert systems and fuzzy systems employ rule-based techniques for problem solving. In fact, fuzzy development tools, combined with conventional, rule-based expert systems tools, are available for developing fuzzy systems. These systems employ fuzzy rules, fuzzy sets and membership functions, fuzzification and defuzzification techniques, as well as conventional forward and backward chaining techniques. Both Metus Systems and Togai Infralogic offer such tools.

Neural nets and fuzzy systems are good at processing data. By their very nature, neural nets handle imprecise data both during training when the connections between processing elements undergo adjustment and during operation when processing large data for patterns. In addition, research incorporating fuzzy techniques into neural-net algorithms is currently being conducted. What appears to be most promising is the combined use of neural nets and fuzzy logic for developing fuzzy, rule-based systems. In this method, neural nets are used to create membership functions for fuzzy systems by analyzing user-specified input and output requirements. Fuzzy rules and membership functions are then generated by mapping the neural net's learned weights to fuzzy logic methods. National Semiconductor is currently selling a tool for fuzzy software and fuzzy microcontroller development that accomplishes just that.

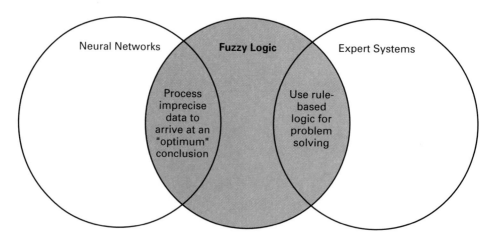

Figure 16.11   The similarities of neural networks, fuzzy logic, and expert systems.

APPLICATIONS OF FUZZY LOGIC

Tables 16.1 and 16.2 list some fuzzy applications which are divided into two main categories: fuzzy control applications and fuzzy I.S. applications.

Fuzzy Control

Control processing is currently the largest area of use for fuzzy logic. Table 16.1 lists some fuzzy control applications currently in use, being marketed, or under development in the following domains or areas:

- Industry.
- Aerospace.
- Transportation.
- Automotive.
- Consumer appliances.
- Consumer electronics.

At the second annual IEEE Fuzzy Conference on Fuzzy Systems, all these areas were the focus of many papers and experience reports. As indicated in Table 16.1, fuzzy logic controllers (implemented in low-cost microcontroller chips) are in use in a wide range of consumer appliances and electronics. This is especially true in Japan and, to a somewhat lesser degree, in Germany.

The automotive industry is also exploiting fuzzy systems for controller design problems involved in providing smoother shifting of automatic transmissions and in modeling the behavior of antilock braking systems during the design and implementation stages. Some of the payoffs claimed from using fuzzy control techniques are better fuel consumption and shifting of automatic transmission systems, and improved braking and road handling for antilock braking systems. In all of the fuzzy controller implementation areas, engineers are claiming that the use of fuzzy development techniques and fuzzy control systems significantly reduces development times as well as time-to-market costs/considerations.

The Japanese automakers are not the only ones involved in applying fuzzy systems. Most U.S. car manufacturers are also investigating their use to solve some otherwise unsolvable problems. One of these seemingly intractable problems looms on the horizon. As of 1994, all automobiles sold in California had to be equipped with on-board diagnostics to state whether they comply with vehicle emission regulations. In 1996, this law goes into effect nationwide. Automotive engineers are now investigating the use of fuzzy logic, as well as neural networks, to help handle this task.

Fuzzy Information Systems

The use of fuzzy logic in more traditional I.S. processing tasks is not nearly as well established as its use in fuzzy control. This is mainly because the technology is still very young,

Table 16.1 Some representative fuzzy-control applications.

Company/Industry	Application/Comments
Industrial	
Fuzzy Machine Tool Diagnostics, Komatsu, Japan	Fuzzy system to check machine tools for worn-out gears and dirty oil filters. Developed for Komatsu by Omron (Japan's leading manufacturer of factory controllers). Omron reps claim fuzzy logic allowed them to slash development time by 75%. (Omron applied for over 700 fuzzy logic patents in Japan, and projected sales of over $750 million or nearly 20% of total revenues, from products incorporating fuzzy logic by 1994.)
Aerospace	
CRIM, NASA	One of the first successful fuzzy logic applications in the industry; component of the system used to monitor and control the temperature environment of the Commercial Refrigeration Incubation Module aboard the space shuttle Endeavor, launched on May 7, 1992.
Transportation	
Sendai Subway, Sendai, Japan	Fuzzy control system that allows subway trains to brake more swiftly and smoothly. Developed by Hitachi. In use since July, 1989.
Automotive	
INVECS, Auto Transmission System, Mitsubishi Motors	"Intelligent and Innovative Vehicle Electronic Control System" uses sensors to detect when driving conditions change, and a microchip adjusts the gears and speed. For example, when rounding an uphill turn, the controller keeps the AT in gear for as long as the car needs it (rather than just for a preset period— the way conventional cruise controls systems do. Should a driver round a tight curve in the rain too fast, the microcontroller will prevent spinout by reducing the power to the drive wheels and adjusting the rotation speed of the rear wheels to match the radius of the turn.
Fuzzy Automatic Transmission, Nissan	"Bluebird" model of the Nissan Maxima, currently available in Japan, with a fuzzy automatic transmission.
Consumer Appliances	
Fuzzy Air Conditioner, Mitsubishi, Japan	Consumer air conditioner with microcontroller-based fuzzy controller jointly developed by Togai InfraLogic and Mitsubishi Heavy Industries. Monitors/controls room temperature using 25 fuzzy rules for cooling and 25 for heating. Mitsubishi claims that improved thermostat control using fuzzy logic has led to reduced heating and cooling times by a factor of five and a reduction in energy consumption of 24%.
Fuzzy Washing Machine, Matushiata, Japan	"Fully automatic" washing machine. After loading, user simply pushes the start button. Two optical sensors analyze the dirt in the wash and the size of load. Information is fed to fuzzy

Table 16.1   *(Continued)*

Company/Industry	Application/Comments
	microprocessor that selects wash, rinse, spin and cycle times from among 600 possible combinations. Matushiata claims that fuzzy washers account for over half of their washing machine sales.
Siwamat 3773 Fuzzy Washing Machine, Siemens AG	Embedded, fuzzy microcontroller system for spinning poorly balanced loads. Uses two fuzzy classification systems, one for washing and rinsing motion and one for various aspects of spinning motion. Developed using Togai InfraLogic's TILshell and MicroFPL product. Siemens estimates the product development cycle was shortened by several months using fuzzy control. Available.
Fuzzy Vacuum Cleaner, Siemens AG	Uses fuzzy control circuits for dust sensing (selecting the suction level), suction stabilization, and for motor temperature limitation. Achieved quality control is superior to the best available conventional control (i.e., the target suction is established with less deviation). Fuzzy components developed with Togai's TILshell software.
Consumer Electronics	
Fuzzy Autofocus VCR, Cannon, Japan	VCR camcorder. Fuzzy autofocus provides better focusing when point-of-interest is not at the center of view finder. Developed by Cannon and Togai InfraLogic.

implementation of the technology for I.S. is still not understood, and the majority of the software tools currently being sold are targeted primarily at developing fuzzy control systems. Additionally, these tools and fuzzy logic technology, in general, lack any standard methodologies for developing I.S. applications. (It is worth noting that several companies are selling, or soon will be selling, tools specifically designed for I.S. domains.)

Table 16.2 lists some representative fuzzy I.S. applications. These systems are being used in a number of industries—financial, transportation, and shipping—as well as in more exotic applications pertaining to law enforcement and nuclear risk assessment. The use of fuzzy logic for financial applications in areas such as credit and loan analysis as well as marketing is receiving a lot of attention. The major benefit associated with using fuzzy techniques for such I.S. applications is the ability to model, using conventional language, complex situations that are difficult, if not impossible, to model using traditional programming techniques. This difficulty can stem from a variety of situations and phenomena. First, it may be too difficult to develop a conceptual mathematical model. Second, the ability to model will suffer drastically due to the complexity of such a system's size. Consequently, the model would require both a huge knowledge base and rule base, which can result in an unacceptably large overhead in computing resources. In addition, the learning curve required of the end user can also be prohibitive. In other words, marketing analysts, traders, administrative personnel, and other managers, who

Table 16.2   Some representative fuzzy I.S. applications.

Company/Industry	Application/Comments
Financial	
Company Acquisition & Credit Analysis	Developed by Metus Systems Group, this fuzzy modeling system isolates candidate companies for investment or acquisition. Operates in two stages: a fuzzy DB manager and a fuzzy policy analyzer. DB component allows analysis, using the same linguistic vocabulary, to interrogate large DB2 DBs. Once a set of candidate companies has been isolated, this information is fed into a fuzzy financial analyzer that combines information from the company's P&L operating statements, and source and application funds statements with public data from S&P's, D&B, and Valueline. System ranks companies in terms of risk, stability, viability, and actual worth.
Loan Evaluation Advisor	Used by a "large bank" in the Washington, DC area, system employs a fuzzy model to evaluate commercial loan applications. The analyst compares the application profile with the company's financial behavior over the past 24 months. The fuzzy approach allows a loan officer to deal with fluctuations in account balances, overdrafts, delinquent payments, number of preexisting loans, collateral appraisals, and so forth in approximate terms rather than sharp cut-off points, providing a much clearer view of the company's assets, its financial management, and its potential for future stability (the measure of whether a significant loan should be made).
Managed Health Care Provider Fraud Detection	Originally developed for a major Connecticut insurance company, this system is now independently and jointly marketed by the original developer and IBM's Insurance sector. System reads several million provider claim forms from a DB2 DB and reduces the information to a few hundred thousand "behavior" patterns. Distributed system running on IBM mainframe and Graphical analysis interface under Presentation Manager on OS/2 workstations.
Yamaichi Trading System	Decision support system for selecting stock options. Uses approximately 800 fuzzy rules and handles 65 industries and a majority of the stocks listed on the Nikkei Dow. In use since 1987.
Transportation/Shipping	
GEM Containerized Management System	Developed for a consortium of 14 shipping lines based in London, England, this system solves supply-and-demand model for +280,000 containers of 15 different types across 93 ports in Europe, the Far East, and the U.S. Handles requests from users for quantities of containers throughout the world. Develops a least-cost and least-risk recommendation. Makes extensive use of fuzzy logic in representing nearly all operating characteristics of the model (i.e., high/low tariffs, distance to next port, yard size, number containers onsite, ETA, etc.).

Table 16.2 *(Continued)*

Company/Industry	Application/Comments
Retail	
Product Pricing Model	Developed for a major British retailing firm this model establishes a price for new products, reprices products based on changes in the market and/or demographics, and predicts changes in the pricing of competitive products within the same or adjacent market regions. Model uses advanced fuzzy logic techniques to develop a consensual recommendation from multiple cooperating, collaborating, and conflicting agents in the fields of finance, marketing sales, manufacturing, transportation, and administration.
Risk Assessment/Law Enforcement	
Fuzzy Fail-Safe System, Los Alamos National Labs	Decision support system to assess the risk of theft or misuse of nuclear materials, specifically plutonium and enriched uranium, from nuclear facilities. System is designed to help users apply resources—accounting, budgetary and operational restraints, etc.—to create the optimum solution for safeguarding against misuse.
Criminal Identification System	Developed by Knowledge Based Technologies for a European police force, this system allows victims of crimes to interrogate a DB of convicted and known criminals in fuzzy terms (for example, the mugger was fairly old, rather tall, etc.). The fuzzy model also incorporates perspective shifts so that the interrogator could say "old from a young perspective," etc.

have neither the time nor the inclination to master the learning curve required of complex programs, can benefit greatly from logic applications.

One particularly interesting and very successful system, developed by the Metus Systems group for a very large British retail firm, uses fuzzy techniques combined with traditional, rule-based inferencing to establish prices for new products based on such factors as competitor's price and market demographics. Using this system, a market analyst can rapidly develop a marketing and pricing strategy for a product by describing the situation using English-like conventions.

Another system was developed by the Metus Group. This risk assessment model, developed for a large insurance company, shows the reduction in overhead that can be obtained using fuzzy logic. This modeling application was originally written in a conventional, expert-systems shell using 181 rules. The new system, developed using a fuzzy model, accomplishes the same task using only 12 rules.

The use of fuzzy system techniques for I.S. applications is still in its infancy and should still be considered very experimental. However, the technology is beginning to be applied and has been done so successfully in a number of cases. As more suitable tools become available supporting fuzzy techniques as well as client-server architectures and business-rule development, the use of fuzzy techniques will begin to receive more attention.

SUMMARY

Fuzzy logic is not a trendy technology or a completely unproven fad that should be passed off or similarly brushed aside with complete skepticism. Rather, fuzzy logic is another subset of AI, as are expert systems, neural nets, OOP, natural language and so on, whose roots can all be traced to AI research. In reality, fuzzy logic should probably be considered more of a technique for representing and handling data than a technology per se. (In the same way, case-based reasoning is really an AI technique closely associated with expert systems technology.) Regardless of how it is classified, fuzzy logic should be viewed as simply another technique that can be integrated into or alongside other computing methods to complement and enhance them. Those who cannot accept the contradictory sounding name fuzzy logic might try referring to it as *continuous logic*.

OO IMPLEMENTATIONS

Rules can be implemented in an OO environment in several ways. Rules can become methods on instance variables. Since a rule can affect many variables in many classes, the rule must also be associated with those same variables and classes. This is particularly true when the rule requires evaluation whenever any variable changes (an *eager* evaluation). Instead of duplicating the same code in each class, the code could be placed in one class (usually the output variable's class) and referred to by the others. When the evaluation occurs only upon request (a *lazy* evaluation), the method implementing the rule is typically placed in the output variable's class. On the other hand, some designers prefer to have one large class that maintains all of the fuzzy rules. However, this can quickly become unwieldy when many rules are used. To accommodate this problem, some designers add a *blackboard* system to access these rules whenever a variable has changed or an output variable is required.

Chapter **17**

Genetic Algorithms[*]

INTRODUCTION

Genetic algorithms (GAs) are computer models based on biogenetics and the principles of Darwin's theory of evolution. They solve problems by maintaining a population of candidate solutions that evolve over time through competition and controlled selection. GAs were conceived in the 1970s by John Holland, a professor at the University of Michigan. Since then, researchers worldwide have worked to further their development and application. Current research focuses on applying GAs to a number of application areas—primarily those requiring an optimum or near optimum solution in a large search space. Problem domains that have proven difficult to solve using traditional programming and knowledge-based system (KBS) techniques include: planning and scheduling, design and configuration, sequencing, machine learning, and formula or process optimization. Genetic algorithms are also providing promising results in assisting other AI development techniques, such as tuning neural networks and selecting fuzzy-membership functions associated with fuzzy-systems development.

Products that support GA research and application development have been on the market for several years now and more seem to appear each month. Consequently, these tools have sparked much ongoing research on applying GA techniques to more conventional applications.

This chapter examines one of AI's newest search and optimization techniques inspired by the concepts of evolutionary programming. First we will provide a background discussion of the underlying theory and concepts of GAs. At the same time, we will consider how GA techniques have been implemented. We will also examine a commercial GA tool to see how it can be used to solve a traditional optimization problem. We will conclude with a list of some available products.

Much of the language used in discussing genetic algorithms is based on biological terminology. Some critics would comment that the complexity of the computer-based, evolutionary processes found in GAs is a far cry from those occurring in the biological world. However, the ability to make the analogy of GAs to biology does provide a familiar context in which to discuss this new search technique. In addition, most of the GA tools on the market rely to some degree on this terminology as well. The basic concept of a GA is that the program works toward finding better solutions to problems in the same manner that species evolve to adapt themselves better to their environment. As in biogenetics, this process takes place in an iterative manner—evolving over time. The potential or *candidate* solutions that are most fit survive and continue to adapt. The less optimal solutions perish. Hence, GA argot often refers to the survival of the fittest analogy.

Before examining how a GA operates, we will first define some of the key components and terminology used by GA researchers and application developers. Figure 17.1 provides an overview of the basic functionality of a simple GA and its relationship to operational computer terminology. (Though there are many different variations of GAs, we will use a simple model common to most GA algorithms.)

GAs are accumulating search algorithms that:

- Represent possible solutions as strings *(chromosomes)* comprised of input values *(genes)*.
- Create generations of solutions using operators from genetics—through *crossover* and *mutation*—in order to create new variations in a population.
- Evaluate each solution *(individual)* based on fitness criteria related to a specific problem (the *environment*).
- Simulate an "environment" using appropriate constraints and *fitness fuctions*.
- Use the fitness information to favor the best individuals *(strings)* when creating the next new *generation(s)*.

Figure 17.1 An overview of GA functionality and terminology.

In a genetic algorithm, candidate solutions to a problem are represented as a string of parametric values (ordinal, real, or index). Such a string is referred to as a *chromosome* and the parameters or input variables within it are called *genes.* Specific chromosomes within a given population are called *individuals.* The population's environment is simulated in a GA by using constraints, rules, and fitness functions appropriate to the task at hand. Genetic algorithms are developed in any number of languages, ranging from C and C++ to Lisp and other specialized AI languages.

Figure 17.2 shows a chromosome comprised of nine genes. As in biology, each gene contained in a chromosome in a GA controls one specific property and has well defined positions within that chromosome. Each gene can have different *values.* In the natural world, a gene could contain the code or value for blue eyes. In a computer-based, GA-modeling program, it could contain a value representing some input variable, such as

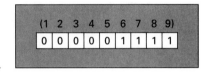

Figure 17.2   A chromosome with nine genes.

the distance between two points (e.g., 85 miles between San Francisco and Sacramento, California) or the profit margin for a line of products (e.g., 30 percent). Depending on the number of genes contained within it, a single chromosome can contain a huge amount of information. (for example, if a chromosome contains 9 genes and each of these genes has 3 values, then the total number of combinations is 3 to the 9th power or 19,683 possible combinations.)

HOW GENETIC ALGORITHMS FUNCTION

Genetic algorithms undergo four primary stages in their problem-solving cycle. These steps can be (loosely) compared to the evolutionary processes occurring in species in the real world. They include:

1. Creation of a population of candidate solutions.

2. Evaluation of each solution.

3. Selection of solutions based on their "fitness."

4. Reproduction of solutions using the genetic operators for crossover of genes and mutation for random changes of genes.

Figure 17.3 shows the main stages in the GA cycle. In simple computer parlance, a GA maps a problem onto a set of strings, each representing a potential (or candidate) solution. Candidate solutions are then manipulated by the GA in its search for the best or most "fit" solution. This process occurs over a number of iterations until the GA finds an acceptable solution.

In the first stage, the GA cycle creates an initial population of candidate solutions for a particular search problem. In the next stage—evaluation—each solution in the population is evaluated and assigned a measure or value, called a *fitness function,* that represents its fitness as a solution. Individual solutions in the population are probabilistically selected on the basis of their fitness relative to the environment (the constraints and rules imposed by the problem). Individuals with high-fitness functions are selected for replication, possibly more than once, while those with low-fitness functions may not be chosen at all.

In stage three—genetic reproduction—some individuals are selected for manipulation and alteration using idealized genetic operators in order to create a new generation of solutions. During this stage, the genetic information or variables, which we refer to as genes in GA and biology, are manipulated. There are two types of genetic operators: *crossover* and *mutation.* Although they differ in operation, both ensure that

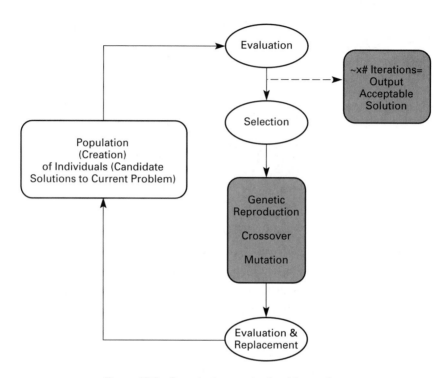

Figure 17.3   Steps in the genetic algorithm cycle.

individual solutions with high-fitness functions are retained for future generations and that new, promising solutions with high-fitness functions are introduced into the population.

Crossover takes place when part of one chromosome is combined with part of another. This "mating of two chromosomes" is similar to species' sexual reproduction, because it involves the exchange of the digital information contained in the genes. In Fig. 17.4, we see two parent chromosomes—C1 and C2—which have swapped genes in order to form a new offspring chromosome—C3. In this example, the crossover point has taken place at position five. In most GAs, the position for crossover can vary. Typically in GAs, the occurrence of a crossover, as well as the position in which it takes place, is randomly or probabilistically selected. The crossover mechanism is arguably the most important operator in creating variation within a population.

Other selected individuals may be altered using the mutation operator for the same purpose as crossover—the creation of more generations of offspring (individuals). However, rather than simply swapping some number of genes among chromosomes, the mutation operator introduces new genetic structures into the population by randomly or probabilistically modifying one or more of an individual chromosome's genes. Since this modification is not related to any previous genetic structure of the population, it creates new individuals representing other sections of the search space. Figure 17.5 shows the mutation operation taking place at position six in a chromosome. As in the occurrences of

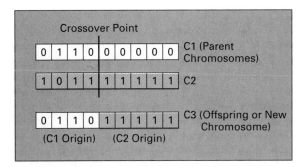

Figure 17.4   Crossover at position 5.

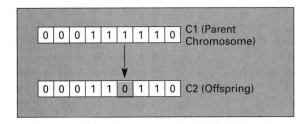

Figure 17.5   Mutation at position 6.

crossover and mutation, the position carried out is usually selected by probability. In a computer-based GA model, mutation occurs by altering a random gene (bit) in an individual (string).

In the fourth step in the GA cycle, the resulting offspring produced by genetic reproduction are evaluated and inserted back into the population—replacing older, less fit individuals. This cycle of creation, evaluation, selection, and reproduction is repeated until the GA reaches an acceptable solution or until the GA cycle has undergone a specified number of iterations (usually determined by the user). Upon evaluation, if an acceptable solution (an individual with a high-fitness function) is found or after a number of iterations have been completed, the best solution (in effect, the "answer") can be output.

WHY USE GENETIC ALGORITHMS?

All this talk of evolutionary-inspired programming that uses bits and strings to model genes and chromosomes is very interesting in itself, but why would you want to use it? What practical problems can GAs be used to solve? Most current research and development focuses on using GAs to solve problems that are impossible to solve using traditional programming concepts or have proven difficult using knowledge-based systems (KBS) techniques. For the most part, such problems involve huge search spaces.

Figure 17.6 provides a simple way of examining the applicability of a solution to a problem's search space. It shows that traditional programming pays off handsomely when

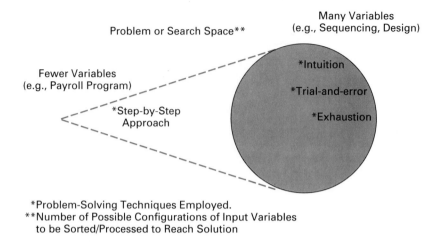

*Problem-Solving Techniques Employed.
**Number of Possible Configurations of Input Variables
to be Sorted/Processed to Reach Solution

Figure 17.6   Applicability of problem or search space size to GA techniques.

there are few input variables involved or the number of possible configurations is small or well defined (e.g., payroll or accounting programs). However, to attempt to solve problems involving large search spaces using traditional step-by-step programming in which every configuration is analyzed and exhausted is not practical. Likewise, certain types of problems that involve intuitive thought or creativity (such as problems in design, scheduling, market advisory, or prediction) have also proven elusive to KBS techniques. The number of rules necessary to account for the many possible variables and their configurations can literally explode, making them impractical to model. Genetic algorithms, on the other hand, can be applied successfully to problems with large search spaces. These are discussed in the next section.

PRACTICAL GA APPLICATION WITH C DARWIN II

In turning from theory to actual problem using a GA tool, we will look at a product called C Darwin II. It was developed by NovaCast, AB, at the Soft Center in Ronneby, Sweden, and is marketed in the U.S. by Itanis International in Pittsburgh.

C Darwin II is a GA shell program for solving problems. It is targeted at users who want to apply the problem-solving techniques of GAs to practical applications, rather than researchers who may want to experiment and further define GA techniques. C Darwin II is a GA program for end users, not experienced programmers, who want an add-on library of GA functions. The tool runs on a PC under DOS. It can also be run in DOS mode under Windows, and it comes with icons for integration with the application manager found in the Windows operating system. C Darwin was selected here because it offers a way to illustrate GA techniques without resorting to actually writing application code. The tool does, however, include a runtime application generator for serious application development.

The basic evolution technique used in C Darwin requires that the solution be represented as gene values in a chromosome. There are four main steps involved in setting up C Darwin to solve a problem.

Step 1. Define the problem in detail and select a suitable representation.

Step 2. Select and define the chromosome. Define the basic constraints. Define the genes.

Step 3. Select data. Enter problem-specific data. Enter functions and constraints. Set up the fitness function.

Step 4. Select evolution. Use default values for evolution parameters. Run a test to check that the functions are working as planned. Modify if needed. Select Run and follow how the program gradually converges to a solution. Press Best to see the best solution so far. The solution is now encoded in the genes of the chromosome.

The first step involves defining the problem. In C Darwin, the actual data defining the chromosomes is entered into a "data sheet" screen. The environment that will test and select the individuals is set up by defining the appropriate formulas, constraints, and fitness functions that will be maximized or minimized depending on the problem. For certain types of problems, the fitness function values can be entered manually for each individual in a generation. For larger problems, data can be imported from ASCII files.

Once the kind of solution desired has been defined and the appropriate formulas, constraints, and fitness values have been entered, C Darwin is ready for evolution. This takes place in the manner specified in the traditional GA paradigm, in which the program first randomly generates an initial population of solutions. Next, a fitness value is calculated for each individual in that generation. The fitness values are then used when producing the next generation. Pairs of chromosomes are then selected by probability based on their fitness values, with special variations being induced by means of crossover and mutation. New offspring resulting from this reproduction process are then subjected to the environment where the suitability of each individual is tested by the fitness function and so on.

C Darwin's evolution process allows the programmer to execute a single-step approach, individual by individual, one generation at a time, or generation after generation. The progress of the evolution step can be followed in a screen that displays the best solution so far by means of values or in a bar diagram at any time. Once a solution or model for solving a particular problem has been developed, it can be saved for later use or modification. It can also be converted to a runtime program that can be embedded in other applications.

Genetic algorithms are quite adept at solving sequential problems where the order of events is important. The classic example of such a problem is the Traveling Salesperson Problem (TSP). The C Darwin tool uses an example of the TSP as an introductory problem to users who want to familiarize themselves and develop an understanding of the problem-solving capabilities of GAs.

The basic idea of the TSP problem is that a salesperson wants to find a short route for a planned business trip. In the tutorial provided in C Darwin, a salesperson wants to pay a visit to customers located in 12 different cities: Boston, New York, Detroit, Buffalo, Pittsburgh, Chicago, St. Louis, Atlanta, Memphis, Dallas, Cincinnati, and Los Angeles. Because she will be making the trip by car, the salesperson wants to find the shortest route in order to minimize the mileage. Because she is intelligent, she knows that the number of possible routes can be expressed as the factorial of the number of cities to be visited: $12 - 1$, or $1 \times 2 \times 3 \times 4 \times 5 \times 6 \times 7 \times 8 \times 9 \times 10 \times 11$. This amounts to a startling 39,916,800 possible routes. Realizing that this problem is an ideal candidate for solving with a GA, our salesperson starts to define and solve the problem as outlined in the following step-by-step approach.

The first step is to design the chromosome. Since the salesperson wants the result to be represented as a list of the cities, in the order in which they should be visited, the chromosome will have 12 genes (because there are 12 cities). Since each chromosome should be able to represent any of the 12 cities, the value for each one could be any number between 1 and 12. In this aspect, the genes can be identical except for the fact that the salesperson does not want to visit the same city twice. Therefore, a constraint is put on the chromosome stating that no two values of the genes should be the same. In other words, each gene must contain a value different from the others. At this stage, C Darwin is started and the chromosome screen is selected from the program's main menu. This chromosome screen is where the necessary chromosome and associated genes are defined in order to solve the TSP problem (see Fig. 17.7). For number of chromosomes, enter 1. For number of genes, enter 12 for the 12 cities to be visited. Also, specify that each gene type is identical.

The next step in modeling the TSP problem is to enter the names of the cities as well as the data representing distances between the cities that the salesperson intends to visit. Data defining these distances are entered into C Darwin's data sheet screen in a triangular table format, which shows every possible distance between cities. Figure 17.8 shows a partial view of the data sheet screen. The left of the screen lists the names of the genes. Note that column A, appearing under the Route heading, is reserved for the chromosome.

At this stage, the program can present possible solutions in the chromosome and also the distances (between the cities). In this instance, the chromosome shows the values (9, 12, 10, 6, 3, 5, 11, 8, 2, 1, 7, 4). These values indicate the sequence for a route. Also note that the route can begin at any point as the chromosome represents a sequence. For example, starting at city number 11, St. Louis, the next nearest city is Atlanta (8), and the next is Memphis (2), and so on.

Next, the fitness function must be defined in order to tell the system what and how we want to optimize. For the TSP problem, the program is asked to minimize the route distance to be driven. Therefore, it is necessary to create a population of chromosomes like the one above. To accomplish this, the data about distances is used to calculate the total distance for each chromosome. The total distance will be the fitness value. Basically, the program is being asked to favor those chromosomes which have a low fitness value so that the best solutions (individual chromosomes) will be more frequently used for each successive generation created in the GA cycle. This task is easily accomplished in C Darwin because the program includes a special function for collecting data defined in a chromosome in order to calculate distance. (It specifies in which column and row headers data are located. In addition, C Darwin has a Formula submenu with predefined formulas for computing such functions as minimizing and maximizing, etc.)

```
+ C DARWIN II                          NONAME                    Chromosome Description +
Description              :   Route Planner1
No. of chromosomes      :   1 (maximal:   5)
  Chromosome no.        :   1
  No. of genes          :   12
  Gene types            :   identical (identical, different)
  Different value for every gene:  yes
  Sum of genes must equal to              , if not,  adjust gene      0
```

# Name	Type (index, ordinal, real)	Leading digits	Decimal digits	Precision	Minimal value	Maximal value	bit
1 gene 1	index	2	0	2	1	12	4
2 gene 2	index	2	0	2	1	12	4
3 gene 3	index	2	0	2	1	12	4
4 gene 4	index	2	0	2	1	12	4
5 gene 5	index	2	0	2	1	12	4
6 gene 6	index	2	0	2	1	12	4
7 gene 7	index	2	0	2	1	12	4
8 gene 8	index	2	0	2	1	12	4
9 gene 9	index	2	0	2	1	12	4
10 gene 10	index	2	0	2	1	12	4
11 gene 11	index	2	0	2	1	12	4
12 gene 12	index	2	0	2	1	12	4

Figure 17.7   C Darwin II chromosomes description screen.

This problem could be made more complex by pinning down the city where the salesperson lives. To keep things simple, let it be assumed that she is French and that she will fly to whatever city is best, rent a car, and then travel from city to city in the recommended way.

At this stage, the program is ready to begin the evolution process. If desired, the process can be started using the existing default values that specify the population size, which has a default value of 300 individuals, or a screen can be entered specifying particular population-size parameters. Once the evolution is begun, it is possible to watch how the minimum and average values for the fitness functions gradually improve in the Fitness Function window. In the right hand portion of the screen (in Fig. 17.9) is the value showing which generation has the best solution so far.

Switching back to the data sheet screen (Fig. 17.8), you can see the route itself represented in the chromosome. Other screens show the mileage for the best route so far or view the evolution process graphically. It is important to point out that a GA approach to problem solving may not always result in the absolute best solution, but rather an acceptable one. C Darwin also permits addition of other formulas to the TSP program to increase functionality (e.g., to indicate how much time it will take to drive between various cities, etc.).

The TSP is only one example of the type of problems that can be solved using C Darwin's GA techniques. Others possibilities include composition-related problems in which several ingredients need to be chosen in order to meet certain specifications, design problems, and planning and scheduling problems.

cell:B!1   TOT.KM   KM/HOUR   HOURS
status: 0   16650.0   60.0   277.5É

# gene	A ROUTE	B CITY #	C NAMES	D BOSTON	E NEW YORK	F DETROIT
1 gene 1	9	1.0	BOSTON		350.0	1200.0
2 gene 2	12	2.0	NEW YORK			1100.0
3 gene 3	10	3.0	DETROIT			
4 gene 4	6	4.0	BUFFALO			
5 gene 5	3	5.0	PITTSBURGH			
6 gene 6	5	6.0	CHICAGO			
7 gene 7	11	7.0	ST. LOUIS			
8 gene 8	8	8.0	ATLANTA			
9 gene 9	2	9.0	MEMPHIS			
10 gene 10	1	10.0	DALLAS			
11 gene 11	7	11.0	CINCINNATI			
12 gene 12	4	12.0	LOS ANGELES			
13						
14						
15						

/, F2-menu   F10-help +

Figure 17.8   C Darwin II, data-sheet screen.

ind: 70   100   TOT.KM   KM/HOUR   HOURS
generat: 28   11300.0   60.0   188.3É

Fitness Function

# gene	#	min	avg	max	best	#	% max
	13	−15350.0	−12521.5	−11300.0	−11300.0	7	2.0
	14	−16900.0	−12611.5	−11300.0	−11300.0	7	10.0
	15	−15500.0	−12362.5	−11300.0	−11300.0	7	10.0
1 gene 1	16	−16500.0	−12669.5	−11300.0	−11300.0	7	9.0
2 gene 2	17	−15300.0	−12460.0	−11300.0	−11300.0	7	7.0
3 gene 3	18	−15750.0	−12401.0	−11300.0	−11300.0	7	11.0
4 gene 4	19	−15750.0	−12498.0	−11300.0	−11300.0	7	10.0
5 gene 5	20	−15050.0	−12258.5	−11300.0	−11300.0	7	13.0
6 gene 6	21	−14800.0	−12257.5	−11300.0	−11300.0	7	15.0
7 gene 7	22	−16250.0	−12365.5	−11300.0	−11300.0	7	15.0
8 gene 8	23	−15250.0	−12149.0	−11300.0	−11300.0	7	20.0
9 gene 9	24	−14950.0	−12117.5	−11300.0	−11300.0	7	28.0
10 gene 10	25	−15450.0	−12013.0	−11300.0	−11300.0	7	38.0
11 gene 11	26	−14600.0	−11916.0	−11300.0	−11300.0	7	48.0
12 gene 12	27	−15400.0	−11659.0	−11300.0	−11300.0	7	64.0

Single Generation Run Inspect eDit Best sEmigraphics: off sHow

Figure 17.9   C Darwin II, fitness-function window.

SUMMARY

A genetic algorithm is a search and optimization technique that is still primarily being used in research settings. Although it will probably be some time before we see any real breakthroughs in their commercial application, there are a number of products on the market that are helping to inspire continued research and application development. Several companies have already implemented GA techniques into their development tools, and this trend will likely continue and lead to the acceptance of the technology. In addition, several vendors of massively parallel computing, including Thinking Machines, have announced products employing GAs integrated alongside other search and optimization techniques for managing large amounts of data associated with MPP applications.

OO IMPLEMENTATIONS

Genetic algorithms can be implemented directly in OO languages. In fact, many OO-GA products are already commercially available. Here, classes are implemented for chromosomes and genes along their respective contraints and fitness functions. Of course, a non-OO GA application can be wrapped and placed for use within an ORB environment.

PART **V**

TECHNIQUES FOR INDIVIDUALS AND TEAMS

The modeling process is supported by various other techniques. Part V discusses workshops and ways of facilitating them, interviewing techniques, prototyping, and timebox management. It also discusses the profile required for a user who participates in a system development project.

Chapter 18

Workshops with End Users

INTRODUCTION

A major goal of I.S. today should be getting business people involved in all aspects of business system design. Businesses cannot be redesigned effectively without their thorough involvement. Consequently, enterprise models are needed that reflect business policies. Making these models easy for business people to understand should be a major goal of OO-CASE tools. Those models must be quickly translatable into working software. The changes that occur constantly in a business and its rules must be reflected quickly in the working systems. The era when computerized systems put business in a straitjacket must end.

To involve the end users in OO analysis and design, a workshop technique is employed. Key end users participate in a workshop that progresses through a structured set of steps for reviewing models, planning systems, or designing systems. While the users or business people are encouraged to do most of the talking, an I.S. workshop leader, or "facilitator," guides the session—moving it toward the goal of a model, specification, prototype, or design represented in an OO-CASE repository. The users understand and debate the evolving models and designs. Often these workshops are highly creative and enjoyable. They have been taking place successfully for years in non-OO requirements planning and design and can be even more effective with OO techniques.

Three types of workshops are called JEM, JRP (pronounced "jerp"), and JAD:

- JEM: Joint-enterprise modeling.
- JRP: Joint-requirements planning.
- JAD: Joint-application design.

They are sometimes collectively referred to as facilitated workshops, meaning workshops organized, controlled, and moderated by a professional facilitator.

JAD was the first of these to become popular and has progressed through four generations (as indicated in Fig. 18.1). The early workshops were done with no computerized

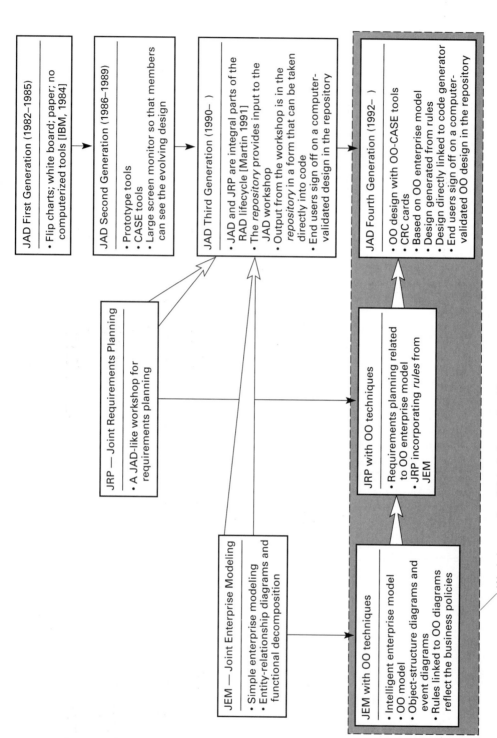

Figure 18.1   The evolution of JAD and end-user workshops.

tools [IBM, 1984]. The second generation of workshops used either prototyping tools or CASE tools or both, but did not use integrated CASE. The third generation used integrated CASE tools with which code could be generated directly from the design that is built in a repository. In this third generation, JRP and JAD were an integral part of a repository-based lifecycle. The term RAD (rapid-application development) was used for this lifecycle that had the goals of high quality, high speed, and lower cost [Martin, 1991].

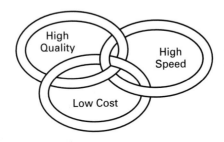

The fourth generation uses the OO techniques. JRP and JAD should both use the knowledge established in joint-enterprise modeling with business rules and usually help add to these models. Particularly important, the JEM, JRP, and JAD workshops should use the same OO-CASE tool, and this tool should generate code.

THE BEST OF COMPUTERS AND PEOPLE

The goal of such workshops is encouraging human creativity and linking it to the power and rigor of repository-based tools.

> We need to create the maximum synergy between human creativity and the power of computerized tools.

To aid human creativity, the diagrams must help users to visualize the enterprise's complex operations. A major goal of OO-CASE is designing diagrams that effectively communicate with business people. These diagrams help to represent a growing body of knowledge that resides in the CASE repository.

The JEM workshops should help executives to think creatively about how their enterprises can be streamlined, made more competitive, or made to function better. The workshop examines the goals, problems, critical success factors, and strategic opportunities—possibly analyzed in a separate study [Martin, 1990]. The JRP workshop focuses on the requirements of a specific system. Business executives and end users brainstorm the possible functions of the system, identify the most useful functions, and eliminate or defer those of questionable value. The JAD workshop helps to ensure that a system fully meets its users' needs and that the design will work well. It is also concerned with producing low-cost systems that can be modified and maintained inexpensively. Box 18.1 lists the benefits of JEM, JRP, and JAD.

BOX 18.1   Benefits of JEM, JRP, and JAD.

Benefits of JEM

- Executives learn to visualize their enterprise in ways that help them think about how it can be redesigned, streamlined, and made more competitive. They also learn to understand the business value of building better I.S. architectures.

- JEM encourages brainstorming about how the enterprise might become more automated and take advantage of information technology in different ways—especially emerging technologies.

- Business people are encouraged to think creatively about the rules for running the business. Their input is essential before I.S. can devise the best set of rules.

- Attention is focused on the need to eliminate certain operations and unify others.

Benefits of JRP

- JRP ensures that business executives are intimately involved in the system-planning process.

- System planning is linked to the top-level analysis of goals, problems, critical success factors, and strategic systems opportunities [Martin, 1990].

- JRP encourages brainstorming to determine the most valuable system functions and to eliminate those of questionable value.

- JRP helps get the requirements right the first time. Changing them after a system has been designed or implemented is expensive and harmful.

Benefits of JAD

- System specification and design require much less time than traditional system analysis. For example, JAD replaces voluminous paper specifications with live screen designs, report designs, prototypes, concise structures, and design diagrams that are easily edited. When created with rigorous design tools, these greatly help programmers or system implementors.

- JAD helps get the design right the first time. Changing the design after a system is built is expensive and harmful. Design errors caught early lower the cost.

- The resulting systems, therefore, have a higher quality and greater business value.

- When used with RAD, the computerized design feeds directly into the construction phase. In other words, the implementation employs the JAD output directly.

- JAD helps integrate and unify the needs of different parts of the organization.

- JAD results in user satisfaction. Because users design the system, they take an interest in it, feel ownership, and help in the construction phase.

- Because end users are involved to the design process, JAD helps increase the computer literacy of a user community. Users often become more imaginative and inventive about creating better procedures.

- JAD relieves the I.S. analyst from having to resolve political conflicts between end users, who can work out potential differences in a JAD workshop.

- JAD is done with a toolset, so the design uses classes, rules, and enterprise models already in the repository. The toolset enforces consistency and rigor in the design and can link precisely to other systems designed with the toolset.

In corporations that conduct them well, the advantages of these workshops with computer users and business people are so great that it would be unthinkable to build systems without them. Surprisingly, many I.S. organizations do not yet use such workshops, and consequently they experience higher costs, longer development times, lower quality, fewer business improvements, and users who are less happy. Some I.S. organizations have used JAD, JRP, and JEM workshops for many years, steadily learning how to do them better.

Currently, many of these workshops still do not use OO techniques—relying on conventional data modeling, process modeling, and structured techniques. OO techniques have many advantages and are rapidly being adopted. OO models are more intuitive to most business people than conventional structured techniques. Facilitators using OO techniques report that they obtain high-quality results, often with a higher level of creative debate about the redesign of processes or business areas.

REPOSITORY, NOT PAPER

The workshops should generate a computerized model or design—with little paperwork. When designing a system, the users sign off on a design *in a repository* that can be used directly with a code generator. RAD lifecycles often have a *requirement-planning phase* using a JRP workshop, separate from a *user-design phase* using one or more JAD workshops. For systems where the requirements are already well known or obvious, JRP and JAD may be combined into one workshop. The lifecycle for one system can be faster and better if enterprise modeling has already been done with the help of JEM (joint-enterprise modeling) workshops. All these workshops should use the same repository.

THE EXECUTIVE SPONSOR

When systems are built, a high-level user executive should be the owner of the system. Though sometimes called the *executive sponsor,* the term *executive owner* might be preferable. It emphasizes that the executive's budget pays for the system. Establishing this end-user executive, who is at a suitably high level and *committed* to the system, is an essential prerequisite to the workshop activity.

Because of this financial commitment, the executive sponsor is entitled to kill the system after the JRP workshop if the planning indicates that the system will not provide a high enough return on investment.

The executive sponsor should ensure that the right people attend the workshops and should motivate the participants appropriately. When disputes or political arguments occur, the executive sponsor should resolve them, off line. The executive sponsor should open the workshops and review their conclusions, but usually not be present during the body of the workshop.

THE FACILITATOR

Particularly critical to the success of these workshops are the skills of the person, referred to as the facilitator, who organizes and oversees them. Being a facilitator should be regarded as a profession, needing professional skills that require time to develop. The facilitator should stay in that job full time until her promotion or relocation, and then a new facilitator should work alongside early enough to learn the skills. Large I.S. organizations have a Facilitator Department with skilled facilitators who are allocated to one project after another.

A facilitator is not likely to do a perfect job in the first session. After the third or fourth, confidence and skill increase to make the activity as effective as possible. When JEM, JRP, or JAD fails, the facilitator is usually at fault; more skilled leadership could have made it work. Appointing different facilitators for each project team often results in unskilled leadership and inadequate results. The most successful use of JAD is generally in organizations that have a full-time facilitator doing one project after another. Often this person conducts a JRP workshop and continues with a JAD for the same system.

The facilitator should be chosen primarily for skills in communication along with the additional characteristics listed in Box 18.2. The facilitator needs to be diplomatic and not associated with any politics that might affect the session. Above all, the facilitator must appear to be *impartial.* The job includes preparing and orchestrating the session, making discussions occur within a structured framework, and having the session move reasonably quickly to the required conclusions. The facilitator acts as the focal point for tying together the views of management, end users, and I.S. professionals (see Fig. 18.2).

Thorough preparation is extremely important. The facilitator needs to research and prepare the meeting well—providing the participants with a suitable level of printed detail.

The facilitator needs to be comfortable standing in front of a group of people, confident in the task and capable of directing discussion and fact-finding activities. The respect of all parties at the session is essential. This can be gained by being well prepared, knowledgeable about the business area, and competent in the techniques used. The ability to control controversies and stay flexible is also important.

A good facilitator can eliminate the effects of politics, power struggles, and communication gaps. I.S. and end users are put on equal terms and made partners. The facilitator assumes the role of a referee at times, arbitrating debates. Constantly eliciting questions, the facilitator should encourage the quieter members to participate, ask questions, and respond when the more aggressive members take a position. The facilitator must prevent domineering participants from overpowering the meeting, draw out shy participants, and redirect participants who have a hidden agenda. The facilitator should have a well thought-out agenda and stick to it.

A good facilitator knows that certain goals must be accomplished by a given time. He moves the session forward until the requisite designs are completed, along with screens, reports, and, possibly, prototypes—obtaining users' concurrence on these designs. The goal is to discuss the ideas fully and reach agreement as a group without too much delay or haggling. The facilitator must be enthusiastic about the session and convey this excitement to the participants about how well it can work.

BOX 18.2   Characteristics of a good workshop facilitator.

- Excellent human communication skills.
- Impartial, unbiased, neutral.
- Good negotiating skills, sensitive to corporate politics, diplomatic.
- Good at conducting a meeting.
  — Has leadership qualities similar to those of a good board chairman.
  — Makes the meeting move quickly to conclusions and avoids tangents.
  — Can turn a floundering meeting into a productive session.
  — Can summarize what has been said.
- Understands group dynamics and can excite the participants, getting them to work hard on items that need detailing.
- Lively in front of an audience.
- Capable of organizing the research, documents, and people.
- Not an expert on the applications but capable of researching and learning quickly.
- Fully familiar with the diagramming techniques used in the workshop and familiar with OO modeling.
- Has become skilled at the job by practice—a professional facilitator.

Figure 18.2   JEM, JRP, and JAD sessions need the commitment of management and the partnership of management, end users, and I.S. professionals. Their cooperation is facilitated and coordinated by an impartial session leader who needs the skills listed in Box 18.2.

THE SCRIBE

The user workshop needs a professional who is highly skilled with the CASE tool that is used. The medieval word *scribe* is often used to describe this person, because in the earliest JAD workshops the scribe wrote down what was said and produced paper documentation. Today, the scribe builds the CASE representation of the models, plans, and designs, updates the repository, and uses the tools to ensure integrity and consistency in the repository information. The scribe must be able to operate the CASE tool quickly and accurately. The scribe may create a prototype screen during a JAD workshop. Some documentation at high-level workshops may be done by the scribe without a CASE tool, but having documentation in the repository has major advantages.

A good integrated-CASE toolset correlates the information entered with knowledge already in the repository, indicating any flaws or inconsistencies. Because of this, the scribe may interrupt the meeting frequently and indicate whether what has just been said is consistent with previous decisions or is already in the repository. The scribe is thus an active, not a passive, participant.

The facilitator is highly dependent on the scribe. It helps if the same facilitator and scribe always work together as a team—understanding and enhancing each other's capabilities.

FACILITATOR TRAINING

An organization that incorporates JEM, JRP, and JAD into its development methodology should train one or more facilitators and make this their job for two years or more. Experience increases the facilitators' skills.

The facilitator should be trained in areas listed in Box 18.1 and have had on-the-job training in other workshops. A mock-up session should put the facilitator in a variety of problematical situations which are videotaped and then critiqued. A thorough knowledge of the automated tools used is essential. The facilitator should have management skills, business savvy, and a good reputation, because credibility will make the job of working with a variety of end users, executives, and I.S. staff much easier.

A facilitator should be regarded as a trainee until the fourth workshop. In the first, as an apprentice working with and helping an experienced facilitator, the trainee observes the initiation, research, preparation, as well as the final workshop. In the second and third, the trainee co-leads with an experienced facilitator to build skill and confidence. In the fourth, the trainee becomes the facilitator. If a corporation is doing its first workshops, it may employ an outside consulting firm to run them until its own facilitator becomes experienced.

WHO ATTENDS THE JRP WORKSHOP?

Selecting the best user participants is very important. The participants should have the right mix of knowledge about the business and have the authority to make decisions about the design. All should communicate well. Often, one or more key people are critical for creating the design and having it accepted. *If these key players are not available, the workshop should not be run.* (See Chapter 22 on domain experts for more information.)

Workshops are particularly valuable for projects that span user organizations or for applications that affect multiple locations or disciplines. The workshops are useful for resolving operational, organizational, or procedural differences. The end users or managers in the workshop confront each other under the guidance of a facilitator trained in negotiating skills and must sign off on a design that both sides accept. Systems analysts should not be trapped in the middle of political conflicts. Conflicts are brought into the open in a constructive planning or design session.

Often, contentious political issues are known before the workshop. They should be addressed by identifying the *sponsoring executive* and having this person meet with the parties in question, seeking consensus on the issues, or motivating the parties to achieve consensus during the workshop. The workshops attempt to achieve consensus among participants with different experiences, needs, or visions.

A goal of a JRP or JAD workshop is to get the planning or design *right the first time* or, at least, as close as possible to the final system. It is expensive and time consuming to change the requirements of the system after it has been designed or to change the design after it has been constructed. To get it right at the workshop, those end users and managers who really understand the requirements *must* be present.

Increasingly today, electronic document interchange (EDI) systems are being built that transmit data electronically among enterprises. Corporations are placing workstations on the locations of agents, wholesalers, retailers, buyers, suppliers, or dealers. Online cooperation between organizations is important for minimizing inventory costs and improving service. When such systems are designed in JRP or JAD sessions, including representatives of the external organization can be valuable.

A COHESIVE TEAM

Teams play an important part in the development lifecycle. A team must become cohesive and share a common goal. Team members need to develop respect for one another, know each other's talents, and like to call on those talents to address a situation collectively. The facilitator needs to establish the team's goal clearly and motivate the team members to achieve it. Any of the participants' hidden agendas should be temporarily set aside. When a team of talented people focuses on achieving a single, clear goal, it can do so with great energy and find the experience rewarding.

An important principle is that all members of the team are equal for the duration of the workshop. However, various individuals in the team may provide leadership—taking charge temporarily when dealing with subjects relating to their expertise. Except for the facilitator, no individual should dominate for more than periodic bursts, or the contributions of the others may be lost. The facilitator must preserve the right balance.

A cohesive team usually has fun. It enjoys addressing problems in concert, with different team members peeling off periodically to prepare a presentation, invent a chart, or create a segment of a design. In some cases, such teams enjoy working on tasks that could otherwise be dull. The skilled facilitator knows how to help the team and build up momentum.

It usually takes two days for the team to become cohesive. Teams spend much of the first two days becoming comfortable with one another. If the first workshop lasts five days, the real work is usually done on the last three days.

WORKSHOP DURATION

JAD workshops typically last three to five days. JRP workshops vary in length depending on the complexity or newness of the requirements. They typically range from one to three days.

Workshops with top management are shorter than workshops with lower-level users. High management has less available time, more impatience and outside pressures, and often a lower attention span.

Corporations conducting facilitated workshops for several years often state that the workshops have become shorter as experience and skills have increased. Good OO modeling often requires multiple short JEM workshops interspersed by periods of detailed work. The workshops help to validate the models and deal with many questions raised in the modeling process.

GROUP DYNAMICS

Workshop sessions succeed because of the group dynamics. The facilitator needs to know how to use group dynamics constructively. (For more information on facilitation techniques, see Chapter 19.) The participants are shut away in a workshop knowing that they have a given task to accomplish by a given time, with a given agenda. This task-oriented environment helps participants concentrate on sharing ideas and achieving the established goals. It helps to ensure that the information provided is complete. When appropriately motivated, such groups tend to police themselves and avoid the bickering and pettiness of politics.

The facilitator may follow the agenda by asking questions of the users at each stage:

- What business rules apply here?
- What are the responsibilities of this object?
- What information is needed to improve decisions?
- What other control conditions could affect this operation?
- Could this step be eliminated or delegated to another object?
- Should this decision be made in a different place?

The answers and discussions should be made tangible by quickly generating and displaying screens or reports that future users could employ. As new flows or structures are designed, they should be printed by the design tool so that session members can study and make notes on them.

The main participants of the workshop must attend *full time*. If they miss a day, they cannot contribute fully and others waste time updating them. They may also cause earlier decisions to be reexamined which wastes time. Since each day in a workshop builds upon the previous day, participants must be present full time each day to maintain continuity.

Some JRP and JAD workshops have observers who come in to see what is happening. This practice should be discouraged. If keeping out observers is impractical, they should be kept quiet and not allowed to interrupt the meeting. The group dynamics depend upon intense, full-time participation.

The number of participants varies from one system to another. The session should not be too big. Large groups tend to argue too much or waste participants' time. The most effective sessions usually have fewer than nine people plus the facilitator and scribe.

The group should follow a structure with agreed-upon stages, goals, and deliverables. In this way time-wasting, ad-hoc debate is avoided. (For more guidelines on such workshop techniques, see Chapter 20.)

OPEN ISSUES

The workshop should move along at a rapid clip. When an issue comes up that cannot be resolved, the meeting should not become bogged down in discussion. After declaring the problem an open issue, the scribe should note the following:

- Issue number.
- Issue name.
- Person assigned to resolve the issue.
- Date for resolution.
- Description.

The scribe may have forms or computer screens for recording open issues.

THE FIVE-MINUTE RULE

When arguments threaten to slow down the progress, the facilitator should stop them and declare them an open issue. Some facilitators impose a five-minute rule: *No argument is allowed to continue longer than five minutes.* If it cannot be resolved within five minutes, it is declared an open issue.

Open issues are reexamined at the end of the day. If an issue still cannot be resolved, the person to whom the issue has been assigned must try to produce a solution. Major disagreements among participants should be taken to the *executive sponsor* for resolution.

BOX 18.3   Facilities in the workshop room.

- Large white board with colored pens.
- Flip-chart board, colored pens, and space to display multiple flip charts.
- Overhead projector and screen with both prepared and blank transparencies as well as colored pens.
- Possibly, a magnetic or felt board with a kit for building diagrams.
- Small round table if CRC cards are used.
- PC or workstation.
- Large-screen monitor or projector so that all participants can see and discuss what is on the screen of the prototyping and OO-CASE toolset.
- Printer so that designs can be printed for the participants.
- Photocopier so that all participants can be given copies of information created.
- Polaroid camera to record white-board drawings or wall charts.
- Slide projector if the facilitator has prepared slides.
- Videotape player and television monitor if the facilitator has planned to use videotapes.
- Coffee and refreshments.
- Name cards and stationery for participants.
- *No telephone!*

THE WORKSHOP ROOM

The workshops need an appropriately equipped room. Facilities in such a room are listed in Box 18.3 and its typical layout is shown in Fig. 18.3. This layout may be varied. For example, when CRC cards are used, a small round table is needed.

OO-CASE and prototyping tools should be used by the scribe in the workshop. The participants should be able to see, periodically, what is on the toolset screen and discuss it. The personal computer should thus have a large-screen monitor or projector. This is not permanently switched on, because the scribe wants to build the design in private much of the time.

The projector may project onto a white board so that participants can scribble on the design. The workbench tool has a printer so that parts of the design, specifications, agenda, and so on can be printed and distributed to users.

Large white boards to create sketches and lists, as well as flip charts, should remain visible throughout the session. An overhead projector is used to make prepared presentations and sketch diagrams during the session. A slide projector or videotape player may also be included. The facilitator may arrange for slides or videotapes to be available of the processes that need automating. A PC printer and a copying machine should be available.

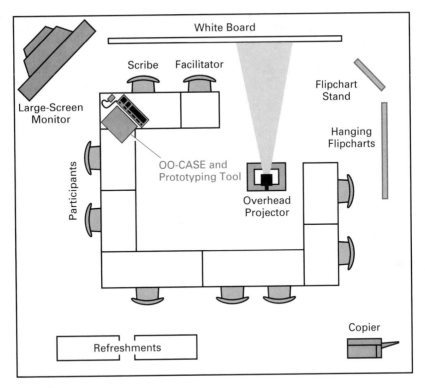

Figure 18.3 Layout of a room for JEM, JRP, and JAD. A small round table should be used when CRC cards are employed. There should be no telephone.

The room has refreshments, but no telephone. An important aspect of the workshop is its isolation from the interruptions of daily business. A permanently established JAD room may be designed to serve other functions, such as other meetings, training, demonstrations, and sales presentations.

TRAINING THE PARTICIPANTS

Non-I.S. people participating in workshops may need some training prior to the workshop, since they must be able to read and think constructively about the types of diagrams used.

A criterion for tool selection is that the diagrams should be easy for non-I.S. people to use. Complex details should be displayable in windows so that they do not clutter the main diagrams. End users can be taught to read these diagrams, so that they can use them as a basis for discussion in a four-hour training class. They may then do some studying of relevant diagrams prior to the workshop.

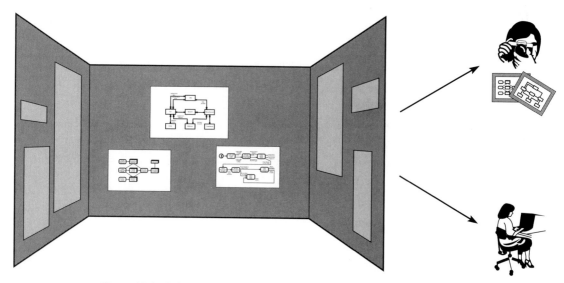

Figure 18.4   Information on wall charts, flip charts, and white boards may be photographed with a Polaroid camera. The scribe enters this information into the OO-CASE tool. The tool detects inconsistencies and helps build a design with overall integrity.

WALL CHARTING

Groups discussing complex subjects commonly use wall charts. Participants stand in front of white boards or pin flip charts to the wall. Kits especially designed for wall charting are available. Blocks of different shapes can be written on with an erasable pen and stuck to the wall to create a chart, such as an object-relationship or *composed-of* diagram, event diagram, class-hierarchy diagram, or class-communication diagram. With some kits, the blocks are stuck on a metal board with magnets; with others, pieces of cardboard are stuck to a wall with a gummy adhesive. The workshop room should have a wall-charting facility which makes charts easy to change.

When viewed from a distance, a large wall chart gives an overview of the subject. When viewed up close, it gives detail. The scribe or facilitator may have a Polaroid camera so that temporary wall charts can be recorded. The scribe enters information from the wall-chart discussions into the OO-CASE tool (see Fig. 18.4).

SUMMARY

JEM, JRP, and JAD are three similar techniques for achieving creative end-user participation in OO-modeling, planning, and design and combining this with the power and rigor of OO-CASE and prototyping tools. (JRP and JAD are discussed in more detail elsewhere [Martin, 1991].)

REFERENCES

IBM Overview Pamphlet, *JAD: Joint Application Development,* IBM, White Plains, NY, 1984.

JM&Co., *RAD Expert,* a methodology in hyperdocument form adaptable to different toolsets, available from James Martin and Company, Reston, VA, 1991.

Martin, James, *Information Engineering, Book II: Planning and Analysis,* Prentice Hall, Englewood Cliffs, NJ, 1990.

Martin, James, *Rapid Application Development,* Macmillan, New York, 1991.

Chapter 19

Group Facilitation Techniques

INTRODUCTION

Facilitation techniques are employed by a workshop leader for user workshop sessions, such as intensive planning sessions, joint requirements planning (JRP) workshops, and joint application design (JAD) workshops. The user workshop leader employs facilitation techniques for two primary reasons: to speed the gathering of planning, analysis, and design information and to ensure that session participants work effectively together.

User-workshop facilitation is the process of harnessing the participants' knowledge while managing their behavior to accomplish a set of predefined objectives. It is concerned with both workshop content and execution.

Benefits

The benefits of using group facilitation techniques include:

- Eliminating the effect of politics and power struggles on the decision-making process.
- Enhanced communication among session participants.
- Balanced participation to ensure true group consensus.
- Moving the session forward to ensure progress.
- Enhanced creativity.
- Resolving conflicts in planning or design issues.
- Greater commitment to session results.
- Managed expectations.

Facilitation Tools

Group facilitation techniques are practical applications of the principles and concepts of group dynamics, behavioral psychology, and communication science. The collection of techniques a facilitator acquires over time is sometimes referred as a toolkit or kit bag. A facilitator must understand both the conditions under which each technique may be applied and the mechanics involved in its use. A facilitator is always adding to his or her toolkit, trying techniques as required. Since the dynamics of each user workshop will be different, each situation will call for a unique set of techniques to facilitate progress and success.

QUESTIONING

Questions may be asked for a variety of reasons: to suggest ideas or alternatives, to test ideas, to identify and clarify issues, to synthesize information, and to analyze similarities, differences, agreements, discontinuities, paradoxes, or contradictions. Questioning techniques can provide feedback, build group consensus, and lead groups to make decisions. Questions are a powerful tool to collect information and control individual behavior and may be used to gain commitment either from individuals or the group.

There are six basic questioning techniques:

- *Tie-down.* Looks for a response to get commitment, agreement, stimulate thinking, or follow up on an issue.

- *Alternate advance.* Suggests a choice and is used to confirm a statement.

- *Porcupine or boomerang.* A questioning technique so named because a graph of the alternatives presented resembles a porcupine. A boomerang answers a question with a question. The response to the question confirms commitment.

- *Involvement.* A positive question that may address intangibles to confirm facts.

- *Discovery.* A method used to uncover additional information.

- *Leading question.* Requests that the responder confirm an idea before the questioner states it.

INFORMATION COLLECTING TECHNIQUES

Several information collection techniques may be employed during a user workshop. A facilitator may structure an exercise or activity using one or more techniques to generate ideas or solutions. These techniques speed up the collection of valuable information within a structure while maintaining a high degree of creativity.

Brainstorming

Brainstorming is a workshop activity where a group attempts to produce an uninhibited stream of ideas. Perhaps the most widely used form of idea generation, brainstorming is intended to generate as many ideas as possible. It promotes creativity when a group is bogged down or unaccustomed to new ways of doing business. One idea tends to generate another as participants spark creativity in each other. A brainstorming session encourages everyone's participation and does not evaluate the practicality of the suggestions. The activity, however, may become chaotic and the effectiveness of the exercise may be compromised. Brainstorming does not include a mechanism for converging and evaluating ideas. Techniques such as *displayed thinking* and *nominal group technique* are alternatives that provide structure and more control.

Displayed Thinking

Displayed thinking is a fast-paced, two-step process used to generate or collect ideas and subsequently organize them. Participants write down their ideas, which are then collected and categorized. The results can therefore be structured in a meaningful way for the group. Displayed thinking involves everyone and is fast and thorough (see Fig. 19.1).

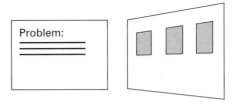

Figure 19.1   An example of displayed thinking.

The following steps are used in displayed thinking:

1. Distribute markers and Post-it™ note pads to each participant.
2. Write the issue to be considered on a white board, easel, or overhead transparency, so that all participants can see it.
3. Instruct participants to write each of their responses on a separate sheet and to raise their hands when they come up with a response. Encourage multiple responses from each participant.
4. Post each response on easel paper or white board, underlining one or two key words.
5. When all responses have been generated, ask participants to decide how to categorize them. Make header labels on stickies for the categories.
6. Ask the group to discuss each item and move the item to an appropriate category. New categories may be created and old ones deleted until a consensus is reached on an appropriate organization.
7. Prioritize the categories and (optionally) prioritize items within each category.

Nominal Group Technique (NGT)

With *nominal group technique (NGT)* people work silently to generate ideas. The facilitator collects them from each participant, and then the group discusses and prioritizes them.

This technique is an outgrowth of research that showed that people came up with more and better ideas working silently in a group than when they worked alone. Each participant contributes. NGT separates information collection from information analysis. Evaluation occurs only after all ideas have been exhausted. NGT may be used in dyads or in groups (see Fig. 19.2).

Figure 19.2   Using NGT.

The steps in using the nominal group technique are as follows:

1. Post the issue and instruct each participant (or dyad) to silently generate a list of responses.

2. Collect the responses and post or rewrite them on easel paper or white board. As each participant or dyad gives a response, instruct the others to check off duplicates from their lists.

3. After all response items have been collected, review each response by asking:
   - What does this item mean?
   - Is this item dependent upon or related to another item?
   - Categorize as appropriate.

4. Review the categories and check for clarification and sequencing.

5. Prioritize the categories for action.

Small Group Proposal

Small group proposal is a technique to divide the group into subgroups to tackle certain kinds of problems. This technique can be used for those types of problems which are better solved by small teams with a common background, interest, expertise, or focus. Once a situation has been identified where small teams are appropriate, the following steps apply:

1. Divide the user workshop team into meaningful subteams.
2. Give each subteam an assignment and monitor its progress.
3. Regroup and have each team present its ideas.
4. Lead the entire group to consensus.

Strawman Model

The *strawman model* technique harnesses creativity by providing a starting point for discussion or analysis. An additional advantage of the technique is that the model can encompass certain assumptions that may need to be supported in a solution to a problem or in answer to a question or issue.

DECISION-MAKING TECHNIQUES

Overview

Together with the facilitator, the workshop participants should choose the techniques they wish to use for decision making. This increases participants' commitment to the decision and makes the group more effective. A good group decision should have the following characteristics. It must:

- Take into account both facts and opinions and be derived from input from those parties that will be affected by it.
- Be understood by all members in the same way.
- Take principles of self-interest into consideration.
- Be carried out.
- Have few harmful consequences.

Consensus Building

A consensus is a decision that takes into account the ideas, facts, and opinions of all workshop participants. All participants must be able to live with the outcome. In other words, the participants may not be happy with the decision, but they must abide and support the decision.

Consensus is one of the essential means by which decisions are made within a group setting such as a user workshop. A facilitator's job is to ensure that a consensus decision-making environment is maintained. Every participant within a user workshop must have an equal opportunity to influence the outcome.

The four essential building blocks for achieving good, consensus-based decisions are skilled leadership, objectification, three-stage decision process, and the pyramid model.

1. *Skilled leadership.* The facilitator provides skilled leadership by using a structured agenda, by clearly defining roles and responsibilities of the team, and by participating actively but in an unbiased fashion.

2. *Objectification.* Objectification is the removal of subjective elements and personality factors from the statements made regarding issues. It may help to use Post-Its™ to divorce the idea from the person who came up with the idea.

3. *Three-stage decision process.* The three-stage decision process consists of collection, evaluation, and reaching a decision. The key to success is executing each step separately. Specific rules should be given to the participants for each step. For collection, all ideas should be of equal value and comments should not be allowed. During evaluation, all ideas should be owned by the group. Ideas may be added or deleted, but no final decision made. During the decision step, discussion should be focused and facilitated. Voting is not used for consensus-based decisions.

4. *Pyramid model.* The pyramid model for decision making works from the bottom up and may be useful when user workshop groups are large. The group is divided into subteams to reach consensus within each subteam prior to reaching consensus at the total group level.

The steps in consensus building are as follows:

1. Identify the issue to be addressed that requires group consensus. Post it.

2. Work in dyads or in subteams and instruct each subgroup to address the issue.

3. Each subgroup must agree to one response to the issue. Alternatives should be discussed and evaluated.

4. Collect the single response from each group. Open and lead the discussion to evaluate all responses.

5. Reach agreement on one response in the total group.

Decision Matrix

This technique assists participants in structuring their ideas and decisions. A *decision matrix* is a matrix of possible decisions arrayed against the criteria used to influence the decisions. A decision matrix may be created to identify criteria for decision making or criteria for evaluation. Criteria may be either qualitative or quantitative. The advantage to using a decision matrix is the focus of thought it provides, thus forcing participants to evaluate each criterion carefully.

The steps in using a decision matrix are as follows:

1. Create a matrix structure (either manually or with a spreadsheet). Identify each axis of the matrix.

2. Identify acceptable codes for each cell on the matrix (e.g., H or 5 = high priority, C = critical impact, etc.).

3. Have the group or subteams fill in the cells.

4. Review results. Calculate any applicable mathematical results.

Forced Choice-Paired Comparison

A *forced choice-paired comparison matrix* is a variant of a decision matrix, where each decision is paired with every other decision. An example is illustrated in Fig. 19.3. Here,

Which vacation spot should I choose? Rio, The Bahamas, Florida, Hawaii?

	Rio	The Bahamas	Florida	Hawaii
Rio	———	0 / 1	1 / 0	0 / 1
The Bahamas	———	———	1 / 0	0 / 1
Florida	———	———	———	0 / 1
Hawaii	———	———	———	———

Rio = 2 The Bahamas = 1 + 0 = 1 Florida = 1 + 2 = 3 Hawaii = 0

Figure 19.3 An example of a forced choice matrix.

individuals or the group must express a preference for one of the choices in each pair. It may be used for analysis, priority setting or final decision making.

The steps in using forced choice-paired comparisons are as follows:

1. State the issue as a question.
2. List all the choices for the issue.
3. Map the choices on a matrix with the choices listed both in rows and columns.
4. For each row and column pair place a "1" in the cell half you would choose and a "0" in the cell half you would not choose.
5. Add the bottom cell halves across. Add the top cell halves down. Add the two results for each choice together. The choice with the largest numbers has the highest priority.

Force Field Analysis

Force field analysis is a means of describing a decision in terms of the forces that promote the proposed action and forces that hinder it. This method provides a framework for problem solving and assists in the evaluation process for making decisions. This technique has the advantage of forcing participants to examine both positive influences (supporting forces) and negatives (impeding forces). In addition, participants are forced to examine relationships among the different components of a given solution. A factor may be supporting force in one case and an impeding force in another, depending upon the change that is proposed. This analysis is performed using a force field analysis worksheet, like that displayed in Fig. 19.4.

The steps in using force field analysis are as follows:

1. Specify the change, goal, desired state, or solution in measurable terms.
2. List all the forces working against the attainment of the goal (i.e., impeding forces).

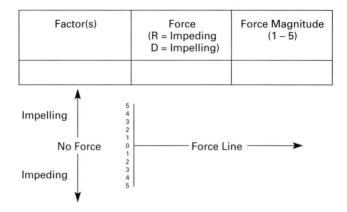

Figure 19.4   Example of a force field analysis worksheet.

3. List all the forces working for or promoting the goal (i.e., impelling forces).

4. For each impeding force list all the possible factors that could possibly reduce or eliminate the force.

5. For each impelling force list all the factors that could possibly increase that force.

6. Determine the magnitude of each force on a scale of 1 to 5 (or 1 to 10). That is, identify those forces that seem to be most important to the successful outcome of the change, process, goal, or desired state and identify those factors most likely to reduce an impeding force and increase an impelling force.

7. Plot the factors on a force line with impelling forces above the no force line and the impeding factors below.

8. Analyze the results and develop a strategy to convert impeding factors with a high magnitude or impact into impelling or supporting forces.

T-Charting

T-charting is a technique to define an issue or to evaluate the pluses and minuses of a proposed solution. The vertical bar of the T represents the issue or solution, and the pluses and minuses are arrayed on opposite sides. T-charting may also be used to evaluate workshop results. Normally, T-charting is conducted following force field analysis rules.

Impact Analysis

Impact analysis focuses participants on one aspect of decision making through an examination of the impacts of the various solutions to a given problem. This technique assists participants in seeing the end result of the decision-making process. Impact analysis reduces clutter in the decision-making process and takes into account solution implementation issues. It is normally used for complex decisions and may involve the calculation of probabilities. However, mathematical results are only part of the analysis. Qualitative factors must also be assessed.

The steps in using impact analysis are as follows:

1. Identify specific proposed solutions (either ahead of time or with participants).
2. Identify critical impact categories with the participants and post for the group to see.
3. Identify qualitative and quantitative measures to evaluate impacts within each category.
4. Lead participants to identify impacts. Alternatively, instruct small groups (or dyads) to work on specific categories, then collect round robin style.
5. Use the measures to lead participants through an evaluation of the impacts.

Voting

Voting is a quick way to reach a decision. It may require a simple majority or some larger percentage. It is not often used in user workshops where the goal is consensus. However, this technique can be extremely valuable in difficult situations where interaction among participants would result in additional problems or where time is too limited to allow full group discussion. Voting is perceived as being fair or equitable and can be carried out quickly. Voting is best used for noncritical issues or when discussion would provide few benefits.

MEETING MANAGEMENT TECHNIQUES

Meeting management techniques pace the activities of a user workshop, build commitment, enhance credibility and rapport, and manage behavior. Some of the techniques previously discussed can also be viewed as meeting management techniques.

Ice Breaker

Ice breaker techniques or activities are used to warm up the workshop team, break up the action or pace of activity, and to control the group. Typical ice breakers last no more than five or ten minutes at the beginning of each workshop day or module (e.g., morning, afternoon).

Facilitators often rely on their own creativity to construct various ice breakers. A joke may be told, a story related, or a specific interactive exercise executed. Care must be taken to choose appropriate ice breakers. Touchy-feely exercises are usually turn-offs and may work against the objective of establishing credibility and rapport.

Ice Breaker Exercise: The Nine-Dot Problem

The *nine-dot problem*, depicted in Fig. 19.5, is an ice breaker exercise whose purpose is to get participants to overcome perceived boundaries. The problem is to connect the nine dots using four continuous straight lines. A variant of the problem is to connect the dots in three lines. This variant requires big dots and long paper.

Credibility and Rapport

Techniques for establishing credibility or trust and to build rapport or commitment include *self disclosure*, *expectation*, *solicitation*, and *rules of operation* techniques. Facilitator self-

Problem: Connect the dots
with continuous straight lines.

Solution: with four lines.

Solution: with three lines.

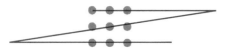

Figure 19.5   The nine-dot problem.

disclosure and honesty can create a positive atmosphere. Eliciting participant expectations can serve as an energizer. Establishing rules of operation with the group, rather than imposing the rules upon the group, serves to create an atmosphere of mutual respect and tends to open the doors for commitment building and consensus-based decision making. The "five-minute rule" is the most commonly used rule of operation in user workshops. The rules of operation is also the most effective technique to manage the meeting flow and group participation.

Behavior Management

Behavior management techniques head off or turn around actions that tend to disrupt the workshop. They are used to diffuse aggression (unite group), bring the group back to the agenda (focus group), and equalize participation (mobilize group).

LEADERSHIP STYLE

Leadership style is a pattern of behavior as perceived by the group. It is a balance between directive (autocratic) and supportive (democratic) leadership.

Effective facilitation requires the proper mix of leadership styles. A facilitator must be flexible and apply the style most appropriate to the state of team development despite the natural tendency to rely on one's primary style. Effective leadership also requires an understanding of personality types in order to determine how best to motivate user workshop participants.

There are four primary leadership styles (see Fig. 19.6):

- High directive, low supportive *(telling)*.
- High directive, high supportive *(selling)*.
- High supportive, low directive *(participating)*.
- Low supportive, low directive *(delegating)*.

Supportive Behavior	Directive Behavior	
	High	Low
High	High Supportive High Directive (developing team)	High Supportive Low Directive (effective team)
Low	Low Supportive High Directive (new team)	Low Supportive Low Directive (self-sufficient team)

Figure 19.6 An example of basic leadership styles and team development.

GUIDELINES FOR GETTING COMMITMENT

Marketing can be viewed as preparing the environment (or group) for gaining commitment or decision making. A sale is the achievement of that commitment or a decision. The following selling techniques can be used to get commitment.

Ben Franklin Close (Modified T-Chart)

The example in Fig. 19.7 shows that a modified T-chart can be used for the *Ben Franklin close*. The steps to create a Ben Franklin close are as follows:

1. On a white board or on easel paper draw a line down the middle. Write "Yes" on one side and "No" on the other. Write the decision statement at the top.
2. Collect all "Yes" factors and accentuate the positives or benefits.
3. List all the "No" factors.

Do we build the system?	
Yes	No
———— 5	———— 5
———— 3	———— 7
———— 10	
———— 5	
———— 5	
———— 2	
———— 5	
35	12

Figure 19.7 An example of a Ben Franklin close (modified T-chart).

4. Total up each side and say something like, "When we weigh the facts, the wise decision is obvious, isn't it?"

Bridging to overcome mistakes:

1. Admit the mistake. Summarize the items agreed to already. Ask a closed question.

2. Ask a lead-in question.

3. Resume presentation and discussion.

Can we live with this?

1. State the proposed solution or decision.

2. Poll each participant.

3. Tally the responses and state the final decision.

GUIDELINES

Guidelines for Strawman Models

Based on available information, construct a strawman solution or model and present it to the group. The model can be outrageous and provocative if the situation is appropriate.

1. Solicit responses to the model. Use an open-ended questioning technique to individual participants or to the group at large.

2. Responses can alternatively be generated using small groups or subteams. Responses may initially be limited to "positives" or "negatives."

3. Solicit substitutions or modifications to the model as appropriate.

Guidelines for Meeting Management

Review the agenda with the group on at least a daily basis. Inform the participants how much progress has been made. Identify potential problems and keep the project manager apprised.

- Never let participants take phone calls except in emergency situations. Use a message system and allow time at lunch and the end of the day for message follow-up.

- Always explain the purpose of each structured exercise and how it relates to the objectives of the workshop. Walk through an example of each diagramming technique.

- Vary exercises throughout the workshop to keep interest and enthusiasm levels high.

- Encourage participation, but limit rambling conversations. Be firm but polite.

- Avoid yes/no questions whenever possible. Use open-ended questions as appropriate.

- Summarize discussion often to keep on track.

- Do not permit side conversations. Physically move towards the participants engaged in side conversations. Do not embarrass nor insult them when being direct with the participants.

- Follow the rules of operation such as the "five-minute rule" for issue tabling.
- Strive to start and end on time. Be aware of body language and other nonverbal and verbal clues when participants are tired.
- Always remember to thank participants for their time and contributions.
- Pace the activities, but keep the workshop flowing, adjusting the agenda as needed.
- Observers are there to observe, not participate. Enforce the observers rules to mitigate workshop disruption.

Guidelines for Handling Conflict

To handle conflicts effectively:

- Be alert and recognize when conflict among participants is present.
- If appropriate, indicate to the group that conflict exists. Otherwise, diagnose the conflict silently.
- Identify individual needs or wants and mutually exclusive needs and wants.
- Highlight areas of agreement.
- Develop an action plan for the areas of agreement. Follow up on actions.

Guidelines for Obtaining Feedback

Feedback should be provided to:

- Clarify communication. The receiver rephrases what he or she believed was the intent of the sender's message.
- Indicate how a person's behavior and comments affect others. The receiver describes the reactions rather than evaluating them.
- Identify specifics without being judgmental and avoid generalities.
- Direct behavior within the receiver's control.

Feedback should be solicited rather than imposed. Feedback should be provided at the earliest opportunity after statements have been made or a behavior occurs.

Guidelines for Listening

Keys to developing good listening skills include training yourself to:

- Assume the subject is important and interesting.
- Accept the speaker's delivery or style of presentation and remain calm, even if you disagree.
- Acknowledge the speaker physically and verbally and remain alert and focused.
- Pay attention to the feelings or emotions behind the detailed facts.
- Acknowledge your feelings or reactions prior to speaking.
- Ask for a restatement if you did not hear clearly the first time and ask for clarification if the message is complex.

MEETING DANGERS

To ensure the success of meeting management, avoid three chief dangers: aggression, getting off focus, and squashing. The following guidelines may help.

Unite Group

When participants become overly aggressive with each other (or with the facilitator), the *unite group* technique must be used:

- Let off steam: Allow the venting of frustration and anger.
- Do not take sides: Focus on being impartial.
- Bring in others: Directly question neutral players.
- Stick to facts: Avoid focusing on personal opinions.

The temperature of the situation should be lowered quickly.

Focus Group

When participants go off on a tangent topic or start to lose focus (usually because they are tired), use the *focus group* technique:

- Stay alert: Avoid drifting. Rely on your listening skills.
- Steer the group: Monitor the group, keeping a hand on the wheel with feedback.
- Test comprehension: Use questioning to check the group's understanding of the discussion.
- Paraphrase: Check back with the group by rephrasing feedback comments.

Refer to the agenda mentally, as well as verbally, to keep the group from getting off the point.

Mobilize Group

When a participant becomes overbearing, dominating the conversation or criticizing others' ideas outright, mobilize the group quickly before intervention becomes ineffective. Use the following techniques:

- Protect the weak: Do not allow participants to squash one another. Keep criticisms in check directly.
- Check around the group: Bring all participants into the discussion.
- Record suggestions: Have the scribe document the new suggestions to balance the overbearing participant's comments.
- Build up ideas: Provide feedback to ensure meaningful results.

Be aware of the dysfunctional behavior that could potentially inhibit effective group communication and interaction. Handling difficult behavior quickly is critical to effective meeting management.

Chapter 20

User Workshop Techniques

INTRODUCTION

User workshops bring together all the key people in a project, both from the business community (users) and the I.S. community, at a session facilitated by a professional moderator. This avoids serial interviewing and the potential for misinterpreting important information. The user workshop technique can be used for any situation which requires something more than a simple meeting or round table discussion.

There are many benefits of employing the user workshop technique, both qualitative and quantitative. Providing a structured environment where key stakeholders can openly discuss important topics results in improved decision making, ownership, and consensus, improved deliverable quality, more effective project teams, and reduced time and cost.

ROOM FACILITIES AND LAYOUT

The room should be large enough to contain the number of participants at a U-shaped table. Adequate walking room should be provided along with separate areas for a refreshment table, an observer's table, and breakout areas. Neither the participants nor the facilitators should feel cramped or closed in. Lighting should be variable for use with slides, overheads, and/or PC-screen image projection. Figure 20.1 shows the basic layout of a user workshop room. User workshops require a partnership of management, end users, and I.S. professionals.

Equipment

Appropriate equipment is needed in the rooms in which user workshops are conducted. Traditional items of equipment include:

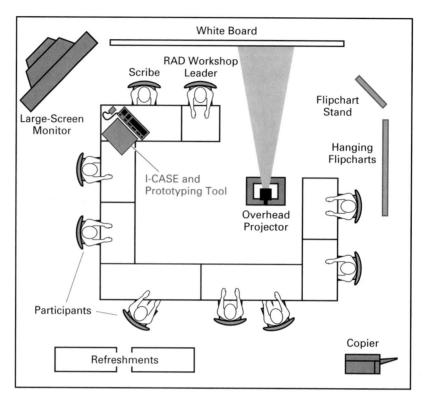

Figure 20.1   A sample layout of a workshop room.

- One or more large white boards with dry erasable colored markers (printable white boards are preferred, if available).
- A kit for building diagrams and specially shaped blank magnets for modeling exercises.
- At least two flip charts with extra pads of paper, colored markers, and enough wall space to hang and display multiple flip-chart sheets. Lined or graph-paper sheets make it easier to write legibly. (More flip charts may be required if the group works in subteams during the workshop.)
- Stickers for structured exercises. Stickers come in multiple colors, and large and small sizes. A stapler, scissors, paper clips, and related office equipment are usually included in the kit bag.

Computer items include:

- PC with word processing, graphics, and software development tools. A large screen monitor or projector device helps all participants view the screens clearly and easily.
- Printer to provide participants with models, screen designs, and supporting materials.

Electronic items include:

- Access to a copier (if not provided in the room) to produce copies of information created.
- Slide projector if the user workshop facilitator or executive owner has prepared slides.

- Videotape player and monitor if videotapes are to be used.
- Overhead projector and screen, transparency markers, prepared and blank transparencies. An extra projector bulb and enough electrical cords are helpful.
- Tape recorders should not be used. There should be no telephone in the room. An instant camera may be useful for photographing white boards and flip charts.

Amenities include:

- Separate refreshment table.
- Name card badges or tent cards for participants. Writing materials and markers may also be provided.

LOCATION AND DURATION

Location

User workshops are best held off-site, away from the normal work location of the business and system participants. Most hotels and conference centers provide facilities outfitted with the equipment listed above. Many enterprises have created JAD rooms, group decisions support centers, or facilitated workrooms which can also be used. If held on-site, take care to keep the participants from checking back with their desk to avoid group disintegration.

Duration

User workshops vary in their duration. Four-day or three-day sessions tend to be the most frequently used—allowing participants to have at least one day in the office or for traveling from a remote location. Complex system applications or applications which cut across multiple business organizations (often where politics are of concern) may require multiple user workshop sessions.

Specific Hours

Each workshop day should be typical business or working hours, such as 8:00 A.M. to 5:00 or 6:00 P.M. Some sessions go late into the night, but common sense should be used when making these scheduling decisions. User workshops are intense events and participants' motivation and attitude has to be managed properly to maximize their usefulness.

Full and Half-day Sessions

Full-day sessions are always preferred, but some cultures and availability constraints may dictate half-day sessions. One advantage to half-day sessions is that the facilitator has time to prepare for the next session. Another advantage is that deliverables can be reviewed, modified, or produced by the scribe(s) and/or I.S. team. With half-day sessions, however, employing meeting management and behavior control facilitation techniques is essential. Group effectiveness needs to be maintained.

Marathon Sessions

Great results can be achieved in marathon sessions. However, experience shows that participants (and the facilitator) are not at their best the following morning. Client culture, level of participants, and type of user workshop will also affect the length of the workshop day.

USER WORKSHOP STRUCTURE

User workshops involve more than the time spent in the workshop sessions. Enough preparation time must be allocated before the workshop sessions to maximize their success. After the workshop sessions, finalize the documentation and prepare for the next step. The following three-stage model can be applied to any type of user workshop.

Preworkshop Activities

Preworkshop activities include:

- Planning and project scoping.
- Research and background analysis (may include interviewing).
- Executive owner identification and kick-off.
- Participant selection, briefing, and training.
- Logistical arrangements.
- Selecting and preparing workshop exercises.

The facilitator will normally require two to five days of preparation time for each three-day session. Initial user-design sessions may require one to four days of preworkshop activity per five days of scheduled workshop time. Subsequent user-design workshops may require one to two days of additional preparation.

User Workshop Format

Each agenda will differ. However, all user workshops will have an opening module, a work module, and a closure module. The work module itself may be composed of sub-modules or structured activities depending on the topics to be addressed.

Postworkshop Follow-up

For proper closure and to build ownership of the workshop results, follow-up should include:

- Deliverable finalization and validation checking.
- Prototype extension (for design user workshops).
- Expectation management.
- Open issue resolution.
- Executive commitment and decision to proceed.

Depending on particular responsibilities and assignments for deliverable construction and presentation, allow one to three days of facilitator time for follow-up.

PARTICIPANT SELECTION AND PARTICIPATION

Selection

Participation should be full-time during the workshop, whether full-day or half-day sessions. Participants from the business community (users) should be selected based on their value and ability to contribute to the creation of workshop deliverables. The actual workshop should not be held until all the key participants are available. This may often require the executive owner to clear calendars/schedules to get the most knowledgeable users in the workshop.

Visiting participants may be allowed to attend the workshop as silent observers or as subject area experts. Subject experts may be part-time and only scheduled for certain workshop modules or activities.

Preparation

Participants should be briefed prior to attending a user workshop. Formal briefing meetings may be held either in conjunction with kick-off meetings or separately. Any available materials pertinent to the project such as a list of objectives or supporting documents should be provided. Any existing models may also be distributed.

Participants should also be trained in all diagramming conventions which will be used during the user workshops. Example walk-throughs may be required depending on their familiarity with system development concepts.

Typically, only one half-day briefing session is required. Individual participants may be given assignments, if required for the workshop's success. Roles and responsibilities, objectives, and user workshop concepts should also be introduced. A formal briefing meeting packet is typically distributed to all participants.

Kick-Off Meeting

Holding a formal *kick-off* meeting is one key to successful use of the user workshop technique. Whether or not the kick-off meeting is merged with a briefing and participant training meeting, the meeting should be conducted several business days prior to the actual workshop (unless logistics and cost constraints are prohibitive).

The executive owner should open the meeting and then turn it over to the facilitator. The expectations of all participants, both users and systems professionals, must be established. Kick-off meetings should last no more than two hours. When combined with a participant briefing session, allow one full day.

Materials Assembly

A formal briefing book may be prepared and distributed to all participants at the briefing or kick-off sessions. Subsequent documentation or useful model extracts may also be prepared and distributed to participants prior to each subsequent workshop. Special packages should be assembled for the executive owner. Materials required to conduct user workshops, such as overheads, scripts, exercise walk-throughs, and/or strawman models, are the responsibility of the facilitator and scribe. These materials require preparation, reproduction, and possibly distribution time.

USER WORKSHOP AGENDA MODEL

Opening Module

Start-up items should be limited to 15 to 20 minutes. These include:

- Welcome remarks from project manager(s) and/or facilitator.
- Housekeeping items (rest room locations, message system, smoking areas, etc.).
- Schedule review.
- Executive owner kick-off speech (optional, may be performed during preworkshop activities).

Prepare to Work

The steps for work preparation include:

- Introduction to the user workshop technique and overview of the project's purpose and approach. Allow no more than 30 minutes.
- Review agenda and make changes as required (helps to establish rapport with group).
- Review and set rules of operation.
- Review the scope and objectives (i.e., check expectations) when the sessions start in the morning, resume after lunch, and close each day.
- Execute ice-breaker or start-up exercise (optional).

Work Module

The work module agenda is customized based on the type of user workshop, the particular objectives, and special client needs. Moderators should use facilitation techniques to manage the work items performed during this module. Keep to the schedule, but remain flexible for modifications.

Closure Module

At the end of each workshop day, allow a minimum of 15 minutes to accomplish the following:

- Review agenda.
- Summarize progress and modify as appropriate.
- Elicit participant feedback and check expectations.
- Always thank participants for their time and contribution.

At the end of each user workshop, allow at least one hour to bring closure:

- Always review objectives, goals, and agenda items.
- Summarize results to build up ownership.
- As an option, have the executive owner give a five-minute closing wrap-up.
- Review open issues and check assignments.
- Prepare action plan.
- Evaluation and closure. (By current convention, a one or two page user-workshop evaluation form is distributed to all participants. Their comments are invaluable for improving the workshop technique.)

RULES OF OPERATION AND HANDLING OPEN ISSUES

Rules of Operation

This technique works best when the participants assist in determining how they would like to operate during the workshop. Normally the facilitator lists one or two suggested rules and then solicits additional rules. (It is often useful to ask the participants to think of all the bad meetings they have attended.) Then, participants consider what useful guidelines they would like employed to manage the meeting better. Some common rules are:

- Everyone participates equally.
- One conversation at a time.
- Critique ideas—avoid criticizing people.
- Five-minute rule for issue tabling.
- Observers contribute only when requested by a participant via a facilitator or during a participant's break.
- Keep on time.

Handling Open Issues

User workshops should be well paced and move quickly. When an issue cannot be resolved within a reasonable time frame, it should be boarded for future resolution.

If there is a five-minute rule of operation, the facilitator and other participants need to invoke it when the discussion becomes bogged down or when an argument threatens progress. Issues can be either within or outside the scope of the workshop's objectives or project's scope. All issues should be written down for subsequent action.

- State the issue in a clear, concise statement or question. Check with participants for proper wording.
- Put the issue on a white board or flip chart. Keep an issues list posted around the room.
- For each issue list: issue number, issue statement, person assigned to resolve issue, date for resolution, suggested solution (if appropriate).

- Examine the issues list daily and at the close of the workshop.
- Rank issues for executive owner resolution or for a later workshop.

DOCUMENTATION CONVENTIONS

Deliverables are driven by the methodology, workshop objectives, and particular client needs. Typical documentation from user workshops should include:

- List of objectives (project and/or system).
- System/application scope including preliminary (and final) list of system functionality.
- Tangible and intangible benefits, return on investment.
- Business model diagrams.
- User interface designs.
- Interface to other systems.
- Open issues list.
- Implementation priorities, action plans, and target dates.
- Executive summary.

Typically user workshops generate one to two days of documentation time for each eight to ten hour workshop day. Allow enough resources during and after the workshop for completing the documentation.

CRITICAL SUCCESS FACTORS

Critical factors affecting the success of the user workshop technique include:

- Executive commitment (resources, time, and people).
- Skilled, experienced facilitator or session moderator.
- Reasonable scope.
- The appropriate selection of full-time, committed participants.
- Business focus.
- Methodology concepts, principles, and conventions are followed.
- Easily understandable diagramming conventions.
- Proper environment and room layout/facilities/tools.

GUIDELINES

Contentious political issues may be known before the workshop. An executive owner at a suitably high level should deal with these issues by meeting with the parties in question, seeking consensus on the issues, or motivating the parties to achieve consensus during the workshop.

Teams often require a period of incubation in order to become comfortable and work well together. If adequate preparation time is not provided and/or if a briefing meeting was not conducted, workshop progress may be slow the first day or so. Some teams will require a team building exercise to get them together. (Refer to Chapter 19 on facilitation techniques for sample exercises.)

Some tips for user workshops include:

- Based on their expertise, various participants may provide temporary leadership or team up with the facilitator. Use sparingly when practical.

- Project managers and executive sponsors should not be facilitators for user workshops in which they have a stake in the outcome. Unbiased facilitation and impartiality will be compromised.

- To improve clarity, avoid technical jargon.

- Plan for anticipated cultural changes.

Chapter 21

Interviewing Techniques

INTRODUCTION

This section describes structured interviewing techniques: the participants' roles, the information and preparation required, running the interviews, and analyzing and confirming the results. System development places great emphasis on user involvement. Thus any task that gathers information about user requirements is vital to a project's success.

Interviewing is a major technique for gathering facts and opinions from business stakeholders about the enterprise, its future developments, its work environment, business activities, and information requirements. The objectives of interviewing are to:

- Gather perceptions of important business facts from individuals whose responsibilities are within the project scope.
- Improve the insight into and commitment to the project and its results from people involved.
- Provide a common basis for further analysis.

Interviewing users individually is more flexible, less "make or break," than user workshops and more likely to cover the whole project scope. Each user gives a small amount of time, which is easier to schedule, and additional interviews can be arranged as omissions are discovered. The keys to successful interviewing are good preparation and immediate documentation and feedback.

The specific interview topics, the people to be interviewed, and the analysis of the results depends upon whether the interview is for a planning project or an analysis project. Interviewing a representative selection of users may involve significant effort.

In addition to structured interviewing, another technique for gathering information is to hold a user workshop (see Chapters 18 and 20). Both techniques may be used in the same project and may be supplemented by questionnaires.

TRAINING FOR STRUCTURED INTERVIEWING

Two interviewers are selected from the project team for each interview: one leading the discussion, another taking notes and controlling the topic list. If team members have not conducted structured interviews, spend a day holding an interview training session. Practice interviewing a user team member and analyzing the results. This activity reminds the interviewers of what to look for and helps them develop a common style for handling interviews and recording results.

An experienced interviewer leads the questions while the trainee team members record the interview. At the end of the interview, select one trainee recorder to analyze the interview. Ask the other recorders to add anything else that they recorded. Finally, ask the interviewee to comment on analysis errors and omissions and any activities omitted in the interview. Use the trial interview to improve the questioning, the interview analysis form, and other aspects of the technique.

PREPARATION FOR INTERVIEWS

Interview Topics

The topic selection depends upon the project's objectives, the tasks to be performed, and the interviewees' level of responsibility. Top management interviews usually focus on business direction, objectives, and priorities. Middle management interviews also touch on those topics, but emphasize functions, information requirements, performance measures, and the current system support. Topics for user managers emphasize business concepts and behavior.

Selecting Interviewees

Use the organization chart, project scope, recommendations of the project sponsor, and knowledge of user team members. The expertise and responsibilities of the selected interviewees must cover the project scope.

The interviewers must study all available material on the business activities for which the interviewee is responsible and on their relationship to the project scope. They also must know the interviewee's role, function, and experience. Knowing both the interviewee's attitude to his or her job and the length of time in the job is also helpful.

Depending on the level of the planning task, the interviewees should be either the most senior executives of the respective business units or those people who report to top management. Sometimes a few additional managers of the next-lower level may be selected. The interviewees may also include some senior employees. Interview a key manager for each business function in the project scope.

The interviewees for an analysis project must have enough experience to understand the processes. If a key manager lacks this experience, consider including an experienced subordinate in the interview.

If several users or organizational units perform similar functions, select at least two interviewees in order to identify variations.

Arranging Interviews

Interviews must be scheduled at an early stage and should be grouped by organizational unit or business function. If possible, work in a top-down order beginning with senior managers. Topics can be clarified further in interviews at the next level.

After the project has been announced and the project sponsor has made a statement of support, the interviewees should be briefed about the interviews' purpose and content and introduced to the interviewers. Ask that examples of relevant documents be available.

Interviewers should be introduced to senior management when the interview is scheduled, stating the purpose of the interview and presenting a short list of topics. Introduce interviewers to middle management and user managers by sending the detailed topic list before the interview. A collective briefing session may also be useful to gain attention and commitment.

Ideally, interviews are held at a location free from interruption, such as a project interview room. Interviewing in the morning is best, because the interview can then be analyzed on the same day. For each interview, allow an hour and a half for senior management and three hours for lower-level management.

Each interviewer must allow one day for each interview, including preparation, documentation, and analysis. Each interview thus requires two work days from the project team.

CONDUCTING THE INTERVIEW

The interview itself consists of three parts: introduction, discussion of prepared topics, and final arrangements.

Introduction

At the beginning, make personal introductions, check the interviewee's expectations concerning the interview, and remind the interviewee of the project's objectives and scope. Emphasize that you need to know the goal of the interviewee's activities and not the details of how they are carried out.

- Explain the purpose of the interview to the person interviewed.
- If necessary, modify the topics list or questionnaire.
- Discuss whether certain confidential information should be documented.
- Explain the roles of the interviewers.
- Agree to the time frame for the interview.

Discussion of Prepared Interview Topics

The interview leader tries to go through the list of topics or the questionnaire in as much order as possible. The note taker controls this process while documenting the answers according to the standard, as well as leaving room for digressions, which sometimes reveal important information. Note emphatic statements verbatim. Both interviewers must make note of issues that should be raised later in the interview.

Document the interview using a standard form called an interview analysis worksheet, supplemented by more conventional minutes of the interview, if necessary. The standard documentation form is needed as a common framework for subsequent analysis of all interview results. It eases the final check for completeness to the answers on the interview topics. It may also serve as a summary for feedback to the interviewee.

During the interview, identify the interviewee's principal responsibilities, and then ask to work through each responsibility in some logical sequence, such as time. Use open-ended questions and keep the conversation flowing. Note issues to return to when the flow stops or when it is appropriate to the discussion.

Final Arrangements

When concluding the interview, check that the scope of responsibilities has been covered and ask any additional questions. Ask about any impending changes to the business. Agree on the sample or background documents that will be provided. Thank the interviewee and arrange for the interviewee to review and comment on the interview analysis, either in writing or another interview.

ANALYZING THE INTERVIEW

A clear set of interview results is a sound basis for starting the analytical tasks. Analyze the notes as soon as possible after the interview, while the material is still fresh.

Evaluation of the Interview Results

The two interviewers discuss the results, considering their notes and individual perceptions of answers given during the interview. If necessary, additional issues needing clarification can be raised at a subsequent feedback session.

Obtaining Interviewee Confirmation

Send the analysis to the interviewee with a note that includes thanks, an explanation of any technical terms used (e.g., critical success factor), and a request for comments. Include diagrams only if the interviewee is already familiar with the diagramming notation.

The interviewee should be allowed to modify and confirm the documented results. Depending on the completeness of the results, an additional, brief interview may be needed. Encourage the interviewee to write comments on the analysis manuscript and to keep a copy to help you both discuss any additional questions. Follow up on any unreturned analyses or outstanding documentation.

GOOD PRACTICE

Most interviews go smoothly. It is possible to deal with many of the following issues by consideration of the interviewee's viewpoint, and by good organization.

Keep to the Interview Schedule

The most common problem is the interviews running overtime. At the start of the interview, confirm the expected duration. About ten minutes before the end of the interview, determine how much more material is to be covered. If extra time is needed, ask whether extending the interview would be convenient now or later.

Respect Confidentiality

Interviews in a business analysis project are not normally confidential within the business. Ask the interviewee at the start to indicate any subject that should not be used outside the team, or any comments that should not be attributed to particular people. If any team member is not employed by the business directly, assure the interviewee of commercial confidentiality.

Avoid Information Engineering Jargon

Ask "What must go right for the work to go well?" instead of "What is your critical success factor?" Talk about activities instead of processes or functions, and about concepts or information instead of object types.

Set Expectations

Some interviewees may have optimistic expectations about the delivery of a new information system. Make it clear that the immediate focus of the project is requirements (both existing and potential), and that system design will follow.

Other interviewees are so frustrated with current system problems that they will complain during the interview. Ask whether the problems are known to the people who service the system, and, if they are not, offer to pass on that information. Then return to the main subject.

Keep to the Interview Scope

The interviewee may have responsibilities outside the project scope. When the discussion touches on these areas, determine the relationship between the responsibilities and the project scope before gently guiding the interview back to the main theme.

Interview the Appropriate Person

Occasionally you will find that you are talking to the wrong person—the job is not what it appears to be or someone else knows the details. Apologize, but waste no more of anyone's time. Identify the right person to contact and leave.

Ensure that the Documenter Can Keep Pace

Make sure that the documenter does not fall behind. If the interviewee is going too fast, say "Let's be sure we are getting all this," or "Have I understood this right?" and slow the interview down.

Evoke Responses

Perhaps the most difficult situation is when the interviewee does not respond or cooperate. The interviewer must quickly discover what is wrong; it may be something concerning the interviewee's job, or it may be a problem with service from the I.S. organization. To stimulate the discussion, try asking an open-ended question like "What is the biggest problem you have in doing your job?"

Abandon False Starts

Be prepared to abandon any incorrect initial assumptions, if they are causing problems, and ask again for the interviewee's own view of the job.

Lines of Questioning

Many approaches to questioning are possible, and questions can be worded in many different ways. The interviewer must try alternatives until the interviewee provides adequate responses.

FORMAT OF INTERVIEWS

The analyst must adapt the interviews to the enterprise's environment. The interviews can be either formal or informal discussions, individual or collective briefings, or formal meetings with minutes or standard-form documentation.

INTERACTING WITH TOP MANAGEMENT

- Always act respectfully to top management.
- Their time is more important than your time; act that way. If you have to wait for them, wait and don't complain.
- Prepare, prepare, prepare. Know what you want; know what you are going to say; get to the point; be brief; accomplish your mission; leave. Remember, your half-hour appointment may suddenly become five minutes. Executives have bosses too, and when they are called, they go.
- Never see top management without a good reason. Overexposure can be worse than underexposure.
- Never criticize other members of top management, and do not be critical of company personnel, at any level. Enemies are never useful.

- Always assume that there are no secrets. Everything you say or write will sooner or later be known by everyone.

- Try to determine the personal objectives and motivations of the executive. You must work through these. Study and understand your own objectives and motivations.

- Some points take a long time and many meetings or memoranda to communicate. Think in the long term as well as the short term. Have a plan, a strategy, and a program.

- Learn from your exposure to top management and adapt your approach.

- Anticipate even casual contacts (e.g., lunch, the tennis club, the corridor) with top management. What might you be asked? What might you say?

- Don't agree with top management if it conflicts with what you think is right, but be sure you are right.

TYPICAL QUESTIONS FOR ANALYSIS INTERVIEWS

- Tell me about the main kinds of activity in your area.

- What happens when you finish this activity? What happens then? What is the usual outcome? What can go wrong? What do you do if it goes wrong?

- Can this activity happen in any other way? (This highlights alternative mechanisms.)

- What triggers the activity? What do you do at (give some particular time, such as end of month)? What else do you do?

- What are you sent? What is done with it?

- What information do you need to enable you to do the activity? What do you do with the information? What details are relevant?

- What decisions have to be made (to make things happen)? What information do you need to help you make the decision?

- Are you interested in information about . . . ?

- What exactly is a . . . ? How do you tell them apart?

- Can a . . . have more than one . . . ? (For example, can an Order have more than one Item?)

- Would you want to keep the same information about an earlier one or a later one? (For example, a job applicant or a pensioner as compared with an employee.)

- Do you want to retain information about it? For how long? Why?

- How many are there? How often does it happen? Where are they to be found/does it happen?

- Can it have several of these features? (For example, can a machine operative have many skills?)

- Do you always have to have one of these with it? (For example, Invoices for a Delivery.)

- If a (consultant) can (work on) many (projects), and a (project) can (have) many (consultants), do you need to keep any details about how one is allocated to the other?

Chapter 22

Domain Experts*

INTRODUCTION

Domain experts apply their practical experience by formulating concepts to solve real-world problems. Frequently, they are the end users of an application, since most I.S. development responds to an internal or market requirement. To ensure the success of a project, domain experts should be business or technical experts senior to those just using the delivered application, for example, team leaders, managers, and other senior staff.

The practical viewpoint of domain experts is important, because many aspects of a problem are not captured in manuals or current systems. Those who take part in a certain business or technical process presumably understand the complex concepts, relationships, and rules that apply. For example, in the development of a bond-trading application for a Wall Street firm, bond traders served as domain experts. They indicated that they often grouped securities and sold them as a block to regular clients, which increased the traders' sales. While the technique of packaging of securities was an important aspect of the problem to the traders, it was not documented in the detailed requirements assembled by the development staff. Using traders as domain experts uncovered this requirement.

Where requirements *are* well documented, guidance from a domain expert is still essential. Since the aircraft-maintenance process has an enormous number of manuals, procedures, and diagrams, an analyst would find it difficult to learn enough about maintenance without the assistance of engineers. Here, the domain expert acts as a filter for the necessary information. After a brief analysis, the CDM Authoring System was able to produce a comprehensive model. (The project is detailed below.)

Finding and retaining good domain experts can be difficult. Individuals with a deep understanding of a process are in demand. Such people are usually willing to participate

---

*This chapter was contributed by J. Bradford Kain of Quoin, Inc., Boston, MA.

Clinical process projects.

In 1989, the Information Management Centre of the U.K. National Health Service started a number of development projects. The goal was introducing object-oriented models into the development of clinical applications. Project teams were set up in several clinical specialties including: diabetes (Eurodiabeta/AIM and St. Thomas's Hospital), pediatrics (Hospital for Sick Children), and nephrology (Dulwich Hospital). The work was part of an effort to develop a conceptual model for clinical care known as the Common Basic Specification [IMC, 1992]. The projects continued for over two and half years under different sponsors. A Smalltalk/V and Gemstone prototype for a tissue-typing application was completed in 1992 [Fowler, 1993].

The projects built object-oriented models of each clinical specialty, using Ptech object and event diagrams in the analysis. The key to the effort was the participation of doctors and nurses on each specialty project. The clinicians were senior staff members at the hospitals including registrars and consultants. The staff had no background in OO analysis or I.S., but they were trained during the project. The clinicians quickly became familiar with the approach and worked daily with the analysts to develop the diagrams and supporting documentation. The resulting models were validated through a peer review led by the IMC. In addition, the models produced by the Eurodiabeta project were validated in a wide clinical audience that included health care organizations from the European Union.

in development work—if their time and experience are used effectively. Management provides the more common obstacle, which is particularly true when the domain experts and developers are in separate cost centers. The development group should make access to domain experts a priority.

When dealing with complex problems, working with a range of domain experts can be useful. Having numerous domain experts will increase the variety of experiences and perspectives that can contribute to effective problem solving. However, since analysis is usually done best in small working groups, some limits apply. Relying on a single domain expert may limit the analysis. For example in the Clinical Process Projects, a few clinicians worked directly with the analysts while a larger group of clinicians reviewed the models. This worked well and gave the project teams some useful exposure with their colleagues. In contrast, at Bank of Boston a single person represented all the loan officers. This senior loan officer proved very capable at eliciting requirements from the other staff and creating a consensus on the needed functions for MarketManager. However, the disadvantage of using a representative domain expert was the gulf created between the users and I.S. staff.

Using domain experts is one way to gain support for development projects. For example domain experts were the driving force behind the MarketManager application at Bank of Boston and the development of a payroll application at Chrysler [Fowler, 1994b]. In each of these cases, the client was another unit within the same company. Here, the users were not only involved in the specification, they also paid for the development of their applications.

MarketManager.

Bank of Boston, a large retail and commercial bank, needed a desktop application to help its loan officers manage the sales process for commercial banking services, such as loans, cash-management accounts, and lines of credit. In addition, the bank wanted the sales staff to make use of the information collected by the other loan officers. MarketManager was intended to manage customer and service information for each loan officer and provide a repository for the entire sales staff.

The project began in early 1993 with a team consisting of a project manager and developer, four additional developers, and a consultant who acted as a design mentor. The basic architecture was MS Windows that clients developed in C++ and Borland Object Windows Library with MS SQL Server running under OS/2. The team did an informal analysis and design, producing simple object diagrams from the initial analysis. The application design was done at the code level through header file and code reviews.

A senior loan officer was selected to represent the business side. This officer conferred regularly with the other loan officers, who would be the new application's users. This individual managed the collection of requirements and reviews done with the development staff.

MarketManager was completed in approximately seven months, just one month over the original schedule. The application is extremely successful and is now used nationally by more than 200 loan officers.

DEVELOPERS AS DOMAIN EXPERTS

Project teams often avoid using domain experts. Finding and managing the right people is a challenge. However, the real reason is usually that the team has built a number of applications and feels that it already knows the users' requirements. In this case, domain experts might be asked to validate a list of functional requirements produced by the project team, but they have no substantial role in development. All knowledge about the problem is supplied by the development team.

The notion of developers as domain experts should be rejected. Analysts or programmers might have much experience in a particular field, but their perspective is necessarily that of building systems. While this background might include some of the knowledge that a true domain expert might provide, it is fundamentally different. Analysts, designers, and programmers focus on how to provide functionality within the limits of available technology. Developers are skilled at using specification and implementation tools. Conversely, domain experts focus both on the problem and on the concepts, relationships, and rules that define it. I.S. is just a means to support the process of doing their job. This difference in perspectives can lead to misunderstanding—even antagonism. For example, at a medical informatics conference several years ago, a developer claimed, "there are no patients, only patient records." This remark did not reassure the clinicians present that the systems being built would improve their work.

As I.S. supports more complex problems, it will be necessary to rely more on domain experts. Increasing complexity will mean that developers cannot fulfill both roles. Few individuals are capable enough to be a good air traffic controller and a talented C++ programmer or a skilled bond trader and an expert in distributed systems. More complex applications will require the participation of domain experts. Complexity will force the partition of responsibilities for understanding a problem and knowing how to implement systems based on that understanding.

An example of a highly complex system that required domain expert involvement is the ten-year effort by the Federal Aviation Administration to replace the aging legacy systems that comprise the air-traffic control system in the U.S. The Advanced Automation System (AAS) project is currently under development by an IBM software engineering team of more than 500 developers.

> What IBM devised, according to one controller, was a perfect electronic facsimile of the paper flight strip. The database contained all the information that can be listed on a flight strip—about 140 separate units of information, or fields, enough to keep the controller tapping on a keyboard all day. "The controller should be paying more attention to watching aircraft than to inputting information," says Mitch Coleman, a controller . . . brought in a year ago to help streamline the system. Controllers suggested a version of the electronic flight strips with a more manageable 35 fields. The . . . National Air Traffic Controllers Association has cited the lack of controllers' full-time involvement early in AAS development as a reason for these snags [Stix, 1994].

Using developers as domain experts can reduce the support for changes to the process. Developers focus on I.S. systems, which limits their ability to conceive of changes. Furthermore, any changes suggested by developers to the underlying process would probably not be taken seriously because of their bias toward I.S. By contrast, domain experts naturally tend to explore improvements in the process as part of the analysis. In short, developers think in terms of the existing systems, while domain experts think in terms of the process itself.

Domain experts will likely improve a process without being constrained by implementation. For example, the analysis for the CDM Authoring System resulted in several changes in the semantics of the underlying model. Although the CDM was then at version five and stable, the analysis process raised several questions. This led the engineer involved to refine some of the concepts in the CDM. The changes were captured in the object diagrams and became part of the implemented application [ADT, 1990]. This improvement to the model might not have happened without the domain expert, because there was no obvious reason to question the requirements specification.

When domain experts are not involved, the delivered system is often just the old system reimplemented in new technology. An example of this is the bond-trading application mentioned above. The project was successful in that it delivered a robust application on schedule and within its budget. The developers considered the application successful, because it used new technology (C++ and Motif) and had improved connectivity with the back-office systems. However these criteria only addressed the application with no consideration to any improvement in the underlying business process.

Content Data Model (CDM) authoring system.

The U.S. Air Force IMIS (Integrated Maintenance Information Systems) project was started to build sophisticated applications for the maintenance of military aircraft and other systems. An initial part of this large project was a context-sensitive, multimedia database for maintenance data. In 1990 an authoring system for this component was developed by a team of contractors led by SAIC. The authoring system consisted of database, presentation, and navigator/editor subsystems. The system was implemented using the object-oriented database Ontos, C++, Motif, and Smalltalk-80.

The U.S. Air Force had developed a conceptual model of maintenance information known as the Content Data Model (CDM). The CDM was a detailed model expressed in SGML and was used as a starting point for the analysis. Ptech object diagrams were developed by a two person team of an analyst and engineer. The model was extremely complex, containing more than 200 types. However, it was completed in one month's work, because the domain expert had a deep understanding of the CDM. This model was then used to generate the C++ for the database and integrated with the other subsystems. The authoring system was completed in 1991 and was a successful part of the IMIS program. The IMIS project was completed in 1993.

Another example of how the poor use of domain experts can sabotage a project involves the development of a real estate portfolio application at a commercial bank. This project was the company's first use of object technology. During development, the domain experts were not consulted after the initial requirements were gathered. Although the project was eventually completed, no one was interested in using it. Had domain experts been included in the development, they would have gained a sense of ownership of the application and more readily adopted it. Few projects fail when they are supported by both the I.S. and business or technical staff.

However, developers should serve as domain experts in two situations. First, the problem itself is software engineering, such as programming environments or CASE tools. Second, applications that support new technology might not yet have any domain experts.

STRUCTURE VERSUS BEHAVIOR

The project team should consider how to interact effectively with domain experts. With a given domain expert, a key issue is which to specify first—the structure of a problem or its behavior. Some methods prescribe specifying the object diagrams first, followed by a state-transition or other behavioral diagram. In practice, a project team can start analysis with either kind of representation. Choosing a structural or behavioral approach depends on the domain experts involved. Individuals use different means to understand and relate knowledge about a problem. Selecting the optimal approach for representing the problem will affect the amount and quality of information gained in analysis.

Some domain experts think in terms of concepts and relationships and express themselves by defining terms and giving examples. Classifying the examples into a hierarchy comes naturally. This category of domain expert handles abstractions well—quickly comprehending the OO constructs of types, associations, and subtype relations. Object diagrams are the most useful representation in this case, since almost all OO methods support some kind of object diagram. The engineer on the CDM Authoring System project fit this description. He was very capable at developing an object model, because his understanding of the problem was very concept based. Similarly, the doctors on the Clinical Process Projects—experienced with classifying diseases or defining standard data sets—were able to develop object diagrams. In general, senior domain experts tend to have the experience to work at this level of description.

The second category of domain expert thinks in terms of the process. These individuals will express their knowledge of a problem by relating use cases [Jacobson, 1992]. The constructs of event types, cause-and-effect rules, and conditions are most meaningful to these individuals. A representation that captures the control aspects of the problem is appropriate here. Event diagrams [Martin and Odell, 1992], state-transition diagrams [Booch, 1994], or structured text [Jacobson, 1992] are common techniques for representing the dynamics of a problem.

Two Clinical Process Projects made extensive use of event diagrams. Both the diabetes and pediatrics specialty projects produced about the same number of object and event diagrams. Event diagrams were created first and were used to drive the subsequent development of object diagrams. The clinicians on these projects were registrars who spent a great deal of time working with patients at their hospitals. The doctors and nurses were focused on the daily practice of medicine, while the clinicians on the other teams were more involved in research. Overall, the teams found event diagrams were good for communicating with the review groups.

NOTATION

Since domain experts differ in their tolerance for complex notations, choosing the right notation is important. The notation should be clear to the domain expert, yet powerful enough to capture the meaning, or *semantics,* of the problem. This often requires striking a balance between using a method's complete set of notation elements and a simplified set. The analyst should not consider implementation characteristics such as accessibility and reference semantics. Private versus public accessibility and pointer versus direct references are germane to detailed design and implementation. However, the domain expert does not have to work at this level of detail. Object diagrams should use only the basic constructs of object types, association, specialization, and composition; attributes and operations can be omitted. (Figure 22.1 shows an object diagram which omits attributes, operations, and other constructs for the sake of simplicity.) However, these characteristics of each type would still have to be discussed with the domain expert.

In the Clinical Process Projects, for example, less complex diagrams were needed because a wide audience reviewed the models. The project teams met this requirement in

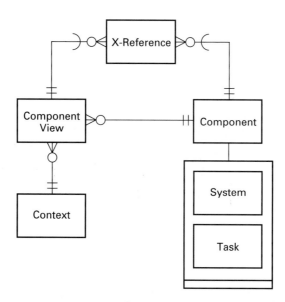

Figure 22.1　An object diagram can be used just to express object types and
their relationships. Attributes, operations, and other constructs have been omitted for the sake of simplicity.

several ways. First, a high-level diagram described the dynamics of the problem using a
simple object-flow diagram. This style of diagram uses activities and products to describe
the basic functional decomposition of a problem. The clinicians reviewing the models
found this representation accessible. Second, some diagrams were simplified, reducing
clutter by eliminating graphic constructs. This step has been particularly important on
other projects where a detailed notation such as Booch was used.

The MarketManager project was more constrained. Since the domain experts were
uncomfortable with any kind of notation, traditional requirements documents had to be
used. This tactic was adequate on this project because of the strong user interest, but in
other situations it could have significant drawbacks. Typically, conventional analysis
begins with collecting the users' requirements through interviews or source documents.
The analyst then produces a list of functions that the application should support. These
lists can be vague and usually include a mix of problem and implementation requirements. For example, "support multiple accounts" (i.e., for each loan officer) and "use a
graphical user interface" were in the same list of requirements for the MarketManager
application. The functional requirements were seen only as an important starting point for
the real analysis activity of producing data-flow or entity-relationship diagrams. Thus the
role for the domain experts was limited to an initial representation of what the application
should do. Frequently, the domain expert was not involved past this first phase. Because
of their interest and financial support, the domain experts for the MarketManager project
stayed involved. The use of text descriptions or requirements lists should be used with
care.

ANALYSIS PROCESS

The project team can use a variety of techniques to gather analysis information from domain experts:

- Written information.
- Interviews.
- Comments on draft models.
- Analysis sessions.
- Prototyping sessions.

The choice of approach depends on the preference of the domain experts. A project with many domain experts might use more than one technique.

In the first technique, the application is described solely by some form of text, such as written problem statements or other documents. This approach is demanding for both the project team and domain experts, because a typical problem statement requires so much effort to develop and interpret. Because of this, some domain experts will resist the task. Additionally, resulting problem statements are often vague or poorly written. The project team must then decipher the description. Existing applications or manuals can provide a source of knowledge about a problem. However, the project team should not limit its understanding of the problem to existing software. Relying too much on an existing application could reduce the scope for improvement in the new implementation. An advantage of this approach is that the analysis process is fully documented and could be audited.

Interviewing domain experts is the second technique. Although it requires more preparation than using text, interviews develop an understanding of the problem more effectively. They are particularly useful when the domain experts have limited time to take part in development.

These interviews should have a definite structure. The analysts should prepare by identifying specific issues through reviews of available documents, existing systems, or procedures. The resulting list of specific questions should elicit the key problem concepts. For example, the analyst should ask "what kinds of products interest you" and "what characteristics of products matter to you" instead of an open-ended "tell me about products." This focused list will help avoid a tendency of domain experts—to describe in one session everything that is important about a problem. This tendency can lead to an overload of information and overlooked requirements. Limiting interviews to one-hour sessions is also a good tactic.

Domain experts can also provide comments on draft models, though they will need training to read the notation. If the domain experts are committed strongly enough, this can be effective. In the Clinical Process Projects, the clinicians reviewing the Eurodiabeta models became familiar with the notation after a two-hour introduction. At that point, the reviewers understood enough of the diagrams' meaning to ask specific questions of the project team. After several reviews, the clinicians were quite adept at understanding the models.

Using domain experts to review models is a more productive approach than interviews. The domain experts can spend as much time as needed in reviewing the diagrams.

A formal author/reader cycle such as the Structured Analysis and Design Technique (SADT) is often useful [Marca, 1988].

The participation of domain experts in the analysis sessions is the fourth technique. This approach requires greater commitment from the domain experts but can be the most effective of the different modes of interaction.

Building consensus within a group of domain experts is ultimately the responsibility of the analyst. This can be difficult, because each domain expert brings a different perspective to the problem. In the Clinical Process Projects, the respective views of the clinical specialties was a constant concern. The teams were either upset about the lack of consensus on some issue or tried to ignore the issue. For each issue, however, the conflicts in the model were resolved in a way that accommodated all viewpoints.

A simple example involved the use of generalization to support differing concepts of who or what was the recipient of care. After some discussion, the type Object of Care was specified as the supertype of Patient, Group, Population, and Organ. This new supertype allowed the different specialties to focus on their own issues. Figure 22.2 shows the basic structure of this solution. While the use of generalization is a simple example, more sophisticated techniques include application views [Fowler, 1994a] or meta-models.

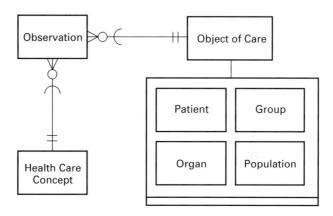

Figure 22.2   The use of generalization for consensus.

ANALYSIS GUIDELINES

Analysts should follow several guidelines when working directly with domain experts. In interviews and analysis sessions, analysts should focus on understanding the problem. The analyst should make an effort to express the semantics of the problem in everyday language at the expense of technical accuracy. A good analyst develops a set of phrases that use common terms but correspond to the object-model constructs. Technical jargon should be avoided. Furthermore, the domain experts should not consider implementation issues.

Extensive use of examples should be made. Whenever a domain expert suggests a type, identify several instances to make it more tangible. Types without identifiable instances are immediately suspect. To describe the behavior, examples can take the form of a scenario or event trace. In the diabetes specialty project, numerous scenarios were developed that showed one particular invocation of the process. These event traces were text descriptions of different encounters between clinicians and objects of care.

Analysts should respect the domain expert's knowledge and not enforce their own preconceptions. One good tactic is letting the domain expert name the types. If a domain expert suggests a vague or even obtuse name, the analyst can gently suggest an alternative. This can be done by looking at some of the instances and restating the question "what would all these things (i.e., objects) be called?" If the domain expert insists on the first name, accept it.

An example of a debate over naming the concept of a Channel comes from the MarketManager project. To the analysts, Channel seemed a natural term for the association between Customer and Product. The domain experts thought of a channel as just any path *to* a customer. Although the domain experts used the association between Customer and Product, the particular name was new. The domain experts needed some time to accept this idea, but it eventually became an important part of the object model. Figure 22.3 depicts the Channel relationship recommended by the analyst.

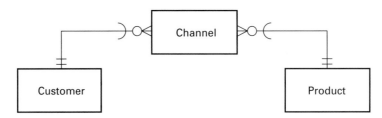

Figure 22.3   Relationships can introduce new concepts, such as, the relationship type between Customer and Product could also be represented as the concept of a Channel.

CONCLUSION

The inclusion of domain experts in the analysis process has been a critical success factor for many projects. As I.S. applications become more complex and users demand applications that better serve their business or technical process, domain experts will become increasingly more important. Developers need to understand the role of domain experts and how to make the best use of their practical understanding of the problem at hand.

REFERENCES

ADT (Ptech Inc.), *CDM Process Description.* Associative Design Technology, Report Prepared for SAIC, 1990.

Booch, Grady, *Object-Oriented Analysis and Design with Applications* (2nd ed.), Benjamin/Cummings, Redwood City, CA, 1994.

Fowler, Martin, "Application Views: Another Technique in the Analysis and Design Armoury," *Journal of Object-Oriented Programming,* 7:1, 1994, pp. 59–66 [1994a].

Fowler, Martin, "Experiences in Three OO Projects," *Proceedings of Object Development Experiences,* London, SIGS Publications, 1994 [1994b].

Fowler, Martin, T. Cairns, and M. Thursz, "Prototyping a Health Care Enterprise Model with an ODBMS," *Proceedings of Object-Oriented Data Management,* Brunel University, U.K., 1993.

Gold, G., Personal communication during the Eurodiabeta Stage 2 review, 1990.

Goldberg, A., and D. Robson, *Smalltalk-80, The Language,* Addison-Wesley, Reading, MA, 1989.

IMC, *Common Basic Specification Generic Model,* National Health Service, Information Management Centre, Report, 1992.

Jacobson, I., M. Christerson, P. Jonsson, and G. Övergaard, *Object-Oriented Software Engineering: A Use Case Driven Approach,* Addison-Wesley, Wokingham, England, 1992.

Lippman, S. B., *C++ Primer,* Addison-Wesley, Reading, MA, 1991.

Marca, D. A., and C. L. MacGowan, *SADT: Structured Analysis and Design Technique,* McGraw-Hill, NY, 1988.

Martin, James, and James J. Odell, *Object-Oriented Analysis and Design,* Prentice Hall, Englewood Cliffs, NJ, 1992.

Rumbaugh, J., M. Blaha, W. Premerlani, F. Eddy, and W. Lorensen, *Object-Oriented Modeling and Design,* Prentice Hall, Englewood Cliffs, NJ, 1991.

Stix, Gary, "Aging Airways," *Scientific American,* 270:5, 1994, pp. 96–104.

Chapter 23

Prototyping

INTRODUCTION

Prototyping is a technique for building a quick and (if need be) rough version of a desired system or parts of that system. The prototype illustrates the system to users and designers and also allows them to see flaws and invent ways to improve it. As a communications vehicle, it allows people who require the system to review the way users will interact with it. Prototyping is far more effective at this than reviewing paper specifications.

- A prototype is used where the functions and detailed design of a system are not yet fully understood.
- The prototype is used to explore and solidify the functions and design.

If a picture is worth a thousand words, a prototype is worth ten thousand words. But a prototype is fundamentally different from a paper description, because it is real and can be manipulated, adjusted, and modified. Would-be users get a feel for what their system will be like. Its flaws are visible and tangible rather than buried in boring text. These advantages make a world of difference to system development. If the right tools are used, prototypes can also be created much more quickly than written specifications.

Prototyping in a RAD lifecycle is fundamentally different from prototyping in some lifecycles, because the prototype must be part of the evolving system. Sometimes, prototypes are built with a tool different from the final development tool and are eventually thrown away. In RAD lifecycles, they should be built with the final development tool, so that they pass directly from the design to the construction phase.

Without exception, prototyping ought to be used in the development of all interactive systems. When end users seriously review a prototype, they almost always change something. This implies that, had they not reviewed the prototype, a system would have been built that was less than adequate. Prototyping does much to solve the problem of inadequate communication between designers and users.

The term prototyping suggests an analogy with engineering, where prototypes are used extensively. However, fundamental differences exist between the prototyping of software and that of machines. In engineering, a machine prototype usually takes longer to build and is much more expensive than the ultimate product. The ultimate product may come from a mass-production line, and the prototype is needed for testing the product before the production line is built. In software, there is no manufacturing production line. Prototyping is practical only if the prototype can be built quickly and cheaply. Unlike production engineering, a software prototype is not a full-scale version of the eventual system. It is usually an incomplete or simplified version that has the essential functions of the working system—but not the scale or performance. It lacks such features as security, auditability, and recoverability.

Prototyping can be employed in various phases of system building. During system design, prototyping is used extensively to develop screens, dialogs, and reports—checking that the functions of a system conform to what the users really want. Often, prototyping reveals the need to add or enhance functions. When used in joint application design (JAD) sessions, discussions become more tangible.

Prototyping can also be used in the analysis phase. Partial prototypes can help to check the system's desirability before funds are committed and can be used to stimulate user ideas or compare alternative ideas. They can act as a catalyst to stimulate creative thinking about the system.

Prototyping should be part of the construction phase, because an iterative lifecycle with a steadily evolving prototype should be used for construction. During *construction,* a tool that permits the prototype to evolve into the final working system should be used. Some construction methodologies are based on prototyping/code-generation tools. This approach to construction is powerful, highly recommended, and will probably become the predominant means of building systems.

With powerful code generators, distinguishing between prototyping and construction is difficult. During the construction phase, a developer designs and generates the code for processing a transaction. The users examine the transactions and may suggest modifications. The developer adjusts it until the users agree that it is what they want. The resulting code is part of the final system. The developers then work on a different transaction. The final system is thus a prototype consisting of smaller prototypes.

USES OF PROTOTYPING

Prototyping is more valuable with some systems than with others. It is less valuable with batch processing than with interactive systems. Most batch systems, however, produce many reports, and these can be prototyped quickly with a report generator. Online data entry may also be prototyped. Prototyping is of limited use in some logic-intensive systems although, in these cases, partial prototypes may verify the human interaction. Users may check portions of the logic to see whether it behaves as they expect.

Prototyping is particularly valuable where users are unsure of exactly what they want. For example, an end-user dialog should be tried out with the users to see if it can be improved. Screens and reports should be checked with management to see if they can be made more useful or easy to use. Because the functions are subtle, users understand them better than the analysts do. The prototype, then, can act as a catalyst to elicit alternative ideas that need to be explored. It is a form of experimentation that can achieve better business practices.

TOOLS FOR PROTOTYPING

Software prototyping became practical when fourth-generation languages and code generators emerged. With them, a working model of a system could be built quickly. As these tools improved, building and changing aspects of systems could be done very quickly. Thus a designer, skilled with a prototyping tool, could react to users' suggestions and show them modifications—almost immediately in some cases.

Prototyping tools have screen painters, for example, with which a specimen screen can be created quickly. Screens can be linked to form dialogs. Reports can be generated on the fly. Database structures can be created and modified very quickly. Some tools can generate screens and reports during a meeting and display them with a large-screen monitor. This high-speed interaction encourages creative dialog with the intended users.

Expert system shells or OO-CASE tools like OMW from IntelliCorp have been used for prototyping because changes to logic can be made easily. Since the rules specifying the logic are independent of each other, business functionality can easily evolve without concern for details such as process control logic. Also these shells sometimes provide highly interactive development environments. This includes support for incremental rule compilation, which allows program changes to be made and retested—all within subsecond response times.

Fourth-generation languages and code generators are designed to create fully working systems rather than mere prototypes. Most of them, however, have facilities for creating prototypes quickly. When such tools are used, the prototype can evolve into the final working system. This is essential for RAD. Some tools sold as prototyping tools are far from having such capability.

Commitment to a fourth-generation language or code generator for full-scale development is a much broader decision than the choice of a tool for prototyping. A major criterion is machine efficiency. Can the tool handle enough transaction volume, large enough databases, and enough simultaneous users?

For RAD, the prototyping tool must be an integral part of an I-CASE toolset that designs, generates, and optimizes the final code. The objective of prototyping is to adapt the prototype to the users' requirements as quickly and flexibly as possible.

> From the viewpoint of prototyping, tool selection should be based upon its ease and speed for users and how easily the prototype can be modified and fine-tuned.

BOX 23.1   Characteristics of the prototyping tool.

The prototyping tool should:

- Be an integrated part of the I-CASE toolset and use a repository.
- Be interactive and fast and easy to use.
- Facilitate quick screen design and report design so that it can be used in a JAD session.
- Support desirable dialog structures, such as scroll bars, mouse operation, action bar, drop-down menus, and so on.
- Encourage stepwise refinement.
- Facilitate quick building of prototypes that can evolve into the final system if the platform and efficiency is acceptable.
- Support installation standards, such as IBM's Systems Application Architecture (SAA).
- Provide facilities for testing.
- Give good machine performance (with an optimizing compiler).

So that the prototype can become the final system, the tools should be able to:

- Support the database structure of the final system.
- Support appropriate networking access.
- Handle a suitably large number of users, large databases, and high-traffic volumes.
- Link legacy code.
- Provide utilities for extracting data from files or databases and loading them into the prototype database, or online access to other files or databases.

The system generated by the tool should have these features:

- Backup and recovery facilities.
- Security and auditability.

PARTIAL-SYSTEM PROTOTYPING

Some prototyping efforts create a version of a complete application. Some tackle only one facet of an application. Partial-system prototyping has proven particularly valuable on some systems. Sometimes project managers have not considered this approach, because they assume that a complete system prototype is needed. Partial-system prototyping can be easier, and there is no excuse for not using it.

Partial prototypes are of a variety of different forms:

- *Dialog prototype.* The prototype reveals the intended user interaction. This is probably the most common form of partial prototyping. It allows the users to see what they will be receiving, play with it, suggest omissions, generally react to the dialog, and finally sign off on its design. Many software products have been used as dialog simulators.

The design of the dialog greatly affects the usability and users' perception of the system. Many systems are partial failures because of poor user dialogs. Many analysts and programmers are not trained in what constitutes a psychologically effective dialog. They often create dialogs that are muddled, that are not clean, and that lay traps for the unwary. It helps to build a prototype dialog that can be tested, criticized, and improved before final implementation.

- *Data entry.* One group of users may perform data entry. The data-entry subsystem may be prototyped, adjusted independently, and linked to an existing system. Data-entry prototyping may be done to check the speed and accuracy of the data entry. Validity and integrity checks may be tested.

  Some systems have been split into a *front end* and a *back office.* The front end is interactive. The back office consists of multiple batch updating runs. The front end may be prototyped independently of the back office.

- *Reporting system.* The reports provided to users may be tried out on them before full system implementation. They may be either batch or online. Often many adjustments are made in the reporting subsystem. Report generators may be used.

- *Data system.* A prototype database may be implemented with a small number of records. Users and analysts interact with it, generating reports or displaying information that might be useful to them. This interaction often results in requests for different types of data, new fields, or different ways of organizing the data.

  With some prototyping tools, users or analysts can build their own files, manipulate them and display information from them. Such tools are used to explore how the users will employ information and what should be in the database.

- *Calculations and logic.* Sometimes the logic or the calculations of an application are complex. Actuaries, engineers, investment analysts, or other such users may use a language such as Lotus 1-2-3, Javelin, or Focus to build examples of the computations they need. These may then be incorporated into large systems and perhaps linked to other applications. The users may employ their calculation prototypes to check the accuracy of the results.

- *Application package.* An application package may be tried out with a small group of users to determine whether it is satisfactory. At this time the need for various modifications may become clear. These are tried out before the package is linked to other applications or put into volume use.

- *Concept.* Sometimes the concept of an application is in question. It needs testing and refining before too much money is spent on building the system. The testing may be done with a quick-to-implement data management system. Standard data-entry screens and standard report formats may be used so that the concepts may be tested and refined without too much work. Later, application-specific reports or screens may be built.

WHO WILL BUILD THE PROTOTYPE?

Many prototypes are built by one person who is fast and competent with the prototyping tool. This person is often an I.S. professional but could be an end user. The prototype may be built by a two-person team, one end user, and one I.S. professional. It is generally not appropriate to have large teams working on a prototype. Two people should be the maximum for most situations. The prototype builder should be skilled and fast with the prototyping tools, able to modify the prototype quickly while interacting with the users. Initial prototypes are often built while a JAD workshop is in progress.

BUILDING THE PROTOTYPE

Good prototyping tools ought to enforce cleanly structured design—but many do not. A prototype should never be an excuse for casual work in which structured design is abandoned. Where this rule is not followed, a prototype that grows complex, written in languages such as Focus, Ramis, Nomad, and so on becomes difficult to modify or convert to a working system. The prototypers should first build something simple. This starts a debate early in the evolution that may flush out misconceptions. The initial prototype is successively enhanced. With complex systems, the functionality should be built first and then the human factoring should be polished. OO-CASE tools, such as IntelliCorp's OMW, are particularly useful here.

Prototyping should be a way to introduce end users' creativity into the design process. To achieve this, the reviewers should be motivated appropriately, to excite them about their role in developing the system and encourage them to think inventively about how the system could improve their procedures. Brainstorming sessions may be used for discussing the potentials of the prototyped system.

WHO WILL REVIEW THE PROTOTYPE?

As part of the planning process, the reviewers should be selected. The main reviewers are end users who will employ the eventual system. Some of the reviewers should be very knowledgeable about the application procedures.

A potential problem in prototyping occurs when reviewers do not spend the time or have the enthusiasm to do a thorough creative review. It is necessary to select reviewers with sufficient commitment who are determined that the system will meet the needs of their area as effectively as possible.

In its final stages, the prototype may also be reviewed by:

- Technical staff who will build the final system.
- The human factoring expert, who may operate a usability laboratory.
- Management.
- The executive owner (executive sponsor).
- Possibly external reviewers such as customers.
- Possibly an external consultant.

STEP-BY-STEP OR CONTINUOUS EVOLUTION?

Prototypes can evolve either continuously or in a succession of discrete releases. The left side of Fig. 23.1 shows discrete step-by-step evolution; the right side shows continuous evolution. Step-by-step evolution progresses from one planned prototype to another. Each prototype is reviewed until the final system is achieved.

Continuous evolution progresses with a sequence of modifications, continuously adjusting the prototype until the target is reached. This requires intelligent, understanding

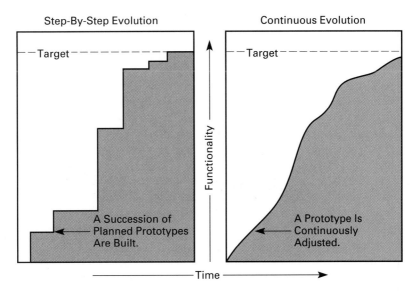

Figure 23.1 Prototyping can evolve in a succession of discrete releases, or continuous evolution can occur. The RAD lifecycle normally employs continuous evolution, which is faster and more satisfactory but requires the users who work with the prototype to be available at any time.

end users working as a team, with the developer(s) reviewing the evolution. These reviewers should be available every day.

With step-by-step prototyping, a list of desirable enhancements is created for each prototype, and a target date is set for when the next version will be available for review. In one highly complex financial system, six prototypes were built over a period of six months. The prototypes steadily converged to the required system, and the last prototype became the working system.

With continuous evolution, the reviewers work regularly with the prototype builders, examining each enhancement when it is working. Continuous evolution tends to be used when there is a closely knit relationship between the builders and users. Sometimes in continuous evolution it is necessary to suspend the interaction while the builders step back, rethink, and re-architect their system.

> Continuous evolution is generally the fastest form of iterative evolution and is recommended for the RAD lifecycle, but it needs to be well managed so that there is no inflation of requirements.
>
> When the feedback loop is too short, it may destabilize the project.

Selected users should be available whenever needed to validate or change the evolving prototype.

When demonstrating a prototype, the analyst may create small files of made-up data to illustrate what the system will do. In other cases, made-up data are not good enough. The users need to update real data or explore complex databases in order to experience what the proposed system will do for them. If real data are required, the users may be given prototypes connected to a *live* data system or may be given data that have been *extracted* from a live data system. The latter is generally safer and more flexible.

If the users do not update the data, they may be given report generators or other facilities that use data in a live database but that cannot modify the data. Often, however, the users want to manipulate or update the data. They should then be given extracted data to use, not live data.

When prototyping decision-support systems, the users ask for information relevant to the decisions. The analyst must find out where such data exist, capture them, and reconstruct them in the data management system of the prototyping tool. Sometimes they exist on batch files, sometimes in corporate databases; sometimes they can be obtained from external sources.

FROM PROTOTYPE TO WORKING SYSTEM

When the prototype is regarded as complete, there may still be much work to do in building the operational system. System features missing from the prototype should be listed and may include:

- Features for recovery and restart.
- Security features.
- Features for auditability.
- Features for ease of maintenance.
- Machine efficiency.
- Facilities for having multiple users.
- Facilities for high-volume usage with adequate response times.
- Larger database facilities.
- Networking facilities.
- Operation on a different machine.
- Documentation.

In some cases, the prototype becomes the working system; in other cases, it needs rearchitecting before it is usable. In other cases, an entirely different system is built in a different language.

> In the RAD lifecycle, the prototype should evolve into a solid final system with a code generator that gives good machine performance.

EXPECTATION MANAGEMENT

A danger of prototyping is that the users, motivated to be excited about the prototype so that they make constructive suggestions, acquire expectations that cannot be fulfilled. They may expect a working system similar to the prototype to be available almost immediately and cannot understand why they have to wait so long. The expectations of the users should be managed correctly.

PROTOTYPES AND TRAINING

The prototype may be a useful training vehicle. People who will eventually use the system can work with the prototype for training and practice so that they are ready for the system when it eventually arrives.

PILOTS

The term *pilot* is also used for a system not yet fully operational.

> A *pilot system* is a preliminary system in which the functions and design are thought to be understood. It is implemented in a limited form so that experience can be gained with it before the full system is cut over.

A pilot system is a fully working system deployed at first with only a small number of users, a small number of terminals, or a small database. When the pilot system is found satisfactory, the number of users may be increased and the database expanded. For example, if the final system will have 500 terminals, a pilot system might be initially operated with 5. If the system will be installed in 1000 dealerships, it might first be operated in 10. As a result of this pilot operation, modifications are usually made before the system is fully deployed. A prototype is used where the functions and detailed design of a system are not yet fully understood. The prototype is used to explore and solidify the functions and design.

Sometimes a powerful prototyping tool enables its users to build a great deal of functionality into the prototypes as they progress through multiple iterations. The system designers may decide to cut down on some of the functions when the first pilot system is built. They may do this because some functions have limited value or may duplicate other functions or because some functions would worsen machine performance or increase implementation difficulty. Enthusiastic prototyping sometimes results in overengineering. This should be avoided in the expensive implementation phase.

Figure 23.2 shows a typical progression of a complex system for which the functions were only partially understood at the beginning. There are six prototypes of growing functionality. After the sixth prototype, the system is rearchitected and some functions

Chapter 24

Timebox Development

INTRODUCTION

Creative people in many walks of life have deadlines. A magazine writer, television producer, or seminar developer creates material for a certain date. Whatever else happens, this person must not fail to meet the deadline.

To meet the deadline, he may allow the contents to slip. There may be items he wants to include but cannot do so in time. The producer of a television documentary or a seminar broadcast by satellite may say "I wish I could have interviewed so-and-so" or "I wish we had better footage on this." However, there is no time to obtain the extra interview or footage. The deadline is absolute. The show must go on the air.

There is much similarity between television production and the building of information systems. Television production employs a planning phase, design and story boarding, then construction. A difference is that most I.S. development does not have a firm deadline. Sometimes developers claim for a year that the system is "95 percent complete."

Timebox Methodologies—A Variant of RAD

Timebox methodologies apply a similar constraint to the building of I.S. applications. There is a deadline that is immovable, but the functionality of the system may slip. The system must work, carrying out its basic functions, but the fancier refinements may have to be postponed for a later release.

The first 75 percent of a system's functionality can be created relatively quickly with a code generator—especially if reusable structures are employed. The next 15 percent may take as long to create as the first 75 percent. The system may go through much refinement before the last 10 percent is completed. Many of the features in the last 10 percent could be dropped or postponed for a subsequent release. This will give users a chance to work with a system and change their minds about what they want its detailed functions to be.

In RAD methodologies, the core of a system is built quickly and the refinements are then added. New transactions and new screens are added. The system grows like an onion, with successive layers of refinements being implemented. This refinement makes the setting of a firm deadline practical. The timebox lifecycle allows refinements to be made until the deadline is close, and by then a working system *must* be delivered.

The Need for a 90-Day Lifecycle

The term *timebox* was first used at DuPont. In moving to a highly automated manufacturing environment in the Textile Fibers Division, it was necessary to create complex application software quickly. If applications took two or three years to build, this would prevent the rapid evolution of an integrated manufacturing environment. DuPont decided that many of their applications, operating on a DEC VAX, should be built in 90 days. Later this became 120 days, largely because of the time needed to reorganize the end-user activities.

The move to the automated factory environment was a step into the unknown. There were bound to be midcourse corrections. There would probably be applications that did not work well. To find out that an application was misconceived after two or three years would be a disaster. If the problem were found in 90 days or so, then rapid evolution was possible. Having a system of limited functionality working quickly is better than waiting two years for a comprehensive one.

If an application were built in 90 days and put into operation, the need would soon arise to have a second edition of that application. Rather than making the first version rich in functionality, it is better to get a basic version of it working, learn from the experience of operating with it, and then design a second edition. This implies that the first version must be built quickly so that it can be changed and added to quickly.

These constraints apply to most applications. The faster the rate of change and the greater the competitive pressures, the more important they are. In the DuPont Textile Fibers Division, building applications fast was considered essential for competitive success.

A timebox methodology has been used with great success in DuPont. DuPont developers stress that the methodology works well for them and is highly practical. It has resulted in automation being introduced more rapidly and effectively. DuPont quotes large costs savings from the methodology. Variations of timebox techniques have since been used in many other corporations.

Creeping Functionality

One of the dangers of prototyping methodologies or iterative development is that the functions of a system can grow in an uncontrolled fashion. Because users or developers often keep adding functionality, the design does not converge quickly into a usable system. This is sometimes referred to as *creeping functionality*. The more powerful the prototyping tools, the more the developers are encouraged to experiment, to add functions, or to overengineer the system. This can become expensive and can prevent a system from being delivered on time.

Perhaps the best way to combat creeping functionality is to place a rigid limit on the time permitted to produce a working system. Within a defined timebox, a working system must be built.

THE TIMEBOX

Many organizations apply the timebox approach only during the construction phase. Here a team is given a timebox within which a system must be constructed. Before the timebox, the functions and design framework of the system are defined. After the timebox, the system is evaluated and a quick decision is made whether to put it into production. Figure 24.1 illustrates this process. However, system development projects are usually divided into subprojects, each of which is timeboxed. Here, each subproject is given a timebox in which its analysis, design, and construction—as a whole—will be constructed.

The timebox is not extendable. A system must be produced within the time allocated. The system's functionality may be trimmed back in order to complete it within the timebox. The system produced by the end of the timebox must be a system that the team intends to implement.

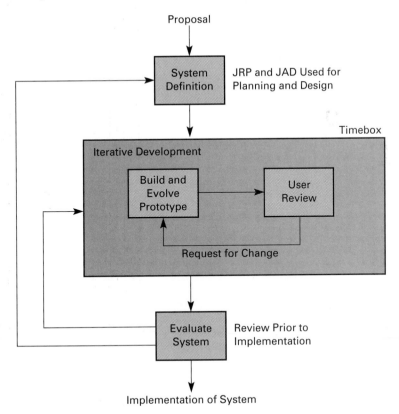

Figure 24.1　Timebox methodology.

Within the timebox, continuous iterative development is done, as shown in Fig. 24.2, with end users and I.S. developers working closely together. This team is under pressure to produce a working system by the end of the timebox.

The timebox methodology, like RAD in general, depends upon having a powerful, easy-to-use development tool that generates executable code. It must be easy for developers to build and evolve prototypes with this tool. The tool must be capable of generating systems with good machine efficiency so that the prototype evolves into the final working system. The development techniques employed by the tool should be sufficiently user-friendly that users can easily participate in the development process. An I-CASE toolset will speed up the development process, check the design, and generate code from the design.

A typical length for the timebox is 60 days. For a subproject, the typical timebox is 120 days. The team working within this period should not be large. From one to five people are appropriate. The timebox team is told that on Day 60 (or 120), they will decide how much (if any) of a working system can be delivered.

For those portions of the system that are not completed, a new timebox can be established to produce subsequent versions of the system with greater functionality. After users work with the system, the requirements for subsequent versions can often change.

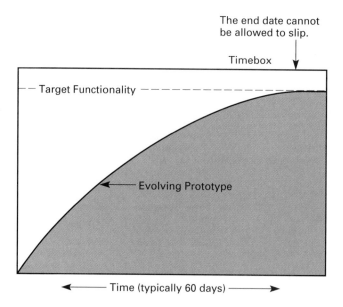

Figure 24.2   During the 60-day timebox, continuous evolution is used. Continuous evolution progresses with a sequence of modifications, continuously adjusting the prototype until the target is reached. This requires an intelligent, understanding team of end users working with the developers reviewing the evolution. The team must produce a fully working system before the end of the timebox.

Quality: Not Limited with RAD

Limiting functionality in order to meet the deadline does *not* mean limiting quality. Pride in their work is essential for teams, and no self-respecting team would put out work of less than the highest quality.

The delivered system must be as bug-free as possible, excellently human-factored, and must provide a set of functions that will do useful work when the system is put into production. I-CASE tools make it much easier to achieve technical quality. Functionality can vary substantially without reducing the usability of the system.

The analogy with television production applies. A self-respecting team making a television program will not put out work of less than excellent technical quality. However the amount of detail and polishing of the subject matter can vary over a wide range. The same applies to system development. One could go on adjusting and refining for months, but it is necessary to call a halt in order to meet the deadline.

The timebox approach uses tools that enable the core functionality to be built relatively quickly and then successively refined. The refinement continues until a certain date and then the system must be handed over to the review board.

Many software and electronic products today have excessive functionality, which bewilders the users. The return on development investment goes down when unwanted or marginal functions are added. A television-VCR-laserdisk system can have up to five hand-held controllers, each with 30 to 40 buttons. Since only about six buttons are used on most of the controllers, the other buttons are a nuisance because they can easily be pressed incorrectly in the dark. Some users put tape over the control buttons that are not used. The timebox approach to development helps control the technician's enthusiasm for adding functions that have little value and which may make the product more difficult to learn and use.

The Team Does the Estimating

A timebox approach, or team development in general, does not work well if there is pressure to meet an impossible deadline. Setting of the deadline, or selection of functions to be accomplished in the timebox, should be done by the timebox team (or systems analyst) before the timebox starts. The team, where possible, should be familiar with the tools and techniques and confident about what they can accomplish with them.

When an enterprise is just starting to use the timebox approach, as least one member of the team should be experienced with the tools. Other members should be well trained and prepared to accept mentoring from their skilled colleagues. Estimating and establishing what can be accomplished in the timebox should be done *by the timebox team.*

After the Timebox

After the timebox, implementation should proceed quickly—resulting in a full system if it is small, or a pilot system if it is large. New functions may be requested as implementation or usage proceeds. These may give rise to a further iteration of the entire lifecycle. A brief summary report may be written after implementation, documenting experience that may help with subsequent implementations.

Multiple Timeboxes

Some systems are too complex to finish in one timebox and are split into subsystems. Each subsystem performs a function in its own right which can be demonstrated and is small enough so that a small team can build it in one timebox of 60-120 days. As team members gain experience with the prototyping and code-generation tools, they become more adept at estimating what they can accomplish in a given timebox.

The separate subsystems all use the same data model. The system should be split into subsystems using an I-CASE tool. The I-CASE tool, with its repository, coordinates the interfaces among the separately developed subsystems.

TIMEBOX PARTICIPANTS

The Review Board

The development is controlled by a group called the review board. The review board signs off on the system design prior to entering the timebox. When the system is complete at the end of the timebox, it is evaluated by the review board. The review board (or individual members of that group) examine the prototype periodically as it evolves in the timebox. They should monitor progress to make sure that the prototype is on track, making helpful suggestions where they can.

When evaluation is done after the timebox, it is hoped that the system can be approved for immediate implementation. In some cases minor modifications may be needed. For unavoidable reasons the requirements may have changed slightly. If the modifications can be made with another iteration of the development, the review board permits the timebox to be re-entered, setting a deadline for the change being completed. If the system proves unsuitable for implementation, another system definition workshop is held to determine what the problem is and how to modify the system definition.

The review board should be relatively small. An end-user leader and an I.S. leader, both decision makers, should be represented on it. The review board *should* include:

- The executive owner or a representative—the person who provides the money and has the final vote on resolving major end-user issues.
- A user who will be primarily responsible for the system's use.
- An I.S. professional responsible for application quality—a professional who ensures that the system conforms to the data and process models in the repository.

The review board *may* include or call upon:

- Other users.
- A technical support representative.
- An auditor, if the system is sensitive from the auditors' point of view (many are not).

In some cases, the review board is the same as the team that participated in the JRP workshop.

The User Coordinator

The user coordinator is the lead end user in the construction activity and may be a member of the construction assistance team. He also serves on the review board. He represents the end-user community and may involve other end users, where appropriate, to help review the prototypes and the evolving system. He arranges for user documentation and training.

In some cases the user coordinator spends all of his time on the project. In other cases he has another job to do and commits to spending a portion of his time on the project.

The Timebox Team

The timebox team should be strongly motivated to succeed. Management should create pressures for the timebox team to complete the system within the timebox. They are told that success or failures is judged by whether they create—by the deadline—a system that is, in fact, implemented. They are told that most timebox efforts do indeed succeed and that they must not distinguish themselves by being one of the rare failures. They should be assured that success will be rewarded and that their efforts are very visible to higher management. They should be told that if they succeed, a major victory celebration will be held.

Prior to developing the system, the timebox team will help plan it. After the timebox, they participate in implementing the system. They may participate in a new JAD to define a new edition of the system after the first has been put into operation.

PART **VI**

OTHER ISSUES

This book has been primarily devoted to discussing techniques of various kinds. Included were techniques for modeling, oo and non-oo design, and people-related situations. In contrast, Part VI is devoted to several other considerations that are necessary for building oo systems. In particular it addresses reusability, standards for object interaction, and the future of software.

Chapter 25

Concepts of Reuse[*]

Organizations need to increase system-development productivity and reduce the cost of building software. The software crisis is real, because software costs too much to develop and maintain. Once these costs are lowered through reuse, software becomes more of a company asset. However, to achieve reuse a development organization must understand the technical and management challenges.

Many organizations are starting to pursue systematic reuse actively. Many aspects of system development involve reuse—including component libraries, frameworks, domain analysis, project management, and distributed architectures. Furthermore, reuse is not limited to code. It affects the entire development lifecycle of planning, analysis, design, construction, transition, and maintenance.

This chapter examines the fundamental concepts of reuse. The discussion will provide definitions of key concepts that capture the evolving consensus on reuse. The next chapter will discuss pragmatic techniques for achieving reuse using object technology, including the kinds of reuse, required infrastructure, metrics, methods, and tools.

Background

Software reuse is not a new idea, as reuse has been a factor in the design of languages and tools since the advent of computing. Researchers recognized the importance of reusable software libraries as early as 1950. Practical reuse began with support for the programming construct known as the *function*. Developers used functions to decompose a program into logical units of work. Functions implemented numerical calculations and other common procedures. The developer could then use a function throughout the program without rewriting it each time. Although this form of reuse had a narrow scope, it reduced programming effort and showed the potential for common solutions.

[*]This chapter was contributed by J. Bradford Kain of Quoin, Inc., Boston, MA.

Researchers quickly recognized the potential for more systematic reuse. Functions and other module constructs (e.g., macros or procedures) became part of most languages. Development groups built libraries of mathematical, statistical, and engineering modules. The use of libraries was the accepted practice in many areas of development.

In 1969, Doug McIlroy called for standard catalogs of modules similar to those used in automotive engineering. However, the limitations of this approach soon became apparent:

- Libraries worked only if individual developers were committed to finding and using the modules.

- The modules had to support a usage broader than just scientific and engineering applications—requiring a greater number and variety of modules. This also required a broader expertise from the developer.

- Documentation was not always available or complete. Developers often had to examine the source code, which was difficult to understand because it was designed to handle any case.

Faced with these problems, programmers would develop their own code instead of investing in the effort to use a library. The complexity and effort required to understand these modules limited the potential for reuse.

Object technology introduces a fundamentally different unit for the description and construction of software. OO applications use the construct of an *object type* that represents a collection of like objects. Each object type can then be implemented as a class and used to fabricate the application. In this process of specification and implementation, the concepts defined in the problem domain determine the application's structure. This correspondence between a problem and its software solution supports reuse.

An application that reflects the real-world problem is easier for developers to understand, build, and maintain. The developer does not have to understand both the problem and an arbitrary structure for its solution. The semantics of the problem are key to understanding an implementation. Furthermore, object types and classes provide natural units for reuse, because types exemplify everyday experience. Developers and domain experts understand a problem in terms of types (e.g., **Account**, **Telephone Line**, or **Engine Part**)—not functions. This change in the kind of software module enables reuse as a practical aspect of application development.

COMPONENTS

Reuse is the process of exploiting the products of the development process from one application to another—a product being any part of the specification or implementation of an application. A reusable product must fulfill two basic requirements. First, the product must not depend on the context in which it is used. Second, the product must also be useful in other applications. A *component* is any product that meets these requirements. Thus, a component is a distinct and useful development product.

Components, then, are the basic units for reuse. The capability to find and take advantage of useful components determines the capacity for reuse in an application. Fig-

Why is reuse so hard to achieve in practice?

Developers resist reuse.

- Contribution is measured by lines of code or other measures for creating new code. In this situation, reuse is perceived to *reduce* productivity.
- University and professional training emphasizes individual problem solving and implementation.
- Perceived value in creating an application without relying on other developers.
- View of development as similar to writing or other art forms (as opposed to engineering).
- Project managers do not encourage reuse.
- Benefits of reuse accrue to the organization, not the individual developer.

Developing reusable components is time-consuming.

- Difficult to define a general and reusable component.
- 30 percent to 200 percent additional effort to build a reusable domain-specific component.
- 1000 percent additional effort to build a robust generic component.

Finding and understanding reusable components is time-consuming.

- 20 percent additional effort to find components in a library or directory.
- Lack of tool support including repository, cataloging, and search tools.
- Difficult to acquire components from other development groups.

Lack of support in the development lifecycle.

- Domain analysis is often not done.
- No prescribed steps for reuse in analysis, design, implementation, or maintenance.
- Lack of usable analysis, design, and implementation specifications.

Components are not always suitable.

- Verification and validation of components is not always done.
- No standard means to describe the quality or reliability of a component and difficult to judge suitability of a component without time-consuming testing.
- Design of a component is not apparent due to lack of specification or documentation.
- Attempt to generalize a component has made it too complex or difficult to adapt.

Every application is perceived as unique.

- Lack of understanding of the problem domain (as opposed to the solution).
- Different execution speed, security, fault tolerance, or other implementation constraints for different applications.
- Changes in implementation technology.

ure 25.1 illustrates different kinds of components. The development process yields useful products in all phases. Thus, components result from both the specification and implementation of an application. Components are typically paper documents or digital files. (However, paper-based components are more difficult to manage.)

Specification components describe some aspect of the problem or structure of the application. Typical specification components include requirement documents, object types, patterns or models, and complete designs. By definition, all of these components are stand-alone specification elements. A developer should be able to understand a component independently of the application in which it used. However, components can be constructed out of other components. This allows a hierarchy of subcomponents and more complex components. For example, patterns and models can be constructed from object types, or a design might comprise several distinct models.

Specification components can be more or less formal. For example, application requirements can be written up as informal text or expressed in a graphical notation using defined syntax and semantics. The result could then be a design specification using a formal language such as Object Z [Spivey, 1992]. Although this variation in the components' formality does not preclude their use, it will affect the components' capacity for reuse. A component specified with formal syntax will generally be easier to reuse and maintain. However, formalization increases the cost of building the component. This trade-off between initial development cost and future reusability is a key consideration in component specification.

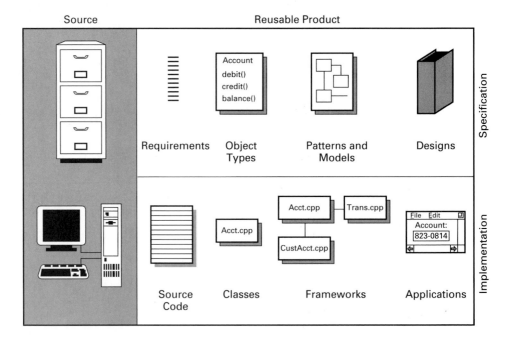

Figure 25.1   The kinds of components that form the basic units for reuse.

Implementation components must either be executable or translated directly into an executable form. These include such reusable units as source code, classes, frameworks, and applications. Furthermore, an implementation component may comprise other components, such as the construction of an application framework from constituent classes.

Specification and implementation components are both important in reuse. However, research and industry have focused on implementation components to date. The reuse of classes, class libraries, and frameworks is a relatively well-understood process. Yet, given that reuse emphasizes the leverage of existing products, specification components could provide greater benefits. Analysis specifications represent knowledge about the problem that is independent of implementation technology. This fundamental understanding of a domain is typically stable and only evolves over time. On the other hand, the implementation requirements and supporting technology tend to change rapidly.

An example of this dichotomy is the clinical care process. The basic practice of investigation and diagnosis has changed only gradually over the years. In contrast, the techniques, tools, and scientific methods have changed rapidly. While the underlying *problem* endures, its *solution* is dynamic. A specification component should capture the fundamental structure of a problem. Thus, if the component represents a basic problem, it should be more reusable.

REUSE PROCESS

Figure 25.2 shows the reuse tasks for both the *producer* and *consumer* of a component. The producer is responsible for creating the component. If the objective were simply to create a stand-alone application, the producer's responsibility would end. However, to

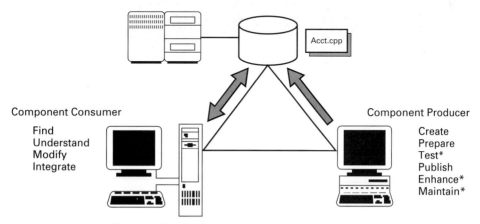

Component Consumer

Find
Understand
Modify
Integrate

Component Producer

Create
Prepare
Test*
Publish
Enhance*
Maintain*

* Done by the producer or by another development group

Figure 25.2   Reuse tasks for the *producer* and *consumer* of a component.

provide a reusable component the producer must also prepare the component for reuse. This task involves the additional responsibilities of design and construction for reuse. Generalization, selection of the component interface, and defining implementation parameters are some of the specific techniques applied here. Initial testing of the component is also done by the producer.

The producer must then publish the component in some way. Most simply the component could be placed in a public directory, or *repository*. Alternatively, the producer might be required to submit the component to a group that manages reusable components or to enter it into a repository. (The latter approach is suggested in Fig. 25.2.) In this case, the producer might also be required to catalog the component or provide additional documentation. After their initial publication, components can require such continuing tasks as enhancement, maintenance, and subsequent testing. These tasks might be assigned to the producer, the consumer, or a specialist group.

At this point, the component is available for reuse. However, for reuse to occur, the consumer must be aware of both the available components and the retrieval mechanism. The consumer must also recognize that an aspect of the new application could resemble some existing specification or implementation. The first task is to find an appropriate component. The consumer might automate the task by using a catalog or searching tools. However, most developers simply search for candidate components in shared directories or other locations. The search might involve reading the specification of the component and perhaps testing it. Developers also read the source code, although this step is really an indication that the specification was inadequate to judge the component. If the component is suitable, a local copy is made.

The developer can then start to gain a detailed understanding of the component. This process often requires understanding the implementation. Improved specification techniques and more thorough validation of components might eventually obviate this need. Once the consumer understands the component, it is integrated into the application at hand. This task can require modifications to both the new application and the component. However, a careful developer would introduce local modifications only through a specialization or some other useful extension of the component.

DOMAIN ANALYSIS

Reuse occurs when a component is used to construct two or more applications. The reuse of the components clearly depends on common requirements. However, the current experience in reuse is predominantly with implementation components (e.g., collection or user-interface class libraries). Reuse within this limited scope is insufficient. A mature software-engineering process should enable the reuse of components acquired from the business or technical problem. These are the components that are meaningful in the *domain*. For example, a securities application could include Security, Trade, and Agent components, while Part and Change Order components could be part of an engineering application. These components, then, are specific to the securities and engineering domains and represent particular concepts. While the domain components can be more difficult to build, once created they should be highly reusable within that domain.

Therefore, understanding the domain is a prerequisite to reuse. *Domain analysis* is the activity that studies the fundamental nature of a domain. It uses the same techniques of abstraction, composition, and generalization that OO analysis does for an application. However, domain analysis does not address particular applications. As a result, domain models are completely independent of implementation concerns. The domain model is not abstract and impractical but simply avoids any constructs specific to implementation. For example, a domain model would not include specification of collections, iterators, or exceptions. A useful test for a domain model is whether each object type is meaningful to a user or domain expert.

A domain model is important, because it clearly describes the problem for both analysts and domain experts. This analysis is the first step in understanding potential components and the overall problem supported by future applications. Figure 25.3 shows an example of a domain model for clinical health care [Cairns, 1992]. The model resulted from the effort made by the National Health Service in the U.K. to understand clinical care before they started implementing applications.

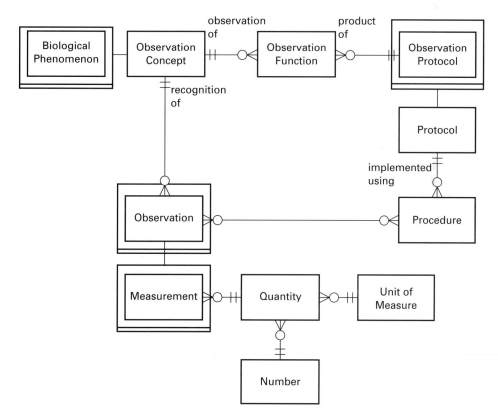

Figure 25.3   A clinical, health-care domain model.

KINDS OF REUSE

Both the organizational resolve and the kinds of components affect the degree and quality of reuse. Developers practice reuse, from ad hoc approaches to increasingly more systematic ones [Comer, 1994]. Ad hoc reuse is opportunistic and driven by the developer's own effort. It typically involves copying code or algorithms and depends on a commitment to reuse.

As an organization matures in its approach, reuse becomes part of a more systematic, software-engineering process. The first stage is the creation of a component library for shared reuse. This library often contains implementation components but gradually adds domain-specific components. However, a commitment to use the library is necessary—developers must access and use the common components.

The next stage is engineered reuse across projects. Project teams construct and use generic architectures and domain-specific components. At this stage, project teams begin to use existing domain models and patterns. Integrated reuse depends on reuse being or becoming part of the normal development process throughout an organization. The reusable components increase in size and complexity.

The stages of reuse represent increasing commitment and improvement of the development process. Case studies have shown that large organizations take seven to ten years to progress from ad hoc to strategic reuse [Comer, 1994]. Fifty percent of the organizations that pursue reuse are in the personal reuse stage. The number of organizations that have achieved some shared reuse is 35 percent. The remaining 15 percent of organizations have achieved systematic reuse, with less than 1 percent treating reuse as part of their business process. This measure indicates the difficulty in achieving reuse.

Reuse involves components of varying formality and complexity. Although a correlation exists between the stages of reuse and the kind of component, a development group can practice ad hoc or systematic reuse with any kind of component.

Code Reuse

In code reuse, existing programming statements are included in an application. The statements are not part of a defined component. This form of reuse is widely practiced by developers and is the least rigorous approach. Code reuse is not proper reuse. The developer does not maintain the connection between the original code and its subsequent inclusion in another application. Also referred to as the *copy-and-paste* approach, code reuse is unpredictable in cost and benefits to an organization.

Despite these drawbacks, code reuse should not be discouraged. This style of development supports the natural tendency to avoid unnecessary work by not rewriting code. Furthermore, a cache of useful code is one advantage that senior developers can provide to a project.

Component Reuse

Component reuse requires including a development product in an application. As described, components are distinct elements of a specification or implementation. Components include object types, collections of related object types, models, classes, applications, tests, and documents. The component's producer should provide a precise specification, describing it through text or graphics—including its purpose, role, and capabilities. Certain components such as classes might also include instructions on how to integrate them with other components.

Components are units distinct from any application. While a developer may derive a component from an existing application, it must be identifiable and separable from its original context. By analogy, a chapter is part of a book, but not necessarily a component for reuse. For the chapter to be a reusable component, it must be able to exist as a stand-alone unit and exist in multiple contexts. Therefore, to define a separable—yet multipurpose—component, an additional design effort is required. Not all software designers or authors make this investment.

A component is either a *black-box* or *white-box* component. Black-box components are used *without* knowing or modifying its implementation; white-box components may be examined and modified. Understanding the internal aspect of a component is a significant burden for the component consumer. For example, understanding the internal aspect of a class component requires examining the source code. This presents further difficulties when the source code is not provided by the component vendor. Black-box reuse, then, is the ideal mode for component reuse.

Model and Pattern Reuse

Developers construct complex components from subcomponents. The more developers create and use such constructs, the greater the potential benefits from reuse. Models and patterns are specific kinds of complex components and warrant particular attention.

A *model* is a collection of object types, relationship types, and other constructs that conveys a particular quality of the domain. A model implies a broad context involving multiple types, relationships, and other semantic building blocks. Furthermore, a model represents some cohesive set of problem concepts.

A *pattern* is a structure recognized in different domains—an identifiable form present in many contexts. Patterns are useful because they allow the recognition of familiar forms during system development. When people find a pattern, they can use a predefined structure to describe or implement the part of the problem that matches the pattern. The use of patterns in design started with Christopher Alexander, who proposed a methodology for architecture and the construction of complex structures [Alexander, 1975]. He identified 253 patterns, such as family, office connection, beer hall, accessible green, and work community. These patterns combine to specify a building. The Programmer's Apprentice Project at M.I.T. used similar notions of programming *clichés* or *plans*.

Model and pattern are not entirely distinct concepts since some components can be considered a model or a pattern. An example is from the Clinical Process Model developed for the U.K. National Health Service [Fowler, 1994]. A significant part of the complete specification was a model of clinical observations and measurements. More than 100 object types were used to describe the concepts and processes clinicians employ when they test or make judgments. Yet the model was expressive enough to describe observation and measurement in general.

Evidence of this came when the entire model served as a basis for a subsequent, financial-analysis application at Xerox Corporation. This example of reuse was significant, because it crossed over the domain boundaries of clinical care and financial analysis. However, the basic structure of observations that relate an applicable observation concept to an object with some result also provides a useful pattern. The pattern consists of **Observation Concept**, **Observation**, **Object**, and **Result Object Types**. Besides clinical care and financial analysis, the pattern could be meaningful in other domains as well. This example illustrates very large-scale reuse and a benchmark for reusable specifications.

The intuition that reusable patterns can improve development is very strong. Yet the industry is still waiting for useful abstractions. Proponents counter that it will take time to identify higher level patterns. Perhaps this is true. In the OO programming arena, Gamma is one of the first such contributions [Gamma, 1995].

Framework Reuse

At the higher level of granularity is the reuse of a complete design or *framework*. Although a framework is intended to be used intact, it includes other components—typically classes in one or more class hierarchies. A framework prescribes a solution to describing or constructing applications. Application developers refine a framework through specialization and extend it by adding new components.

A *specification framework* describes some problem or subject. An example of a specification framework is the Common Object Request Broker Architecture (CORBA) which defines an approach to distributed systems. An *application framework* is a collection of implementation components that provides a basis on which to construct an application. Applications built on a framework usually inherit from particular components, in contrast with component libraries that rely on requests. Application frameworks are also responsible for managing the event loops that provide the default flow of control within an application. Windows/Microsoft Foundation Classes and the Smalltalk development environment are examples of application frameworks. The construction of application frameworks is central to the current work at Taligent, IBM, SunSoft, and other software vendors.

APPLICATION GENERATORS AND LANGUAGE-BASED APPROACHES

The first high-level (nonmachine) languages were referred to as *automated programmers*. The implication was that the compiler did the programming, while the developer only had to write the assembly-language code. The subsequent development of third and fourth-generation languages continued this trend toward successively higher levels of abstraction. The approach is essentially another form of reuse in which a particular compiler takes the specification and produces an implementation. The generation of the output relies on predefined transformation rules.

Reuse depends on codifying knowledge about the transformation rules of the compiler's language. The goal of this approach is that some language will provide the expressiveness and flexibility needed to produce any application. Although this view is somewhat unpopular today, efforts are still being made to support reuse through new high-level languages and other tools. In the Draco system, for example, the developer defines the particular domain language and transformation rules that work with the target language. Draco then translates the specification into an executable form. Modern application generators and graphical development environments also fall into this category.

REFERENCES

Alexander, Christopher, *The Oregon Experiment,* Oxford University Press, New York, 1975.

Cairns, T., A. Casey, M. Fowler, M. Thursz, and H. Timimi, *The Cosmos Clinical Process Model,* National Health Service, Information Management Centre, 15 Frederick Rd, Birmingham, B15 1JD, England, Report ECBS20A-B (ftp: /cosmos at dka.sm.ic.ac.uk), 1992.

Comer, E. R., *Five Stages of Software Reuse,* Software Productivity Solutions, Report, 1994.

Fowler, Martin, "Experiences in Three OO Projects," In *Proceedings of Object Development Experiences,* London, SIGS Publications, 1994.

Gamma, Erich, Richard Helm, Ralph Johnson, and John Vlissides, *Design Patterns: Elements of Reusable Object-Oriented Software,* Addison-Wesley, Reading, MA, 1995.

McIlroy, Doug, "Mass-Produced Software," *Software Engineering Concepts and Techniques: Proceedings of the NATO Conferences,* J. M. Buxton, P. Naur, and B. Randall, eds., Petrocelli/Charter, 1969, pp. 88–98.

Spivey, J. M., *The Z Notation: A Reference Manual* (2nd ed.), Prentice Hall, Hemel Hempstead, England, 1992.

Chapter **26**

The Practice of Reuse[*]

The practice of reuse has been historically difficult, because the solutions involve both technical and organizational issues. To address this problem, software vendors are developing browsers, repositories, object request brokers, and other tools. However, the managerial and economic impediments to reuse are more serious and often harder to solve [Balfour, 1993].

Developers resist using components for many reasons, such as:

- The difficulty in finding appropriate components.
- The cost of building reusable components.
- A lack of trust in other developers.
- The perceived value in creating applications without relying on other developers.

Development organizations must resolve these issues through improving management techniques and supporting the necessary infrastructure for reuse.

INFRASTRUCTURE

To practice reuse, an organization must define the needed *infrastructure* for reuse. Infrastructure refers to the assignment of staff, the definition of roles and responsibilities, the reporting, and the mechanism for sharing components. A working infrastructure for reuse is necessary and separate from any technical support for reuse.

The importance of a reuse infrastructure is demonstrated by the experience of a large brokerage firm. This company constructed several trading applications using object technology. The organization started another project, and senior management decided that this effort should reuse part of a recently built application. However, the developers of the earlier project refused to give up the code. They argued that their

[*]This chapter was contributed by J. Bradford Kain of Quoin, Inc., Boston, MA.

project had created the software and that giving it to a subsequent project would deny them credit for its construction. This response surprised management, since they thought that using C++ and object technology would automatically provide software reuse.

Thus, defining the relationship between component producers and consumers in an organization is a prerequisite to reuse. Several different models [Fafchamps, 1994] are illustrated in Fig. 26.1. The developers responsible for reuse are either part of the conventional, project-team structure or an independent team. As part of the existing team structure, one or more developers have responsibility for building and maintaining reusable components. These *nested producers* must work with other reuse specialists and might also report to a second manager who is responsible for reuse. With this approach, the reuse specialists have a defined niche in the project-team structure, and they participate in delivering an application. However, conflicts between the project versus reuse make this approach untenable for producers.

Alternatively, a separate reuse team is established that is either an extension of other teams or a distinct team in the organization. A *shared producer* uses members of the consumer-project team and reports to the shared-producer team. An *independent producer* has its own manager and reports directly to the independent-producer team. In both cases, the producer team models components separately from the consumer applications. These approaches place more emphasis on reuse, but also have problems supporting requests from consumers and allocating resources to application and reuse teams.

A variant on the team and nested models is having a development group coordinate reuse by project teams throughout the organization. Such a coordinating group, called a *Center For Reuse (CFR),* enables project teams to produce and consume components (see Fig. 26.2). The CFR provides a shared resource for design expertise, specifications, and software components. Senior analysts, designers, and programmers with experience in object technology constitute the CFR staff. These individuals act as *mentors* to different development projects. Ideally, a mentor participates on each development project as a full team member. A mentor's role is encouraging reuse during the initial system design. Reuse design is a difficult task, involving trade-offs in the application specification. For example, a deep hierarchy of relatively simple classes will emphasize reusability. However, this structure will generally reduce the ability to test and maintain the classes. An experienced project mentor can resolve this kind of conflict.

A mentor could also suggest that certain components be used in the design of particular applications. However, in order for CFR members to choose the right component, they must maintain a repository of reusable components. To do this, the CFR must be able to prepare components for widespread use in the organization. One such preparation could be to generalize the component—which might require redesigning and changing it. The CFR would thus require the necessary resources. Keep in mind that the benefits of component generalization are not immediate, because the work is outside the scope of a particular project. In this way, the CFR is a shared resource for the organization.

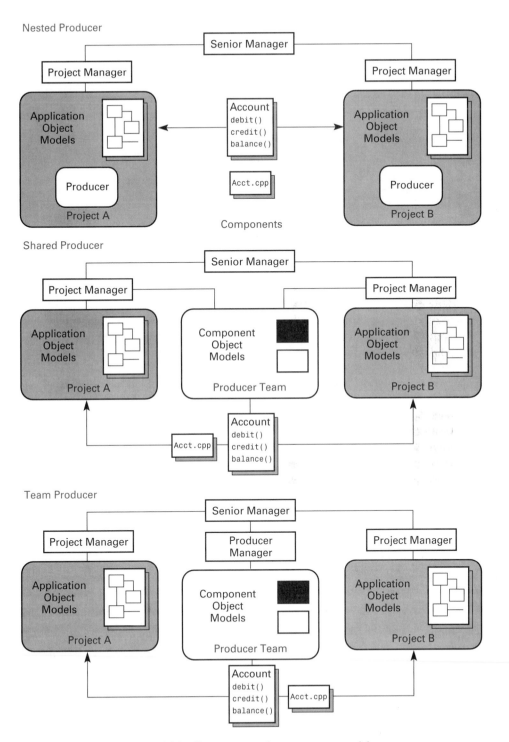

Figure 26.1 Component producer-consumer models.

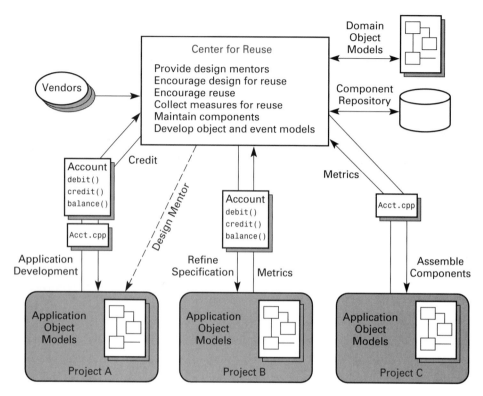

Figure 26.2   Reuse infrastructure.

SPECIFICATIONS

A significant barrier to reuse is that developers lack confidence in the component's functionality, because it lacks proper specification. If the component's interface and capabilities cannot be described, a developer cannot judge its usefulness. Without a component specification, a developer must understand the internal aspects of the component. This approach breaks down the separation of interface and implementation and invites inappropriate changes to the component implementation.

Many development organizations have no defined approach to specification. Project teams use whatever techniques they know. In many cases, specifications do not go beyond block architecture diagrams and the code itself. The latter approach is particularly dangerous if the application code gives the only specification. Using header files or class descriptions to specify a component has usually been unsuccessful, because an interface description in source code strongly encourages a developer to investigate the implementation.

Therefore, to practice reuse, an organization must adopt a defined specification approach. However, a single specification technique is not sufficient. An organization needs a set of formats to describe the developed components and to reflect both the user requirements and the analysis and design work products. Each specification should be complete and represent the component approach. Figure 26.3 gives possible specification formats for different component consumers. Since most organizations still develop or maintain conventional software, developers who support these applications are also component consumers.

These specifications should be interchangeable to maintain the greatest flexibility. Ideally, a specification format is generated from another equivalent view. This capability remains beyond most development environments, though reverse engineering capabilities in several CASE tools have recently become available. This book contains examples of many other formats. An example of an OMG-IDL (Interface Definition Language) is given in Fig. 26.4.

OMG-IDL is an expressive language for the specification of component interfaces. The language was created by the members of the OMG as a formal specification technique for distributed objects (see Reuse and Distributed Computing, below). Although it uses

Consumer	Format	Description
Conventional Developer	Text	OMG-IDL or function prototype
OO Developer	Text	OMG-IDL
	Graphic	Object diagram in a particular nota-
tion		
Data Modeler	Text	Data Dictionary
	Graphic	Data models
OO Data Modeler	Text	OMG-IDL or Object-Z
	Graphic	Object diagram in a particular nota-
tion		
Process Modeler	Text	Use Case in structured English
	Graphic	Event diagrams
OO Process Modeler	Text	Use Case in structured English
	Graphic	Interaction or event diagrams
Domain Expert	Text	Any form they prefer
	Graphic	Any form they prefer

Figure 26.3   Several specification techniques.

```
interface Account {
    exception overdrawn { float amt_over; };
    readonly attribute string owner;
    readonly attribute string number;
    readonly attribute float balance;
    void debit ( in float amount );
    void credit ( in float amount )
    raises ( overdrawn );
};
```

Figure 26.4   An OMG-IDL example.

many of the class definition constructs from C++, OMG-IDL is language independent. A specification in OMG-IDL provides a complete description of what functionality a component supports but does not necessarily expose how the component is implemented. The language preserves the separation of interface and implementation by giving only the operations and any exceptions that must be understood to use the component. There is increasing experience in using OMG-IDL as a specification technique. For example, the members of the OMG who are developing request brokers have been using OMG-IDL since 1991 to specify additional elements of the OMG architecture.

DEVELOPMENT GUIDELINES

As part of an overall approach to reuse, an organization should define a set of guidelines for development staff. While detailed technical guidelines are beyond the scope of this section, those given below provide a starting point. Furthermore, these management and technical guidelines suggest the scope and level of detail for an organization.

- Conduct a domain analysis of one or more application areas important to the organization.
- Throughout the development process, make use of available assets, structure the components to take advantage of existing lower-level components, and emphasize the creation of reusable components as part of each phase.
- Suggestions and constraints for adapting a component should be recorded along with that component.
- Generalize the component. Ensure that its semantics are context free. Factor out commonality.
- Set verification and validation process standards.
- Use concurrent testing and development.
- All dependencies on the environment should be isolated using parameters.
- Classify components according to concurrency, space utilization, reclamation, iterator availability, and other implementation requirements.
- Use higher level abstractions when adapting a particular component, that is, use design when adapting code.
- Each component should represent a single coherent abstraction. The name should reflect this abstraction.
- Instances of the subtypes should be valid instances of supertypes. For supertype operation A1 and subtype operation A2, precondition A1 implies precondition A2 and postcondition A2 implies postcondition A1.
- Operations should act on attributes, private operations, public operations on other classes in this order of preference.
- Use a layered architecture consisting of at least the following layers: user interface, application, and supporting technology.
- Separate components should be used to handle interactions and effects on the environment.
- Define interfaces at an appropriately abstract level. Minimize operations. Define a minimal public interface that calls more specific operations.

- Maintain encapsulation. Define attributes as private. However, operations can be public or private. Define separate operations to return attribute values, modify attribute values, and test for a value. Avoid providing access to other components (including components related through specialization).

- Use separate specification and implementation files.

- Adopt a standard code format for each component including purpose, revision history, assumptions, performance, diagnostics, attributes, and operations. For each operation, include parameters, precondition, postcondition, exceptions, return value, and side effects.

- Define operations with the normal exit at the end of the operation. Group exceptions together.

- Provide a name for each formal parameter to an operation.

- Group defaults at the end of the operation protocol.

- Minimize operation overloading.

- For widely used operations, create a component where the instances represent an invocation of that operation. In other words, treat the instances of an operation as an object.

- For each assumption, define an exception. For each exception, define a function to test whether the exception will be raised.

METRICS

The appropriate use of metrics is important to any reuse initiative. Organizations use metrics to assess both software products (e.g., cyclomatic complexity and software-science metrics) and software process (e.g., COCOMO). The available object-oriented metrics focus on estimating the size of an application and development effort. These metrics count the number of classes, attributes and operations, requests, and other implementation features [Chidamber, 1991]. Recent work has given more consideration to project and design metrics [Lorenz, 1994]. However, no consensus exists on object-oriented metrics and their use in development.

Clearly, reuse metrics must identify the inclusion of a component in an application and its related cost. Conventional, source-code control systems can monitor the reuse of software components. This tactic relies on the check-out mechanism to count reuse of a component. However, once the component is checked out, any subsequent duplication and reuse are not monitored. Furthermore, a source-code control system cannot determine any changes to a component unless it is checked in. These problems limit support for anything beyond black box reuse.

A tactic to alleviate this problem is designing components for *superdistribution* [Balfour, 1993]. Superdistribution means that a component can track its own usage, though each requires a built-in counter to track its use. This tactic avoids counting duplication, because it is easy to do and hard to detect. However, the producer would still need a mechanism to collect the data on use obtained by the software.

Metrics must track the different kinds of reuse including modifications to the components. The list below contains the metrics collected in some significant efforts to measure reuse.

- Number of times a component is reused with changes *(white-box* reuse).
- Number of times a component is reused without changes *(black-box* reuse).
- Number of times a component is reused with extensions.
- Number of times a component is reused without extensions.
- Percentage of an application built from components.
- Effort versus cost to create a reusable component.
- Effort versus cost to find and reuse a component.
- Number of reuses for a positive return on investment.
- Net Present Value (NPV) for investing in reusable components.

Cost of Reuse

Reuse exists within the context of multiple teams and the entire development organization—not just as an individual programmer's activity. Any measurement of reuse should address this *macro-development process.* The key issues of the macro process include measuring the effort required for the producer and consumer of the reusable component. For the producer, this includes the tasks of defining and building the reusable components. The tasks of finding, understanding, and making proper extensions to the reusable components are the responsibilities of the consumer. In addition, someone in the organization must manage the storage, recording, and maintenance of the components. Of course, these costs will offset the benefits to the consumer and the organization. The savings will include not having to recreate similar functionality in other applications and using proven components. This balance of the costs and benefits to the producer, consumer, and organization will determine if reuse is worthwhile.

Therefore, the cost of the reuse tasks is important. The time and effort that producers and consumers of components must commit will determine whether reuse is worthwhile. The component originator must expend substantial extra effort, which varies depending on the type of component, the domain, and the intended reuse. Reported metrics of design for reuse range from 125 percent [Balda, 1990] for domain-specific components to over 1000 percent [Vermuelen, 1994] for highly leveraged components such as data structures.

The effort required to prepare a component depends on the requirements placed on the developer by the organization. For example, an organization might require a separate component specification using a graphical or textual notation. A specialized language such as OMG-IDL can describe the component. This approach takes an extra step, but the component is then described in a form independent of language.

Other organizations use the header file or class description to describe the component interface. This approach takes less effort but can make the component less accessible to analysts and developers who do not know the particular language. Similarly, publishing a component depends on the requirements of the organization. Experience has shown that the greater the effort required to prepare a component for reuse, the less likely that developers will provide such components.

Figure 26.5 gives some typical values for the cost of reuse. The metrics are informal and derive from project experience during the last few years. Furthermore, the factors that affect the actual cost of reuse depend on the specific approach used at an organization. Tools, specification requirements, and allocation of responsibility for reuse tasks can significantly change the results on a project. However, the suggested range gives some idea of the challenges of reuse.

Cost to Component Producer	Additional Effort
Create	10%–500%
Prepare	10%–400%
Publish	10%–100%

Cost to Component Consumer	Additional Effort
Finding	5%–10%
Understanding	5% –10%
Integrating	10%–20%
Modifying	0%–20%

Figure 26.5   The additional effort required to reuse components.

REUSE AND DISTRIBUTED COMPUTING

Reuse provides a key factor for distributed computing. With reuse, existing applications can be more easily leveraged in a distributed system. A developer achieves the greatest leverage when an existing application satisfies some new requirements. The integration of existing applications into a distributed system eliminates the need for redevelopment. The resulting system consists of new and legacy applications that collaborate to fulfill end-user requirements. Reuse at the level of stand-alone applications can be highly effective in reducing development cost and effort.

However, the development of distributed applications is difficult and time-consuming. Distributed applications require the developer to use low-level network protocols and arcane tools. Furthermore, developers have not had a standard architecture to structure distributed applications. The lack of a standard approach means that the typical architecture is just point-to-point integration of applications. In this approach, a new application must provide a separate interface for each legacy application in the system. Adding applications or changing the interfaces is therefore prohibitively expensive.

The Object Management Group (OMG) is working toward a solution to this problem. Founded in 1989, the OMG has developed a standard architecture for distributed computing. The organization is a consortium of more than 400 vendors and end users of object technology. Their approach is to adopt specifications based on available technology and agreed on by the member companies. The OMG has defined common terms, interfaces, and a framework for distributed computing in the Object Management Architecture (OMA). In this framework, objects interact through an object request broker

The Workspace Manager and Project Editor allow the user to define a hierarchical project structure. The developer can then file individual classes under a specific project. The Symbol Browser provides a mechanism to investigate classes, operations, attributes, or any other user-defined symbols. The browser lists all symbols in a project with a particular name and symbol type (e.g., classes). The Class Browser shows the defined operations or attributes of a class. The browser also indicates whether each symbol was defined locally or inherited from another class. The inheritance hierarchy of the classes can be shown in both the Class Browser and a separate Hierarchy Browser. This browser can display the entire project hierarchy or just the classes for a subproject, or it can mark the classes that override a particular method. A double click on a symbol in any of the browsers will load the corresponding code into the Source Editor/Browser. The editor allows the developer to control the compilation and debugging of the code without leaving the environment. Although the tool ships with the GNU compiler and debugger, it also supports a number of other commercial tools.

A particularly strong aspect of SNiFF+ is the Retriever. This editor provides the capability to search the project source code for all occurrences of a symbol. The initial search uses a simple name match. The Retriever will list all source locations that match a supplied regular expression. A filter defined by the developer is then used to narrow the locations. This process of name matching and filtering provides a powerful search function. For example, a developer can retrieve all the locations where a particular object is instantiated, attribute assigned, or operation invoked. All SNiFF+ browsers use the filter mechanism. Filters provide a flexible mechanism to find the appropriate code constructs.

ResourceCenter

ResourceCenter provides a facility to search and catalog reusable components. The tool supports reuse of all kinds of assets including source code, object code, components, and documents. ResourceCenter endeavors to minimize the effort to reuse components. In particular, the tool does not require the user to create an initial classification scheme for components. Asset indexes are maintained by the tool as components are added or modified. The tool is shipped with predefined indexes for the Rogue Wave and Dyad class libraries to encourage reuse. Version 1.0 of ResourceCenter was released at the end of 1994 (CenterLine Software, Cambridge, MA). Figure 26.7 contains examples of ResourceCenter screens.

ResourceCenter uses lexicon-assisted searches to locate assets anywhere in the user environment. Developers will be able to define search expressions including wild cards, Boolean operators, and relevance ranking. The product will include a computer-science lexicon. Users can define their own domain-specific terms to control searches. Developers can create catalogs of reusable components for specific projects or domains. The tool will manage the configuration and security for the component catalogs—each having a security level designated private, project, or corporate. The tool will also provide reports on asset usage. This capability will be important in measuring and evaluating the reuse process.

A key feature is the ability for the tool to access almost any type of asset. Besides code, ResourceCenter supports searches on text and other documents. Examples include

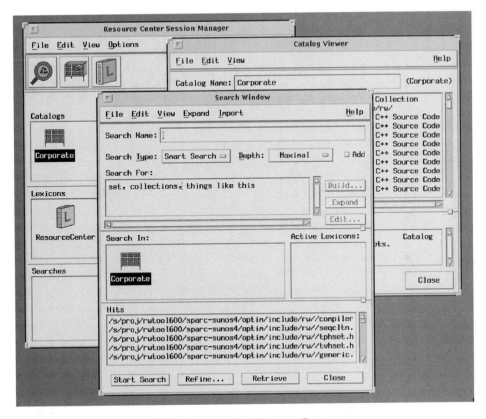

Figure 26.7   An example of ResourceCenter screens.

UNIX manual pages, Internet news, problem reports, designs, Frame or Interleaf documents, and electronic mail messages. The tool also allows user-defined asset types. To support the use of design documents as reusable assets, the vendor integrates Resource-Center with IDE and Rational tools. CenterLine integrates the tools with other configuration managers, editors, and browsers.

InQuisiX

Another tool for managing reusable components is InQuisiX. This tool takes a more formal approach to reuse but also provides facilities for integrating with the user environment. Its principal feature is support for a sophisticated classification scheme and search facilities. InQuisiX was developed as part of the U.S. Department of Defense STARS (Software Technology for Adaptable, Reliable Systems) program by Software Productivity Solutions, Indialantic, FL.

InQuisiX requires the user to create an initial catalog of assets. The tool structures components in a hierarchy. Each component has associated name, text, faceted classification, keyword, file, and link fields. The developer can browse any of the cataloged assets in its native format. As provided by the vendor, the tool supports only text files such as source code. However, InQuisiX can also support assets of any format by integrating other indexing and browsing tools. Assets can be related through appropriate field values. The link fields connect design diagrams and test specifications to related assets. File fields can also refer to external data files. However, the tool automates any additions to a catalog.

The search facility for InQuisiX supports a flexible query mechanism. Queries can locate assets using a single word or entire phrase. Searches can also be performed using multiple fields and simple Boolean expressions. Queries can be iterative. This allows the user to refine the query after each result set is shown. The tool allows the user to store queries for later searches. The tool will automatically reflect any catalog changes in query results.

OMG INFORMATION BROKERAGE

Proponents of object technology have envisioned a component market where application developers could purchase reusable components from vendors. This future market would consist of a large selection of components for different application areas and requirements—offered largely online. Vendors and independent developers would supply useful components, and end users could browse, buy, and download needed components through an electronic service.

The components would include classes for data structures, graphical user interfaces, and other similar components for building applications. Furthermore, the available components would support useful business and technical concepts. For example, the components might include an Account object type, a Switch class, and a Security Transactions framework. These domain-specific components could be provided by banks, telecommunications, and other end users. The component market would enable these organizations to place their reusable components into the market and offset the cost of development. Furthermore, the proponents claim that this efficient market would reduce the cost of software and increase the quality of OO applications. The problem with this goal is that no electronic market exists, and recent attempts to use the Internet in this way have been disappointing.

The Object Management Group (OMG) intends to meet this need. In 1995, the OMG began developing an electronic component market known as the Information Brokerage. The Information Brokerage works comparably to an electronic, stock-trading system. Component vendors provide a specification and price for each of their components. Users will search the market for components using a browser. If users find a component that meets their requirements, they can make arrangements for payment and download the selected components. Although the user may negotiate with the vendor on price, transactions will typically use the listed price of the component. Purchases will be made predominately through credit cards, but the system will also support purchase orders set up for a user in advance.

Users will also access software services through different forums in the system. The forums resemble those in CompuServe, Usenet, and other networks—each forum focusing on a particular company, product, or topic. Service providers, including software and consulting companies, will post information and answer user questions. The posted information will include company background, white papers, product descriptions, and other documents. As part of the available services, the OMG will support registration for Object World and the text of ComputerWorld.

Access to the Information Brokerage is through the Internet at www.omg.org on the World Wide Web. Users can download the desired components directly from the Web. No membership fee or commission is charged for this service. The OMG uses vendor advertising as the primary way to pay for running the system.

Components

The success of the Information Brokerage depends on the number, quality, and usefulness of the offered components. To provide the initial components in the system, the OMG is asking large system vendors to provide components. Among the vendors who have already agreed to participate are Fujitsu, Hewlett-Packard, IBM, and Sun. The OMG has convinced these vendors that the system will provide a new sales channel for internal and commercial products. As the system matures, the OMG expects that the component vendors will include more independent software developers and end users of object technology. However, the large system vendors are needed to create initial interest in the market.

A simple classification scheme will ensure that the system is easy to use. The categories will include financial services, health care, manufacturing, software engineering, and other application areas. The system will offer different kinds of components, such as classes, objects, and parts (components without an explicit class). The initial components will be coarse grained, that is, they will provide large units of functionality. Examples of coarse-grained components include OMA-compliant object services, frameworks, and applications. More fine-grained components such as individual classes will be available as more specialized vendors participate. Some vendors will package objects and classes into larger components, for example, a class library.

The OMG will only require that components are object oriented and that vendors provide a component specification in OMG-IDL. However, the judgment is subjective whether or not a particular component is OO. Components will generally meet this requirement if they fit within a broad category of software considered OO by the industry. For example, the system will not include Visual Basic Controls (VBXS). Although a VBX provides an element of functionality in a Visual Basic application, custom controls do not exhibit the characteristics of encapsulated state and behavior of objects.

The purpose of the OMG-IDL requirement is to promote the language as a general specification technique. OMG-IDL is the key element of the OMG approach to distributed computing. It is the mechanism for integrating applications with an ORB and using other object services. The language is a subset of C++ but provides a general expressive capability. The OMG recognizes this potential and wants to extend the use of OMG-IDL from application integration to general interface definition. In addition, OMG-IDL specified components in the Information Brokerage will provide a ready source for end users interested in Application Objects or Common Facilities. The system will then provide a market for OMA-compliant objects for integration with existing CORBA environments. In this context, the Information Brokerage is a part of the overall OMG strategy of adopting available technology as industry standards. With the exception of the OMG-IDL requirement, other specification notations may be chosen by the vendor. OMG will ensure that the component specifications use OMG-IDL. X/OPEN is completing a compliance test suite that will be available at the rollout of the Information Brokerage.

OMG will not measure the quality of components. While it will establish standard terms and conditions for purchasing components on the system, these will not prescribe warranty or liability. Such a warranty of correctness, robustness, or other implementation qualities will be the vendor's responsibility. Most vendors will opt for their own, more exhaustive terms and conditions. Thus, components will be offered in its present condition unless the vendor gives some added assurance of quality. However, if the Information Brokerage is successful, the OMG will consider defining a general approach to software quality and licensing.

The Information Brokerage started operations in early 1995. The OMG considers the system a pilot for a long-awaited component market. OMG President Chris Stone, says "the Information Brokerage is an experiment in access and electronic distribution of software, services, and information that we expect to evolve as the industry understands user requirements" [Stone, 1994]. No organization has thought through all the issues in the electronic distribution of software. However, the nascent component market has to start before many of the promised benefits of object technology will arrive.

REFERENCES

Balda, D. M., and D. A. Gustafson, "Cost Estimation Models for the Reuse and Prototype Software Development Life-Cycles," *ACM SIGSOFT Software Engineering Notes,* 15:3, 1990, pp. 42–50.

Balfour, Brad, Sam Adams, David M. Wade, and Brad Cox, "Developing Software for Large-Scale Reuse," *OOPSLA '93 Conference Proceedings, ACM SIGPLAN Notices,* 28:10, 1993, pp. 137–143.

Biggerstaff, T. J., "An Assessment and Analysis of Software Reuse," in *Advances in Computer Science,* Alan Perlis, ed., Academic Press, Vol. 34, 1992.

Biggerstaff, T. J., and A. Perlis, eds., *Software Reusability,* Addison-Wesley/ACM Press, Reading, MA, 1989.

Biggerstaff, T. J., "The Library Scaling Problem and the Limits of Concrete Component Reuse," In *Proceedings Of International Conference on Software Reuse,* IEEE Computer Society Press, 1994.

CenterLine Software, ResourceCenter, *Delivering on the Promise of Software Reuse,* CenterLine Software, Presentation, 1994.

Chidamber, S. D., and C. F. Kenerer, "Towards a Metrics Suite for Object-Oriented Design," In *OOPSLA '91 Conference Proceedings, ACM SIGPLAN Notices,* 26:11, 1991, pp. 197–211.

Fafchamps, D., "Organizational Factors and Reuse," *IEEE Software,* 11:5, 1994, pp. 31–41.

Favaro, J., "What Price Reusability? A Case Study," *Ada Letters,* 11:3, 1991, pp. 115–124.

Frakes, W. B., and C. J. Fox, *Software Reuse Models and Metrics: A Survey,* Computer Science Dept., Virginia Polytechnic University, Report 94–27, 1994.

Frakes, W. B., and S. Isoda, "Success Factors of Systematic Reuse," *IEEE Software,* 11:5, 1994, pp. 15–19.

Frakes, W. B., and T. Pole, "An Empirical Study of Representation Methods for Reusable Software Components," IEEE Transactions on Software Engineering, August,1994.

Gamma, E., R. Helm, R. Johnson, and J. Vlissides, *Design Patterns Elements of Reusable Object-Oriented Software,* Addison-Wesley, Reading, MA, 1995.

Grass, J. E., "SNiFF+: A Development Environment for C++," *C++ Report,* 6:3, March-April, 1994, pp. 75–79.

Henderson-Sellers, B., "The Economics of Reusing Library Classes," *Journal of Object-Oriented Programming,* 6:4, 1993, pp. 43–50.

Hooper, J. W., and R. O. Chester, *Software Reuse Guidelines and Methods,* Plenum, New York, 1991.

Joos, R., "Software Reuse at Motorola," *IEEE Software,* 11:5, 1994, pp. 42–47.

Kain, J. Bradford, "Measuring the ROI of Reuse," *Object Magazine,* 4:3, 1994, pp. 49–54.

Kain, J. Bradford, "Pragmatics of Reuse in the Enterprise," *Object Magazine,* 3:6, 1994, pp. 55–58.

Lewis, J. A., S. M. Henry, D. G. Kafura, and R. S. Schulman, "On the Relationship Between the Object-Oriented Paradigm and Software Reuse: An Empirical Investigation," *Journal of Object-Oriented Programming,* 5:4, July/August, 1992, pp. 35–41.

Lim, W. C., "Effects of Reuse on Quality, Productivity, and Economics," *IEEE Software,* 11:5, 1994, pp. 23–30.

Lorenz, M., and J. Kidd, *Object-Oriented Software Metrics,* Prentice Hall, Englewood Cliffs, NJ, 1994.

OMG, *Object Management Architecture Guide,* OMG, Report OMG TC Document 92.11.1, 1993.

Poulin, J. S., and J. M. Caruso, "A Reuse Metrics and Return on Investment Model," in *Proceedings of Second International Workshop on Software Reusability,* Lucca, Italy, 1993, pp. 152–166.

Pree, W., *Design Patterns for Object-Oriented Software Development,* ACM Press/Addison-Wesley, Wokingham, U.K., 1995.

Prieto-Diaz, R., and G. Arango, *Domain Analysis and Software Systems Modeling,* IEEE Computer Society Press, Los Alamitos, CA, 1991.

ReNews, an electronic software reuse newsletter, is available via anonymous ftp at ftp.vtu.edu in pub/reuse.

Schaefer, W., R. Prieto-Diaz, and M. Matsumoto, eds., *Software Reusability,* Ellis Horwood, Chichester, U.K., 1994.

Staringer, W., "Constructing Applications from Reusable Components," *IEEE Software,* 11:5, 1994, pp. 61–68.

Stark, M., "Impacts of Object-Oriented Technologies: Seven Years of SEL Studies," in *Proceedings of OOPSLA,* Washington, DC, 1993, pp. 365–373.

Stone, Chris, Interview, Framingham, MA, 23 September 1994.

Tracz, W., "Software Reuse Myths," in *Proceedings of Workshop on Software Reuse,* Boulder, CO, 1987.

U.S. Army CECOM, "Automated Reusable Components System," *Army Phase III SBIR Program Review,* pp. 64–65.

Vermuelen, A., "Reuse and Extensibility," in *Proceedings of Object World 1994,* San Francisco, CA, 1994.

Wessale, W., D. Reifer, and D. Welter, "Large Project Experiences with Object-Oriented Methods and Reuse," *Journal of Systems and Software,* 23, 1993, pp. 151–161.

Chapter 27

Standards for Object Interaction

INTRODUCTION

Object-oriented technology cannot begin to reach its potential until there are industry standards that enable classes from one vendor to interact with classes from other vendors. When this occurs, the classes will be able to execute on networked machines, from different manufacturers, with different operating systems, database systems, and user interfaces. Software vendors creating new classes will likely do so by employing existing software from other vendors. International standards enabling classes to intercommunicate are as important as international "open" standards for networks.

CASE tools for OO design and code generation should help to enforce the standards, generating requests of standard format, and employing standard classes from a repository for object services and common facilities.

THE OBJECT MANAGEMENT GROUP

The organization primarily concerned with establishing industry standards is the Object Management Group (OMG). The OMG is a nonprofit, international, trade association, funded by about 200 computer and software companies. Its mission is stated as follows [Soley, 1992]:

- The Object Management Group is dedicated to maximizing the portability, reusability, and interoperability of software. The OMG is the leading worldwide organization dedicated to producing a framework and specifications for commercially available object-oriented environments.

- The Object Management Group provides a Reference Architecture with terms and definitions upon which all specifications are based. Implementations of these specifications will be made available under fair and equitable terms and conditions. The OMG will create industry standards for commercially available object-oriented systems by focusing on remote object network access, encapsulation of existing applications, and object database interfaces.

- The OMG provides an open forum for industry discussion, education, and promotion of OMG-endorsed object technology. The OMG coordinates its activities with related organizations and acts as a technology/marketing center for object-oriented software.

The members of the Object Management Group, Inc. (OMG) have a shared goal of developing and using integrated software systems. These systems should be built using a methodology that supports modular production of software; encourages reuse of code; allows useful integration across lines of developers, operating systems, and hardware; and enhances long-range maintenance of that code. Members of the OMG believe that the OO approach to software construction best supports their goals.

To achieve an industrial revolution in software the world needs many software factories all using off-the-shelf software components from many vendors to create new software which is reliable and inexpensive. We need an end to the age of monolithic software in which software vendors write all their own code. Buying software in the future will be like buying a car; it will consist of components from many vendors, worldwide. To achieve this, we need standards for the interfaces to objects so that all vendors can use objects from other vendors. We need standard mechanisms by which objects transparently make requests and receive responses. This interoperability needs to function over networks between different machines and different environments.

THE OMG OBJECT MODEL

The goal of the Object Model Task Force is "to facilitate portability of applications, reusability of object-type libraries, and interoperability of software components in a distributed heterogenous environment" [OMG, 1991]. A goal is that the OO products now evolving, such as OO database management systems, OO-CASE tools, OO preprocessors, and OO-GUI (Graphic User Interface) tools, should employ the model definitions. The OMG acknowledges that programming languages, at least those with ANSI or ISO standardization, "will be slower to evolve than some of the other system software products not so constrained."

OBJECT MANAGEMENT ARCHITECTURE

The OMG has a Reference Model for an *Object Management Architecture* [Soley, 1992]. The goal of the architecture is to enable different software from different vendors to work together. It is intended to influence the design of components only to the extent of achieving interoperability. Diverse design solutions can be accommodated.

The Reference Model addresses:

- How objects make and receive requests and responses.
- The basic operations that must be provided for every object.
- Object interfaces that provide common facilities useful in many applications.

The Object Management Architecture consists of four major parts as illustrated in Fig. 27.1.

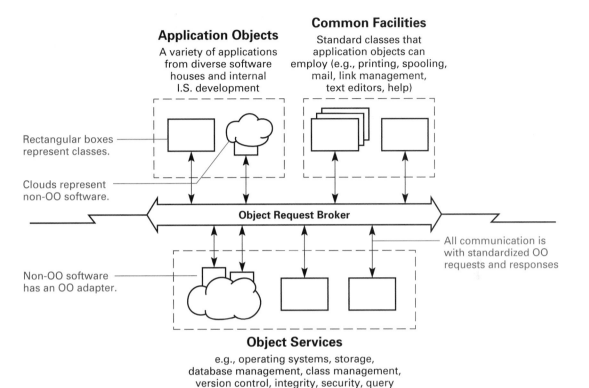

Figure 27.1   The OMG's Object Management Architecture is attempting to achieve industry standardization for OO interoperability.

Application Objects (AO)

Application Objects are end-use applications that may be built by diverse vendors or by in-house I.S. organizations.

Common Facilities (CF)

Common Facilities are objects and classes providing general purpose capabilities useful in many applications. It is a shared library of commonly used functions and includes functions that were once in applications and are now migrating into operating systems or systems software. Various application objects may become common function (CF) when they become popular enough to become de facto standards. This could include such things as 3-D graphic routines, spelling checkers, and hypertext. Types of facilities that are candidates for CF include:

- Cataloging and browsing of classes and objects.
- Link management.
- Reusable user interfaces (e.g., text editors).

- Printing and spooling.
- Error reporting.
- Help facility.
- Electronic mail facility.
- Tutorials and computer-based training.
- Common access to remote information repositories.
- Agent (intelligent macro) facilities.
- Interfaces to external systems.
- Object querying facilities.
- User preferences and profiles.

Object Services (OS)

Object Services is a collection of services that provides basic functions for creating, storing, maintaining, subtyping, and managing objects. They include file or database management systems, transaction managers, directory services, and so on. OMG lists examples of the operations that Object Services can provide:

- *Class management.* The ability to create, modify, delete, copy, distribute, describe, and control the definitions of classes, the interfaces to classes, and the relationships between class definitions.
- *Instance management.* The ability to create, modify, delete, copy, move, invoke, and control objects and the relationships between objects.
- *Storage.* The provision of permanent or transient storage for large and small objects, including their state and methods.
- *Integrity.* The ability to ensure the consistency and integrity of object states both within single objects (e.g., through locks) and among objects (e.g., through transactions).
- *Security.* The ability to provide (define and enforce) access constraints at an appropriate level of granularity on objects and their components.
- *Query.* The ability to select objects or classes from implicitly or explicitly identified collections based on a specified predicate.
- *Versions.* The ability to store, correlate, and manage variants of objects.

THE OBJECT REQUEST BROKER (ORB)

The Object Request Broker is the heart of the Object Management Architecture (shown in Fig. 27.1). It allows objects to communicate independently of specific platforms and techniques. The goal of the Object Request Broker is to guarantee that objects can interoperate with one another, whether they are on the same machines, different machines, or diverse networks of heterogeneous systems.

An object makes a request in a standard fashion, and the Object Request Broker arranges for the request to be processed. The Object Request Broker causes some *method* to be invoked and conveys the results to the requester.

The ORB supports the view that objects of diverse types should be able to communicate but not reveal their insides. The objects may be relatively simple, such as print mechanisms, or highly complex, such as production scheduling systems. They may communicate within the same computer, across LANs, across corporate networks, or across multinetwork systems spanning corporations. The communicating objects may be implemented in different languages, on different vendors' hardware, with different operating systems.

The Object Management Group states (with *emphasis* added):

> The ORB is responsible for all mechanisms required to find the object implementation for the *request,* to prepare the object implementation to receive the *request,* and to communicate the data making up the request. The interface the client [requester] sees is completely independent of where the object is located, what programming language it is implemented in, or any other aspect which is not reflected in the object's interface [OMG, 1991].

Most software systems are not designed to work in an all-encompassing environment; ORB systems are designed to span diverse environments and hide the implementation details of these environments. It is as though mechanisms were encapsulated, thus extending the benefits of OO across diverse platforms and networks.

The ORB standards say nothing about the network mechanisms over which the requests and responses are delivered. Networks are defined in different standards.

The ORB has to find the objects to which a *request* refers. In order to do this, there must be standard formats for requests and responses. In this way, ORB systems are rather like electronic mail systems in which messages travel over diverse networks between diverse computers. The difference is that OO systems make sure that the mail is read.

Box 27.1 lists functions that the Object Request Broker must address, at least to some degree.

BOX 27.1   Functions of the Object Request Broker.

- *Name services.* Object name mapping services map object names in the naming domain of the requester into equivalent names in the domain of the method to be executed, and vice versa. The OMG Object Model does not require object names to be unique or universal. Object location services use the object names in the request to locate the method to perform the requested operation. Object location services may involve simple attribute lookups on objects. In practice, different object systems or domains will have locally preferred object naming schemes.

- *Request dispatch.* This function determines which method to invoke. The OMG Object Model does not require a request to be delivered to any particular object. As far as the requester is concerned, it does not matter whether the request first goes to a method that then operates on the state variables of objects passed as parameters, or whether it goes to any particular object in the parameter list.

- *Parameter encoding.* These facilities convey the local representation of parameter values in the requester's environment to equivalent representations in the recipient's environment. To accomplish this, parameter encodings may employ standards or de facto standards.

(Continued)

BOX 27.1 *(Continued)*

- *Delivery.* Requests and results must be delivered to the proper location as characterized by a particular node, address, space, thread, or entry point. These facilities may use standard transport protocols.

- *Synchronization.* Synchronization primarily deals with handling the parallelism of the objects making and processing a request and the rendezvous between the requester and the response to the request. Possible synchronization models include: asynchronous (request with no response), synchronous (request; await reply), and deferred synchronous (proceed after sending request; claim replay later).

- *Activation.* Activation is the housekeeping processing necessary before a method can be invoked. Activation and deactivation of persistent objects is needed to obtain the object state for use when the object is accessed, and to save the state when it no longer needs to be accessed. For objects that hold persistent information in nonobject storage facilities (e.g., files and databases), explicit requests can be made to objects to activate and deactivate themselves.

- *Exception handling.* Various failures in the process of object location and attempted request delivery must be reported to requester and/or recipient in ways that distinguish them from other errors. Actions are needed to recover session resources and resynchronize requester and recipient. The ORB coordinates recovery housekeeping activities.

- *Security mechanisms.* The ORB provides security enforcement mechanisms that support high-level security control and policies. These mechanisms ensure the secure conveyance of requests among objects. Authentication mechanisms ensure the identities of requesting and receiving objects, threads, address spaces, nodes, and communication routes. Protection mechanisms assure the integrity of data being conveyed and assure that the data being communicated and the fact of communication are accessible only to authorized parties. Access enforcement mechanisms enforce access and licensing policies.

In the world of large-scale networks, the need for a global naming and directory service was discovered, and this led to the widespread adoption of the CCITT x.500 standard. The ORB needs something equivalent to x.500. The ORB itself need not have all the information required to locate objects. It may use a directory or a service which can search for objects based on attributes, including changeable attributes such as *not-busy* or *within 200 feet*. It may use a service similar to the telephone yellow pages or call on a runtime library.

DIVERSE ORB IMPLEMENTATIONS

There are likely to be diverse types of implementations of ORB from different vendors. An ORB could be designed to operate in one machine, on a LAN-based system, on one vendor's network systems, or on far-flung multinetwork systems linking diverse environments. It could be seen as a normal program by the operating system, or it could be built into the operating system as an underlying service which could enhance security, robustness, and performance. It may be linked to an OO database management system or a class library system. It may be an integral part of software for distributed operations or system management. It could be built into system software such as Open Software Foundation's DCE (Distributed Computing Environment).

The different ORB implementations will have to intercommunicate. Like objects, their internal mechanisms can assume any form, but the requests and responses they transmit must be of standard format. The OMG *Common Object Request Broker Architecture (CORBA)* assumes that the *Core Model* of the ORB will be implemented in fundamentally different ways, but there are certain components above the Core Model which provide common interfaces. The common interfaces hide the differences in ORB Core Models, and so the architecture gives the maximum freedom in ORB implementation.

The OMG architecture thinks in terms of *client* and *server* objects. A *client* object requests services of a server object. A *server* object accepts the request and performs the service. The client and server could be on the same machine or on separate machines.

When a client issues a *request,* it names an object, an *operation* of that object, and zero, one, or multiple parameters for that operation. The input parameters are passed to the operation and output parameters and return values are passed back to the client object (unless the request is invalid or cannot be processed, in which case an exception message and parameters are sent back to the client).

The format of the request and response needs to be standardized. Objects can then communicate even though they may be implemented in different languages, on different platforms, by different vendors.

The request may be sent to the Object Request Broker, which arranges for the request to be processed and conveys the results to the requester. This may be a simple operation. However, the Object Request Broker sometimes has to contact Object Services in order to find the class and requested operation. The Object Services may include a class dictionary service or might search runtime operation libraries.

OMG gives an example [Soley, 1992]:

> Consider the request "print layout_312 laser_plotter." This could be sent to the object "layout_312" whose "print" method would then print it on "laser_plotter." Or the request could be sent to "laser_plotter" whose "print" method would access "layout_312." Or the request could be sent to the generalized "print" routine that would figure out a good way to arrange the printing, based on some attributes of these two objects. Or instead of relying on a generalized "print" routine, the Name Service in the ORB could determine an appropriate method jointly owned by the (the classes of) "layout_312" and "laser_plotter."

Clients can create objects by issuing requests. The response is then an object reference that identifies the new object. Similarly, objects can be destroyed.

OPERATIONS

Each operation has an *operation identifier.* If may be referred to with an *operation name.* The operation might be implemented in different ways in different objects.

An operation has a *signature* which describes legitimate values of request parameters and returned results. The signature consists of:

- A specification of the parameters required in requests.

- A specification of the return results.

- A specification of the error messages (exceptions) that may be raised and the types of parameters accompanying them.

- A specification of additional contextual information that may affect the performance of the request.

- An indication of the execution semantics—for example, the execution can be:
  — *At-most-once:* it returns a successful result once only or else an error message.
  — *Best effort:* the server does its best to perform the request but cannot return any results; the requester never synchronizes with the completion, if any.

OBJECT INTERFACES

An *interface* to an object type is the set of possible operations that a client may request of the object type. A client knows only the logical structure of a server object as defined by its interface. The server object might provide its service by itself acting as a client to other objects.

INTERFACE DEFINITION LANGUAGE

Interfaces are specified in IDL, the Interface Definition Language. This language defines the object type in terms of the operations that may be performed on it and the parameters to those operations. IDL fully defines the interface between client object and the server objects.

The programmer of a client object may write an IDL stub. The stub is used by the ORB which finds the required server object, relays the *request* to it, and returns the results. The stub should work with multiple ORBs which may be implemented differently. Clients are maximally portable. They can work without source changes with any server object that implements the desired interface and any ORB that supports the IDL. Clients have no knowledge of the implementation of the server object or the implementation of the ORB or the mechanism, networks, and so on which the ORB uses to locate the server object.

IDL is the means by which a particular object implementation tells its potential clients what operations it makes available and how they should be invoked. The IDL definitions may reside in a *runtime repository* which is part of the ORB.

IDL is a declarative language. It does not include any algorithmic structures or variables. IDL grammar is a subset of ANSI C++ with additional constructs to support mechanisms for invoking remote operations. Because most analysts and programmers are unfamiliar with C++, it is desirable that IDL should be generated by OO-CASE tools.

IDL supports inheritance. An interface can be a subtype of another interface, inheriting all of its characteristics and adding characteristics of its own.

THE ORB REPOSITORIES

The ORB needs a database, or persistent store, of information that enables it to function. The *Interface Repository* stores IDL representations and makes them available to the ORB at runtime, so that they may be used by the ORB to perform requests.

The Implementation Repository contains information that allows the ORB to locate objects and activate them. Other information may be in the Implementation Repository; for example, information which aids in maintaining security, resource allocation, and possibly charging for the use of objects.

ORBS AND OODB

ORBs are likely to use OO databases. There is a strong argument for integration of an OODBMS and ORB.

The ORB should use an OODBMS both as part of Object Services and for its Interface Repository and Implementation Repository. The act of registering an object in the OODBMS should simultaneously register it with the ORB and vice versa. The capabilities of the ORB enhance those of the OODBMS by adding distribution capability, and the OODBMS helps implement the ORB by assisting with versions, naming, location, security, and so on. The language for accessing objects in the OODBMS should be the same as that in the ORB. There seems no point in having separate languages for the ORB and OODBMS.

MULTIPLE ORBS

Complex systems are likely to use multiple ORBs. These ORBs may be implemented by different vendors in different ways.

Classes are built in an ORB-independent way and use an IDL (interface definition language) defined in an ORB-independent way. Because of this, requests and responses can pass through multiple different ORBs and preserve the semantics necessary for client objects to interact with target objects.

Figure 27.2 shows various possibilities. The first two diagrams relate to OO software with no ORB. Classes interact with other classes directly without the overhead of an ORB. Most software packages or modules will be built so that the classes interact directly; only when they interact with a different package or service will an ORB be used.

The third diagram of Fig. 27.2 shows classes interacting via an ORB in one machine. The fourth shows classes interacting via the same ORB in different machines. Here, both implementations use the same object references and communication mechanism. An object reference can be passed freely from one machine to the other—no transformation is needed.

The fifth picture shows two ORBs. Some objects are implemented by ORB 1 and some by ORB 2. When an object connected to one ORB invokes an object connected to the other ORB, the object reference is passed as a parameter from one ORB to the other. Each

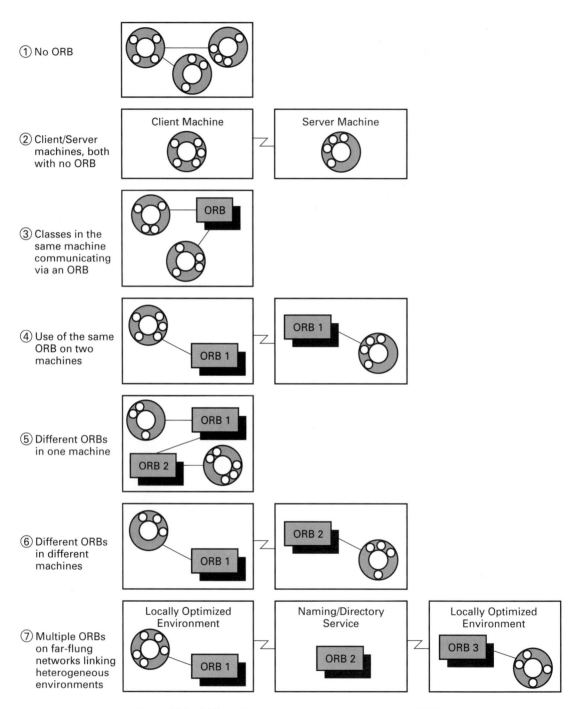

Figure 27.2   Different interconnections among objects and ORBs.

ORB must be able to distinguish its own object references from those of other ORBs and be able to pass other ORBs' object reference parameters. The sixth diagram is similar to the fifth except that the ORBs communicate between separate machines.

The seventh diagram might relate to the far-flung network. ORB 1 and ORB 2 might each operate on an environment which is optimized locally, but objects on ORB 1's environment need to make requests of objects on ORB 3's environment. To find the requisite object, another ORB, ORB 2 provides a networkwide naming/directory service. The ORBs may have no commonality. It may be necessary to have gateways to translate object references and requests used in one ORB to those understood by another.

In ways such as these, ORBs from different vendors may intercommunicate. A class implicitly chooses an ORB when it binds to that ORB's object adapter.

The use of separate ORBs managing objects separately avoids the need to unify and optimize on a global scale. Instead, it allows locally optimized systems to be interlinked.

INTERFACE TO NON-OO SOFTWARE

If OO software is to have widespread use, it must interact with other software that is not OO in nature. A vast amount of non-OO software exists, including basic software such as operating systems, database management systems, network software, and so on. Object-oriented software will ease its way steadily into a world that is largely non-OO. It will be a long time before all of the software that needs to interact is object-oriented.

The *Application Objects* and *Object Services* of Fig. 27.1 will often be non-OO. In order to connect to the Object Management Architecture, they must have an OO interface, sometimes called an *adapter* or *wrapper,* which accepts OO requests in their standard format and translates them to whatever form the non-OO software uses. Similarly, the wrapper translates the responses into standard OO responses.

Figure 27.1 draws non-OO software as clouds and shows it having a square-cornered OO interface. Providing software has an OMA-compliant interface, it can participate in the Object Management Architecture.

The Object Management Architecture does not define the screen interface for the end user. A variety of graphic or other user interfaces could be employed. These are the subject of standardization efforts outside the OMG. The user interface must interact with the Object Request Broker using standard requests and responses. Eventually, Common Facilities may provide standard user interface classes.

Basically, the goal of the OMG is providing the "glue" that enables classes from all vendors to interoperate. Standards for this glue are needed quickly and must have the widest industry support, so that the object-oriented revolution can gain maximum momentum.

REFERENCES

OMG, *Common Object Request Broker Architecture and Specification,* Object Management Group, Document 91.12.1, December 1991.

OMG, *The OMG Object Model,* Object Management Group, Document 92.11.1. September 1, 1992.

Soley, Richard Mark, ed., *Object Management Architecture Guide* (2nd ed.), Object Management Group, Document 92.11.1, September 1, 1992.

Chapter 28

The Future of Software

INTRODUCTION

The human brain is good at some tasks and bad at others, while the computer is good at certain tasks that the brain does badly. The challenge of computing is to forge a creative partnership using the best of both.

The electronic machine is fast and absolutely precise. It executes its instructions unerringly. Our meat machine of a brain is slow and usually imprecise. It cannot do long, meticulous operations of logic without making mistakes. Fortunately, it has some remarkable properties. It can invent, conceptualize, demand improvements, and create visions. Humans can write music, start wars, build cities, create art, fall in love, dream of colonizing the solar system but cannot write bug-free COBOL.

The future challenge in most human endeavors will be merging human and machine capabilities—to achieve the best synergy between people and machines. This synergy will evolve rapidly, because machines are becoming more powerful and networks are growing at a furious rate.

The computers of the future will be nothing like the robots we see in the movies. They will not have the human abilities of an automated Arnold Schwarzenegger. In many ways, they will be more interesting, because they will use worldwide networks of immense bandwidth and have access to vast amounts of data and vast libraries of complex object-oriented software that are absolutely precise in their operation.

Today's software is relatively trivial. To make computers into synergistic partners for humans, they need complex software. Software of the necessary complexity probably cannot be built using traditional structured techniques alone. In the mid-1980s, authorities of structured techniques claimed that building the proposed systems of 50 million lines of code was impossible [Parnas, 1985]. Our future requires software in which systems of 50 million lines of code will be commonplace. Object-oriented techniques with encapsulation, polymorphism, repository-based development, design automation, and code generators are essential for this.

OPTICAL DISKS

In the near future, desktop machines will have optical disks capable of holding hundreds of millions of lines of code. Billion line-of-code disks will eventually be commonplace. Software will probably be sold on optical disks, with one disk containing multiple related products: for example, a general office worker's set of tools, or an I.S. professional's set of tools. If a COBOL programmer had been coding at today's average rate for the last two thousand years, all the object code produced would not fill one CD-ROM.

Future developers will have CD-ROMs containing libraries of applications and objects designed for reusability These libraries will appear in I-CASE format, so that their design can be displayed on the screen, modified, and linked to other system components. Mainframe and LAN server repositories will contain much larger libraries. The tools will need search mechanisms and expert systems to help the developers find the reusable components most appropriate to their needs. Computer users will also have CD-ROMs full of software. More than 100 million lines of object code can reside on one CD-ROM. Disks will be sold with many applications and tools integrated together. Cars, tanks, planes, robots, building controllers, household machines, security devices—machines of many types will have their own optical disks of software.

THE NEED FOR POWER TOOLS

We could not build today's cities, microchips, or jet aircraft without power tools. Our civilization depends on power tools. Yet, the application of computing power to corporate systems is often done by hand methods. Design of the interlocking computer applications of a modern enterprise is no less complex than the design of a microchip or a jet aircraft. To attempt this design using hand methods is ridiculous.

Power tools change the methods of construction. Object-oriented modeling and design change the basic way we think about systems. Now that such tools exist, the entire application development process should be reexamined and improved. Advanced power tools give rise to the need for an engineering-like discipline. OO techniques are the foundation for this discipline.

Important from the business point of view is that power tools for software change *what can be constructed,* just as power tools for building enable us to create skyscrapers. These changes need to be understood by management at every level. Making the changes is a critical success factor for business. Top management needs to ensure that its I.S. organization is adopting the new solutions as quickly as possible.

> Power tools change what is possible. They enable far more complex software to be built.

EVOLUTION OF SOFTWARE PRODUCTION

Since the industrial revolution, manufacturing techniques have evolved in an extraordinary way: from hand tools to power tools, from mass production to flexible robotic factories. Software building will also evolve from hand methods; the evolution will be very much faster. In both manufacturing and software production, four phases may evolve:

Phase 1: A Craft Industry

Most software today is designed and coded with manual techniques; each program is a unique piece of craftsmanship, rather like the making of clothes in cottages before the industrial revolution or the building of guns by individual gunsmiths in the eighteenth century.

Phase 2: Power Tools and Engineering Methods

I-CASE represents the coming of power tools to software building. Designs are synthesized with the help of a computer, and code with no coding errors is generated from the designs. The tools enforce structured techniques and apply rigorous checks to the design, bringing a much needed engineering-like discipline to the building of software.

Phase 3: Mass Production

In the early use of I-CASE tools, each program is still designed on a one-off basis. Later, repositories become populated with reusable classes, and libraries of reusable classes evolve. Applications are built by assembling preexisting building blocks.

Phase 4: Robot Production

As object-oriented design matures, classes of great complexity are created. Vast libraries of reusable classes are built. Tools assist the developer in specifying requirements and then automatically select and assemble the classes and class methods that can meet the requirements. The toolset carries on a dialog with the designer, enabling him to modify the design, selecting parameters and options.

This evolution could be compared to four generations of a family business making furniture. In the first generation, each piece of furniture is built by hand. In the second generation, lathes, drills, and power tools become available (such as I-CASE tools), but craftsmen still build each piece on a one-off basis. In the third generation, an inventory is built of reusable parts: table tops, legs, chair seats, and so on. Furniture is now assembled from reusable parts with minor custom work. Orders can be filled quickly. The capital required is higher, but the manufacturing cost is lower. Similarly, I-CASE tools will be used with a repository of reusable classes and minor custom work. In the fourth generation, robotic factories assemble the components and allow great variability in what can be built from the components. This is like software tools automatically synthesizing much of the design to meet high-level statements of requirements.

Software tools have not yet evolved to this fourth phase. It could be accomplished by combining object-oriented techniques with:

- A standard repository capable of storing many thousands of classes.
- Classes of extreme reliability built with mathematically based techniques.
- A powerful repository coordinator.
- Intelligent enterprise models that express business rules.
- Expert system techniques for guiding the developer in stating requirements and translating them into design.

INHUMAN USE OF HUMAN BEINGS

Norbert Wiener, the great pioneer of computers, wrote a book with the memorable title *The Human Use of Human Beings* [Wiener, 1954]. In his view, jobs that are inhuman because of drudgery should be done by machines, not people. However, among these jobs, he omitted that of the COBOL programmer.

In a sense, the programmer's job is inhuman, because programmers are required to write large amounts of complex code without errors. To build the strategic and competitive systems that business needs, we want complex new procedures programmed in three months. This is beyond the capability of COBOL programmers.

Many of the tasks that I.S. professionals do are unsuited to our meat-machine brain. They need the precision of an electronic machine. Humans create program specifications that are full of inconsistencies and vagueness. Computers should help humans create specifications and check them at each step for consistency. Humans should not write programs from specifications, because they cannot do that task well. A computer should generate the code needed. When humans want to make changes—a frequent occurrence—they have real problems changing the code. Seemingly innocent changes have unperceived ramifications that can cause a chain reaction of errors.

If the programs needed are *large,* we are in even worse trouble, because many people work together on them. When humans try to interact at the needed level of meticulous detail, communication errors abound. When one human makes a change, it affects the work of others. Often, however, the subtle interconnection is not perceived. Meat machines do not communicate with precision.

The end user perceives problems of the I.S. department but does not know how to solve them. A major part of the problem is that humans are so slow; they often take two years to produce results, and they are delayed by the backlog. It is rather like communicating with a development team in another solar system where the signals take years to get there and back.

Error-free coding is not natural for our animal-like brains. We cannot handle the meticulous detail and the vast numbers of combinatorial paths. Furthermore, if we want thousands of lines of code produced per day, then the job is even more inhuman. It is a job for machines. Only recently have we begun to understand how to make machines do it.

The era of code generators, specification tools, mathematically based design, and software design automation is still in an early phase. The era of artificial intelligence is just now beginning to mature, with machines that can reason automatically using large numbers of rules. As these capabilities mature, machines will become vastly more powerful.

CHAIN REACTION

> The automation of software development is the beginning of a chain reaction.

When developers build software out of building blocks, they can create more complex building blocks (whether this is done with object-oriented design or other techniques). High-level constructs can be built out of primitive constructs. Still higher level ones can be built out of these and so on. Highly powerful constructs will evolve for different system types and application areas.

Essential in this is the rigor of the mechanism that enforces correct interfacing among the modules. This rigor allows pyramiding, so that modules can be built out of other modules. The rigor may be achieved by using rules and rule-based processing to enforce integrity in the designs and ensure consistency when separate components are linked. It may be achieved using mathematically based constructs of provable correctness, using design techniques which scale up to large systems. As designers of rule-based, I-CASE tools have discovered, a large number of rules are needed to enforce consistency and integrity.

Essential to the chain reaction is an intelligent repository that stores a large quantity of reusable designs from which procedures can be built. Many developers will use large central repositories as well as repositories on LAN servers.

As the software pyramids grow, software must be made as easy to use as possible. The complexity of software will become formidable, but must be hidden from the users just as the complexity of the telephone network is hidden from telephone customers. Higher-level semantics will be needed for instructing computers to do complex tasks. High-level design languages will allow fast, very complex design. Decision-support dialogs will help complex decision making. Each category of professional will employ an appropriate computer dialog. Click-and-point, object-oriented dialogs using icons will be employed. Speech input and output will mature. The pyramiding of complex software will evolve along with the human-interface tools for making the software easy to use.

Libraries of constructs need to be built for different classes of applications. Some examples of application classes that need their own libraries of operations and control structures are:

- Commercial procedures.
- Financial application.

- Design of operating systems.
- Automatic database navigation.
- Query languages.
- Design of circuits with NOR, NAND gates, and so on.
- Control of robots.
- Cryptanalysis.
- Missile control.
- Building architecture.
- Design graphics.
- Network design.
- Avionics.
- CAD/CAM, computer-aided design and manufacturing.
- Production control.
- Project management.
- Decision-support graphics.

The list is endless.

REPOSITORY STANDARDS

At the heart of CASE tools is the repository, providing libraries of reusable classes and facilitating reusable design. The repository should be an object-oriented database, storing information about the objects that appear on the screens of I-CASE tools and using methods to validate integrity and coordinate the knowledge in the repository. The repository, containing many objects and rules, is very complex.

It is essential for the future of software that standards exist for the repository. Having no *open* standard for the repository and its tool interfaces would be like having no standard for music CDs. Sony CDs would not play on Philips equipment, and so on. An open standard for the I-CASE repository and its interfaces is as important to the future of software development as the CD standard is to the music industry.

Open standards should incorporate the following:

- A *repository* with a standard means of accessing and using the information it stores.
- A *repository model* which defines the classes stored in the repository, their methods, and the relationships among classes.
- *Repository services* that use precisely defined methods for checking the consistency and integrity of information stored in the repository.
- *Version control* for managing the separate versions of objects that are stored.
- *Tool services* defining the objects that are created or modified by the tools and then stored in the repository.
- *Standards formats* for object requests and responses. Standard techniques for object interoperability (such as the OMG Object Request Broker).

- A *standard GUI (Graphic User Interface)* to make CASE tools and their diagrams look and feel similar and easy to use.
- *Workstation services* for enabling desktop computers to interact with the repository on a LAN server or mainframe.
- Full use of existing open systems standards.

Development tools will evolve and change. Diverse tools will be built by many corporations—often small, inventive corporations. The repositories ought to be usable with all these tools. Corporate repositories are already growing to a formidable size and are becoming a vital strategic resource, in some cases helping the corporation stay ahead of its competition. Repositories of reusable components will also contain a large quantity of knowledge, sometimes sold as CD-ROMs. If these repositories follow a standard format, they can be used with many different design tools.

PACKAGED SOFTWARE

Object-oriented techniques in combination with standard I-CASE repositories will have a major impact on the packaged software industry. A problem with mainframe application packages is that I.S. organizations buying them often have to modify the package to adapt it to their needs. These packages are difficult and expensive to modify. One survey by EDS showed that modification and maintenance of mainframe package software averaged six times the original cost of the software. To overcome this problem, packaged software should be sold in OO-CASE form, so that its design can be adapted and modified easily and code generated from that design. Having an open standard for the repository will facilitate this greatly.

A problem with the PC software industry is that low prices are dictated by the shops and organizations that distribute software. Creating complex and interesting new software at these low prices is difficult. Only a few items like word processors and spreadsheet tools can generate enough sales to pay for a 100-person-year development effort. Many PC software companies are embroidering their own products with features of questionable value, rather than striking out for a new 100-person-year innovation. They are stuck on a sandbar related to the cost structure of the industry. This dilemma can be resolved by assembling innovative products from licensable object-oriented components.

Recognizing this, Patriot Partners (originally formed by IBM and Metaphor, Inc.) envisioned a new software marketplace. In this vision, many companies create software units that become components of packages that can be used by many vendors on multiple platforms using multiple operating systems, LAN managers, network architectures, graphic user interfaces (GUIs), and so on. A vendor creating a new software product incorporates components from many other vendors. Some of these components may, themselves, represent 100-person-year development efforts. The initial effort of the partnership is called the Constellation project. The goal of Constellation is building a framework to provide interfaces between platforms, networks, operating systems, and GUIs. These interfaces will shield developers from spending their time on these issues.

> We are at the end of the era of single-vendor software. Software of the future, like a car, will contain components from hundreds of vendors.

Patriot Partners visualized a world in which developers build software from many licensed components, rather than creating a monolithic application in house. They described the following needs:

1. The data will include all kinds of text, numbers, and graphics, even video and sound, and will most likely reside in many different locations. The new breed of user will demand comprehensive and transparent access to all these data sources, as well as means to easily organize, analyze, and synthesize the information in persuasive new contexts.

2. Users need entire suites of software tools, able to span broad-ranging, variable tasks. These tools must be built on conceptual models that match the nature of the tasks, and designed so that users do not face the disruptive transitions common today when moving from one software environment to another.

3. Users can create their own high-value application, intuitively and without coding. Business professionals are constantly confronted with context-specific tasks that cannot be satisfied by generic applications. A task may be vital one week and all but forgotten the next. We must give those users the tools to fulfill computing needs as they arise, to attack this week's or this afternoon's new problem [Liddle, 1991].

The vision of Patriot Partners looked promising, and IBM bought Metaphor in July 1991. The Patriot Partners brochure commented:

> The industry's challenge, then, is no less than redefining what an application is, how it is developed, how it gets distributed and how it is used by a new kind of user. If this challenge seems risky, remember that the low-hanging fruit has been picked; there are no more easy million-seller generic applications out there. The greater risk lies in taking today's products from the Baroque to the Rococo, trying to grow by shaving away at competitors' market shares with feature-laden products that add marginal real value at best.

The Patriot Partners' vision is in many ways similar to that of the OMG with its Object Management Architecture. The OMG is creating an open architecture, whereas an IBM-based initiative may lead to a proprietary architecture. OMG's Object Request Broker is a vital resource for linking the software components of many vendors and facilitating client-server interaction among objects.

REUSABILITY

The future of software depends upon being able to build it from reusable components. The best way to achieve reusability is probably with OO components designed to be used with OO-CASE tools. The potential value of reusable object-oriented designs is immense. Applications may one day be built largely with off-the-shelf components that can be assembled and modified very quickly. This opportunity presents a great challenge to the packaged software industry.

> Reusable components should be designed to be modified. The dictum "SAME AS,
> EXCEPT. . ." applies to reusability.

Conversion of the software industry to OO-CASE design will not happen overnight.
The investment tied up in existing software is large, and the resistance of major software
companies to new methods is high. Perhaps, relatively small or new corporations will sell
reusable OO-CASE designs first.

Patriot Partners gave two scenarios for software built from complex OO components
with precisely defined protocols for interlinking the components [Liddle, 1991]:

> **Scenario 1:** An engineer working on a jet aircraft design uses his AeroCAD package's
> drafting assistant, dimension engine and parametric modeling component tools. To get
> a 3-D rendering, he pulls in the rendering component from another favorite applica-
> tion, Stanford Graphics. To complete the drawing, he calls up the blend tool in Stucco
> Illustrator to realistically shade the aircraft skin. Since all three applications use com-
> ponent-and-protocol architecture, the tools interact quickly and cooperatively, without
> forcing the engineer to load different programs, exit applications, or import and export
> files.

> **Scenario 2:** A project team has a problem. The company's best seller bleach bottle is
> too heavy for the new molding machines and needs redesign. Manufacturing designs a
> bottle that meets requirements, and creates wireframe and 3-D views of it. Packaging
> uses those images to figure how many will fit on store shelves, how they look side-by-
> side, and whether labels need changing. Advertising evaluates how the new design
> will work in ad layouts and point-of-sale displays. Finance analyzes manufacturing
> costs and the need for larger boxes to ship the new bottles. The brand manager reports
> the results of the project to management, relying on a database containing bottle
> images, dimensions, financials, and consumer responses. Because all project team
> members use component-based software, they easily share information over their net-
> work, manipulating images and data to contribute to the complete solution without
> recreating or reentering any material.

Box 28.1 describes desirable characteristics of future software development.

FORMAL METHODS

Today's research on formal (mathematically based) methods has led to a few impressive
results. Building software with these techniques has been extremely difficult, so we need
powerful tools which hide the difficulties. Software should be created from provably correct constructs. Designers should assemble building blocks, each of which is known to be
correct, with tools that ensure that the interfaces among the building blocks are correct.

When CASE tools generate code which is untouched by human hand, the language
the code runs in need not be COBOL, PL/I, or C; it could be a language designed to facilitate mathematical provability and parallel processing (such as OCCAM [Roscoe, 1986]).
Chips may be designed to execute such a language (like the transputer). Specification
languages may also be designed mathematically (such as Z [Spivey, 1989] or Object Z).

BOX 28.1   Desirable characteristics of future
software development.

In the near future, desktop machines will have optical disks capable of holding hundreds of millions of lines of code. Software of far greater complexity than today's is needed and will probably be sold on optical disks. Software components from many companies will be interlinked and cross-licensed. In such a world, the following characteristics are desirable:

- *Software is built out of components from many companies.* No one company is likely to build monolithic software of the complexity required. Instead, software companies will create new applications that are assembled from existing components and some new code.

- *Components have OO design with encapsulation and polymorphism.* Components should not only be reusable but also easily maintained and extendable.

- *Many OO components are designed to be modified.* The dictum "SAME AS, EXCEPT. . ." applies. Modification is sometimes achieved with parameters or menus, sometimes by subtyping.

- *OO components are licensed with well structured and controllable licensing terms.* Many corporations should sell reusable classes that other corporations can use in their software.

- *Open standards* should exist to allow objects to intercommunicate.

- *Components should reside on a standard repository.* In the absence of international open standards for software repositories, *de facto* standards from large vendors or industry consortia will define the repository metamodel and user interfaces.

- *A repository coordinator checks the integrity of the repository contents.* Thousands of rules are used with OO methods and inferential reasoning to ensure that the repository contents fit together with integrity (as with today's major I-CASE repositories encyclopedias).

- *All development is repository based.* Integrated CASE tools facilitate the analysis and design of software and the linkage of repository components.

- *Licensed software components have OO descriptions (in the repository) that developers use when building applications.* Components are designed to work with OO I-CASE tools. All development is done with such tools.

- *Software design is generated, where possible, from classes, templates, OO models, rules, declarative statements, and menus.* CASE tools should provide the maximum design automation.

- *Code is generated where possible, not hand programmed.* CASE tools should provide the most powerful code-generation capabilities.

- *Design is independent of the platform on which the code runs.* Code can be generated from the design for many major platforms.

- *Specified interfaces make platform independence possible.* Specified and standard interfaces should enable software to run with:
  — Multiple host machines.
  — Multiple operating systems.

BOX 28.1 *(Continued)*

— Multiple storage subsystems.
— Multiple database management systems.
— Multiple network architectures.
— Multiple LAN managers.
— Multiple GUIs (Graphic User Interfaces).

- *Specified protocols allow objects to work together.* Specified and standardized protocols should exist for both static and dynamic schema linkages.

- *Specified protocols allow interprocess, interhost, and networked interaction.* The same classes may be linked within one machine, within a client-server system, or across an enterprise.

- *Specified protocols allow portability.* There should be smooth portability from small machines to large machines, and from stand-alone systems to enterprisewide systems and interenterprise systems.

- *Software is designed for multimedia platforms.* Multimedia will include text, graphics, images, animation, sound, and video. Many objects will use images, animation, sound, and video.

- *Software is designed for maximum ease of use with a GUI.* Software should be designed for a graphic user interface and be able to work with the different dominant graphic user interfaces.

- *Software is designed for highly parallel processors.* An OO event schema may be used to design how operations execute on different processors simultaneously. Parallel processors should be used for specialized functions such as database management, searching, and display generation.

- *Software is built where possible from executable specifications.* Specifications should be precise enough that code can be generated from them. They should be built with OO I-CASE tools using graphics as well as rule-based and mathematical techniques.

- *Specification techniques provide a way to think about systems that improve conceptual clarity.* The techniques should be easy to use and learn. At higher levels, they should be employed by end users—CASE tools.

- *Formal (mathematically based) techniques should be used to prove the correctness of software, where practical.* Provable code may be generated in languages which are themselves mathematically based (such as OCCAM).

- *Mathematically based techniques for ensuring correctness should be made easy to use.* I-CASE tools should employ an easy-to-use, user interface which invokes mathematically based techniques to achieve maximum precision in specification. Code should be generatable from this specification for different platforms.

- *System design and program design use visual techniques.* CASE users should be given maximum help in visualizing and automating designs.

(Continued)

BOX 28.1 *(Continued)*

- *Fast iterative prototyping is used.* CASE tools should give the fastest, smoothest prototyping capability. They should allow the system developer to progress as rapidly as possible through the following stages:

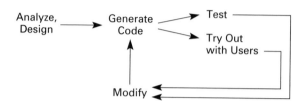

- *Expert systems help developers use libraries of components.* Developers should have access to vast libraries of components, and have an expert system help them to locate the most appropriate components and use them correctly.

- *A comprehensive cataloging scheme is used for software components.* A scheme, perhaps like the Library of Congress classification for books, is needed for cataloging classes that form licensable software components.

- *Developers are able to locate and obtain software components they need via networks.* Software development and cross licensing will be a worldwide industry using worldwide networks.

- *Enterprise models are built with OO techniques.* Enterprisewide information engineering should employ OO modeling. Business people should be able to understand the business models and request changes when needed.

- *The enterprise models form input into a design generator that employs a code generator.* Enterprisewide information engineering should have a high-level OO enterprise model driving OO business area models. These business area models are input to OO system design, where the design tools link to a code generator.

- *A seamless and automated progression moves from high-level specification to design and code.* All stages in the progression update the knowledge in a single repository.

- *End users can validate and help create the high-level specifications.* Specifications may include business rules expressed in English (or other human language), equations, professional drawings, or, in general, the language of the end user. Specifications should show event schemas that users can understand.

It is desirable to have a design chain which progresses from the easiest and most powerful visualization of systems to mathematically formal specifications, to automatic generation of provable code, and finally to chips that correctly execute such code.

Probably the best way to put provable constructs to use is with OO techniques. Classes may be guaranteed correct and designed to check the preconditions and postconditions of every *method* executed.

As such controls to aid software validation are created and improved, it should be made illegal to bypass them. The controls should be applied automatically, and the repository coordinator should enforce consistency. To tamper with generated code should be forbidden. Software builders left to their own devices find reasons to bypass controls; this results in loss of reliability and problems in maintenance, mysterious bugs, and much greater costs in the long run. Reliable software needs "pure" OO tools in which encapsulation cannot be bypassed. The integrity controls should be applied by run-time facilities and OO databases.

> Far more emphasis is needed on formal methods, provable correctness, and enforcement of integrity controls.

PARALLELISM

The PC or LAN server of the future will have many processors. Processor chips of the future will be mass produced in vast quantities. When many millions of one processor chip are made, that processor can be very low in cost. Japan has plans to flood the world with low-cost processor chips. In the future, powerful computers should be built out of many small computers that yield to the economics of mass production. Examples of highly parallel machines have existed for some time, but designing software for applications that run efficiently on them has been very difficult.

The search for ways to introduce a high degree of parallelism into computing is an important one. A million-dollar computer should not be doing one thing at a time; it should be doing ten thousand things at a time. The Connection Machine, from Thinking Machines, Inc., has 65,536 small processors operating in parallel. Other machines with different architecture will be built from mass-produced wafers, each with many chips.

> The evolution of single-processor machines occurred in the first four decades of computing.
>
> The evolution of multiprocessor machines is occurring in the second four decades of computing.

Software for highly parallel machines will necessarily be intricate. However, analysts do not think naturally in terms of parallel processes. The culture of computing and algorithm theory relates to sequential operations, not parallel ones. To bridge the gap between how analysts think and how parallel computers should be used, we need modeling techniques, design tools, and nonprocedural languages, such as SQL and PROLOG, that can be translated by generators into parallel processing. Some types of formal decomposition indicate clearly what steps in complex procedures can take place in parallel [e.g., Hamilton, 1976]. Some processes need parallel machines to be efficient, for example, searching large databases, high-throughput transaction processing, database machines (like Teradata), image generators, compression and decompression of digitized television signals, and possibly human speech processing.

Event diagrams indicate how different operations can function in parallel (i.e., simultaneously) on the same or different processors. A challenge of the OO-CASE industry today is to evolve CASE tools that help to visualize how multiprocessor machines can be used, or to take specifications and implement them with different OO classes running on different machines. We need to evolve techniques that make it practical to use microelectronic wafers or boards containing many advanced RISC processors.

NETWORKS AND DISTRIBUTION OF OBJECTS

The first attempts at interaction between humans and computers were crude. They employed dumb terminals, slow transmission lines, and cumbersome mainframes. The personal computer brought a new world of interaction between humans and machines. The Macintosh demonstrated that computers could be made easy to use. However, personal computers had limited power. The desktop machine was needed, making use of more powerful machines. The desktop machine needed high-bandwidth links to powerful servers.

LAN technology provided the high-bandwidth link—initially, 10 million bits per second; as optical LANs spread, 100 million bits per second; and in the future, a billion or so bits per second. LANs have created islands of computing. If, instead of accessing a machine on the LAN, the user accesses a machine miles away, the transmission speed drops to low figures. A bit-mapped screen can no longer be painted with an interactive response time; thought processes dependent on subsecond interaction with the server can no longer occur. The telecommunications companies of the world are installing optical-fiber trunks. One trunk cable contains a large number of fibers, and each fiber transmits more than half a billion bits per second. A major market for fiber-based telecommunications will be the accessing of servers, previously only accessed with a LAN. Vast networks of optical fibers will be woven around the earth, linking a billion computers—each one a maximum of only 68 milliseconds away from any other.

OO classes in one machine will interact with classes in many other machines. Object-oriented analysis and design is an appropriate way to think about distributed computing. A class will not necessarily know where a request comes from. Each class performs its own methods and is unaware of the effect it may have on other operations that follow. It must, however, protect its own data types.

In conventional distributed systems, data can be accessed in ad hoc ways. There may be little or no assurance of who is doing what to the data via the network. With object-oriented systems, the data is *encapsulated,* as it is in biological cells, and is not available for random manipulation. Without encapsulation, to build distributed systems open to masses of users is dangerous. Encapsulation seems essential to protect the integrity of data.

INTERCORPORATE COMPUTER INTERACTION

Networks have created many new business opportunities. Corporations have streamlined their procedures as it became possible to transmit any information to any location.

Initially, computer network applications were built within one corporation. Then it became clear that major business advantages could accrue from intercorporate networks. Airlines built networks linking travel-agent PCs directly into airline reservation computers. Corporations put software in their customer locations enabling automatic reordering. Supermarket computers transmitted market research information direct to their suppliers. Computers in one corporation became linked to computers in other corporations. Commercial data processing is evolving through the following stages:

1. *Stand-alone batch processing.* Stand-alone machines process batches of work.

2. *Offline telecommunications.* Batches are transmitted off line. Orders are sent by fax.

3. *Online transaction processing.* Terminals for handling transactions are linked directly to computer centers.

4. *Distributed network processing.* Localized processing environments, including client-server systems, are linked to computer centers in the same corporation.

5. *Simple EDI (Electronic Data Interchange).* A corporate computer center is linked directly to the terminals or PCs of customers or suppliers.

6. *EDI networks.* Corporate computers can be connected online to computers in many suppliers, outlets, customers, and trading partners.

7. *Intercorporate computer interaction.* Computers in one corporation interact directly with computers in other corporations.

To achieve intercorporate computer interaction, standards are vital. The world of the future will be one of open systems and standards. Single-vendor, proprietary, vanity architectures will give way to architectures designed for open connectivity, portability, and worldwide access to databases.

Standards for electronic documents will be important, so that machines in one corporation can send electronic purchase orders, invoices, receipts, and so on, to the computers in other corporations. Where such standards are not yet adequate, corporations will be able to make contractual agreements about the format of electronically exchanged data.

SPEED OF INTERACTION

As we progress from the era of stand-alone batch processing through the above stages, business interactions tend to speed up. With online systems, events happen more quickly than with batch systems. With networks, information can flow immediately from where it originates to where it is used in decision making. With EDI, information passes between corporations quickly, facilitating just-in-time inventory control and continuous flow planning in manufacturing. Money passes around the world almost instantly with electronic transfer of funds.

We are progressing to a world in which the computers in one corporation interact directly with the computers of its customers, suppliers, and service providers. A manufacturer's purchasing application scans the possible supplier computers to find goods of the best price and delivery schedule. Computers in hospitals and clinics automatically reorder supplies by transmission to supplier computers (such as the pioneering system at American Hospital Supply, bought by Baxter). Travel-agent computers are online to airline computers, and soon, a secretary's computer can do everything that a travel agent's computer does. While travel agents' or secretaries' computers search for low fares, airline computers, in turn, adjust seat fares and bargain flights in an attempt to maximize the load factors on planes.

Trading rooms in stock markets and futures markets become automated, so that traders worldwide can make deals. Brokers worldwide can make trades, and often the public can buy stocks online, bypassing brokers and their commissions.

Bar scanners inform computers in stores what goods are selling, and stores adjust their prices constantly in an attempt to maximize profit. Computers in stores send details of sales to manufacturers' computers, bypassing traditional market research. Buyers' computers search for deals, and sellers' computers constantly adjust prices and terms. Both sets of machines try to maximize profits or provide the best service. When computers in one corporation interact directly with computers in another corporation, middlemen can be bypassed. Business transactions happen instantly. The windows of opportunity are much shorter. Prices, set by computers, change constantly. Complexity increases because the interacting machines can handle complex airline fares, price structures, manufacturing schedules, and so on.

An order placed in Ireland with an order-entry computer in Germany triggers a manufacturing planning system in New York to place items into a manufacturing schedule in Dallas that requires chips from Japan built into circuit boards in Taiwan for final assembly in the robotic factory in Dallas and shipment from a warehouse in England.

Society will be laced with networks for computer-to-computer interaction among separate enterprises—worldwide. These networks will decrease reaction times, decrease inventories and buffers, bypass middlemen and bureaucrats, and increase complexity as the machines handle ever more elaborate schemes to try to maximize profit. Small corporations will plug into the networks of computers that offer specialized goods or services at competitive prices.

In this world of interacting computers, software reliability and security will be vitally important. OO encapsulation will be essential.

THE NEED FOR FAST DEVELOPMENT

As commerce speeds up because of automated systems interacting worldwide, many new competitive opportunities emerge. An era of rapid change is always an era filled with new opportunities. Slow-moving corporations are bypassed. Entrepreneurs and inventive I.S. professionals will invent new systems with new ways to compete.

New competitive systems are needed. These systems need to be flexible, built quickly, and controlled by business people or end users. Avoiding the straitjacket of traditional mainframe development with its multiyear backlog and maintenance problems is vital.

To achieve fast development, new systems, as far as possible, should be built out of classes that already exist and can be adapted to circumstances. Repository-based development is needed—with automated tools. The tools should make it quick and easy to customize a standard graphic user interface. Systems should be built so that they can be changed quickly and easily, without the maintenance problems of the past.

The methodology for RAD (rapid application development) is very different from traditional methodologies [Martin, 1991]. It should be designed to maximize the efficiency of OO repository-based techniques.

> RAD methodologies will be increasingly essential for business survival.

INTERNATIONAL STANDARDS FOR REUSABLE CLASSES

Large enterprises will have hundreds of thousands of computers, with many millions of MIPS (million instructions per second) worldwide. Managements that fail to build an efficiently functioning organism with this power will not survive. The efficient corporate organism will have repositories storing large amounts of knowledge about the enterprise, its classes, methods, and business values. The classes and operations will be designed for reusability across the enterprise. Commercial paperwork will be replaced by electronic documents in the format of international (or de facto) standards, because computers everywhere will exchange such documents with other computers.

Today, standards for EDI (Electronic Data Interchange) are evolving rapidly. In some cases, standards committees are starting to define documents in object-oriented terms. ODA (the Office Document Architecture) from ISO (the International Standards Organization) defines MO:DCA—the *Mixed Object Document Content Architecture*. This includes an Object Contents Architecture defining image formats, graphics, fonts, and so on, and an Object Method Architecture, defining methods for employing fonts, images, and so on.

As stage 7 of the above stages becomes widespread, changing the world's patterns of commerce, standards should be established for many of the reusable classes used in commerce: customers, accounts, orders, parts, locations, and so on. Millions of transactions will pass between corporations every second. Corporations whose computers interact need not have common classes. This commonality could come from mutual agreements or from large vendors such as IBM, DEC, or possibly large telephone companies. International standards for the major classes of commerce will become increasingly desirable.

CODE GENERATION FROM THE ENTERPRISE MODEL

Executable program code should be generated from the highest level specification possible. A major evolution in I-CASE tools will be the generation of code from higher level specifications. If the enterprise model contains rules expressing the way the enterprise functions, code can be generated directly from the enterprise model. The enterprise model should be understood by the business managers. It should clarify thinking about how they want the enterprise to operate. A precise expression of how the enterprise operates should reside in the repository and should be discussed in workshop sessions. Code should be generated directly from this. A change in business procedures should then be directly translated into the code for implementing the procedures.

The term *Code Generation from the Enterprise Model (CGEM)* has been used to describe this higher level code generation. It requires object-oriented modeling and design. The design chain should progress as automatically as possible from intelligent enterprise modeling and visualization to the generation of bug-free code.

Events, objects, and business rules provide a way of describing the enterprise that business managers and staff can understand. We have stressed that object-oriented techniques provide *a way to think about systems*—a way to think about a business. As such, the subject ought to be taught in business schools and management training courses, as well as in computer science schools and system analyst courses. At its different levels, it can be understood by both business people and computer professionals and provides a vital way to bridge the gap between these two cultures.

Business schools should teach how businesses work with diagrams showing object types, operations, event types, and trigger rules. The courses should use CASE tools for planning and analysis. New types of charts will probably be devised that help human communication. To become a basis for system specification, they should be designed so that they have the precision that enables repository-based tools to check their integrity and consistency with other diagrams.

As we acquire the capability to generate code from the enterprise model or business area model, the development lifecycle will become faster. The libraries of reusable classes will become more mature and enterprise models will evolve, representing business rules more comprehensively. Much development will consist of the successive refinement of existing applications, rather than the creation of entirely new applications.

THE EVOLUTION OF PROGRAMMING TECHNIQUE

Generating code from the enterprise model is one example of programming techniques reflecting *the way users think* rather than *the way the machinery works.*

In the beginning, humans had to program using the computer's instruction set. When computer programs changed from switches to languages, the new programs were organized around the machine instruction set. Therefore, the first languages and machine instructions were very similar. A process-oriented programming model was the result. For example, programs for addition were organized around the machine process of addition: loading registers with numbers, executing the add instruction, and dealing with overflow and underflow. As shown in Fig. 28.1, the programming technique steadily became more remote from the way the hardware operates. It moved closer to human language, to the way humans solve problems, and to human professional disciplines. As this happened, programming became more dependent on interpreters, compilers, and then code generators and CASE tools.

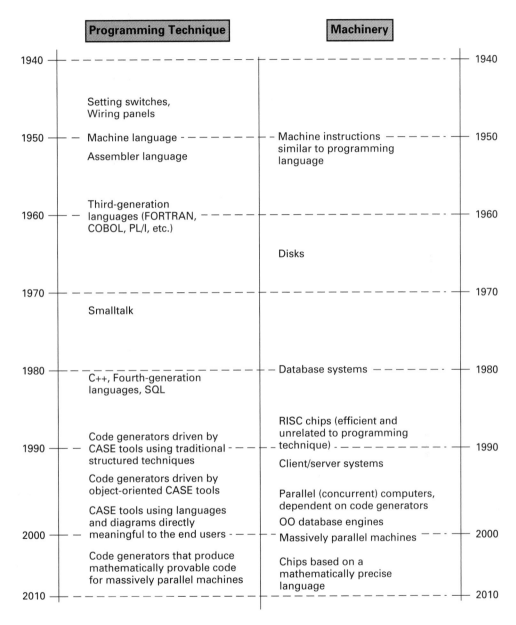

Figure 28.1 In the beginning, humans had to program using the machine's instruction set. The programming technique and the machine steadily diverged, the hardware becoming more cost efficient and the programming methods becoming closer to the way users think about their world.

Meanwhile, the machinery evolved away from an instruction set that was good for humans to technology that was as fast and cost effective as possible. We had generations of RISC (reduced instruction set computing) chips and then concurrent computers with many processors. The RISC chips drifted far from what humans could have programmed easily without software translation. Concurrent computers carried the trend further. It would be difficult for humans to write code that executed on multiple independent processors simultaneously. We have a tradition of *sequential*—not parallel—logic, mathematics, algorithms, and languages. Processor chips of the future may be designed to execute mathematically based languages to enhance verifiably correct behavior in software. CASE tools can generate code for such chips.

Object-oriented analysis and design help users to think about their world in terms that can be represented naturally on the CASE screen and help code generators to produce code for concurrent computers, leading eventually to massively parallel machines with large numbers of cheap processor chips. An object-oriented database engine may be one way to take advantage of parallelism. Corporations of the future may be run with vast networks of object-oriented database engines.

As users become familiar with using the icons and panels as objects on the computer screen, using computers and building applications becomes easier. The users should model their world in an OO fashion with tools that allow models to be expanded into detail and made to run actively. In this way, the distinction between modeling and executable systems blurs.

At the same time that system building techniques become closer to human thinking, the code generators should become more rigorous and based on formal (mathematical) techniques. In the future, the language that the processor chips execute may be a mathematically-based language which facilitates proofs of correctness and for which system builders never normally write code.

PYRAMIDS OF COMPLEXITY

The complexity of living things built by nature is awesome to a computer professional. The brain is so intricate that it cannot be mapped, imitated, or understood in detail. It is rich in diversity—yet self-protecting and self-renewing. The things of nature are complex, because they are grown using organic components. Similarly, we can develop software and information system components and grow complex automated systems. However, we need disciplines and tools that facilitate and enable us to manage such growth.

> The designers of the future must stand on the shoulders of the designers of the present.

As the pyramids of complexity grow, we will reach very high-level OO constructs, often designed for parallel RISC engines. Vast libraries of such constructs will exist. Sophisticated tools and languages will enable developers to employ the constructs they need. Many millions of computers linked by worldwide data networks will exchange constructs from these libraries. Knowledge-based systems will acquire ever more knowledge and become self-feeding. Intelligent network directories will allow machines and users to find the resources they need.

The programmer of handmade COBOL with his ad hoc designer will become part of the romantic past of computer history like the weavers in their cottages when the industrial revolution began.

REFERENCES

Hamilton, M., and S. Zeldin, "Higher Order Software: A Methodology for Defining Software," *IEEE Transactions on Software Engineering,* 2:3, March 1976, pp. 25–32.

Liddle, David E., *Patriot Partners: A Vision of a New Software Marketplace,* brochure from Patriot Partners, Mountain View, CA, 1991.

Martin, James, *Rapid Application Development,* Macmillan, New York, 1991.

Parnas, David L., "Software Aspects of Strategic Defense Systems," *Communications of the ACM,* 28:12, December 1985, pp. 1326–1335.

Roscoe, A. W., and C. A. R. Hoare, *Laws of OCCAM Programming,* Monograph PRG-53, Oxford University Computing Laboratory, Programming Research Group, February 1986.

Spivey, J. M., *The Z Notation: A Reference Manual,* Prentice Hall, Englewood Cliffs, NJ, 1989.

Wiener, Norbert, *The Human Use of Human Beings: Cybernetics and Society,* Da Capo Press, New York, 1954 (reprinted Avon Books, 1979).

AN OO METHODOLOGY COOKBOOK

Chapter 1 discussed why and how methodologies should be adapted to the needs of development projects—and not the other way around. However, the technology to adapt methodologies is not yet widely available. In response, this part contains a methodology cookbook that can be used right now for a large variety of projects. The methodology addresses the complete system development lifecycle discussed in Chapter 2. It contains method fragments for developing object-oriented and client/server systems. Additionally, it suggests ways in which BPR and AI efforts can be integrated into the system development project.

Part VII is called a *cookbook* because it is meant to be a guide and reference for developing systems. As such, this document is not meant to be the ultimate authority for system development. This methodology must still be adapted to the particular needs of each project. In other words, this text can be taken and modified appropriately. With an automated tool, the task is easier.*

The cookbook describes five phases of system development: planning, analysis, design, construction, and transition. Additionally, it defines two distinct sets of procedures for each system development phase—one for the system engineer and one for the manager.

The name given to this methodology is *corporate object engineering.*

---

*This methodology is available from James Martin & Co. on a computer automated method-engineering (CAME) tool.

Chapter 29

Methodology Overview

INTRODUCTION TO CORPORATE OBJECT ENGINEERING (COE)

The methodology defined in Part VII is based on an approach from James Martin & Co. entitled *corporate object engineering (COE)*.

> *Corporate object engineering* is a cookbook for successful business systems delivery. It presents a full set of ingredients (including object-based and other essential techniques) and a recipe (including a process addressing planning, analysis, design, construction, and transition). COE focuses on building distributed, commercial, and business-driven solutions. It is best suited to iterative development with small, multidisciplined teams.

WHAT MAKES THIS METHODOLOGY DIFFERENT?

The COE methodology described in this part was not produced by merely modifying an information engineering (IE) methodology to include OO. Instead, IE was completely reengineered. Methods have been improved, technology has changed, and system-development philosophies have evolved. As a result, the approach to system development must be rebuilt from the ground up. Some of the following items provide a few primary reasons why information needs to be reengineered and why the COE methodology is different.

Not Just Software Engineering

As discussed in Chapter 2, software is just one way of implementing an enterprise domain. When reengineering an enterprise, all implementation mechanisms must be considered—whether they be people, machines, or computers. Here, traditional developers "take off the blinders" and see that there is more in the world than just data. Developers need to see that there are many kinds of business objects. An object might be automated or nonautomated. It might be a sound bite, a picture, a button, a control unit, a process, an arm on a robot—and it may *even* be a piece of data.

COE is designed to work in a corporate environment as a complement to business reengineering and redesign efforts. That is why the term *corporate object engineering* was chosen for this methodology. Many practitioners also refer to this methodology using such names as *information engineering with objects* and *object-oriented information engineering (OOIE)*. This is fine. However, by using the word "information," these practitioners must ensure that they are clear about the scope of their methodologies. If the name means that the methodologies are restricted to information-related development, the practitioners must realize that such methodologies are a *subset* of COE. If they use the definition above, COE is but a synonym.

Heterogeneous Environments

Until the mid-1980s, most systems were developed for mainframes and mainframe software. This monolithic environment has given way to great varieties of automation platforms and their connecting networks. With this change, new or different sets of issues arise in such areas as configuration management, version control, security and integrity, distribution of both data and process, backup and recovery, and transaction management. Furthermore, because of the diversity of environments, even the approach to testing has changed. We still need unit, integration, system, and acceptance testing, but now we also need *beta* testing. Acceptance testing insured that the application features and functionality are correct. Beta testing goes further by checking application performance and timing due to the diverse configurations. The nature of prototyping must also change because of this diversity. Here, prototyping will not be limited to demonstrating proof of concept—it will also demonstrate proof of technology. It will demonstrate whether the application will both work and interface. Using prototyping in this manner will assist the designer to determine tradeoffs as early as possible.

Top-down Development is not Required

For many years, top-down development used be considered the only correct way to develop systems. The principal reason for developing in this manner was to identify the major application requirements before proceeding to a more detailed level. If any requirements were discovered after implementation, retrofitting the application would be very costly. This problem has been reduced substantially using an OO approach, because every data and process component is located one time in a single, predictable place. Modifying and extending components is thus simplified.

In most situations, top-down development is still preferable. There is no substitute for having a good, clear understanding of an application domain. If a developer's concepts are not sound, the resulting OO classes will not be either. Therefore, an application's requirements should be understood as thoroughly as possible. With this kind of understanding, a bottom-up or middle-out approach to OO development can and does work effectively. Moreover, a bottom-up or middle-out approach might be the *only* way to solve certain kinds of problems effectively. Domain experts cannot always fathom new and complex problems by starting at high levels of abstraction. Instead, they need to start at their own level of competence. From this point, development can proceed in both a downward and upward manner—compliments of the extensible and reusable nature of oo.

Not Just Iterative Development

COE supports not just iterative development, but also concurrent engineering. As discussed in Chapter 2, there are iterations to keep each project to a manageable size. However, the project phases can overlap which shortens the time. It also allows for learning within the project and makes effective use of today's rapid development tools. Additionally, this approach has other essential implications: it has shorter time frames (four to six months), smaller teams (four to six persons), and multidisciplined teams.

Modular Component Approach

OO enables developers to employ a *component* approach to system development. Here, a given component can be used in many different situations. Put another way, the same component can be reused by many applications and in many contexts. To accomplish this, a component should not require any knowledge of how or why it is being invoked. Nor should it contain knowledge of what should be invoked after its completion. By being context free, the component does not have to be changed when its context is changed.

Another property of components is that they should be seen by requesters as *blackboxes*. When viewed in this way, their requester does not need to know how the component works—only its preconditions and postconditions, plus input and output variables. The component, then, can be reused without the burden of knowing every detail of its inner workings and data requirements. The only data requirements that must be known should be the minimum required to request the component. The remaining data requirements should be the concern of the component itself—not the requester. For example, a Fill Order operation would require the requester only to provide an order that has been accepted and not filled. In return, the operation will return a filled order. All the other concerns, such as bill of materials, customers, back ordering, make-or-buy decisions, and so on, are solely the concern of the operation—not the requester. This is a major departure from conventional, structure-development approaches where the requester must specify all the internal and external requirements of a component. (The process of checking the leveled model and specifying all input and output flow requirements was known as *balancing*.)

A final note is that components are not limited to being program code. They can also be business models and patterns. In other words, COE supports reuse *in the large*.

Evolution, not Revolution

The notion of change is certainly predominant in the above discussion. Notions such as objects, events, business rules, and reengineering add to our methodology "soup." However, even with the goal of reengineering IE methodologies, many of the established diagrams, methods, techniques, and guidelines still support system developers usefully. For instance, entity diagrams can be enhanced and used as object diagrams. This was primarily done by expanding the diagram to incorporate an OO philosophy—not just by changing the word *entity* to the word *object*. The *structural* approach used by traditional IE is relevant to COE. So, while the IE reengineering effort tried to start over, it found the COE was doing many of the same or similar aspects as IE.

In summary, COE can be seen as an evolution, not a revolution. A little enhancement here, a little addition there eventually adds up to a lot of change. Yet in the end, COE retained a similar look and feel so that transition from IE to COE is facilitated. In fact, one could argue that if COE were massively different, there was something very wrong with the way we traditionally developed business. Yet, IE was a useful way to develop systems—in its time. But as we learn and grow, change occurs. The goal of COE is not only to reflect that change, but to provide a platform and foundation for future change. To change now, yet be indifferent to future technological developments, would result in a stagnant methodology. In response to this, COE represents not only an evolution in methodology, but is *itself* evolvable. Method engineering (see Chapter 1) plays an important role in the COE approach.

Figure 29.1 depicts a projection of how COE will replace IE over time.

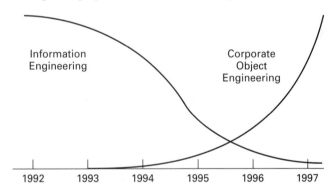

Figure 29.1   A method for a full lifecycle methodology.

SUMMARY OF DEVELOPMENT PHASES

The methodology contained in the following chapters covers the phases required for a full lifecycle development and are illustrated in Fig. 29.2. (The purpose and overall content of these phases was presented in Chapter 2.) There are no events defined in this figure, because one phase does not have to be completed before the next can begin. (A discussion of waterfall, spiral, and concurrent methodologies was also presented in Chapter 2.)

Figure 29.2   A method for a full lifecycle methodology.

Chapter 30

Strategy Planning: Engineering Tasks

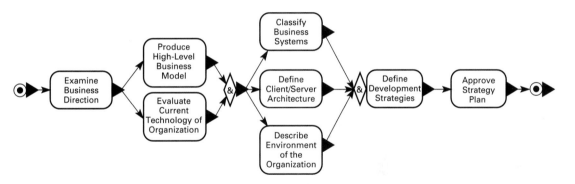

A method for the engineering tasks of strategy planning.

EXAMINE BUSINESS DIRECTION

Too often, people decide to plan systems without understanding the objectives of the business. Any proposed system should be defined in business terms—with its constraints specified and its priorities justified. Top management must understand the system's impact on the organization and support the outcome of this planning project.

One significant objective of this task (illustrated in Fig. 30.1) is getting management involved in both the strategy planning (SP) project and the resulting plan. Another is that of identifying the groups and individuals who should supply information and whose support will be needed for this project's success. In face-to-face meetings, team members will elicit the stakeholders' requirements, objectives, priorities, and future business directions.

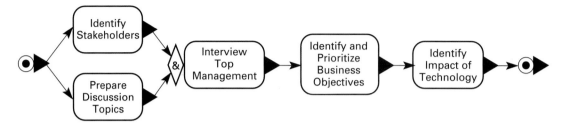

Figure 30.1   A method to Examine Business Direction.

Identify Stakeholder Representatives

Stakeholders are those people, or groups of people, that either affect or are affected by the business in some way. They have a major impact on the way a business sets its objectives and priorities. Those stakeholders *external* to the business should be represented by key individuals having real business power, such as managers and advisors. These representatives must be committed to the strategy planning project for it to succeed.

Stakeholders within the business involve *formal* as well as *actual* business structures. The formal structure of the business unit(s) involved in the project should be identified within the overall structure, such as the division or geographical area. Since the formal structure generally exists only on paper, differences between it and the actual structure must be clarified. Particularly important are the formal and actual responsibilities and authorities of the people who head the organizational units.

Special attention should also be paid to organizational structures that are superimposed on some primary, generally hierarchical, structures. Among the forms these can take are matrix organizational structures, such as those oriented by products or geography. Another form would be temporary structures, such as task forces or project groups. In any case, key individuals having real business power, such as managers, directors, executives and consultants, should be identified to represent both formal and actual business structures.

Prepare Discussion Topics

Discussion topics for management interviews should be based on an analysis of the business issues, of current and expected developments in technology, and of competitor practices.

Familiarity with the business issues is critical—especially the stated objectives, strategies, critical success factors, and inhibitors for the area targeted by the strategy planning project. Internal documents, such as annual reports and business plans, should be reviewed.

Studies from industry and technology should be examined, so that current practices and future directions can be identified for both the business and its supporting technology. In reviewing the state of technology, it is necessary to become familiar with the plans of today's major players in networks, hardware, operating systems, and client/server software. This market is volatile, however, and current size is no guarantee of future performance.

Interview Stakeholder Representatives

Top management should be interviewed to elicit their current and future business objectives and to determine the priorities they give to them. While determining management's requirements and expectations for business systems, try to improve their awareness of the technological possibilities and limitations. Finally, gain further management commitment to the strategy planning project.

A variety of information-gathering techniques can be employed for interviewing top management. Private interviews are useful for reaching key players who are difficult to schedule, or where confidentiality is required. Facilitated workshops combine information gathering with consensus on the issues and priorities.

Identify and Prioritize Business Objectives

From the information gathered, identify the business objectives, critical success factors, and inhibitors. Check the individual interviews, workshops, and business documents for discrepancies and differences of opinion. These differences can be clarified using an objective/organization matrix.

The business objectives should be summarized and ranked by priority. To develop the ranking, another matrix may be helpful: one that lists the objectives and the priority given to them by each person or organizational unit. Verify the ranking with top management. The prioritized objectives will be used to help determine and schedule the subsequent projects in the strategy plan.

Identify the Impact of Technology

From the information gathered, identify the managers' expectations of the benefits and drawbacks to using technology. Compare these expectations with technological usage in similar organizations. Then assess how the organization will be affected by the managers' expected use of technology.

PRODUCE HIGH-LEVEL MODEL OF BUSINESS

This task provides a high-level model of the business within the project scope (see Fig. 30.2). An overview is included of the inherent business objects and a list of the fundamental activities—independent of the organization's structure. It also includes a description of the way activities and objects interact with each other and with the organization's structure. The task, then, provides the basis for defining data stores and business systems as well as the communications requirements between them for the organizations who use the systems and data. The formal statement of the high-level model of the business will also help justify whether to keep, modify, replace, or abandon current systems.

In addition, this task establishes the basis for defining the scope of subsequent development projects. Enough knowledge of the business structure and behavior must be gathered so that the nature of the business systems and supporting data stores can be understood.

Figure 30.2 A method to Produce High-Level Model of Business.

Model Business Activities and Objects

In interviews and user workshops, identify high-level business activities and their interactions. Several techniques can be used to capture this knowledge. A common technique involves using functional decomposition with process-dependency diagrams. A more object-oriented technique is *object-flow diagrams,* described in Chapter 8. Use these techniques to subdivide the higher level activities into enough detail—typically two to four levels down from the top.

Use-case interaction diagrams are also quite popular [Jacobson, 1993]. However, these are recommended for small business domains. For instance, a large telephone company identified hundreds of use cases in just one area of its business. With so many activities, the company had difficulty identifying processing overlaps and hierarchies. In situations like these a hierarchical, or leveling, approach such as functional decomposition and object-flow diagrams can be useful.

Object types should be identified by considering what the various enterprise activities consume or produce. Think of the ideas or concepts that people employ as they navigate, operate, or control the system. The identification of these object types should be kept at a high level. To identify relationships, consider the nature of the interactions between pairs of objects. Focus on the important relationships and avoid trying to uncover them all. Document objects and relationships using a technique such as object-relationship diagrams.

Business activities create, change, or access objects. From the point of view of systems development, the creation and modification of data have more ramifications than just retrieval. Therefore, distinguish between the activities that produce an object from those that only access the object.

Identify Organizational Involvement

To determine whether the activity view of the high-level model is complete and consistent, analyze how involved the organizational units are with business activities. This analysis will also reveal which organizational units need further activity analysis and the geographic distribution of activities. Distinguish whether each organizational unit is involved with each activity to a high, moderate, low, or no degree. Perform a similar analysis of the degree to which organizational units are involved with business objects.

Associate Business Objectives

Business objects and activities are the vehicle for ensuring that the business objectives (identified in an earlier step) are met. For each business objective, then, identify those objects and activities that affect or are affected by the objective. This will assist the planning team to prioritize the projects that implement these objects and activities. In this way, the business direction drives the plan.

Check Completeness

The definitions of object types and activities should be checked to see that they are correct and complete. This can be done by examining the matrices and diagrams. For each object type, ensure that it is:

- Created by an activity (preferably only one).
- Used by one or more activities.
- Related to at least one other object type.

For each business activity, ensure that it:

- Creates or uses at least one object type.
- Either depends on an activity or another activity depends on it.
- Is performed by one or more organizational units.

For each organizational unit, ensure that it:

- Performs one or more activities.

For each business objective, ensure that it:

- Affects or is affected by one or more activities.
- Is supported by one or more object types.

EVALUATE CURRENT TECHNOLOGY OF THE ORGANIZATION

It is important to understand how technology is currently used by the organization (see Fig. 30.3). Both the technical and people side of the current business environment need to be evaluated. This evaluation will help not only in determining whether and how new technology will improve business operations, but will also help in selecting which equipment and facilities may be reused and which must be eliminated. In this task, constraints on the technical architecture are identified.

For a complete business-reengineering effort, this task is not limited to I.S. technology. (However, the scope addressed by this book is limited to the I.S. environment.) Here, evaluations are made whether to keep, modify, replace, or discard each of the cur-

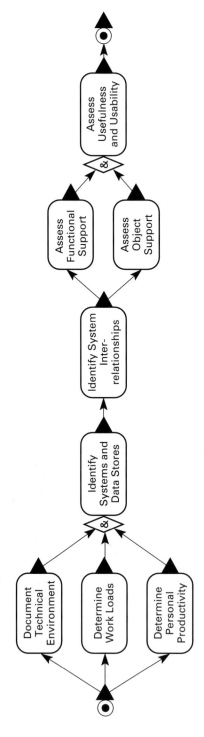

Figure 30.3   A method to Evaluate Current Technology of the Organization.

rent systems and data stores. Identification is made as to where common information is created and used—providing the basis for data sharing and process reuse. All of this is used later in transition planning and design.

Various factors may indicate that the current technology cannot handle the work load. This can be determined by noting how the current technology is used, the work load and work flow for both equipment and people, and how efficiently people work. Where current technology is inadequate, potential business-reengineering projects can be identified that may become one of the development projects in the strategy plan.

Document Technical Environment

Compile an inventory of available technical components and products that either are used or potentially will be used by the organizations, locations, and functions in the scope of the strategy planning project. Usually an organization keeps up-to-date inventories. If so, assemble the material and review it for currency and completeness. If a current inventory is not available, a member of the I.S. department can compile one.

Determine Work Loads

Assess the work loads of the facilities and the people who use them. Look at work flow, frequency of use, permanent and temporary storage, throughput, as well as peak and slack usage. Consider, as well, processing facilities, communications facilities, application-support facilities, and outside resources. Pay particular attention to who the main users are, to what degree the facilities are used, and what future use is expected.

Determine Personal Productivity

Assess the degree of sophistication with which people use technology. While doing this, both end users and management should be aware of trends in information technology. They should also compare their technological usage with that of similar organizations.

In analyzing technological usage, begin with people's use of general components. These technical components include the use of personal, office-productivity tools, such as word processors, electronic mail, spreadsheets, presentation graphics, and database management. Then, move to the more specialized productivity tools used by professionals. These aids include CAD, simulation, mathematical, statistical, engineering, decision support, and project-management tools. Next, assess how facilities are used for advanced systems development for DP professionals and end users. These facilities include languages, tools, CASE, and reusable object libraries. Finally, analyze how well these productivity tools are integrated.

In addition to these productivity and development tools is the area of communications technology. Determine the level of use and integration of communications facilities, such as voice, text, data, and image communications—that is, multimedia. How is the communications infrastructure used?

Evaluate whether the technical components and their use are out of balance. For example, the situation is unbalanced if an advanced, relational-database management system is used with powerful query possibilities—but limited personal computer use. An imbalance also exists if an advanced integrated network is in place, while *no* tools manage data as a company resource.

After evaluating personal productivity, the work load, and work flow, you may discover that certain technologies will not be used appropriately unless the work environment is changed radically. (Client/server is a good example.) This indicates the need for a business-reengineering project.

Identify Systems and Data Stores

Examine existing and planned business systems and data stores. Look at these systems and data stores at the same level of detail as the documentation of the high-level model. Generally, this means subsystems—not programs—should be identified.

Identify both computerized and manual systems. Computer systems are often part of larger business systems that also cover manual procedures. Identify both computerized data stores and formalized clerical files or registers. Analysis should include the history and extract files, but not the temporary and sort files.

Identify System Interrelationships

To develop a transition strategy for the strategy plan, the dependencies between systems and data stores must be understood. Determine where a system gets its data and where it puts the processed data. The data will be contained in some temporary or permanent data store, register, or message depository. Analyze only formal data flows defined in systems and procedures. Show the result of this analysis in a data-flow diagram.

Determine how systems interact with data stores. A system may create or change data in a data store, or it may only retrieve it. (This may involve a whole record or just fields.) Analyze only permanent data stores. One technique for recording these results is a matrix of current data stores and business systems.

Assess Functional Support

This analysis reveals how many of the business activities are already automated. Often, only certain areas of the enterprise have been computerized, such as finance, administration, personnel, and order processing. From this analysis, conclusions can be made about new opportunities for computerized support. These can include product development, logistics management, and decision support systems. The analysis should include only computerized systems. The results of the analysis can be expressed using a matrix of business function and support.

Assess Object Support

Analyze the data stored in computer files to clarify how data about a given object type is dispersed across files. Redundant data storage is likely to be discovered, if application-dedicated data files have been developed in the past. The analysis provides the basis for defining a transition path to a unified database structure. These results can be presented in a matrix of current data stores and objects.

Assess Usefulness and Usability

In a conventional systems environment, data stores are considered part of a business system. Therefore, assessing a system may also result in assessing its data stores.

Assess a system by looking into its usefulness, both from the technicians' and users' points of view. Question both end users and system maintenance personnel using written user surveys or interviews. A system's usefulness can be measured by:

- The degree to which the system meets current business requirements.
- The reliability of its operation.
- Its responsiveness and timeliness.

To measure a system's usability, note the degree to which it is easy to use, modify or enhance, operate, and support. The result of the satisfaction analysis can be depicted using a systems satisfaction chart. If the system is unsatisfactory, it should be reviewed.

From the analysis of function support, object support, usefulness, and usability, the conclusion might be that the system still has business worth. If so, the system is a candidate for systems redevelopment. The strategy plan should specify which systems are candidates.

CLASSIFY BUSINESS SYSTEMS

Business systems should be classifed by how they use and access data stores (see Fig. 30.4). This task serves to envision the likely systems and databases, to provide a basis for the scope of development projects, to establish requirements for the technical architecture, and to determine constraints on and the preferred distribution of the natural systems and stores.

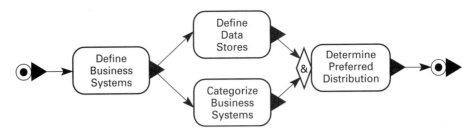

Figure 30.4   A method to Classify Business Systems.

Define Business Systems

A business system tends to be more stable if it is based on business function rather than business organization. A *natural* business system is one in which the activities support a common business benefit (usually one or a limited number of functions) and minimize their communication outside the system. Although a business function may be supported by several systems, question whether such situations are reasonable.

Using the business activities modeled in an earlier step, define the proposed business systems using the natural business systems as a guide. Ideally, they will be the same. While the natural systems may be unacceptable for political, technical, or other reasons, they should not be rejected until their costs have been evaluated.

Categorize Business Systems

Four categories of business systems can influence the choice of technical architecture:

- *Online teleprocessing (OLTP).* Characterized by high volume, rapid response, and typically several changes to the data stores.
- *Decision support.* Characterized by frequent data access but few changes, usually processing intensive.
- *Graphic and multimedia information.* Requiring vast amounts of information to describe a single item.
- *Online complex processing.* Typified by high-volume image processing.

A system may belong to more than one category. However, if one classification does not predominate, try to split the system into subsystems of just one category. The system categories are major factors in determining requirements for the technical architecture.

The high-level model established above provides the means to find the natural business systems and data stores. These are the optimal collections of work and information that are not restricted by how they are actually implemented.

Define Data Stores

A natural data store contains data from object types that are manipulated by a similar set of activities. Often a clustering technique is employed here. Ideally, a data store should be modified by one natural system only, but it may be retrieved by many systems. Define the expected data stores by using the natural data stores as a guide.

Determine Preferred Distribution

Identify whether business systems and data stores should be distributed centrally or locally by evaluating them against distribution factors. There are no hard and fast rules. Any conclusions depend on the management structure and organizational philosophy of the enterprise and on the state of the art of information technology.

Usage-analysis techniques can determine which business systems must be available at a location type to support the local business functions and whether they will be general or specific for a location.

Determine which data stores ought to be accessible at a location type. Also, indicate the expected type of data distribution, whether a master copy of the data stores or a subset is required at the location, or whether the data must be partitioned.

Client/server architecture should be defined (see Fig. 30.5) to determine the appropriate client/server configurations for the systems that will be developed. Conversely, it must be determined where client/server is *not* an appropriate architecture. Finally, because client/server tools are changing so rapidly, the risk of the software selections, must also be evaluated.

When the proposed business systems are classified, several things are determined. These include the nature of the business systems, the communications volume and frequency, and the distribution of processing and data. Now, these requirements can be used to plan the hardware, software, and communications facilities.

The technical architecture affects the organization. In turn, the organization has an effect on the technical facilities. For instance, the organization determines the location and control of the facilities. It also allocates the technical and managerial resources to make technological changes. Finally, it determines how the technical architecture should adapt to organizational changes.

The technical, organizational, and systems requirements should be balanced. The technology may not yet exist that will satisfy the systems and organizational needs. The systems, technical, and organizational tasks can be performed in parallel, revising requirements to meet the restrictions that reality imposes.

This task sets the overall direction for the technical facilities, making sure that it permits flexibility and that the technical facilities can be upgraded. Avoid trying to specify the technical architecture down to the last piece of software. Because the state of the art is changing so rapidly, more and better products will likely be available by the time the design team starts working. The technical architecture can be revisited early in the design stage, after the business has been modeled and a more detailed understanding of the business requirements exists.

Determine Technical Components

Identify the technical components required for the production environment of each business system:

- *Networks.* Their topology, protocols, and interconnections.
- *Platforms.* The combination of hardware and operating system.
- *Database Management systems and database servers.*
- *Middleware.* Including the application program interfaces (APIs), the protocols they support, and the object request broker (ORB).
- *Frameworks or support software.* Including the application area, such as office systems, CAD, and CASE.

Also, determine the facilities needed to develop the systems. Details of the development environment will likely differ from those of the production environment.

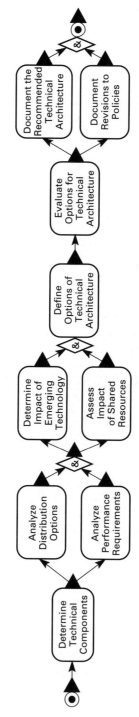

Figure 30.5　A method to Define Client/Server Architecture.

Analyze Distribution Options

Each business system should have an appropriate distribution of presentation, processing, and data access, based on the characteristics of the business system and on the business objectives. To determine what facilities are required at each type of location, examine the preferred distribution of data stores and business systems as well as the technical facilities they require. The results can be expressed with a matrix of technical requirements and location.

Estimate the type and volume of communication between locations. Base the estimate on the systems and data usage at locations and from the interactions between business functions performed at these locations. The results can be depicted in a matrix of locations and communication. The results may show a high level of communication between locations. Based on the performance requirements being analyzed in a parallel subtask, it may be appropriate to revise the architecture distribution and/or determine the need for other technical facilities.

Analyze Performance Requirements

The service level that will be delivered by the technical architecture must be addressed. How many users are anticipated and what response time do they require? What are the average and peak volumes of throughput? How will issues of reliability, security, and integrity be handled? How well can the architecture respond to upgrades and changes in scale? Finally, how will the technical architecture be integrated with existing facilities and architectures?

These requirements can be derived from several sources. The first is the processing, storage, and communications requirements of business systems and data stores. Next are the characteristics of the technical components, and, finally, the current support of facilities for systems. These findings can be documented in matrices of technical requirements to business systems, data stores, and locations.

Determine the Impact of Emerging Technology

Client/server tools and facilities are changing rapidly, as are the client/server players in the marketplace. The decisions made today on the technical architecture must take into account how the architecture will change over time. Consider factors controlled directly by the organization and those determined either by the manufacturers of the technical components or by the marketplace. These include:

- Adding new locations (horizontal scaling) or moving to more powerful machines (vertical scaling).
- How much functionality might be added.
- Emerging standards for components, communication, interfaces, and application development.
- How well old versions of equipment and software are supported.
- Market acceptance of new products and the track record of manufacturers.

On the basis of this list, propose paths for upgrading and assess the risk of each path.

Assess the Impact of Shared Resources

Client/server implies sharing. Evaluate what this means to the organization in terms of information ownership, responsibility for the accuracy and use of information, access to facilities, and the users' technical knowledge. Ideally, facilities should be made available at the location where they are used and will be controlled. Look at:

- Dependencies between business systems and their common data usage.
- The importance of an integrated environment to the organization's operations and competitiveness.
- The current level of integration.
- Where decisions are made.
- Where work is done and controlled.

Organizational considerations often impose special requirements on the technical architecture. Client/server systems almost always result in new roles and responsibilities, because the systems bring new capabilities to the users. To identify the impact of the technology on the organization, look at:

- Changes required in the existing organization to accommodate the new technology.
- How easily the environment adjusts to organizational changes.
- Whether the required technical expertise and managerial competence is available or attainable for technology changes.

Determine any adjustments to the technical facilities that should be made to accommodate these considerations.

Define Options for Technical Architecture

Using the results of the preceding guidelines for the analysis and selection of technical components, define two or three options for a technical architecture. A low-profile option could be introduced and controlled rather easily. In contrast, a challenging option would require considerable effort from the enterprise. It could also be possible to have an intermediate option.

All options must be feasible from a technical, financial, and organizational point of view—within the time frame covered by the strategy plan. Each option for the technical architecture can be represented in a diagram.

Evaluate Options for Technical Architecture

The architectural options should be evaluated against the following factors:

- Cost level—including investment, migration, and exploitation costs.
- Ability to adapt to changes in technology and organization.
- Risks and benefits for business.
- Technical expertise required.

Rank the options relative to each other as high/moderate/low or large/medium/small. No absolute numbers or cost figures are necessary at this point.

Document the Recommended Technical Architecture

Select one option for the technical architecture and give examples of the technical products for each of its components. If the products have been announced but not yet released, note when they are anticipated. Alternatives for such products should also be indicated.

Document Revisions to Policies

Determine the changes to policies that will result from the new architecture. Quite likely, general standards for business-system requirements will be changed significantly and need to be defined.

DESCRIBE THE ENVIRONMENT OF THE ORGANIZATION

Changes in technology often mean changes in the way people do their work. Having a description of the organizational environment will prepare people for changes to their job responsibilities and interactions within the organization. This process is illustrated in Fig. 30.6. Address issues of cultural change early in development. This involves defining the new work tasks and developing the necessary training to prepare the users.

For example, introducing client/server and graphic user interfaces is linked with the decision to empower workers in order to improve customer satisfaction. Client/server technology significantly improves the work environment for data consumers—who are the biggest beneficiaries of office automation. However, the typical data producer often regards client/server technology as a hindrance. Response time may be slower, reliability may become an issue, and a mouse is not the ideal device for entering numbers or text. This is an opportunity to rethink the roles and responsibilities of the data producers.

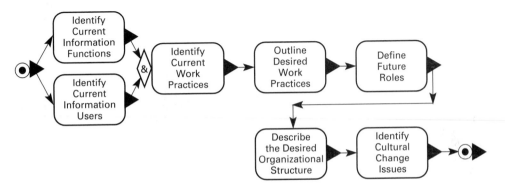

Figure 30.6   A method to Describe the Environment of the Organization.

Identify Current Information Functions

Identify the activities that provide information in a structured way, that is, those activities that produce and manage information. These are the frameworks, or support services, that may or may not be automated. They can potentially be incorporated or affected by the client/server systems that the strategy plan will spawn. In addition to the formalized data environment, consider telecommunications and office management, such as text processing, archiving, and conferencing. A functional view is preferable to an organizational view. Examine the data processing or information-resource management functions. Also, examine those functions that were identified as a result of building the high-level model. Particular attention should be paid to those activities that:

- Manage the implementation of the strategy plan.
- Coordinate information systems development.
- Manage and develop the information resources and information-related facilities.
- Provide user support and promote user involvement in systems development and use.

Identify Current Information Users

Identify the current organizations of the information users. These are the people who control, produce *(data producers),* and access *(data downloaders)* information. Include both the formal organizational chart and any temporary or permanent organizational alliances that have been superimposed on the main organization structure. The formal organization structure is typically documented in organizational handbooks and job descriptions.

In the current organization structure, a barrier may exist between those who *have* access to information and those who *should have* access. Since removing this barrier is a likely objective of developing systems, these potential information users should be included in the analysis. Their requirements should be taken into account when defining future roles, work practices, organizational structure, and cultural change.

Identify Current Work Practices

Review existing work flows, proposed business systems, current technical inventory, and proposed technical architecture to determine the current work practices that will be affected by the systems and technical environment. (Note: The facilities, methods, standards, and policies for planning, development, deployment, operations, and maintenance in the information functions were identified in a previous subtask.)

Determine the information-related roles and responsibilities of the information users. Look at who (i.e., the organizational unit or role) now handles the information functions in terms of their authority, responsibility, expertise, and work. Pay particular attention to the functions that involve end users directly, especially the potential users. These are the areas where systems can result in substantial changes to the organizational structure and behavior. Also, traditional I.S. jobs will likely change.

Outline Desired Work Practices

Identify the deficiencies in current practices for the proposed environment. Situations that need special attention are:

- Where more than one organizational unit is responsible for managing the same function.
- Where a unit has responsibility for a function—but no authority to make decisions.
- Where the people who do the work lack the expertise.

Work practices for systems development and deployment will change. (For example, for client/server installations some specific areas *require* a change.) The first area of change is the maintenance of local facilities which would include repair, configuration, upgrading, backup, and supplies. The second area is the application support facilities, that is, the help desk. This includes both equipment required to reach support facilities, such as bulletin-board access, and policies to acquire outside help. The final area is network support which includes user authorization, disk-space management, remote management, and software licensing.

If the analysis of the current environment identifies the need for business reengineering, then the desired work practices should be determined by a business reengineering project. Such a project may cause substantial changes to user work practices.

Define Future Roles

Determine how existing roles should be modified and what new roles need be added in order to:

- Manage the implementation of the strategy plan.
- Manage the acquisition and deployment of tools and methods.
- Provide user support for applications and facilities.
- Involve users in systems development, deployment, and use.

These roles can be depicted with a matrix that shows users' respective responsibility, authority, expertise, and work.

Describe the Desired Organizational Structure

Determine how the organization's structure must be changed, both temporarily and permanently. Then, outline the division of tasks and roles between the end-user departments and the information-systems department. Within the end-user departments, special structures may be needed for the development of information systems, the control of systems and procedures, data control, and the management of local facilities.

Departments that provide backbone I.S. services to the organization include systems development, computer operations, or user support. They are affected by specific projects for I.S. development, execution, and maintenance. These kinds of changes should be distinguished from changes to departments that plan, coordinate, and provide rules for information activities throughout the organization. The latter affect the way the projects are carried out.

A special task force of high-level stakeholders may be needed to assure that the strategy plan becomes a reality.

Identify Issues of Cultural Change

Identify the cultural issues and assess whether the organization is ready for change. This can be done using the prioritized objectives, the analysis of the current environment, and the organizational changes needed to support the new systems. The priorities of each stakeholder or organizational unit should be compared with the overall priorities. Examine the track record of the organization in adopting new technologies. Technicians who have lived in a mainframe environment are often reluctant to recognize the power of personal computers. Users who have experienced great advances in what they can do with personal computers are often unaware of issues of reliability so vital to the success of systems that share resources. Some issues that have been stumbling blocks are security, privacy, autonomy, authority, and access.

Document the issues and rate the organization's readiness for change. Some measures of readiness are organizational vision and goals, motivation for change, skill level, need for training, use of technology, and support for change.

DEFINE DEVELOPMENT STRATEGIES

This task (see Fig. 30.7) establishes the scope of subsequent development projects. Their relative importance is based on the objectives established earlier. The task also sets forth strategies for incorporating the resultant systems and databases into the organization. Finally, it evaluates the risks, costs, and benefits of each approach.

In examining the current environment, opportunities for business reengineering and system redevelopment may have been identified. Evaluate whether a business-reengineering or a system-redevelopment project should be undertaken. If this is the case, determine the timing of those projects as well as the client/server development projects.

Define Development Projects

In the previous tasks, potential business systems were identified and classified. Typically, systems with different classifications are developed as separate projects, because the systems usually require different technical architectures and may use different development tools. Now, reexamine the systems to determine whether it makes sense to combine the

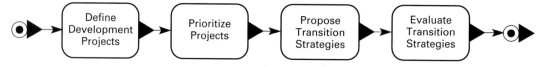

Figure 30.7   A method to Define Development Strategies.

analysis for two or more of these systems in one system analysis (SA) project. If the business objects overlap considerably, it may be more efficient to conduct one system analysis project for several systems in a business area and then split the resulting business model into several smaller system design projects.

The scope of each business area can be determined by inspecting the object/activity matrix and the business-system classifications. Alternatively, depending on the complexity and number of potential business systems, the scope of each business area can be determined using a cluster analysis technique.

Document the scope as business area descriptions. In addition to developing systems, opportunities can be uncovered for:

- Business reengineering or business-process redesign.
- Systems redevelopment.
- Organizational restructuring.

Define the scope and objectives for each of these possible projects.

Prioritize Projects

Looking at the information dependencies between business areas, determine the logical development sequence. An area that supplies information should be developed before the area that uses the information. In addition, consider the logical dependencies of the other project opportunities:

- Any business-reengineering or business-process redesign project should precede further system development, because those projects will radically redefine the scope of subsequent development.
- Systems redevelopment projects, on the other hand, may be carried out simultaneously with other development projects or become part of a future development project.
- Organizational restructuring projects should be synchronized with the systems-development projects that require the restructuring.

The development sequence should be adjusted to reflect the prioritized objectives established above, the restrictions and availability of technical-architecture components, and resource limitations. For example, technological limitations may make it impossible to convert an area that supplies information to client/server at this time. However, great benefits can be gained by converting the area that *uses* the information to client/server. In this case, the development sequence could be changed to add a subsystem requirement that bridges the gap between the first and second area.

Present the development sequences as a schedule of projects, showing the expected duration and proposed start (or end) date of each project.

Propose Transition Strategies

For each project's definition, propose a transition strategy. Consider at least two approaches. The first is an aggressive strategy with maximum project overlap and parallel development. The second is a moderate strategy that requires reasonable effort. Document the transition strategies, describing the approach for system development, use of technology, impact on the organization and its structure, and the phasing from old to new systems and technology.

Evaluate Transition Strategies

Evaluate the reasonableness of the competing strategies. High risks may be associated with the approaches, particularly with the technical architecture. When evaluating transition strategies, the risk of the technical upgrade path should be assessed.

APPROVE STRATEGY PLAN

The strategy plan is established to develop and implement systems projects, to initiate development, and to inform the organization of the plan. It should now be approved (see Fig. 30.8). The goal is to start development—not to produce a planning document. Consequently, the first objective is picking a development strategy. The second objective is lining up actual resources, such as people, facilities, and funds to activate at least one project in that strategy.

Figure 30.8   A method to Approve Strategy Plan.

Select Development Strategy

The alternative development strategies should be reviewed with management, focusing on each strategy's business values and how each meets management's prioritized objectives. Review the proposed technical architecture and upgrade path and how each development strategy meshes with the technical architecture.

Select one development strategy and verify the proposed technical architecture. The technical architecture will be addressed again in the design stage to incorporate new or improved technical components and to select specific products. The selected development strategy is the strategy plan which sets the overall schedule for subsequent projects. It also specifies each project's scope, which provides the control for iterative development.

Set Action Plan

Select the first project and assign the necessary resources, such as people, funds, and facilities. Next, give it a definite start date. In addition to starting the first project, take the necessary steps to start the acquisition process for technical architecture components. Some organizations require a long lead time for product acquisition. The acquisition process should not lock the project team into components or pricing that will be out of date when the facilities are needed.

Communicate Plan to Organization

Management should inform the organization about the strategy plan and the first actions to be taken under the plan. The objectives here are to demonstrate management's commitment to the plan, to gain organizational support for this plan as well as further actions, and to schedule the first deliverables.

The plan can be communicated in one or more ways. First, a memo can be sent from top management throughout the organization. Second, stakeholders can be given a copy of the plan. Finally, a meeting with the stakeholders can be held to present the results.

Chapter 31

Strategy Planning: Management Tasks

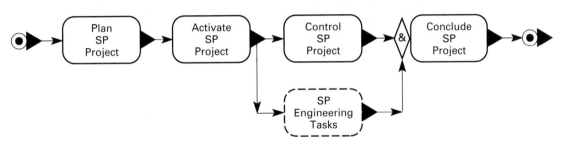

A method for the management tasks of strategy planning.

PLAN STRATEGY PLANNING PROJECT

The first task in the strategy planning (SP) project is to establish the work plan (see Fig. 31.1). This work plan provides the blueprint for the project manager and defines its scope and objectives. Several issues are addressed. Should the plan determine whether business reengineering or system redevelopment projects are needed prior to development? Should the plan be limited to proving the strategy approach for an independent system? Finally, should the plan encompass a wide strategy effort?

Figure 31.1   A method to Plan Strategy Planning Project.

Several steps are required to complete the plan.

- Determine the user involvement, management style, and project organizational structure.
- Identify resource requirements.
- Develop a detailed schedule.
- Assess the project risk and gain acceptance of the plan.

Define Project

Specify the project objectives, scope, constraints and assumptions, deliverables to be produced, standards for the deliverables, and procedures for carrying out the project.

The primary *objective* of a strategy planning project is assuring the success of subsequent system development. More specific objectives include:

- Identifying the business objectives that system development should satisfy.
- Determining whether the current state of system technology can reasonably meet the objectives.
- Eliciting the information requirements, understanding the characteristics of the business systems that support these requirements, and specifying the technical architecture for developing and deploying these systems.
- Identifying the cultural changes that will occur when the systems are introduced.
- Producing a plan that incorporates the iterative development of systems.

A strategy planning project can discover that some systems will not be feasible without radically changing the business. On the other hand, the project can discover that existing systems still have business value. The objectives should state whether identifying and planning for business reengineering or systems redevelopment are part of the strategy planning project.

Next, clarify the *scope* of the strategy plan by specifying the organizations and locations that will be covered. Other limitations are based on such criteria as business function, organizational structure, and kind of technology.

Then detail any *constraints,* such as budget or time limits, availability of skills, knowledge, or equipment. List the *assumptions* employed in developing the project schedule for strategy planning.

The principal *deliverable* is the strategy plan which is based on the other deliverables produced during this project, such as:

- Prioritized objectives.
- Information requirements.
- Assessment of current environment.
- Business-system classifications.
- Technical architecture.
- Future organization and environment.
- Development strategies.

Finally, *standards* and *procedures* must be established for documenting and diagramming deliverables, for reviewing these deliverables, and for revising the project plan.

Make Project Plan

Identify the tasks, effort, and resources needed to produce the deliverables. Establish a schedule and budget. Estimate the risk. Check the plan against the constraints and assumptions identified earlier, and verify that the project plan is feasible.

Identify Effort, Resources, and Scheduling

To identify the tasks required for the strategy planning project, use the steps outlined in Chapter 30. For each task, determine the amount of time, the resources, and the scheduling requirements. Choose the most appropriate technique for each task. For example, one particular method of interviewing may be chosen as a technique for certain tasks.

Do not underestimate the size of nontechnical work, such as the project leadership or the presentation and review of results. In particular, the tasks at the project's conclusion are often underestimated.

Identify and include the milestone reviews. Major milestones for a strategy planning project occur at the end of the Plan Strategy Planning Project task, at the point of gaining approval for the strategy plan, and at the project's conclusion. Other milestone reviews may be scheduled, depending upon the project's complexity and scope.

Estimate the team size and composition. Keep the core team small—ideally three to six people. Outside experts and reference groups can be used for specific tasks, rather than an enlarged team.

Establish the Project Schedule

Use estimates of resource requirements and availability, task dependencies, and effort. Consider timeboxes and user workshops when developing the schedule, particularly for review tasks. The schedule will very likely be adjusted after the specific team is established. Start scheduling any interviews or workshops as soon as possible, as they will be difficult to schedule within the time frame of the project.

Develop a Budget

The project budget should take into account the project schedule and resource usage, equipment and facilities, and other expenses, such as travel and office support.

Identify Areas of Risk in the Schedule

In addition to the risks that apply to all projects, look for the following:

- Lack of top management support.
- A team that is poorly prepared or part-time.
- Inadequate user involvement.
- Users' lack of business knowledge.

- A project having an ill-defined scope.
- Too much time spent in decision making.

Build risk reduction into the project plan. If this is a high-risk project, treat it as if it were a much bigger project. Choose behavioral techniques to achieve consensus quickly. Manage expectations from the start.

Check Plan Against Assumptions

The constraints and assumptions may require adjusting to produce a feasible schedule. In particular, check the project scope.

Obtain Project Approval

Present the project plan to the project sponsor and to other people required for approval. These and other stakeholders in this plan should be identified before the plan is presented. By involving them in reference groups or a steering committee, you can obtain their commitment to the project and the resulting strategy plan.

The stakeholders include the *project sponsor,* who must have both the authority to commit resources and the ability to influence other stakeholders in order to win and maintain the project's charter. Other stakeholders include:

- The ultimate *customers* of information and processes within the project scope.
- Potential *adversaries* of the project. Determine who will lose power or influence if this project succeeds and identify how to gain their confidence and support.
- *Process facilitators* determine who supplies information or otherwise supports the processes. They also clarify how the process will affect them.
- *Guardians of organization standards* incorporate their views into the project standards. A representative may be on both the steering committee and a reference group. The organization may require them to approve the project plan.
- *Budgetary watchdogs* should be considered on a steering committee.

ACTIVATE STRATEGY PLANNING PROJECT

The activation task, illustrated in Fig. 31.2, launches the project. First, the working environment should be set up. This includes the room for the project team, the facilities for interviews, group workshops, or training, as well as the computer equipment and software. In addition, the team must learn and practice the techniques that they will use in carrying out the strategy planning project.

Figure 31.2   A method to Activate Strategy Planning Project.

The secondary purpose of this task is understanding the impact of cultural change. The team will likely be unfamiliar with the techniques and some of the equipment. The team's reaction to the activation task can give them insight into how to prepare the organization's transition to the applications that the strategy plan will produce.

Establish Project Environment

The project environment will require equipment and facilities for interviews, workshops, team training, and team meetings. The productivity of the project team will be increased if each team member has easy access to the following software:

- Word processor.
- Spreadsheet.
- Diagrammer.
- Presentation.
- Project estimation and project management.
- Methodology management software.

A CASE tool is helpful, but not necessary, for some of the diagramming.

Train Team

When training the team members in the techniques they will be using, place special emphasis on information gathering and business modeling. Make sure that each team member knows how to use the software to help produce project deliverables and work products. Combining the project kickoff with a training session is a good idea.

CONTROL STRATEGY PLANNING PROJECT

It is essential to control the progress of the SP project (see Fig. 31.3). This task permits corrective actions within the plan's scope and identifies when the critical project elements, such as objectives, scope, budget, or time span, need to be changed. In addition, the project may have to coordinate with the results of prior projects and concurrent events outside the project. The Control Strategy Planning Project task manages this coordination.

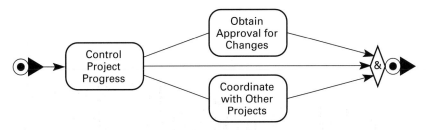

Figure 31.3   A method to Control Strategy Planning Project.

In a strategy planning project, the critical control points are the decision-making tasks.

Control Project Progress

Project control is vital to the success of the project. It involves assigning project tasks, monitoring the status of tasks and deliverables, checking progress against the plan, and periodically reporting progress to the project sponsor and other stakeholders.

The project manager must keep the project moving forward, motivate the team, and keep the support of the project stakeholders. Minimizing bureaucracy is essential to project control. The team should devote most of its time to performing the project, not filling out project-control reports.

A finite time frame and expense budget is necessary for this project. Avoid letting excessive requests for "small" increases in scope derail the project. The requests that are not recommended for inclusion should be recorded as *enhancement requests*.

Assign Project Tasks

The project plan typically includes initial task assignments. These are often adjusted and amended during the project, as the plan confronts reality. Circulating a weekly assignment sheet is a good practice, either before or during the *short* weekly staff meeting. Items to discuss at a status meeting include the following:

- Major events.
- Action items.
- Recap of expected deliverables.
- Actual achievements and variances.
- Overall project assessment.
- Next week's deliverables.
- Action items for the next meeting.

Monitor Tasks and Deliverables

Keep the project's progress and management issues visible. Post schedules, reports, and issues. Assign all issues a due date. Review whether an answer to an issue is overdue.

Check Progress Against Plan

Compare the resources actually used and the time spent to the planned resources and time. Identify progress that is ahead of schedule, as well as tasks that are behind schedule or likely to fall behind. Determine if any delays are externally imposed. Identify any unproductive work.

Report to Sponsor

Give periodic progress reports to the project sponsor and keep influential stakeholders informed, as well. These reports should include the time spent by each team member for each task, the deliverables produced, and an estimate of task completion.

Obtain Approval for Changes

The project plan is a contract between the team and the sponsor of the strategy planning project. Make minor corrections, such as changing meeting times, trying alternative techniques, or getting users more involved, within the original plan. However, the difference between planned and actual performance may be too great to overcome by working "smarter." Corrective actions that change the schedule, the cost, the scope, or the deliverables require formal approval.

Look for early warning signs that the project will not meet the plan. For example, the team might not be completing deliverables by the milestone dates, or the quality may be low. The cause could be inadequate resources, poor productivity, an unreasonable schedule, or an inappropriate scope. The right solution depends on identifying the root cause.

Examine each proposed solution for its impact on the project objectives, scope, benefits, schedule, quality, and resources. Since changes in scope, timing, and resource use may affect other projects, the development-coordination organization should also review the proposal. In reviewing the impact, do not forget to repeat tasks that were considered complete.

Decide which actions to recommend to the project sponsor. Justify the proposed change in business terms. Make the sponsor and steering committee aware of the alternatives to and the consequences of not making the change.

When the project sponsor, steering committee, project manager, and development-coordination group agree to the changes, publicize the new plan to everyone on the project. Notify the project team, reference groups, stakeholders, business users, and technical specialists whose schedules might be altered as a result of the changed plan. Work closely with the project sponsor.

Coordinate with Other Projects

A project does not happen in isolation—even a planning project. The project manager is the liaison between the SP project and other developments that could affect its direction, contents, and schedule. In particular, be aware of other work that will affect the availability of resources, especially those people who provide information to the project team and review its results.

CONCLUDE STRATEGY PLANNING PROJECT

As illustrated in Fig. 31.4, a project needs an orderly conclusion, freeing project resources for other activities, and ensuring recognition for its participants. While most projects reach completion, occasionally a project will be stopped before its objectives are achieved. For example, this could occur when a midproject review indicates that the project should be suspended or canceled. In a suitable environment, the project manager can recommend such an action—if justified.

For high-level strategy plans, the project never really concludes any more than a financial or operational plan would conclude. These kinds of plans are always reevaluat-

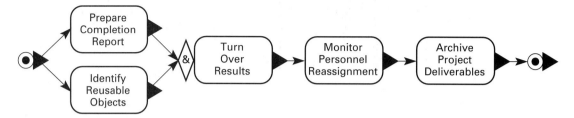

Figure 31.4   A method to Conclude Strategy Planning Project.

ed and restructured on a regular basis. In this way, the strategy plan always reflects the direction of the business. For lower-level plans, however, such a conclusion is sometimes reasonable. For example, an SP project to convert the western regional office over to a client/server architecture would be one such plan.

Prepare Completion Report

The *project completion report* contains various sections. These include management summaries, deliverables for subsequent projects, evaluation of resource performance, project analysis, and project metrics. Prepare these according to the organization's requirements and conventions.

The management summary section should include an overview, summaries of analysis findings, project metrics, and recommendations.

The deliverables section describes the strategy plan: project background, scope, objectives, conclusions, and schedule of subsequent projects. The major deliverables should be placed in an appendix containing the information requirements, business-systems classifications, technical architecture, and future organization and environment.

The project analysis section recaps the project performance. Include the business accomplishments, lessons learned, a summary of metrics, and any unusual or interesting project aspects.

The project is not complete until the steering committee and executive owner accept its results. An executive presentation of the report prior to final sign-off may also be required.

Identify Reusable Objects

Everything produced during this project can potentially be reused. Review the project deliverables with an eye to reusability. Make sure that they are cataloged and stored in a form in which they can be accessed for reuse. In particular, the information requirements and documentation standards should be given to subsequent analysis projects as a starter kit.

Turn Over Results

The *strategy plan* should have recommended follow-on work and specified at least one project to activate. Determine what these projects will require using the deliverables, work products, open issues (documenting compromise decisions), lessons learned, and any other applicable documentation. Plan to meet with those project managers to assure a smooth transition.

Monitor Personnel Reassignment

Take care of project members. This increases the chance of success for other projects. More importantly, it is the right thing to do. Personnel actions to consider include performance reviews, recognition and rewards, as well as the placement of team members at the project conclusion.

Archive Project Deliverables

If it was important to do, it is probably important to keep. Identify how and where to archive project deliverables and work products within the organization. Work with a development coordination unit to ensure that the correct versions of shared objects are passed to other teams and that they know how to access and update these objects.

Chapter 32

System Analysis: Engineering Tasks

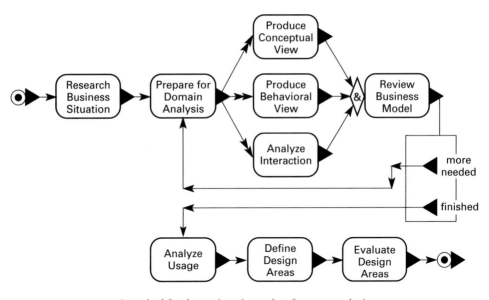

A method for the engineering tasks of system analysis.

RESEARCH BUSINESS SITUATION

Researching the business situation begins with collecting what is already known about the business (as illustrated in Fig. 32.1). This can include such items as an overview of the business, some business terminology, specific queries, and starter models. Such items can make gathering information from users more effective. Additionally, they can pro-

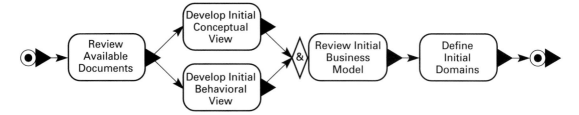

Figure 32.1   A method to Research Business Situation.

vide the team with enough understanding of the business to subdivide the work and facilitate iterative development until more information is known.

In planning for this system analysis (SA) project, start with the *high-level model* of the business that was defined during the strategy plan phase. In this task, other reusable objects and models will be sought that are appropriate to the project, such as those developed in other projects and in commercially available templates.

Two views of the business model should be created. The *conceptual view* contains the objects that the business uses and their interrelationships. The *behavioral view* describes the actions of the business and the circumstances under which they occur. The techniques used in this task are the same used in later model-building tasks. The major difference is the level of detail captured in the model.

Review Documents

Collect documents and papers that provide background and details on the business and the project. Such documents include:

- Models, matrices, and other products from strategy planning.
- Models or components from previous (or currently ongoing) development projects.
- Value-stream definitions from business reengineering.
- Annual reports on the business.
- Business plans and strategy descriptions.
- Business training documents.
- Existing systems documentation.
- Competitive assessments and industry reports.

Review these documents to gain an understanding of the business and its environment. Focus particularly on the material that supports this project's objectives.

Develop Initial Conceptual View

Based on the preliminary information gleaned from the document review and personal knowledge of the team members, develop an initial conceptual view.

Gather the team together and discuss the concepts within the scope of the business. Avoid lengthy discussions or detailed definitions of the concepts. Simply record the concepts as candidate object types and build an initial object diagram. The same steps should be used as those described in detail in the Produce Conceptual View task (presented later in this chapter). Record questions and issues on an open issues list. This list will be used in the information gathering tasks to set the agenda for discussions with the business.

Develop Initial Behavioral View

Based on the preliminary information gleaned from the document review and from personal knowledge of the team members, develop an initial behavioral view.

Gather the team together and discuss the behavior of the business. Avoid lengthy or detailed discussion of the business behavior. Simply record the behavior as candidate processes and events, and if possible build a first-cut event diagram. If a higher level view is required, a use-case diagram can be constructed instead. If an even higher level view is required, an object-flow diagram might be more appropriate. Select the right technique for the problem at hand. Ensure that all underlying concepts are recorded on the object diagram. In other words, this step and the previous step should be performed during the same sessions by the same team. Record questions and issues on an open issues list. This list will be used in the information gathering tasks to set the agenda for discussions with the organization.

Review Initial Business Model

Review the initial conceptual view and the initial behavioral view. Ensure that the language used and the scope of coverage across the two views is consistent. Remember that these initial models are just a starting point. Do not allow debate about the initial models to delay the project. After all, the next tasks involve meeting with the people in the business who know the answers.

The meetings that generate the initial models help build a shared understanding among the project team before it meets with the organization. As the business model is developed, continue to foster a clear understanding among team members with regular meetings.

Define Initial Domains

At this point, the project team should have a reasonable idea of the *initial domains.* Domains are distinctly limited spheres of knowledge or activity. Once defined, each domain identifies a specific system region that can be analyzed. Domains are not applications or projects. In fact, a domain may be implemented by several applications or projects. Furthermore, an application or project may implement several domains. Domains are used to delimit and focus the SA team's efforts—independent of implementation. Once a domain is specified in terms of its structure and behavior, implementation considerations will be examined. Current implementations will be examined in the Define Design Areas task of this project, as well as in the system design and system construction projects.

A domain is usually defined for each process (e.g., use case, operation, or activity) identified in the Develop Initial Behavioral View. However, a domain may also be based on a logical clustering of one or more of the object types identified in Develop Initial Conceptual View. (Such clusterings are often called *subject areas.*)

PREPARE FOR DOMAIN ANALYSIS

Preparing for domain analysis, illustrated in Fig. 32.2, includes:

- Gathering the information needed to assist in building a comprehensive model of the business domain directly from people currently performing or managing the processes in the business.

- Building contacts between the project team members and the business participants, or users.

- Scheduling and preparing for domain analysis sessions.

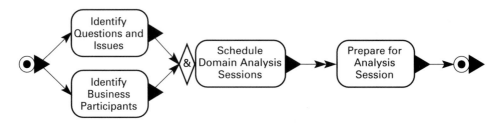

Figure 32.2   A method to Prepare for Domain Analysis.

Identify Questions and Issues

The only way to get the desired result from the domain-analysis process is to *be very clear about what is wanted.* Plan the overall process and identify the kinds of information required. Sources for identifying questions and issues are:

- Project scoping documents, which describe the aims and objectives of the project.
- Preliminary models that are constructed while researching the business situation.
- Experiences of the team members, particularly those with business knowledge.
- Value-stream diagrams and process descriptions that are available if a business reengineering effort has been completed.
- Descriptions of problems with the current systems, customer complaints, and known issues.

Remember that discovering information is an iterative process. The list of questions and issues will be refined each time through. Maintain a list of open issues as a basis for further information gathering. A diminishing list of open issues is one way to measure progress.

Identify Domain Experts

Carefully select the people who will provide input and insight on the business. Involve the project sponsor in identifying the appropriate people. Review the organization structure and map it against the preliminary business models. Identify at least one person as an information source for each component of the business model.

Ensure that the domain experts are senior enough in the organization. While it is important to speak with some operational staff to understand the details of the business, their view is usually rooted in the present. Remember that applications should be built to support the business in the future. Therefore, make sure to talk with people who understand the vision of the future.

Some participants are suggested for political reasons. In other words, their potential to contribute is low, but their potential to be disruptive, if ignored, is high. These participants should be included to ensure that overall confidence in the project's result is high. Beware, however, of letting politics take over. Such participants must be additional to, not in place of, the main contributors. (For more information on this topic, see Chapter 22 on domain experts.)

Consider the impact of additional participants on the project schedule. The number of domain-analysis sessions is *the* most significant variable in the analysis metrics.

Schedule Domain Analysis Sessions

When the required business information has been gathered, some adjustments might be required to the initial concept and behavior models constructed in the previous task. Additionally, the initial domain boundaries might need some refinement. For each of these domains, then, schedule detailed modeling sessions. Analysts and domain experts should work together during domain analysis.

When scheduling the project team members for the meeting, agree on the roles they will play. Assign one to direct the meeting and the another to document the results.

Confirm the meeting participation and arrange for the meeting site and facilities. Do not schedule a meeting to start first thing in the morning or to finish last thing at night. Allow time (30 minutes) for final preparation immediately before the meeting and for a debriefing immediately following the meeting.

If possible, more than one domain analysis session should be scheduled to occur simultaneously. Here, each domain is analyzed in its own right. However, where domains interface, the sessions require a degree of coordination. In manufacturing, this approach is known as *concurrent engineering*. Concurrent engineering permits us to produce more results in less elapsed time than conventional approaches. By carefully monitoring opportunities for reusability and interface requirements, a concurrent engineering approach to system engineering is not only feasible, but necessary, in a world of increasing competition.

Prepare for Analysis Session

The previous step scheduled one or more domain analysis sessions—each of which will require appropriate preparation. Decide whether each meeting should be a single-interview or joint-group session. This decision should be based on the information required, the domain experts involved, the politics of the situation, and the time available. In general, joint sessions are the most productive, because they use time more effectively and the joint discussion accelerates reaching consensus.

Identify precisely the information required from the meeting. Place a structure on the meeting that works through the information requirements in a logical manner. One important consideration is which to model: the domain as it is currently understood or the domain as it should be in the future. Many analysts prefer to produce a "should be" model before the "as is" model. In this way, the domain can be reengineered without a bias from the present. In fact, many analysts do not produce an as-is model. Here, the only places current practice is addressed, then, are during design and construction to aid reuse and during transition to aid migration.

A meeting agenda is essential, even if there is only one participant. The agenda acts as a meeting guide for both sides. Place an item on the agenda for open issues and also one to discuss current problems. The latter must be placed at the end of the agenda. In this way, the meeting is not dominated by a discussion of problems and can focus on a constructive view of the future of the business.

Schedule the project team members for the meeting and agree on the roles they will play. At least two team members will participate in each meeting. One will direct the meeting and the other will document the results. Set up the meeting by confirming the business people's participation and arranging the meeting site and facilities.

PRODUCE A CONCEPTUAL VIEW

For each domain, produce a conceptual view (see Fig. 32.3) to build a formal representation of the business concepts, refining the initial concept view. Domain experts provide the business concepts that become the contents of the concept view. Business analysts give the view its form and improve the representation of the concepts by considering such things as constraints, supertypes, subtypes, immutability, cardinality, and time dependence.

This task captures enough of the concept view to be reasonably confident that it contains all the business concepts that support this domain's business processes—and no more. The concept view of the business model represents the business objects and their associations. Since this view is conceptual in nature, it must not reflect any physical design and implementation considerations. (In the system design phase, however, this view provides the basis for database design, which *is* implementation dependent.)

This view may be expressed on paper or screen. Either way, it should be recorded in an automated form. Furthermore, the concepts should be prototyped to ensure that they are correct and useful. With some of the new OO-CASE tools, it is now possible to prototype directly from the diagram. When the concepts are right, the project's success benefits greatly.

Identify Object Types

Review the results of the information gathering meetings. Identify concepts that may be object types in the business. In the initial pass, do not try to make too many judgments

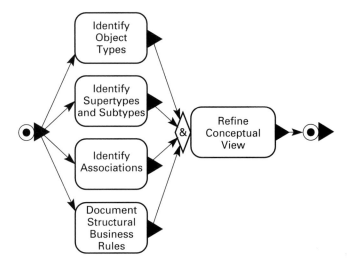

Figure 32.3   A method to Produce a Conceptual View.

about the validity of the object type—just record its existence. This can be achieved initially by annotating the meeting notes with an object type name in the margin. This is a way to check that each business fact is in fact covered by one or more object types.

After listing the possible object types, check against the list of object types already recorded within the project. For each object type already known, review its existing definition and description to ensure that it correctly reflects the business facts recently discovered. If the identified object type is new, create a definition for it. Define the object type in business terms as thoroughly as possible. Check the repository to see if the object type has already been defined and used outside of this project.

At any point in the process, it may be discovered that an object type is synonymous with another, already identified, object type. When this occurs, consider whether it is exactly the same object type or is, in fact, a subtype or supertype of the existing object type. If it is the same, ensure that the facts about the object type are complete and record the synonym as an alternative name. If it is different, add the new object type to the repository.

Identify Supertypes and Subtypes

For each object type, consider its theoretically possible supertypes. For instance, a possible supertype of Book is Published Item, where the supertype of Published Item could be Item, and so on. There are two purposes to this step. The first is determining whether the domain is placed at the correct level. For example, if the domain supports a book check-in process, the object type Book would seem obvious. However, in contemporary libraries other items may also be checked out, such as magazines and audio tapes. Here, the object type Published Item would be more appropriate than Book for this domain. The second purpose of this step is to help identify reusable components. For example, a check-in/check-out process for Items might have already been defined by the library—or

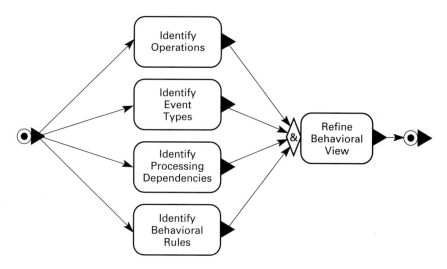

Figure 32.4   A method to Produce a Behavioral View.

This view may be expressed on paper or screen. Either way, it should be maintained in an automated form. Furthermore, the processes should be prototyped to ensure that they are correct and useful conceptually. With some of the new OO-CASE tools, a prototype can now be executed directly from the diagrams. The only way to know that a diagram is correct is if it works. When the analysis is correct, the final product has a better chance of also being correct.

The steps depicted in Fig. 32.4 may occur in various sequences, depending on the modeling technique chosen. A more detailed method for producing event diagrams is presented in Chapter 7. Methods for constructing state-transition diagrams are presented by Rumbaugh [Rumbaugh, 1991] and Booch [Booch, 1994]. If use-case interaction diagrams are preferred, consult Jacobson [Jacobson, 1992]. A technique should be chosen for its clarity and rigor as the best expression of the problem at hand.

Identify Operations

Review the notes from the information-gathering meeting and identify the discussion of business processes. Use this discussion, the initial business model, and the initial domain specification produced earlier. For each domain, identify those operations required to carry out the domain processing.

Operations can be defined at many levels from high-level abstract definitions to very fine-grained, action-oriented definitions. The goal is to understand the processes at a level which provides insight into how business is transacted. The following guidelines will help to set an appropriate level:

- You should be able to identify a single execution of the operation, for example, Take an Order as opposed to Order Processing.

- The operation should be meaningful in a business discussion, not merely a data processing requirement.
- The operation should be simple, but integral. In other words, it should satisfy a simple, single goal in the business and must be completed as a single activity.

All of the operations need not be defined to the correct level in the first attempt. As the project team refines the business model, the operation definitions will naturally evolve towards a consistent level.

Name the operations as they are recorded. The names should have an action verb and an object type name whenever possible. Make sure that the object type name is consistent with the names used on the object diagram. Define operations in a concise but meaningful way, including the purpose for the process.

If the operation is new, create a definition for it. Describe the operation in business terms. Check the repository to see if the operation has already been defined and used outside of this project.

For each operation identified, define its input and output parameters. The input is the information that the operation needs in order to operate, and the output is the result that the operation produces. Express them in terms of concept view components, such as object types, relationship types, and attribute types.

Associate each of the operations with an object type that will serve as its object-oriented *host*. The host should be the object type that is input to the operation. If more than one object type is input to the operation, ask which object types are affected by this operation. Often, the answer will clearly identify a single object type. However, if the answer is more than one object type, associate the operation with those object types. During implementation, a choice might have to be limited. In CLOS, an operation may be associated with multiple object types. In languages like C++ and Smalltalk, an operation must be associated with only one object type. In analysis, such restrictions do not apply. Hosts act as indexes for operations. To find and reuse an operation, the host (or hosts) are the first place to look.

Identify Event Types

Events are the noteworthy state changes that control the execution of processes. They trigger or prevent the triggering of operations. On state-transition diagrams, these are usually represented as arrowed lines. On event diagrams, they are represented as small, solid triangles.

For each operation identified, determine which event triggers the operation. Then, ask whether there are other events which, while not triggering the operation, must precede it. In addition to determining events from processes, the reverse is also possible. Review those events already identified or those which are explicit in the notes from the information-gathering meeting. Then, identify the operations that they trigger.

If the event type is new, create a definition for it. Describe the event type in terms of its state change. In other words, identify the prestate, the poststate, and the kind of state change. Check the repository to see if the event type has already been defined and used outside of this project.

Document Processing Dependencies

In diagramming the behavioral view of the business model, identify dependencies between operations. In event diagrams, when one operation is completed, its event occurs—triggering another operation. This processing dependency, then, is expressed using trigger rules and are represented using arrowed lines. When the dependency is not triggered, the arrowed line may connect two operations without an intervening event type. In this situation, the dependency simply indicates object flow and no triggering. Jacobson and Booch employ different techniques. In pseudocode, this dependency is expressed by placing one line of code right after another.

Define Behavioral Rules

Document the behavioral rules associated with each operation. For each operation, record the triggering rules, control-condition rules, and precondition and postcondition rules. Often, the notes from the information-gathering meeting can be used as a source for these rules.

If the identified rule is new, create a specification for it. Describe the rule in business terms, as well. Check the repository to see if the rule has already been defined and used outside of this project. Reuse when possible.

Refine Behavioral View

After incorporating the additions and changes to the behavioral view of the business model, review the integrity of the model as a whole. For each process:

- Check that the operation is named and its processing described.
- Check that the input and output parameters are specified for each process.
- Check that the precondition and postcondition rules are specified for each process.
- Ensure that the operation is associated with a host object type.
- Ensure that the operation has at least one triggering event associated with it.
- Ensure that the trigger and control condition rules are specified.

Operations are processes that can be requested as units. Ultimately, the processing for each operation must be described in detail. An operation's detailed processing description is called its *method*. For example, Produce Behavioral View is an operation, and its method is depicted in Fig. 32.4. Methods may be expressed using various techniques, such as pseudocode or an event diagram. In this way, the operations on an event diagram may be expressed as yet another event diagram—employing a *leveled* approach to system specification. The decision to go to the next level will be decided in the Review Business Model task. Each operation, then, can define a domain in its own right—requiring analysis steps that produce another level of conceptual and behavioral views.

ANALYZE THE INTERACTION

Analyze the interaction (see Fig. 32.5) to check the quality and completeness of the behavioral and conceptual views of the business model—specifically to detect and correct specification errors. Although the task can be performed after the conceptual and behavioral views have been produced, it is usually performed at the same time.

The techniques used in this task may seem too easy to be powerful. Yet, the few steps performed here often uncover significant errors. In this task:

- Check the actions that activities perform on objects to verify the completeness of the business model.
- Examine the lifecycles of objects to assure that the behavior view includes the processes that affect the objects in the concept view.
- Revise the business model in light of any discrepancies found in performing this task.

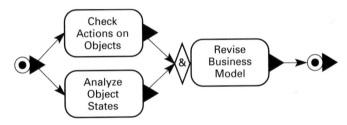

Figure 32.5   A method to Analyze the Interaction.

Check Activity Actions on Objects

Produce a matrix of operations against object types. Typically, this reads best if the operations are placed on the rows and object types on the columns. Record in the matrix the interaction between operations and object types. Read the interactions from the operation definitions. Perform the following visual checks on the matrix:

- Each object type must have at least one operation associated with it.
- Each operation must be associated with at least one host object type.
- Each object type must have at least one operation that creates object instances, or the instances must be generated outside the system.
- Each object type must have at least one operation that terminates or archives object instances.
- Each object type must have at least one operation that queries it.
- Each relationship and attribute type must have operations that query and modify it.

Analyze Object States

Some object types are reasonably critical to the business. Such operations typically have several operations that are associated with them. Since these object types are important to the business, it is also important to ensure that all of its operations are addressed and supported.

Begin identifying the critical object types by reviewing the matrix of operations and object types. These include object types such as **Customer, Product, and Order**. Also, select those object types that host five or more operations. For each object type selected:

- Identify the states in the life of the object type.
- Identify the permitted state transitions.
- Identify the operations that cause the state transition and the states that result from these operations.
- Look for missing operations (desired transitions for which there are no processes).
- Look for illegally defined operations (processes whose effect is an unallowable transition).

For each operation that is missing, create a definition for it. Describe the operation in business terms. New operations should be fully specified, either in this project or another project. Check the repository to see if the operation has already been defined and used outside of this project. For each illegally defined operation, determine how it should be removed from the system and any other system that uses it.

An object type's lifecycle can be viewed in more than one way. Consider whether more than one state diagram is required to represent this. If the Produce a Behavioral View task employs state-transition diagrams, this step will require less work.

Revise Business Model

Record the issues raised in building the matrix and examining the object states. Review the project documents to see if the answers are available. Update the business model with the new information. If the answers are not available, add the issue to the open issues list. These new issues will be addressed in the next task.

REVIEW THE BUSINESS MODEL

After each domain analysis, review the business model to assure that the analysis is progressing. The purpose of this task (illustrated in Fig. 32.6) is to:

- Identify likely business changes and modify the business model to improve its resilience to change.
- Identify what portions of the model and objects may be reused by other projects.
- Choose a form to document that the model is complete and correct and that it can be reviewed and understood by users, management, and quality assurance reviewers.
- Obtain user and management agreement and commitment to the outline business model.
- Confirm the correctness and scope of the outline business model before defining design areas.

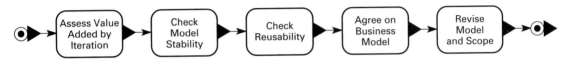

Figure 32.6   A method to Review the Business Model.

Once the model becomes reasonably stable and the rate at which the project team is changing the contents has slowed, the project can concentrate on moving forward to the design stage. The team must recognize that perfection is not the goal here, because the model will be completed in the design stage.

Assess Value Added by Iteration

Business modeling is an iterative process—understood by adding knowledge incrementally. However, generating a perfect understanding would take endless iterations with a process of diminishing returns. Therefore, examine carefully the value added by each iteration.

Review the current state of the business models and assess their completeness. Check the following:

- Are all of the elements recorded?
- Are the elements complete, that is, named, defined, and diagrammed?
- Are the elements consistent?
- Does the business model effectively communicate the business to the business community?

Review the schedule for information gathering and check if all of the key business participants have contributed. Finally, check the most valuable source—the open issues list. The number of outstanding issues should get smaller, as will the scope and significance of items on the list. If significant items remain or a large number of items remain outstanding, analysis should continue.

Ultimately, the business model must be specified thoroughly enough to guide the designers. The component requiring the most iterations is the operation. For each operation, the analyst must specify its procedure, or method. Each method can contain operations that, in turn, may have their methods specified, and so on. As discussed earlier, the operations on an event diagram may be expressed as yet another event diagram—employing a *leveled* approach to system specification. Each operation, then, can define a domain in its own right, requiring its own analysis steps and identifying its own object types, operations, and so on. If analysis does not proceed to the next level, the design team may not have enough detail to produce its design specification. The decision to go to the next level is decided in this step. As a general guideline, the analysis team should schedule each operation to do next-level analysis, unless:

- A primitive operation is reached (e.g., create or terminate).
- The plan dictates skipping.

- The analysis is already done and can be reused.
- Team members do not have expertise.
- A timebox cutoff is reached (see Chapter 24).
- The operation is external to the business (i.e., the operation's method is not executed by the business).
- A level is reached that only design tasks should address.

Check Model Stability

The project team is trying to understand a business that is changing. Because of this, business analysis resembles shooting at a moving target. Meet with the senior business people and ask them about future business changes. The project team should already be aware of definitive, planned changes, and it should seek insight into possible, as yet undecided, changes. These can include business reorganization, legislative or regulatory changes, market growth or change, or personnel changes.

For each anticipated business change, ask what is the probability that the change will materialize. If the probability is low, it can be ignored. If it is high, the potential impact must be assessed. To assess the impact of a business change, take a copy of the business model and assume that the change is implemented. Then, update the model to accommodate it. Examine the implications of the model changes and consider whether the base models should be extended to make them more flexible to accommodate such a future change.

Check Reusability

Throughout the modeling process, the possibility of reuse should be investigated at every step. The business modeling processes look both within and outside the project scope to see if their respective components have already been defined elsewhere. Identifying reuse opportunities at this early stage is essential to exploiting reuse.

In addition to looking for reusable components, the project should also be contributing to the repository of reusable components. This step, then, considers how this project's business model components can be reused in the future. In doing so, it may consider whether any components in the model can be restated or generalized for broader use.

Agree on the Business Model

As each domain is modeled, gather the project team together and review the current state of the business model. This model will continue to evolve. Retaining a perspective on the *whole* model is important, while team members focus on its particular aspects. The objective of these meetings is to share understanding and improve consistency across the complete business model.

At key points in the project, meet with the business community to present and discuss the business models. The business people must agree that the models capture the essence of the business.

Revise Model and Scope

Changes to the business models will be dictated by the review process. The reasons for these changes should be recorded and cross-referenced with the open issues list. This simple step will prevent time wasted later discussing why a change was made.

As understanding of the business improves, the scope of the project may also be refined. Document any changes in scope. The executive sponsor must agree with the changes, and the development-coordination group must be kept informed. Such changes in scope will invariably require changes in domain definitions. Additional domains or domains whose definition has changed must be reprocessed through the Prepare for Domain Analysis task above.

ANALYZE THE USAGE

The reasons for performing this task (illustrated in Fig. 32.7) are to:

- Determine where processes are (or will be) performed in the enterprise.
- Provide the quantitative information needed for designing the distribution of processing and data stores.
- Provide the quantitative information needed for estimating the required use of computer facilities.
- Determine possible distribution strategies for the database.

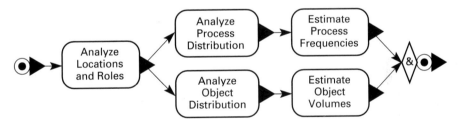

Figure 32.7   A method to Analyze the Usage.

In this task, look at roles (who performs the work), the locations (where it is performed), and the volumes and frequencies (the amount of work). You must also look at the operations (what work is done) and the object types and their associations (what information is accessed).

This task identifies the business requirements for distribution and determines the impact that the distribution paths will have on business operations. The goal is *not* to design the distribution.

Analyze Locations and Roles

Identify the types of locations involved in the business. These can be widespread, as in sales offices in cities across the country, or localized, as in departments in the head office.

At this point, concentrate on logical rather than physical locations. For example, knowing that the business involves the sales offices is more important than knowing that the offices are in Chicago, Detroit, and so on.

In identifying a location type be sure that a common set of characteristics applies to all locations of that type. For instance, the business may use sales offices, but the regional and local sales offices have different roles or are radically different in size. If this is the case, perform the usage analysis for regional sales offices and local sales offices separately.

Identify the roles of people associated with the business at each location type. At some business locations, the roles may not be very significant. This is typically found where business functions are very narrow or the user community is very small.

Check the list of location types and roles to ensure a good understanding of who is involved in the business and at what location they reside. Remember that business processes and people can be relocated. Check if any changes are planned.

Analyze Process Distribution

Create a matrix of the business-location type and role versus the process. Generally, the matrix reads better when the location type and role are placed on the rows while the process is placed on the columns. Record an entry in the cells of the matrix to indicate where:

- The process involves activity at a location type/role—*sometimes* or *always*.
- A location type/role executes the process—*completely* or *partially*.

Estimate Process Frequencies

For each cell filled in on the matrix of location and role versus process, indicate:

- An appropriate time period in which to measure the level of business activity (for example, hourly or daily).
- The average number of times that a process occurs within the time period.
- The maximum number of process occurrences for the time period.
- The likely peak period.
- The expected growth of business activity.

Analyze Object Type Distribution

Create a matrix of business-location type and role versus object type. Generally, the matrix reads more clearly when the location type and role are placed on the rows and the object type is placed on the columns. Record an entry in the cells of the matrix to indicate:

- What information available from an object type is used by a location type/role—*all of the information* or *some of the information*.
- Instances of an object type that must be available at different occurrences of a location type and role—*the same set of object instances* or *a different set of object instances*.

Estimate Object Volumes

For each cell filled on the matrix of location and role versus object type, indicate:

- The number of instances of the object type required.
- The number of instances accessed within a given period of time.
- The expected growth of object instances.

DEFINE DESIGN AREAS

This task subdivides the business model into cohesive areas for subsequent development as business systems and selects the appropriate form for implementing each process in the systems—whether client/server or some other mechanism. Defining the scope of a design area specifies the functionality that will be implemented by the system (see Fig. 32.8).

In Define Development Strategies (see Chapter 30), the approaches to incremental development (also called *spiral development*) were planned. Now, the functionality that must be incorporated into each increment is planned.

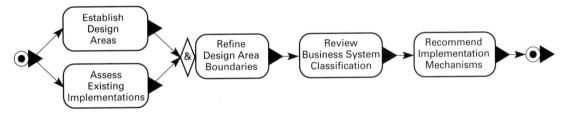

Figure 32.8 A method to Define Design Areas.

Establish Design Areas

In building the business model, a concept view (of object types) and a behavioral view (of operations and events) were defined. The entire business model need not be implemented in a single project. Implementing the business models in iterative stages provides numerous benefits. Shorter projects deliver benefits to the business quicker. Smaller projects prove to be more successful. Lessons learned on early projects can be applied to later iterations.

The iterations are defined in terms of design areas. The business, described by the business model, is subdivided into design areas for iterative implementation. A design area is a collection of interrelated object types and processes. If the business model is small, define design areas intuitively. Such definitions should be based on business goals, locations, and available resources, such as technology and personnel.

Assess Existing Implementations

Examine all existing applications that implement any or all portions of the domains analyzed in this project. Rate the quality of each of these implementations in terms of performance, usability, and space requirements. Determine which should be reused, replaced, or modified for the new system. This determination might cause changes to the design area boundaries defined in the Establish Design Areas task.

Refine Design-Area Boundaries

Review the proposed design area, paying close attention to the boundaries and interaction between design areas. Adjusting the design-area definitions may ensure that each area is complete and provides a consistent business value. The design areas can also be adjusted to optimize the accommodations of existing implementations.

Review Business System Classification

In Classify Business Systems (see Chapter 30), the business systems were categorized as online teleprocessing, decision support, graphic and multimedia information, or online complex processing. For each design area, review the classification based on the information the team now possesses. Classifying the expected systems support for the design areas provides a basis for planning the design and construction. It also helps the business understand what type of support it can expect.

Recommend Implementation Mechanisms

For each design area:

- Consider the characteristics of the object types and business processes within the scope.
- Review the usage analysis and possible distribution of these components.
- Examine the interaction with other design areas.
- Map the design area to the technical architecture.
- Identify appropriate implementation mechanisms.

EVALUATE DESIGN AREAS

The reasons for evaluating design areas are to:

- Verify that genuine benefits will be gained by providing computer support to selected parts of the business.
- Determine the most effective and efficient development path for further design and implementation.
- Ensure that management is aware of the development costs for the proposed business systems and required resources.
- Ensure that management understands the time scales involved.
- Complete the project and get approval for subsequent work.
- Get a starting position for subsequent design-area projects.
- Define the release schedule for implementing system functionality.

The goal of this task (illustrated in Fig. 32.9) is to identify those business areas that will benefit from automated support and to get commitment of actual people, finances, and facilities to start designing a system. Its primary deliverable is a *design-area development plan*. This plan documents the findings of this task.

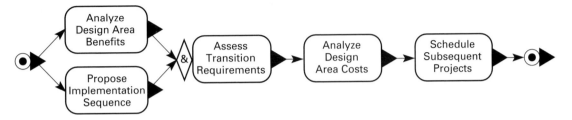

Figure 32.9　A method to Evaluate Design Areas.

Analyze Design Area Benefits

Identify the benefits of implementing the design area. These include:

- Increased business revenues, such as expanding markets, improving customer relationships, and reducing cycle times.
- Reducing business costs—for example, lowering inventory, reducing resource requirements, and lowering communications costs.
- Removing processing problems, such as delays in responding to business changes and incompatible or incomplete information.
- Reducing processing costs—for example, moving to a lower cost platform.

Assign a monetary value to each benefit and calculate the benefits for the design area.

Propose Implementation Sequence

Examine the design-area definitions and the interactions between design areas. This information is available on the matrix of object types and processes. The interactions indicate where a process in one area needs to communicate with an object type in another. Translate the dependencies into a logical sequence for implementation. Sometimes the dependencies are circular, where two design areas depend equally on each other. The choice is either to implement them in parallel or to adjust the scope of the design areas.

Review the logical sequence and check its practicality from a business perspective. Adjust the sequence as appropriate and recommend a project sequence.

Assess Transition Requirements

With an existing system or database, a transition process will likely be required to move data across to the new system. Identify the transition requirements immediately, because transition can be time-consuming. In some cases, it can take even longer than the implementation project itself. These transition costs must be included in the project assessment.

Analyze the Design-Area Costs

Prepare an outline development plan for each of the design areas. Estimate the resource requirements and costs. Design-area project costs will include development costs, operational costs, and transition costs.

Schedule Subsequent Projects

The design-area costs, design-area benefits, transition requirements, and the implementation sequence should be presented to the business decision makers. Be prepared to make adjustments based on their business insight. More than one option may be possible—particularly if more than one design area is done in parallel. If appropriate, present the alternative options together with their implications. Addressing design areas in parallel reduces the benefits of iterative development and entails some additional risks.

Based on the decisions of the project sponsors, continue the planning process by scheduling the projects. Summarize the resource requirements and match them against availability. Consider outsourcing or supplementing the team with external resources as appropriate.

Present the schedule to the project sponsor for approval. Once approved, the *design-area development plan* is completed.

REFERENCES

Booch, Grady, *Object-Oriented Analysis and Design with Applications* (2nd ed.), Benjamin-Cummings, Redwood City, CA, 1994.

Jacobson, Ivar, Magnus Christerson, Partik Jonsson, and Gunnar Övergaard, *Object-Oriented Software Engineering: A Use Case Driven Approach,* Addison-Wesley, Reading, MA, 1992.

Rumbaugh, James, Michael Blaha, William Premeriani, Frederick Eddy, and William Lorenson, *Object-Oriented Modeling and Design,* Prentice Hall, Englewood Cliffs, NJ, 1991.

Chapter 33

System Analysis: Management Tasks

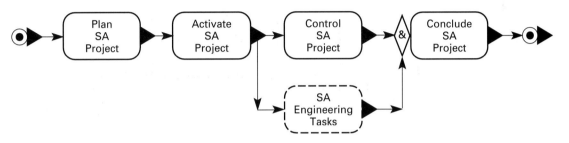

A method for the management tasks of system analysis.

PLAN SYSTEM ANALYSIS PROJECT

The work plan must be established for the system analysis (SA) project defined by the strategy planning project (see Fig. 33.1). The work plan provides the blueprint for the project manager.

The scope of this system analysis project was established in the strategy. The objective for the system analysis plan is defining the business model with just enough detail to move forward to the design stage with great confidence that the users' requirements will be met.

Figure 33.1   A method to Plan System Analysis Project.

To complete the plan, choose the appropriate techniques, for example, object-relationship modeling or entity-relationship modeling. Then determine the user involvement, management style, and project-organizational structure. Identify resource requirements, develop a detailed schedule, assess the project risk, and gain acceptance of the plan.

Define Project

The *strategy plan* has already defined the basic scope of this project. In this subtask, fill in the details of the project objectives, scope, constraints and assumptions, deliverables, and standards for the deliverables and procedures for carrying out the project.

The *primary objective* of a system analysis project is to understand and model the business so that developing systems meet business requirements. The specific goals are:

- Identify the business concepts, their descriptors, interrelationships, and structural rules. The databases derived from these concepts will thus have structural integrity.
- Determine the business activities and the circumstances under which they happen. The resulting applications will reflect the business behavior and support the behavioral rules.
- Determine the scope and sequence of subsequent iterative systems development.

The *scope of this project* is set by the business-area definition specified in the strategy plan. It lists the business activities, objects, organizational units, and locations.

Detail any constraints, such as budget or time limits and the availability of skills, knowledge, or equipment. List the *assumptions* employed in developing the SA project schedule.

The *principal deliverables* are the business model and the design-area development plan.

Establish documentation and diagramming *standards* for deliverables. Standards for deliverable reviews and procedures for revising the project plan were established in the strategy planning project. The same standards and procedures apply to this project.

Make Project Plan

Identify the tasks, effort, and resources needed to produce the deliverables, establish a schedule and budget, estimate the risk, check the plan against the constraints and assumptions identified earlier, and verify that the project plan is feasible.

Identify Tasks, Effort, and Resources

Use Chapter 34 to identify the tasks. For each task, the combination of task and technique determines the effort, resources, and scheduling requirements. For example, one of the various forms of modeling may be chosen as a technique for certain tasks.

Do not underestimate the size of nontechnical work, such as the project leadership and the presentation and review of results. In particular, the tasks at the project's conclusion are often underestimated.

Identify and include the milestone reviews. Major milestones for an SA project occur at the end of the Plan task, the business-model review task, the design-area evaluation task, and at the project's conclusion. Other milestone reviews may be scheduled, depending upon the project's complexity and scope.

Estimate the team size and composition. Keep the core team small—ideally three to six people. At least one of these should have been on the SP project core team. Use outside experts and reference groups for specific tasks, rather than enlarging the team.

Establish the Project Schedule

Use estimates of resource requirements and availability, task dependencies, and effort. Consider timeboxes and user workshops when developing the schedule, particularly for review tasks. Remember, the schedule will likely be adjusted after the specific team is established. Start scheduling any interviews or workshops as soon as possible, since they will be difficult to schedule within the time frame of the project.

Develop a Budget

The project budget should take into account the project schedule and resource usage, equipment and facilities, and other expenses, such as travel and office support.

Identify the Areas of Risk in the Project Schedule

In addition to the risks that apply to all projects, look for the following:

- Involving the wrong users or those without management backing.
- Planned or expected business changes that will affect the project scope.
- The need to analyze many objects that are accessed, but not modified, by the activities in the project scope.
- Spending too much time in decision making.

Build risk reduction into the project plan. If this is a high-risk project, treat it as if it were a much bigger project. Choose behavioral techniques to achieve consensus quickly. Manage expectations from the start.

Check Plan Against Assumptions

The constraints and assumptions may require adjustment to produce a feasible schedule. In particular, check the project scope and team composition.

Obtain Project Approval

Present the project plan to the project sponsor and other people required for plan approval. A task force may have been established to oversee the fulfillment of the strategy plan.

Reconfirming support for development is always a good idea, particularly if the project meets resistance. Identify the other stakeholders whose unofficial approval will help assure the project's success:

- The ultimate *customers* of information and processes within the project scope.

- Potential *adversaries* of the project. Determine who will lose power or influence if this project succeeds and identify how to gain their confidence and support.

- *Process facilitators.* Determine who supplies information or otherwise supports the processes and clarify how the process will affect them.

ACTIVATE SYSTEM ANALYSIS PROJECT

The activation task, illustrated in Fig. 33.2, launches the project. As a first step, set up the working environment: the project team room, the facilities for interviewing, group workshops, and training, as well as the computer equipment and software. In addition, the team members must learn and practice the techniques of model building and information gathering that they will use in outlining the system analysis project.

Figure 33.2   A method to Activate System Analysis Project.

Establish Project Environment

Set up the equipment and facilities for the project, using the same setup as in the strategic planning project. Space and equipment will be required for interviews, workshops, team training, and team meetings. The project team productivity will be increased if each team member has easy access to the following software:

- Word processor.
- Spreadsheet.
- Diagrammer.
- Presentation.
- Project estimation and project management.
- The methodology.

A CASE tool is helpful, but not necessary, for some of the diagramming.

Train Team

The team members must be trained in the techniques they will be using. Special emphasis should be placed on techniques of information gathering and business modeling. Combining the project kickoff with a training session is a good idea. Make sure that each team member knows how to use the software to help produce project deliverables and work products.

This next task (illustrated in Fig. 33.3) controls the progress of the system analysis project. It takes corrective actions within the scope of the plan and identifies the need to change the critical project elements, such as objectives, scope, budget, or time span in a timely manner. In addition, the project may have to coordinate with the results of prior projects and concurrent events outside the project. The control task manages this coordination.

In a system analysis project, the central issue is avoiding paralysis by analysis. The key to successful control is managing scope and controlling iteration.

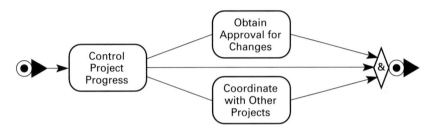

Figure 33.3   A method to Control System Analysis Project.

Control Project Progress

Project control is vital to the success of the project. It involves assigning project tasks, monitoring task and deliverable status, checking progress against the plan, and periodically reporting progress to the project sponsor and other stakeholders.

The project manager must keep the project moving forward, motivate the team, and keep the support of the project stakeholders. Project control should minimize bureaucracy. The team should devote most of the time to performing the project, not filling out project-control reports.

The project should have a finite time and expense budget. Avoid letting excessive requests for "small" increases in scope derail the project. The requests that are not recommended for inclusion should be recorded as *enhancement requests.*

Assign Project Tasks

The project plan typically includes initial task assignments. These are often adjusted and amended during the project, as the plan confronts reality. Circulating a weekly assignment sheet is a good practice, either before or during the *short* weekly staff meeting. Items to discuss at a status meeting include the following:

- Major events.
- Action items.
- Recap of expected deliverables.

- Actual achievements and variances.
- Overall project assessment.
- Next week's deliverables.
- Action items for next meeting.

Monitor Tasks and Deliverables

Keep the project's progress and management issues visible. Post schedules, reports, and issues. Assign all issues a due date. Review whether an answer to an issue is overdue.

Check Progress Against Plan

Compare the resources used and the time spent to the allocated resources and time. Identify progress that is ahead of schedule, as well as tasks that are behind schedule or likely to fall behind. Determine if any delays are externally imposed. Identify any unproductive work.

Report to Sponsor

Give periodic progress reports to the project sponsor and keep influential stakeholders informed, as well. Reports to the sponsor should include the time spent by each team member for each task, the deliverables produced, and an estimate task completion.

Obtain Approval for Change

The project plan is a contract between the team and the project sponsor. Make minor corrections, such as changing meeting times, trying alternative techniques, or getting users more involved, within the original plan. However, the difference between planned and actual performance may be too great to overcome by working smarter. Corrective actions that change the schedule, the cost, the scope, or the deliverables require formal approval.

Look for early warning signs that the project will not meet the plan. For example, the team might not be completing deliverables by the milestone dates, or the quality may be low. The cause could be inadequate resources, poor productivity, an unreasonable schedule, or an inappropriate scope. Identifying the root cause is essential to coming up with the right solution.

Examine each proposed solution for its impact on the project objectives, scope, benefits, schedule, quality, and resources. Changes to scope, timing, and resource use may affect other projects. Therefore, the development coordination group should also review the proposal. In reviewing the impact, do not forget to repeat tasks that were considered complete.

Decide which actions to recommend to the project sponsor. Justify the proposed change in business terms. Make the sponsor and steering committee aware of the alternatives and the consequences of not making the change.

When the project sponsor, steering committee, project manager, and development coordination group agree to the changes, publicize the new plan to everyone on the project. Notify the project team, reference groups, stakeholders, as well as any business users and technical specialists whose schedules might change. Work closely with the project sponsor.

Coordinate with Other Projects

A project does not happen in isolation. The project manager is the liaison between the SA project and other developments that might affect the direction, contents, and schedule of the SA project. In particular, be aware of other work that will affect the availability of resources, especially those people who provide information to the project team and review its results.

CONCLUDE SYSTEM ANALYSIS PROJECT

This last task (illustrated in Fig. 33.4) creates an orderly finish to the system analysis stage, frees project resources for other activities, and ensures recognition for its participants. While most projects are completed, occasionally a project will be stopped before its objectives are achieved. For example, a midproject review might indicate that the project should be suspended or canceled. The project manager should be able to recommend such an action—if justified.

　　The system analysis project enhances the model and may revise the definition of the system's scope created during the strategy plan. Ensure provisions for recording these changes.

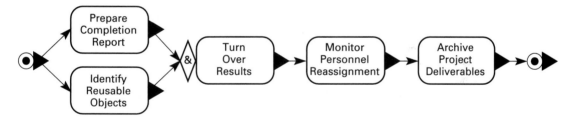

Figure 33.4　A method to Conclude System Analysis Project.

Prepare Completion Report

The *project completion report* contains sections for management summaries, deliverables for subsequent projects, evaluation of resource performance, the project analysis, and project metrics. Prepare these according to the organization's requirements and conventions.

　　The management summary section should include an overview, summaries of analysis findings, project metrics, and recommendations.

　　The deliverables section describes the business model: project background, scope, objectives, conclusions reached, and schedule of subsequent projects. The major deliverables should be placed in an appendix containing both the concept view and the behavior view of the business model and the design-area development plan.

The project-analysis section recaps the project performance. Include the business accomplishments, lessons learned, a summary of metrics, and any unusual or interesting project aspects.

The project is not complete until the steering committee and executive owner accept its results. An executive presentation of the report prior to final sign-off may also be required.

Identify Reusable Objects

Everything produced in the course of this project has the potential for reuse. Review the project deliverables with an eye to reusability. They should be cataloged and stored in a form in which they can be accessed for reuse. In particular, the business model and documentation standards should be given to the subsequent design projects as a starter kit.

Turn Over Results

The *design-area development plan* (produced by the Evaluate Design Areas task in Chapter 32) recommended follow-on work and specified at least one project to activate. Determine what these projects will require using the deliverables, work products, open issues (documenting compromise decisions), lessons learned, and any other applicable documentation. Plan to meet with those project managers to assure a smooth transition.

Monitor Personnel Reassignment

Care for project members increases the chance of success for other projects. More importantly, it is the right thing to do. Personnel actions to consider include performance reviews, recognition and rewards, as well as the placement of team members at the project's conclusion.

Archive Project Deliverables

If it was important to do, it is probably important to keep. Identify how and where to archive project deliverables and work products within the organization. Work with a development-coordination unit to ensure that the correct versions of shared objects are passed to other teams and that they know how to access and update these objects.

Chapter 34

System Design: Engineering Tasks

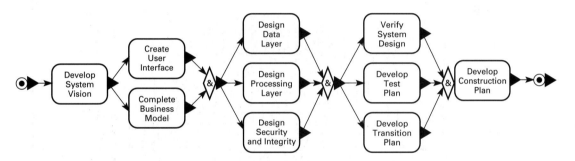

A method for the engineering tasks of system design.

DEVELOP A SYSTEM VISION

This first task specifies how the system will work (see Fig. 34.1). It prepares for development by testing critical elements and by acquiring and testing the development tools. Its specifications form the basis of the system design, establish the parameters for the acceptance tests, and identify the critical elements of the production environment that must be met before the system can work properly. The testing and acquisition will help those people who design the systems be confident that the disparate pieces will work together.

In our rapidly evolving world, major changes to the capabilities of communications, hardware, and software occur every few months. These changes address limitations that implementors of earlier applications have discovered. Because of this, the selections of technical architecture made in the strategy plan should be revisited and, where appropriate, revised.

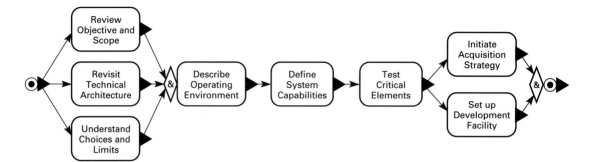

Figure 34.1   A method to Develop a System Vision.

Identify the critical elements and test them before the System Design (SD) project is started. This will ensure that the selected operations' facilities will work as envisioned. This test must be devised and executed in less than a week—running on borrowed facilities, if necessary.

Set the requirements for system operation, such as the look and feel of the systems. These standards are added to the development standards set in the project plan. Since you may have to jump administrative hurdles before the production facilities are in place, take steps *now* to start acquiring the facilities.

Review Objectives and Scope

The whole team reviews the project objectives and becomes familiar with:

- The portion of the business model that will be supported by the business system being designed.
- The existing systems that the new system will replace in whole or in part.
- The existing systems that will interface with the new system.
- The locations and users of the new system.

Ideally, at least one member of the design team worked on the analysis team. If the team lacks continuity or a gap exists between the end of the systems analysis (SA) project and the beginning of this design project, allow extra time for the team members to get up to speed. In addition to reviewing the model and the SA project-completion report, system design team members should interview SA project participants.

Revisit the Technical Architecture

Reexamine the technical architecture in light of the business model that has been developed and the availability and reputation of the technical components. The analysis of business concepts and behavior as well as information usage may suggest that the architectural requirements need adjusting. In addition, new operating software, hardware, and communications facilities and standards will probably have appeared on the market. New releases of development tools may be available. Even the applications that this SD project is expected to reuse, replace, or modify may have changed in some manner. (This should have been minimized by proper high-level coordination, however.)

Review the technical architecture's original selections and evaluate any new options now available. In reviewing the architectural components for the operating environment, pay particular attention to new developments in database integrity, in communication protocols and connectors (including middleware), and in data compression. Advances here may help simplify the design of the distributed systems.

Understand Choices and Limits

Examine the users' working conditions to identify environmental factors that may limit the selection of equipment and facilities. The SD team may visit representative work sites. For example, are users wearing special clothes that limit movement? Can users be connected to the network wiring or must they communicate over the air?

Assess the design's complexity as implied by its scope and objectives and by the technical architecture selected. As the design's complexity increases, the number of places where things can go wrong is compounded.

Describe the Operating Environment

Describe the elements of the user environment:

- *Types of users.* Managerial, secretarial, clerical, and so on.
- *Skill levels of the users.* Casual versus experienced users.
- *Working environment.* Office, factory, open air, and so on.

Specify the location of each architectural component and any environmental considerations. For example, the operating environment might require special desk heights, a secure space for the server, and so on. One organization located their only server next to a secretary's desk to make backing up the server easier. One night the cleaning crew took out the server with the trash.

List the elements of the technical environment:

- *Site requirements.* Such as a secure closet with adequate air circulation or special wiring.
- *User facilities.* Such as an adjustable desk to accommodate keyboard and mouse.
- *Technical components.*

Each component should be allocated to a specific machine—server, client, host, or peripheral. This will become the checklist for configuring the hardware and system software. While the system may continue, people will change jobs and machines will break down. Note which components can be transferred between machines and which have to be replaced, which go with the user and which stay with the equipment.

Define System Capabilities

The business model specifies what the system should do. This is expressed in terms of the business objects and business activities that the system should support. The technical architecture specifies the delivery mechanism. Now the people who must approve the new system should specify how the business functionality will be delivered by defining what an acceptable system should achieve. The system capabilities should conform to the following recognized practices:

- Ease of use and support provided to users and operators.
- Functionality and performance of the software, hardware, and communications.
- Availability, reliability, security, and operating cost of the system.
- Flexibility to change.
- Integration with existing systems.
- Standards for recovery, documentation, and performance audits.

Test Critical Elements

Identify those elements that must perform effectively and efficiently so that the system meets the specified capabilities. This includes elements of both the operating and development environments. To help identify the critical elements, review the selection criteria for the technical architectural components and the performance choke points. Examples of critical elements are:

- Network capacity at peak periods.
- Ability to handle multiple database operations in one transaction.
- Integration of development tools from different vendors.

Devise a simple test to check the critical elements. This test must take less than a week to devise. If the test facilities do not exist in-house, rent them. Disaster recovery companies, testing labs, or an equipment supplier may be able to provide adequate testing facilities. Also, the manufacturer of the critical component may be willing to assist, if the project has a real-world problem that can test the component's limits.

Initiate an Acquisition Strategy

Start the process to acquire facilities and their technical components. A complete facility can be set up in a week or less. However, the organization may have a defined procurement process that must be followed and could take considerably longer.

Expect to use the facilities for testing during the system construction (SC) stage. Determine when and what production facilities must be in place so that the facilities themselves can be checked before any systems or components are tested. Schedule the acquisition of other facilities to correspond with the pace of the system deployment.

Set Up a Development Facility

Acquire the necessary hardware and software to build and test the user interface and to design the rest of the system. The development environment should reflect the production environment. Each developer workstation should have client/server development software, spreadsheet, word processor, a network requester, and database-interface, dynamic-link libraries. The file server should have configuration-management software, a CASE or diagramming tool, and widgets (user-interface components). The database server should have a database-management system.

CREATE A USER INTERFACE

Build a user interface that is effective and comfortable to use (see Fig. 34.3). With many of today's automated tools, designing the interface also creates the actual working interface—not merely a prototype.

To begin, elicit the users' view of how the system should work. With their help identify reusable objects and events, map the business objects and events to interface objects and events and, finally, produce and test the usability of the interface.

If the SD project's objective is limited to placing a GUI face onto existing systems, much of the work has already been done. The user conceptual model describes the behavior of the system in business terms. For example, if the system focuses on the **Order** object, actions that the user may perform in a given role may be *enter, revise,* or *cancel.* In other words, a data-driven technique can be used to determine common business actions, such as example, list, cancel, or submit.

Whether your approach is driven by process, events, or data, the product is always the same: a list of object types, events, and operations to implement in GUI form. Next, identify interface objects (widgets) and interface events (for example, single click, double click, or drag) to represent the business actions and, then, attach widgets to the business objects in the view. This gives the user interface prototype. Finally, users test the prototype for usability.

Model User Tasks

In a workshop, users should describe how they want the system to work. To prepare for the workshop, draw up straw-man scenarios of design options based on the SA deliver-

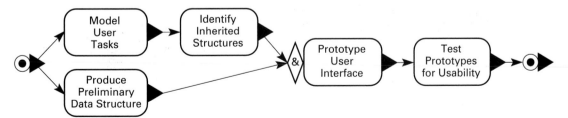

Figure 34.2 A method to Create a User Interface.

ables, the SD team's own knowledge of the design area, and the observations by users in the current working environment. The principal objective for the scenarios is putting the user in control of the system.

For the user workshop select participants who have a broad understanding of the work and whose decisions on the system design will be accepted by other users.

Set up and conduct the workshop. Keep the session focused on developing the user's conceptual model of the system operation. During the workshop, use the conceptual model to direct the users' attention to the objects and, then, to the actions *on* the objects.

The conceptual model describes the users' perception of what the system is doing. In other words, it describes what is presented to them, how they interact with each element, their expectations of what should happen, and the sequence of interactions. The model uses business objects, business actions, and business roles. However, it does not detail how these elements will appear on a computer screen. Each object type or group of object types may eventually become a window or, more likely, some widget in a window. After the workshop, the contents should be diagrammed into a table.

Identify Inherited Structures

Look for common actions that apply to more than one type of object. These are the inherited structures that should be represented by similar widgets when the user-interface prototype is built. Look also for multiple instances of the same object-action pair for a given role. These are reusable structures that should be represented by the same combination of widgets when the prototype is built.

Produce Preliminary Data Structure

Many interface-builder tools require that the database definitions be specified before generating a working interface. This database can be a simple transformation of the object-relationship diagram (or entity-relationship diagram)—ignoring any consideration of distribution or performance. If the team is not using a tool that automatically generates the database definitions from the diagram, follow the appropriate rules for converting object structures into the target database structure. Chapter 14 describes the steps for producing a preliminary relational-database structure from an object diagram. Write the DDL (database definition language) to generate the database structure.

Prototype User Interface

Consider the interface as a metaphor of the business. The closer the interface reflects the business, the easier it will be for the users to understand. The strategy planning project developed overall standards for the systems and their operation. When developing the prototype, follow these standards.

Develop the prototype in one or more user workshop sessions. The team should prepare straw-man prototypes for the workshop—presenting alternative approaches for specific aspects of the interface design, where appropriate. For example, the straw-man prototype might show how to present the same action as a menu choice, a button click, or a drag and drop onto an icon.

The next step is determining how to represent the business objects and behavior as interface objects and actions. The interface builder tool may require that the database objects be mapped to the interface widgets before generating a prototype. The designer may also have to provide methods, albeit minimal, for the actions.

By the end of the workshop, the SD team should have a working prototype that the users can test. Try to keep the functional scope of the prototype as narrow as possible, while still allowing the users to get a real sense of the look and feel of the application.

Test Prototypes for Usability

Devise tasks that users can perform with the prototype and determine usability. The testers might require training before they perform the tests—particularly on unfamiliar equipment. It may also be appropriate to have observers monitoring the tests. The observers should look for signs of poor usability that may not be evident to the testers.

The users should have their role and the tests' purpose explained to them. They should understand that usability testing determines how easy and natural the interface is to use. The tests should also discover:

- If too many actions are needed to accomplish a task.
- If manipulating the system puts a physical strain on the user.
- If information is hard to find.
- If there is confusion, ambiguity, inconsistency, or unfilled expectations.

The purpose is *not* to test for bugs.

Carry out the tests. Depending on facility availability, the tests may take place at a prototyping lab or the users' workplace. The lab should duplicate the users' surroundings as closely as possible. Debrief the testers as soon as they have completed each test. The test results should then be fed back to the team, who will use them to refine the prototype and repeat the test cycle. If users were actively involved in developing the prototype, no more than two rounds of usability testing should be needed to identify and correct the major problems.

COMPLETE THE BUSINESS MODEL

The business model developed in the systems analysis (SA) project is not necessarily complete. The next task, illustrated in Fig. 34.3, recognizes this. Additional information about *what* the business does will probably be discovered while the users develop their understanding of *how* the business works now and should work with the new system. The concept view should be updated, based on business objects that users discover are missing from the user interface. The behavior view should be updated based on business actions identified in the user-conceptual model.

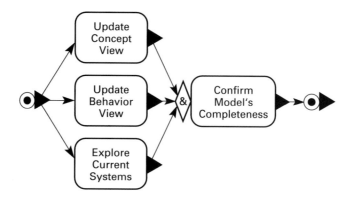

Figure 34.3   A method to Complete the Business Model.

In addition, the current systems and data stores should be explored. This will confirm that the model has not missed identifying behavior or concepts that the new system should support. It will also identify bridges between new and existing systems. Exploring current systems and data stores will not be necessary under two circumstances: first, if the new system is independent of existing systems, such as a pilot project or proof-of-concept project; and second, if this project puts a new user interface on the current system. Here, during the SA stage the team would have drawn on the information from current systems and data stores in order to build the business model.

Update Concept View

As the user interface is being developed, new relationship types and attribute types are frequently discovered that were not included in the model at the end of the systems analysis project. Additional business rules can also be discovered. The same techniques should be used to update the model as were used earlier to create the model. (See Produce Conceptual View in Chapter 32). To update the concept view:

- Identify additional object types.
- Determine if the existing associations (i.e., relationship types and attribute types) should be revised and new associations added.
- Update the business-rule definitions.
- Refine the structure.

Update Behavior View

In developing the users' conceptual model of the tasks, the team will likely discover or refine its understanding of the triggers, preconditions, and postconditions. Additional processes can also be discovered—or that two processes thought to be different are really the same process. To update the behavior view of the model:

- Refine the process definitions.
- Modify the event-dependency diagram.
- Revise the trigger, postcondition, and precondition rules.

Explore Current Systems

Perform this subtask only if this system replaces one or more current systems, in whole or in part, or if it bridges existing systems.

Create business models based on current systems, including procedural descriptions, event-dependency diagrams, and object-relationship diagrams. Examine and document the current systems that support the design area or act on any object types included in the business model for the design area. This can be done to:

- Understand interfaces with systems outside the design area to facilitate bridge construction. This is particularly important for client/server configurations that will interface in real time with legacy systems that use nonrelational databases.
- Put current systems data and procedural descriptions into forms that facilitate transition planning.
- Put current systems data and procedural descriptions into forms that ease comparison with the business model. This comparison is an important part of checking that all the model's components have been included.

Be careful when conducting this analysis on files belonging to old systems. Few people fully understand what is located in a particular file. Such systems sometimes have fields holding information completely different from that indicated by the file name.

In this subtask, the consequences of the decision to replace or bridge the systems are addressed. Do not get sidetracked by current system problems. These were evaluated in the strategy planning project (see Chapter 30), and the decision was made to keep, modify, or discard the systems.

CONFIRM THE MODEL'S COMPLETENESS

Check the Concept View

Check the object types (or entity types), attribute types, and relationship types in the conceptual view of the business model against the equivalent objects in the current systems model. Examine the meanings, not the name, to determine if the two are equivalent. There are three possible outcomes.

1. The object type is in both the old system and the new model. Examine the support of the old system for this object (data or activity). Ensure that no properties were overlooked in the new model.
2. The object type is in the new model and not in the old system. Do a cursory check to determine why the discrepancy exists.

3. The object type is in the old system and not in the new model. Decide whether this represents a missing object. An object type may not actually be missing for a number of reasons:
   — The object type may exist only because of the design of the current system.
   — Different names may have been used for the same object type in the two models, or the same name may have been used for two different objects.
   — The current systems model may artificially merge two different objects into one object.
   — The object type is outside the project scope.

If the object is outside the project scope, keep track of the object for its possible impact on transition planning. If any object types are missing from the concept view, repeat the Update Concept View subtask, above.

Check the Behavior View

For each item in the current systems procedure list, find a corresponding process in the business model. Examine the descriptions and the sequence of actions (triggers, preconditions, and postconditions). Examine, as well, the names to determine whether a process and procedure cover the same activity. Determine the reasons why a procedure has no corresponding process. For example:

- The process may be missing from the activity model.
- The procedure may handle housekeeping functions that are related to design, but not analysis.
- The procedure may simply move information around. A process must transform information.

Determine where a process has no corresponding procedure. If the omission is not due to the scope of the current systems analysis, it may identify weaknesses in the current system that the business model addresses. If processes or events are missing from the behavior view, repeat the Update Behavior View subtask, above.

DESIGN DATA LAYER

A preliminary data structure was defined when a prototype for the user interface was defined. That structure did not consider distribution, integrity, or performance.

The Design Data Layer SD task (illustrated in Fig. 34.4) produces the data structures, including how the data structures will be distributed between clients and servers. Identify the structural business rules that define the database-integrity constraints. However, do not include the definition of any data or program structures that are required for *enforcing* security and integrity or for converting data or bridging. Those are covered in subsequent tasks.

Figure 34.4   A method to Design Data Layer.

Design Database Distribution

This subtask applies only if the data will be distributed.

The ideal distributed database should appear as a single database to the user. This is the principle behind C. J. Date's twelve rules for distributed database management systems.

The first three rules address distribution of control:

1. Local autonomy.
2. No reliance on a central site.
3. Continuous operation.

Review the usage analysis to determine the degree of independence and extent of data sharing between sites. This will help to determine the degree to which the distributed databases can operate independently.

The next five rules address distribution transparency—the degree to which the users and applications are unaware of the actual database distribution:

4. Data location independence.
5. Data fragmentation independence.
6. Data replication independence.
7. Distributed query processing.
8. Distributed transaction management.

Determine the distribution strategies for the database tables, balancing the storage and transmission costs, the retrieval and update efficiency, and the overhead processing. Each distribution strategy has a different impact on the security and integrity design. In documenting the database design, note what issues have to be resolved in the security and integrity design.

The last four rules address the heterogeneity of the operating environment:

9. Hardware independence.
10. Operating system independence.
11. Network independence.
12. DBMS independence.

The technical architecture addresses these rules. Check the impact of the distribution design on the components of the technical architecture. Does the database distribution require additional, new, or different protocol converters, bridges, routers, gateways, database servers, or middleware?

Establish Integrity Constraints

Integrity constraints involve the implementation of the structural and integrity rules of the business model. Enforcement of the constraints maintains the consistency of the database.

Each database technology has different kinds of constraints that must be met. In this step, the constraints for relational databases will be discussed.

In relational databases, integrity constraints apply to column values (null, not null, and domain constraints), rows in a table (primary key and uniqueness constraints), relationships between tables (referential integrity), and combinations of columns, rows, and tables.

Null, not Null

Specify which column values are mandatory attributes, that is, not null, and which are optional attributes, that is, may be null.

Unique, Primary Key

Identify the columns in a table whose values uniquely identify a row. Any key that is unique may be a primary key. Identify the primary key of each table. The primary key will be a foreign key in related tables and must not be null.

Foreign Keys and Referential Integrity

For tables with foreign keys, specify what should happen when a row is inserted in the table and when a row in the referenced table is updated or deleted. The database server may have the insert and update rules built in but provide the flexibility to determine the delete rules: cascade, restrict, and set null.

A table that has a mandatory relationship to a referenced table must have a delete rule of cascade or restrict. Cascade deletes all related rows when the corresponding row in the referenced table is deleted. Restrict prevents the deletion of the row in the referenced table when a related row exists. The delete rule of set null specifies when a row in the referenced table is deleted, the value of the foreign key in the corresponding table is set to null.

Check Other Constraints

Specify any other integrity constraints, such as restrictions on column values and combinations of columns, rows, and tables that the business rules define.

Fragment Integrity in Distributed Databases

When the database-distribution design partitions tables horizontally, different rows in a table are stored at different sites. In this case, the integrity constraints need to handle the migration of a row from one fragment to another. When tables are partitioned vertically, different columns of a table are stored at different sites and each part of the table holds the primary key. Here, the referential integrity rules have to apply to all sites that store the table.

Refine Data Structures

Convert the preliminary data structure (developed above in the Produce Preliminary Data Structure subtask) into a refined data structure. This should be based on the various design options provided by the database software to ensure satisfactory performance:

- Alternative access paths (indexes).
- Methods of indexing.

- Overhead associated with maintaining the indexes when the database is modified.
- Clustering.
- Allocating database components to separate files or disks.

Define the data storage structure in terms of the datasets (physical files) that will be used to store the database. Define the database records that will be allocated to each dataset, as well as the physical characteristics of the datasets and their physical arrangement within the storage medium. Calculate the disk space required for the data, taking into account the expected growth in the number of rows in each table.

DESIGN PROCESSING LAYER

This task produces the program structures, including how the program structures will be distributed between clients and servers (see Fig. 34.5). It also determines which behavioral business rules must be implemented on the client and which on the server. If the database supports stored procedures, this task also determines whether to implement the rule as a process or a database method. If the database does not support certain integrity constraints, this task also decides where those constraints should be implemented. For object-oriented systems, it also considers what is implemented by the common object-request broker architecture (CORBA).

This SD task does not include the definition of any program structures that are required for enforcing security and integrity or for data conversion or bridging. Those are covered in other tasks.

Figure 34.5   A method to Design the Processing Layer.

Determine Business Rule Locations

For each business rule, determine whether it should be enforced on the client, the server, or both. If the database management system (DBMS) supports stored procedures, decide whether to implement a behavioral rule as a stored procedure in the database or as a method in a client or server process.

Determine how both the DBMS and the database server support integrity constraints. In other words, are they automatically enforced by the DBMS, implemented through triggers or stored procedures, or implemented by a method in a client or server process?

If the data will be distributed, specify where the integrity rules should be enforced for distributed data. If the data will be fragmented vertically or horizontally, determine where the fragment integrity will be enforced and where the global integrity will be enforced.

Design Process Distribution

In host-based computing, the raw information is shipped to the host. The host performs all processing and ships the results back to the user. This can result in a great deal of network traffic. In client/server computing, processing takes place where it makes the most sense, and only the results of the processing are sent over the network. The choice of client/server architecture determines the location of the presentation and data access layers and whether the business logic is also distributed.

If the business logic will be distributed, determine what portions of each elementary process are best handled locally (and thus minimize network traffic). Determine, as well, what portions may benefit from off-loading the processing to a remote processor. The architectural components should handle the communication between processes, for example, through a remote procedural call. If this is done, the location of the processing will be transparent to the user and programmer.

Design Program Structures

Specify the structure of the processing logic, describing the modules and the communication between them. Name each module. If the name is not self-explanatory, state what the module does and, then, detail each interprocess communication. Indicate whether the communication is local or remote. The program structures may be represented in a structure chart, network, or table.

DESIGN SECURITY AND INTEGRITY

This next task specifies the requirements that ensure the validity of the data in the databases, thus assuring consistency of both data and applications across the network and establishing rules for database access (see Fig. 34.6).

This is where the heart of the design occurs. The approaches taken in this task will be determined by the features and restrictions of the specific software products that

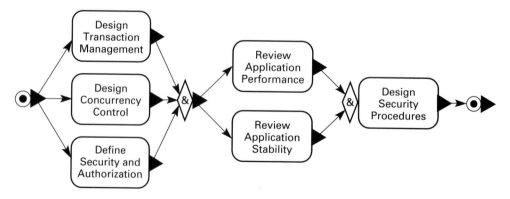

Figure 34.6   A method to Design Security and Integrity.

implement the application. However, no matter what the products support, the design must incorporate the referential integrity of the databases. The design must take into account that the clients may not be active when a transaction occurs. It must ensure that users have the correct version of the application and the database definitions. The design must also allow for controlling access and for checking viruses. It must result in a system that has an acceptable response time.

These design issues may not have been a concern in the past. For instance, they may have been handled automatically by development tools in a host-based system. Furthermore, such issues have not been as relevant on unconnected personal computer (PC) systems. In the more complicated world of heterogeneous databases, client/servers, and two-phase commits, such issues are now a major concern. They mean the critical difference between the success and failure of a system.

Design Transaction Management

Integrity rules must hold before a database transaction takes place and after the transaction is committed or aborted. In designing the data layer, specify what integrity is required. In designing the processing layer, specify where to enforce integrity. Now, specify how and when to ensure database integrity when transactions modify the databases. Database transactions must pass the *ACID* test:

- *Atomicity.* The entire transaction is either committed or aborted.
- *Consistency.* The transaction takes the databases from one consistent state to another.
- *Isolation.* The effects of the transaction are invisible to other applications until the transaction is committed.
- *Durability.* The changes made by a committed transaction are permanent.

Determine the method for committing a transaction and for recovering from an aborted transaction. In a single database environment, the DBMS usually has a defined method to log transactions which handles commits and rollbacks for a single modification to a single table. Design the methods for handling commits and rollbacks to other work packages, such as updates to multiple rows of a single table, updates to multiple tables, and changes to stored procedures.

In a distributed-database environment, the strategies to handle commits and rollbacks are more complex, because each site handles only a portion of the transaction. Despite this, the whole transaction must be treated as a unit.

One approach to guarantee consistency is a two-phase commit. In the first phase, a transaction coordinator issues a PREPARE message. In the second phase, a COMMIT or ABORT message is issued. All participants must acknowledge the messages.

Most database servers do not support an automated two-phase commit that occurs without user or application intervention. Some offer automated support in a limited environment. Others offer commands and procedures to allow the application to implement a two-phase commit.

If the data-distribution strategy involves replicated data, define the method to ensure consistency. Such consistency must be assured even if a node that contains replicated data is not active at the time of the transaction. Even if no other information is replicated, a distributed database often has a replicated distributed-database dictionary. Define the method for synchronizing updates to the database dictionary.

Design Concurrency Control

If two applications try to update the same database object simultaneously, concurrency control guarantees that neither transaction is lost. In client/server systems, the method of concurrency control must guard against lost updates, achieve acceptable performance, and minimize network traffic. Methods for concurrency control are:

- *Locking.* Where the transaction acquires exclusive control of an object mode, such as write lock or read lock.

- *Multiversioning.* Where the second transaction receives a copy of the object and may also employ a locking mechanism—making a new version of the object.

- *Optimistic concurrency control.* Where the state of the database when the transaction begins is compared to the state when the transaction is ready to commit.

Determine which methods the DBMS supports and which are appropriate for the required type of access, for the volume, and for the frequency of access. In decision-support systems, the applications read many objects and modify few. Online transaction processing systems (OLTP) typically have high access volume and frequency, and they modify a high proportion of the objects that they access.

If the method will use a locking scheme, select the algorithm for deadlock detection or deadlock avoidance. Deadlock avoidance or periodic deadlock detection schemes are more appropriate than continuous deadlock detection which requires high network overhead. Deadlock avoidance is better for heterogeneous servers, but it can unnecessarily roll back transactions.

Define the methods for managing concurrency within the transaction. This is particularly important where a single transaction is processed by distributed processors.

Define Security and Authorization

The usage analysis that was performed in the SA stage identified user roles. Review the role definitions and usage from the point of view of data security. Review the fields of each database object to determine which roles should be able to access each field and with what kind of access privileges. (In RDBS, review the columns of each table.)

Determine how to enforce attribute-level security at the user-interface layer, the data layer, and the processing layer. Specify whether the specific security enforcement will be based on the user role (type of user) or the user ID (individual).

User Interface Layer Security

In a GUI environment, the user first selects an object type and then selects actions allowed for that type of object. Users cannot act on anything they cannot select. A certain level of security may be enforced in a GUI environment by limiting both the objects and the actions on those objects.

Define what interface objects and actions are available to the user and the degree to which they are visible. Determine whether the unavailable actions and objects should be "grayed out" or not appear at all.

Review the user interface. Determine if the user-interface security requires any changes to the interface appearance or usability testing, or whether the changes can all be handled in the processing layer.

Data Layer Security

Define who may access each column. The method will depend on the database server. Some databases support access privileges only at the table level. Partition the table vertically to limit column access. Fragmenting a table changes the data-structure design and affects the integrity constraints. If the table partitioning enforces security, revise the database design. The application structure will also need review to determine if additional methods will be needed to enforce integrity. If the data-layer security requires more than minimal changes to the data structure, repeat the Design Data Layer and Design Processing Layer tasks.

Processing Layer Security

Specify what security will be enforced at the processing layer, including those resulting from the interface and data layer security. State which checking takes place at the client and which at the server. Revise the application-structure design to incorporate processing-layer security. If the application structure requires more than minimal changes, repeat the Design Processing Layer task.

Review Application Performance

Examine the architectural design of the database, application, and network from a performance perspective. Determine if design changes can alleviate any problems identified by the team. A client/server environment offers numerous opportunities and places where performance can suffer. The simpler the design, the fewer places where things can go wrong. Check the design for unnecessary complexity.

Review Application Stability

Review the design from both the client's and server's points of view.

- What does the client expect to see on the server, and what does the server expect to see on the client?
- What does the application do if conditions are not right for execution?
- How does the application make sure that the conditions are right for execution?
- Can the users overload the system capabilities?
- What happens when a user upgrades the application? The equipment?
- What happens when clients are added or removed? When servers are added or removed?
- How does the user remove the application?

Design procedures for installation, upgrading, and removal. Then, specify how these procedures can identify the system components that they install, upgrade, or remove. Determine how the procedures should be performed. To the extent that these procedures are implemented as transactions, review how the transaction management and concurrency-control design affect them. Conversely, review how these procedures affect transaction management and concurrency control.

Design Security Procedures

Design the automated and manual procedures for the following categories: authorizing users and granting access privileges, backup, recovery, fallback (in case of a partial or full-system failure), and audit.

VERIFY SYSTEM DESIGN

Verifying the system design (illustrated in Fig. 34.7) ensures the design's quality from both the technical and users' perspective before the plan is developed to construct the system. This is the killer review task.

This is the last chance to make sure that the design is correct. After this point, any bugs that exist in the design will become bugs in the code. Time should not be wasted desk checking where automated tools can catch problems faster, easier, and more accurately. Ascertain that:

- All the specified functionality is incorporated.
- The design follows standards.
- It agrees with the business-system classification and technical architecture.
- The SD team understands where and how this system links with existing systems.

Confirm Design Completeness

Check the design against the business model:

- Does the system functionality support all elementary processes in the design area scope?
- Have the object types, relationship types, and attribute types in the concept view been translated into tables, columns, and foreign keys in the data structures?
- Has the concept view been updated to reflect items discovered in the design? Data elements added only for security or performance should not appear in the concept view.
- Is each business rule implemented in at least one way?
  — Stored procedure.
  — Database trigger.
  — Database-table definition.
  — Database insert, update, and/or delete rule.
  — Method on client and/or server.

If the new system replaces an existing one, check that the design implements the current system functionality. Note any shortcomings and identify the tasks that need repeating in order to correct the problems.

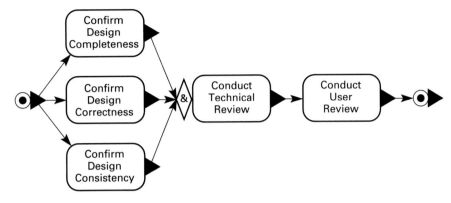

Figure 34.7 A method to Verify System Design.

Confirm Design Correctness

Check that the design is practical and meets requirements:

- Does the design support the requisite users, locations, functionality, and objects?
- Does the design match the business-system classification? Is the design compatible with future requirements and expected growth? Does the design correctly interface with other systems?
- Can the capabilities of the technical architecture support the design?
- Does the design conform to standards, such as user interface, production control, audit, security, and budget?
- Is performance satisfactory? Will data be available when the system requires? Will system executions finish in their allocated time slots?

Note any shortcomings and identify the tasks that need repeating in order to correct the problems.

Confirm Design Consistency

The following questions need to be addressed. Are all parts of the design consistent? To check this, see how consistently the business rules are implemented. In addition, does the design match the users' conceptual model of the system? Note any shortcomings and identify the tasks that need repeating in order to correct the problems.

Conduct Technical Review

The technical SD subteam checks the design against the following criteria:

- Will the system and its components fulfill the acceptance criteria?
- Will the test plan measure the system's quality against the acceptance criteria?
- Will the system perform efficiently?
- Does the system meet shop, industry, and best-practice standards?

- Will system personnel be able to maintain and modify the system easily?
- Can the users be readily trained in the system's use?
- Will the team be successful following the transition plan? Can the old systems be shut down and the new systems brought up with the allocated resources?

Conduct User Review

Users should review the design to verify that the system will meet their needs. The following questions need to be addressed:

- Have the acceptance criteria changed?
- Does the design match the acceptance criteria? Does each output of the system match the acceptance criteria?
- How much will the users need to change their environment or work patterns?
- Will the end users accept these changes to their work environment?
- Does the training address the necessary cultural changes as well as the technical task training?
- Are the work demands during testing and transition reasonable? Will they create a negative feeling towards the system?

DEVELOP TEST PLAN

This task (illustrated in Fig. 34.8) determines the time and effort needed to ensure the quality of the delivered system. Testing takes on a new importance in many systems, because the system environment varies from installation to installation. For instance, the client computers for a single system may have different operating systems. However, they may have the same operating system, but different configurations. Finally, they may have different applications and gateways, running simultaneously with *this* system. Consequently, many more facets must be tested.

In addition to the usual cycles of unit, integration, system, and acceptance testing, client/server systems should also plan for beta testing. This early release of the system is given selectively to sites chosen for their configuration and to users who can cope with

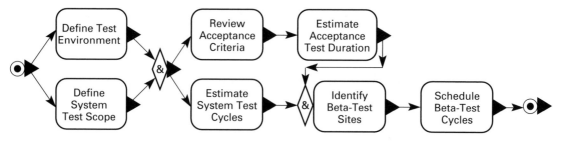

Figure 34.8   A method to Develop a Test Plan.

beta-test software.

This task determines how the tests depend on one another and estimates their duration. The tests' costs, resource requirements, and impact on the system-release schedule can then be established. Identifying the contents of the test is *not* the goal.

Once the system capabilities and user-interface design have been developed, the team should be able to develop the plans for system and acceptance testing. However, allow for adjustments to the plan as the design details emerge. The plans for those tests depend substantially upon the design.

On the other hand, the beta-test plans are more heavily influenced by the release schedule. They should be used for testing the system operation on different configurations—not as a substitute for unit, integration, systems, or acceptance tests. Projects can easily get bogged down in beta tests. Each cycle must be rigidly scheduled (i.e., time-boxed) and have an absolute cutoff point for accepting changes. The number of beta cycles is influenced to some degree by the number of different configurations the system will support.

Define Test Environments

Identify the characteristics of the environment needed for adequate system and acceptance testing. Ideally, systems and acceptance test environments should duplicate the production environment. For client/server systems, this is not usually feasible because the environment has so many potential variables. Specify the technical components of the servers, networks, and hosts, as well as typical clients for the systems and acceptance tests. Limit the client computers to the most common configurations.

The purpose of beta testing is checking the system in a broad spectrum of environments. Determine the range of client configurations, including hardware, software, and communications options. In addition to generic features, such as memory, display, and disk space, identify brands of computer components.

Certain aspects of the system on some client configurations can be tested during unit and integration testing.

Define System Test Scope

List the tests needed in each of the following areas:

- *Environmental testing.* To ensure that the necessary pieces are in place and operate properly for the system test.

- *Integration group retesting.* To ensure that the integration groups still work after test aids have been removed.

- *Merging of the integration groups.* To ensure that the integration groups work together properly.

- *Breakdown testing.* To recognize breakdowns, test recovery, and fallback procedures.

- *Volume testing.* To check performance under peak loads.

- *Bulletproofing.* To check that the system can correctly handle any input and that privacy and security can not be broken.

- *User task testing.* To check that the whole system, both automated and manual, is practical from the users' point of view.
- *Transition testing.* To check that the conversion and bridging works.

Review Acceptance Criteria

Each organizational unit that accepts the system sets its own acceptance criteria and devises its own tests. The acceptance criteria have already been specified. Now, each participating organization specifies its tests, organizes the tests into test cycles, and prepares a test-cycle dependency diagram showing the sequence and purpose of each test cycle.

An acceptance test cycle is a practical, online testing session, batch-test run, or perhaps an entirely clerical trial procedure. A test cycle normally includes many valid transactions plus transactions with user errors. Some test cycles can test only one severe error situation, because that error may halt the system.

Estimate Acceptance Test Duration

Estimate both the elapsed time and effort, that is, person-days, and the technical resources required to conduct each test cycle. The project may have only limited technical resources for the acceptance tests, particularly if new equipment must be acquired for the end users. Develop a dependency diagram for all acceptance tests and calculate the duration, taking resource limitations into account.

Estimate System Test Cycles

Group the testing requirements into manageable sessions, that is, test cycles. Draw a test-cycle dependency diagram to show the sequence and purpose of each test cycle. Try to use data created by one test cycle as input data to another test cycle.

Define the conditions to be checked within each test cycle. Define both the condition and the outcome. Because the modules will have already undergone integration testing, reproducing every integration-test condition as a system-test condition is not necessary. The tests should show that the normal routes through each user task work correctly and that two or three error situations are handled properly. Estimate the elapsed time and effort in person-days to conduct each test cycle.

Identify Beta-Test Sites

The beta-test sites need to be staffed and equipped. The ideal beta tester is a skilled computer user who knows how to seek out and identify problems. However, this tester should also have the perspective of a computer novice who is puzzled by the things that sophisticated users take for granted. Since it is difficult to find both qualities in one person, select a mix of skilled and naive users. The beta testers will be doing their real jobs in the beta tests. Select users who can tolerate working in an unstable environment.

Identify the sites that have access to the equipment configurations identified earlier. In addition to the system being tested, the equipment should contain the hardware, software, communications, and components required for all the other work that the user does.

Good beta testers are harder to find than equipment. Consider giving some beta testers access to equipment that they do not normally have.

To speed construction, a few beta sites should be available for unit and integration tests. List the people and equipment that they will use for beta testing and for assisting unit and integration testing.

Schedule Beta-Test Cycles

Contrary to popular belief, beta testing should not define the system specifications or debug the code. The purpose is uncovering configuration problems that could not be checked in the unit, integration, systems, or acceptance tests. By the time a system reaches beta testing, most bugs should have been caught.

Develop a schedule for the beta tests that shows the required duration and resources. As the configurations become more complex, the number of beta-test cycles increases along with the length of each cycle. However, the number of cycles should be limited. Otherwise, the team may be pressured to make enhancement changes, because the actual release date will be so far in the future. Three or four cycles should be adequate. Each cycle should have a rigid schedule, with an absolute cutoff date for problem reports. Any problems received after the cutoff should go into the next cycle or be saved for maintenance releases. Allow adequate time for bug fixes between the cutoff date and the next beta release.

DEVELOP TRANSITION PLAN

This task (illustrated in Fig. 34.9) clarifies how the new system will integrate with the existing systems and data stores. It also determines the skills people will need to use the new system successfully, the system's impact on the organizational culture, and how to plan for the changes.

Conversion from existing systems to the new system is usually a complex and lengthy process. The team may have to build temporary or permanent bridges between old and new systems. Additionally, it may need to convert from one release level of the system to another that incorporates more functionality. Finally, it may need to perform a one-time conversion of data from current stores to the databases.

To complete the conversion on schedule, it is often wise to start writing the routines as soon as they have been designed. Do not wait for approval of the whole system design.

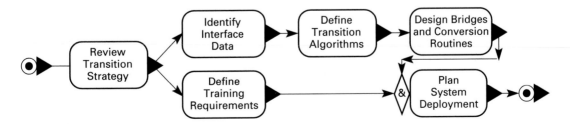

Figure 34.9　A method to Develop a Transition Plan.

This approach has some cost, since the new design may change or the system may not be approved. However, this costs much less than delaying the system, because the conversion routines have not been completed in time.

Review Transition Strategy

The system-transition strategy specifies the approach for converting from the existing operations to the new systems. Review the strategy in light of the scope and contents of the actual system design. Examine all the implementation issues, including system interfaces, organizational impact, contingency plans, alternative schedules, and costs.

Identify Interface Data

Interface data include the corresponding fields in the existing and new systems and the algorithms that make the field values equivalent. In a relational database, a field is a column. The interface data format is not the same in both existing and new systems, and the content may not map one to one. However, a transition algorithm converts the field(s) on one side of the interface to a field on the other side. Use the interface data in the bridges and conversion routines.

Identify the fields in each interface. Determine the source of data for each field and its status when the system is implemented. The field may be input directly, derived from current systems, or present in the database. If the transition is phased, specify the status of the field by location. Specify the field(s) in the existing system and the equivalent database column(s) in the new system.

Define Transition Algorithms

Specify how the existing and new fields translate to each other. The algorithm may be any of the following:

- One-to-one correspondence between existing and new fields.
- A formula that combines the result of multiple fields in the existing system to derive one field in the new system, or vice versa.
- A look-up table.
- For cases in which existing and new fields have no logical correspondence, a formula or look-up table with an acceptable level of error.

Design Bridges and Conversion Routines

A bridge in this context is a module, program, or subsystem that links the data between the new system and the existing systems. A conversion routine is a one-time transfer of data from its existing form into the form required by the new system.

For bridges, determine the frequency of bridging from one system to another, the volume of data and how it is stored in the current system, and the capabilities of the network and hardware. This determines whether the bridge should be a batch procedure or an online transaction. For each bridge, produce the full range of design documentation required, and incorporate all the relevant transition algorithms.

For conversion routines, design the automated and manual procedures to translate data from its current form into the databases for the new system. This may involve a combination of utility programs, one-time programs, and data entry in several forms, such as keying and scanning. Conversion should be a one-time occurrence, although it may be repeated at many locations. Conversion routines should make maximum use of existing utilities. Specify which transition algorithms are used by each conversion routine.

Define Training Requirements

Identify the user tasks and roles that the system will support. The strategy-planning team outlined desired work practices and may have planned for dramatic changes to roles. The new system will likely allow the users to carry out their tasks in substantially new ways—possibly including new technical responsibilities. In addition, new technical roles to support the business users may have been identified. List the business and technical skills that each role requires to use or support the new system. Document the skill requirements in a matrix of skills and organizational roles.

Determine who will operate or supervise the user tasks and their organizational roles. (A person may have more than one organizational role.) For each person who will perform a role, determine whether the person has the required skills. Document the skill requirements for each person in a *training requirements* matrix that lists skills on one axis and individuals on the other. The cells show whether the person already has the skill or requires training. A cell value of *Y* shows that the person already has a needed skill. A cell value of *N* shows that the individual requires training for a needed skill.

Determine the degree of change that the training requirements matrix shows. Compare this to the current situation. Assess the organizational readiness for the degree of change and document the issues (in addition to training) that must be addressed.

Plan System Deployment

Plan the approach for deploying the system that addresses:

- Requirements for cultural change, including training.
- Environmental (that is, software, hardware, communications, and workspace) requirements.
- Initial locations to receive the system.

The strategy must be compatible with the bridging and conversion routines defined earlier.

DEVELOP CONSTRUCTION PLAN

The goal of this task (illustrated in Fig. 34.10) is to develop a realistic system-construction plan that will receive management approval. This plan incorporates only unit and integration testing and does not detail those tests for the whole system (covered in the test plan). Nor does it cover planning any construction necessary to move between existing and new sys-

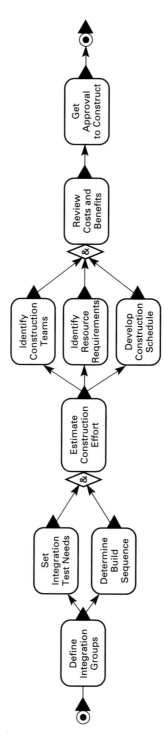

Figure 34.10 A method to Develop a Construction Plan.

tems (see the transition plan). Management approval to construct the system implies acceptance of the test and transition plans, as well as the construction plan.

In planning for construction, identify who will build the different parts of the system—keeping in mind that each part requires different skills:

- The database builders should be familiar not only with SQL but with the optimization algorithms of the database server. This will speed response time.
- The application builders should be able to understand and cope with the different flavors of languages to get the application, database, communications, and operating systems to work as one.
- The network builders should be familiar with the capacity limits of the network pipes and the best way to handle issues of access, bridging, routing, and gateways.
- The writers should be able to explain the system features and operations clearly—but should not feel rejected if no one reads the manuals.

Define Integration Groups

Identify the principal objects in the system. Refer to the users' conceptual model of the system to identify the actions that are performed in a user task. An integration group contains the actions centered around the principal object that a user task manages.

Specify the object and actions that each integration group must test. Include two levels of integration groups: those that act on one object and those that deal with object interactions.

For clarity, redraw the application-structure chart, clustering the actions belonging to the same integration group. Verify that every action belongs to an integration group.

Set Integration Test Needs

Specify the conditions and purpose of each test. In the integration group, determine the lowest level to which the test can be applied. Tests can be classified in two ways. Initial tests check that a method exists to handle the message passed to the object. Detailed tests check that the method handles the message properly.

Determine Build Sequence

The easiest way to test a system, particularly a database/teleprocessing system, is using the system to construct the data. A fully tested part of the system can be used with confidence to load test data for subsequent parts of the system.

Identify the data requirements for each integration group and which integration groups create the data. Construct an integration-group dependency diagram that is based on the data dependency. Estimate the actual testing effort and elapsed time for each test and add the time estimate to the integration-test dependency diagram. Include an estimate for unit testing.

Estimate Construction Effort

Base the estimate of the time required to build and test the system components on the number and complexity of programs, databases, and networks that need to be constructed and the estimates for unit and integration testing. Allow adequate time and effort to test that the databases, programs, and networks work together.

Estimate the time to prepare test data for unit and integration testing and documentation. Test data must be ready when the components are ready for unit testing. Documents, especially online help, also undergo unit and integration testing. They must be ready for acceptance testing.

Estimate the time to prepare and test training material. The estimates for systems and acceptance testing are part of the test plan. The estimates for everything connected with transition are part of the transition plan.

Identify Construction Teams

Determine who will build the system. These people have special skills and talents and must work as a team. They are not just resources. The construction teams should include:

- *Database builders.* Those who must be familiar with the capabilities of the database server, who can write and test DDL, triggers, and stored procedures, and who understand how to tune databases.
- *Program builders.* Those who understand object orientation, who are familiar with the client/server building tools, and who are comfortable working with users on unit and integration tests.
- *Network builders.* Those who are knowledgeable about protocols, hardware, and what goes where, and who know the capabilities and limitations of networks.
- *Documenters and training designers.* Those who can explain how things work so that ordinary people can understand how to use the system. When deciding between someone who knows the system and someone who can teach, pick the teacher. If the teacher cannot explain how the system works, it is too complicated to use.

Identify Resource Requirements

Identify the facilities and equipment that team members need to build their part of the system, and what other resources will be needed to test that the disparate pieces work together. Each person should have at least one workstation equipped with the necessary software tools, testing aids, and environment emulators. Special equipment might be required for testing from time to time. Review the equipment configuration at the proposed beta sites. The resource estimate should include access to selected testers and their equipment as well as travel and support.

Develop Construction Schedule

Draw up a schedule based on the build sequence, dependencies between the construction subteams, time required for testing, and resource availability. Take into account the schedule for both the transition plan and testing plan.

Review Costs and Benefits

Prepare a cost-benefit summary report, incorporating the earlier cost-benefit analysis prepared for the design-area development plan. The remaining development costs can be estimated accurately from the testing, transition, and construction plans. Calculate the total expected development costs. A reasonable estimate of production costs can be derived from the performance assessment prepared in the Design Security and Integrity task. Review the estimate of system benefits. These should not have changed unless the system scope has changed significantly.

Get Approval to Construct

The steering committee reviews the plans and the cost/benefit summary. As a result, it may approve, cancel, or postpone the project, or it may seek changes to the project's scope or plans. If the steering committee seeks changes, it should state:

- What it disapproves of in the plan.
- Areas recommended for modification.
- The nature of the modification required (e.g., different scope, spread-out development, parallel development, or different equipment).
- Required return on investment.
- Whether this project team needs to present alternative plans.

If changes are requested, the team may repeat earlier design tasks to modify the design and prepare one or more new plans.

Chapter 35

System Design: Management Tasks

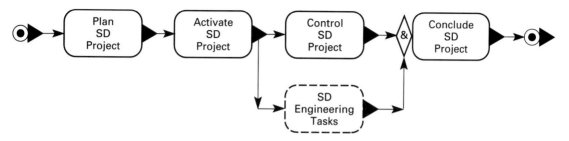

A method for the management tasks of system design.

PLAN SYSTEM DESIGN PROJECT

When planning a system design (SD) project, a work plan must be established based on the scope established at the end of the system analysis (SA) project (see Fig. 35.1). The work plan provides the blueprint for the project manager.

The objective of the system design is to build the user interface and test it for usability, to design the data and processing layers including database security and integrity, and to plan for testing, transition, and construction.

To complete the plan, determine the user involvement, management style, and project organizational structure, identify resource requirements; develop a detailed schedule; assess the project risk; and gain acceptance of the plan.

Figure 35.1   A method to Plan System Design Project.

Define Project

The *design-area development plan* has already defined the basic structure of this project. In this step, fill in the details of the project objectives, scope, constraints and assumptions, deliverables to be produced, and standards for the deliverables and procedures for carrying out the project.

The primary *objectives* of a system design project are to build a usable user interface, to design the rest of the system, and to prepare for building, testing and deploying the designed system. The specific goals are to:

- Specify how the system will work.

- Produce a user interface, that is tested for usability and is a metaphor for the business.

- Design the databases, the applications, and the support structure that will perform acceptably in the system environment.

- Plan the subsequent construction schedule, testing, and transition to integrate the system into the organization environment.

The *scope* is the design-area definition of this project that was specified in the design-area development plan. It lists the business activities, objects, organizational units, and locations. Also included are any current systems that will interface with this system or be replaced by it.

Detail any *constraints,* such as budget or time limits, availability of skills, knowledge, or equipment. List the *assumptions* that will be employed in developing the SD project schedule.

There are two types of *deliverables:* those that design the system and those that plan for its implementation. (See the SD engineering path tasks and deliverables for details of these deliverables and their components.)

Establish documentation and diagramming standards for deliverables. Standards for reviewing deliverables and procedures for revising the project plan were established in the strategy plan discussed in Chapter 30. The same standards and procedures apply to this project. The strategy plan itself includes the standards for the overall look and feel of the systems to be developed under the plan's direction.

Make Project Plan

Identify the tasks, effort, and resources needed to produce the deliverables; establish a schedule and budget; estimate the risk; check the plan against the constraints and assumptions identified earlier; and verify that the project plan is feasible.

Identify Effort, Resources, and Scheduling

To identify the tasks required for the system design project, use Chapter 34. For each task, determine the amount of time, the resources, and the scheduling requirements. Choose the most appropriate technique for each task. Do not underestimate the size of nontechnical work, such as project leadership and the presentation and review of results. In particular, the tasks at the project's conclusion are often underestimated. Any testing can consume time and resources. Schedule adequate usability testing and ensure that the deadlines are both firm and reasonable.

Identify and include the milestone reviews. Major milestones for a system design project occur at the end of this task, the completion of the user interface, the review, the approval of the system-construction plan, and at the project's conclusion. Other milestone reviews may be scheduled, depending upon the project's complexity and scope.

Estimate the team size and composition. Keep the core team small—ideally three to six people. At least one member should have participated in the core SA project team. Use outside experts and reference groups for specific tasks, instead of enlarging the team.

Establish a Schedule

Use estimates of the resource requirements and availability, the task dependencies, and effort. Consider timeboxes and user workshops when developing the schedule, particularly for review tasks. Remember, the schedule will likely be adjusted after the specific team has been established.

Develop a Budget

The project budget should take into account the project schedule and resource usage, equipment and facilities, other expenses, such as travel and office support, and, if needed, test facility rental.

Document Project Risk

Identify the areas of risk in the schedule. In addition to the risks that apply to all projects, look for the following:

- Inadequate user involvement.
- Inexperience with new technology.
- Untested technology.
- Nonstandard "standards."

Build risk reduction into the project plan. If this is a high-risk project, treat it as if it were a much bigger project. Choose behavioral techniques to achieve consensus quickly, particularly in developing the user interface. Manage expectations from the start.

Check Plan Against Assumptions

The constraints and assumptions may require adjusting to produce a feasible schedule. In particular, check the project scope and team composition.

Obtain Project Approval

Present the project plan to the project sponsor and to other people required for approval. A task force may have been established to oversee the fulfillment of the strategy plan.

Reconfirming support for development is a good idea, particularly if the project meets resistance. Identify the other stakeholders whose unofficial approval will help ensure the project success:

- The ultimate *customers* of information and processes within the project scope. Some of them may design and test the user interface.

- Potential *adversaries* of the project. Determine who will lose power or influence if this project succeeds and identify how to gain their confidence and support.

- *Process facilitators* determine who supplies information or otherwise supports the processes. Clarify how the process will affect them.

ACTIVATE SYSTEM DESIGN PROJECT

The activation task (illustrated in Fig. 35.2) launches the project. First, the working environment needs to be set up. This includes the room for the project team, facilities for interviews, group workshops, or training, as well as computer equipment and software. In addition, the team must learn and practice the techniques that they will use in carrying out the system-design project.

The SD team should be familiar with the technology and environment that will be used in the production system. A briefing on this technology is a good way to kick off the project and should include visits to user work sites.

Figure 35.2   A method to Activate System Design Project.

Establish Project Environment

Set up the equipment and facilities for the project. Space and equipment will be needed for interviews, workshops, team training, and team meetings. Each technical team member will need a workstation equipped with the selected interface builder plus access to the workstation components of the technical architecture. In addition, each team member should have easy access to the following software:

- Word processor.
- Spreadsheet.
- Diagrammer.
- Presentation.
- Project estimation and project management.
- The methodology.

A CASE tool is useful, but not necessary, for some of the diagramming and for generating the database definitions (DDL).

Train Team

The team members must be trained in the techniques they will be using. Launch the project with a technological briefing and follow by training in techniques of user interface. During the project, the team can be trained in the other techniques. Each team member must know how to use the software to help produce project deliverables and work products.

CONTROL SYSTEM DESIGN PROJECT

This next task (illustrated in Fig 35.3) controls the progress of the project and allows corrective actions within the scope of the plan. In addition, it identifies the need to change the critical project elements: the objectives, the scope, the budget, or the time span. Finally, the Control System Design Project task manages any coordination with the results of prior projects and concurrent events outside the project.

In an SD project, the designers focus on *how* the system will work, *who* will use it, *where* it will be located, and *when* the users will get the system. One early task is to produce a working user interface, which the users actually help to build and test for usability. Consequently, users may expect to have the rest of the system built just as quickly and easily. The hard part of the control task is managing user expectations. You must ensure that the system design is not compromised under pressure from the users to have the system finished.

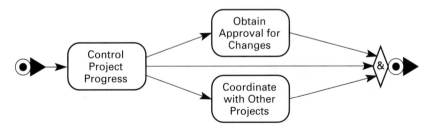

Figure 35.3   A method to Control System Design Project.

Control Project Progress

Project control is vital to the success of the project. The project manager must keep the project moving forward, motivate the team, and keep the support of the project stakeholders. Project control should minimize bureaucracy. The team should devote most of its time to performing the project, not filling out project-control reports.

Project control involves assigning project tasks, monitoring task and deliverable status, checking progress against the plan, and periodically reporting progress to the project sponsor and other stakeholders. Do not let excessive requests for "small" scope increases derail the project. The project should have a finite time and expense budget. Record the requests that are not recommended for inclusion as *enhancement requests*.

Assign Project Tasks

The project plan typically includes initial task assignments. These are often adjusted and amended during the project, as the plan confronts reality. A weekly assignment sheet should be circulated either before or during the *short* weekly staff meeting. Items to discuss at a status meeting include the following:

- Major events.
- Action items.
- Recap of expected deliverables.
- Actual achievements and variances.
- Overall project assessment.
- Next week's deliverables.
- Action items for next meeting.

Monitor Tasks and Deliverables

Keep the project's progress and management issues visible by posting schedules, reports, and issues. Assign all issues a due date. Review whether an answer to an issue is overdue.

Check Progress Against Plan

Compare the resources used and the time spent to the planned resources and time. Identify progress that is ahead of schedule, as well as tasks that are behind schedule or likely to fall behind. Determine any delays are externally imposed. Identify any unproductive work.

Report to Sponsor

Give periodic progress reports to the project sponsor and keep influential stakeholders informed, as well. Reports to the sponsor should include the time spent by each team member for each task, the deliverables produced, and an estimate to complete each task.

Obtain Change Approval

The project plan is a contract between the team and the project sponsor. Make minor corrections, such as changing meeting times, trying alternative techniques, or getting users more involved—within the original plan. However, the difference between planned and actual performance may be too great to overcome by working smarter. Corrective actions that change the schedule, the cost, the scope, or the deliverables require formal approval.

Look for early warning signs that the project will not meet the plan. For example, the team might not be completing deliverables by the milestone dates or the quality may be low. The cause could be inadequate resources, poor productivity, an unreasonable schedule, or an inappropriate scope. The right solution depends on identifying the root cause.

Examine each proposed solution for its impact on the project objectives, scope, benefits, schedule, quality, and resources. Changes to scope, timing, and resource use may affect other projects, so the development-coordination organization should also review the proposal. In reviewing impact, do not forget to repeat tasks that were thought to be complete.

Decide which actions to recommend to the project sponsor. Justify the proposed change in business terms. The sponsor and the steering committee should be made aware of the alternatives as well as the consequences of not making the change.

When the project sponsor, steering committee, project manager, and development-coordination group agree to the changes, publicize the new plan to everyone on the project. Notify the SD project team, reference groups, stakeholders, as well as any business users and technical specialists whose schedules may change as a result of the plan change. Work closely with the project sponsor.

Coordinate with Other Projects

A project does not happen in isolation. The project manager is the liaison between the SD project and other developments that may affect the direction, contents, and schedule of the SD project. Stay in close contact with other projects whose scope overlaps this one. The team's design decisions will likely be affected by the findings of construction projects. If this is not the first design project, maintain a close relationship with any concurrent construction projects. Be aware of other work that will affect the availability of resources—especially those people who provide information to the project team and review the results.

CONCLUDE SYSTEM DESIGN PROJECT

This last task (illustrated in Fig. 35.4) creates an orderly finish to the project, frees project resources for other activities, and ensures that its participants are recognized for their participation. While most projects are completed, a project may occasionally have to be stopped before its objectives are achieved. For example, this could occur when a mid-project review indicates that the best course of action is to suspend or cancel the project. In a suitable environment, the project manager can recommend such an action, if justified.

The clean-up portion of this task ensures that the changes to the business model made in the system design stage have been archived. The start-up portion of the task provides a

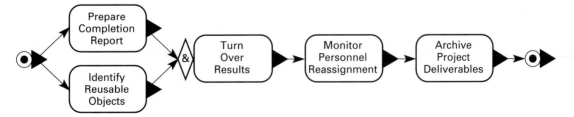

Figure 35.4   A method to Conclude System Design Project.

smooth transition from the end of the design stage to the beginning of the construction stage. In fact, the border between design and construction should have been crossed by the system transition (ST) team. They should have started building bridges and conversion routines as soon as their design was determined.

Prepare Completion Report

The *project completion report* contains sections for management summaries, deliverables for subsequent projects, evaluation of resource performance, the project analysis, and project metrics. Prepare these according to the organization's requirements and conventions.

The management summary section should include an overview, summaries of analysis findings, project metrics, and recommendations.

The deliverables section describes the system design: project background, scope, objectives, conclusions reached, and construction schedule. The major deliverables should be placed in an appendix containing the system capabilities, the components selected for the production and development environments, the user interface, the database design, the application structure, security and integrity design decisions, the detailed business model, and the plans for construction, testing, and transition.

The project analysis section recaps the project performance. Include the business accomplishments, the lessons learned, a summary of metrics, and any unusual or interesting project aspects.

The project is not complete until the steering committee and executive owner accept its results. An executive presentation of the report prior to final sign-off may also be required.

Identify Reusable Objects

Everything produced during this project has the potential for reuse. Review the project deliverables with an eye to reusability. Make sure that they are cataloged and stored in a form in which they can be accessed for reuse. In particular, the user interface standards should be given to subsequent projects as a starter kit.

Turn Over Results

Determine what the follow-on construction projects will require. Use this project's deliverables, work products, open issues (documenting compromise decisions), lessons learned, and any other applicable documentation. Plan to meet with those project managers to assure a smooth transition.

Monitor Personnel Reassignment

Take care of project members. This increases the chance of success for other projects. More importantly, it is the right thing to do. Personnel actions to consider include performance reviews, recognition and rewards, as well as the placement of team members.

Archive Project Deliverables

If it was important to do, it is probably important to keep. Identify how and where to archive project deliverables and work products within the organization. Work with a development-coordination unit to ensure that the correct versions of shared objects are passed to other teams and that they know how to access and update these objects.

Chapter 36

System Construction: Engineering Tasks

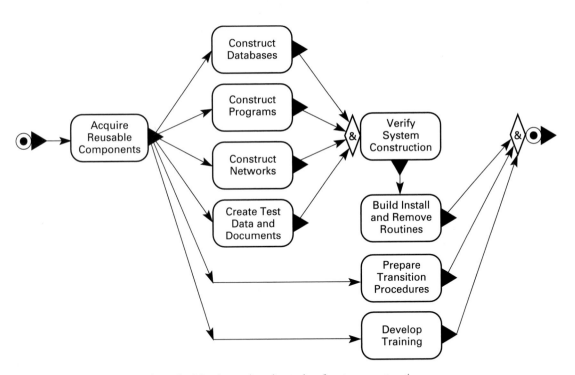

A method for the engineering tasks of system construction.

ACQUIRE REUSABLE COMPONENTS

Acquiring reusable components (illustrated in Fig. 36.1) speeds the construction by reusing tested components. In this task, reusable components are identified and acquired. These can include database objects, methods, and even whole programs and systems.

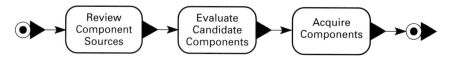

Figure 36.1 A method to Acquire Reusable Components.

This task is one of a series in which the project team actively seeks to benefit from reuse. In the system analysis (SA) stage, the team looked for reusable objects and models. In the system design (SD) stage, it sought reusable interface structures, such as screen widgets and common dialogs. Now, in the system construction (SC) stage, the team looks for reusability in database and application components, set-up and clean-up routines for networks and systems, and even test data and test scripts.

Review Component Sources

Any project deliverable is potentially reusable, if it can be used by the application being developed without adversely affecting its use in existing applications. Look within the team, at other groups within the enterprise, and at outside sources—especially commercial suppliers of component parts. Search for components that can speed development for each construction subteam.

- Examine home-grown and commercial-class libraries, template libraries, and middleware.
- For the database, check existing databases for reusable stored procedures, triggers, table definitions, and data dictionaries. Commercial suppliers also have database objects.
- For the application, review the functionality of commercial applications—particularly, those with a built-in language that permits customization. In addition to applications that supply the business functionality, also consider Help systems, installation and removal generators, and installation scripts. Also look for reusable logic.
- For the network, look for filters, connection interfaces, as well as security and safety routines.
- For testing, examine previous test plans, data, conditions, and scripts.
- For training and documentation, look for computer-based training packages, courses offered by outside organizations, layout templates, style sheets, clip art, and computer-based training algorithms.

Evaluate Candidate Components

Examine each of the candidate components to determine how it matches current requirements and whether it is reusable. If the component belongs to an existing system, consider what will happen to this system if the original component is discontinued or corrupted. Good reusable components have the following characteristics:

- Well documented and follows standards.
- Easy to understand, modify, and supplement.
- Clear, simple, and precise interfaces.
- Flexible, without compromising efficiency.

- Use the best structured techniques.
- Self-contained, black-box usage.
- Know what other components they need.
- Predictable, robust, and verifiable behavior.

Several components may be suitable for a job, and they should be ranked by how well they fit with other components. Component selection should be based on a combined fitness of purpose and reusability. The selection criteria should lead to a quality system that meets the users' needs and reduces the system-development time.

Acquire Components

Before a component can be reused, the owner must give permission and may require a fee. Negotiating the payment method should be part of the acquisition phase. Your negotiating position will be much weaker when the component is already being used in the system. Once you have obtained the component, catalog it and document that the component is reused in all the systems that use it.

CONSTRUCT DATABASES

The Construct Databases task (illustrated in Fig. 36.2) creates the new databases. In doing so, it also promotes object reuse, facilitates legitimate access, ensures the accuracy of the stored data, and verifies the database structure, security, and integrity. Databases store data independent of the programs that use them and also reserve them for as yet unknown management requirements. Therefore, they are *not* restricted to the immediate needs of the new system but are also available for future uses.

Sharing and reuse are fundamental to a database. The previous task may have identified existing database components that could be incorporated into the new database structure. One objective here is taking advantage of reuse—adjusting the database design, if necessary.

However, this task's fundamental objective is developing the physical database, that is, the structure of the containers that will hold the data. Application programs access the database contents through the database server (SQL server), which queries the database structure to find the data. This makes the application independent of the data's physical storage.

The data-definition language (DDL) specifies the database structure and privileges. Depending on the database server, the DDL may also specify integrity constraints. Otherwise, the constraints are specified in the data-manipulation language (DML). Both the DDL and DML are part of the structured-query language (SQL).

Adjust Database Design

If database components have been acquired, modify the data structures or the data-storage structures to incorporate them. Determine the distribution strategy. Will a component

Figure 36.2   A method to Construct Databases.

be replicated or accessed directly? Check how the components affect the requirements for database security and integrity. Should additional integrity checks be performed? Is access to the acquired components restricted?

Write Structural DDL

Using the revised database design, write the DDL to create the databases. For relational databases, you must define the base tables in the database, specifying the columns and indexes. Define the data storage.

Using the security and integrity design, define the authorization for each database along with its views and privileges. Define any integrity constraints that should be specified in the creation statement. Depending on the database server, this may include null constraints, default values, the primary and unique key, the foreign key, considerations of referential integrity, and structural rules.

Write Triggers and Stored Procedures

Using the security and integrity design, write the DDL to invoke integrity constraints that are triggered by the database or its stored procedures. Many database servers enforce referential integrity through database triggers. Write the stored procedures to enforce structural rules as specified in the security and integrity design.

Generate Databases

Generating each database requires a definition of the database schema and of the physical database environment. The database administrator reviews the DDL to see that it conforms to shop standards and can perform the actual database generation. Generate the DDL for the following environments:

- Workstation-emulation environment for unit testing.
- Testing environment for the database server and, if distributed, for the client.
- Production environment for the database server and, if distributed, for the client.

The database administrator generates the database for the production environment and usually generates the database for both the server and the client test environment. The project team may generate the database for unit testing.

Test Databases

Unit test each database in a workstation-emulation environment. Include all of the integrity constraints that can be tested. Check user access, recovery, and all possible triggers and stored procedures during the unit testing. If the database is distributed, most tests will have to be performed in the test environment—rather than in the workstation-emulation environment.

CONSTRUCT PROGRAMS

This task (illustrated in Fig. 36.3) produces modules by building and testing the application piece by piece and group by group to verify that each module or group of modules operates according to expectations. The objective is delivering a system whose components are free of defects and operate correctly. The system will then be tested as a whole during system, acceptance, and beta tests.

Begin testing before all the modules are developed. The team will learn quickly from mistakes and speed the construction by developing one module, testing it, and cloning reusable components. Development can be speeded up if users assist in unit and integration testing. The developer and tester work side by side. On one computer, the developer corrects the errors in the source that the user finds in the application running on another computer.

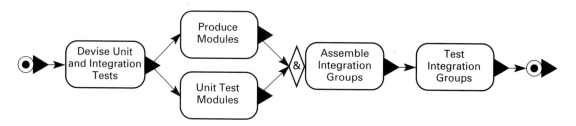

Figure 36.3 A method to Construct Programs.

Devise Unit and Integration Tests

Develop the unit test plan for each module and then for each integration group before writing code. Before developing the unit test plan, do the following:

- Review the requirements for the system acceptance and the overall test plans. (The unit testing plan should support these.)
- Review the description of the module or program. You should understand the function it provides as well as its inputs and outputs.

Then, develop the test plan and record the following:

- Details on the unit being tested (e.g., What is it? Who is doing the test?).
- Business function of the unit.
- Structural functions in the unit (i.e., the technical aspects of how the unit should behave, such as batch or online).
- Type of testing planned based on the type of module being tested. (Generally, test batch programs with a test file and online programs with a script.)
- Based on the functions identified above, note those events or scenarios that are likely to be potential sources of error (e.g., duplicate master records, indexes out of range, incomplete interface parameters, etc.).

- Test(s) and test data prepared to address each function (i.e., conditions, events, transactions, and parameters).
- Test(s) and test data to verify the operation of each interface (i.e., each input and output).
- Results expected from each of the tests listed above.

As the test plans are being developed, list them on a spreadsheet in order to assure that nothing is forgotten. Since the team will not be able to test for everything, concentrate on tests that catch the most probable errors. Include an equal mixture of tests that prove the module functionality and tests that try to break the module or program.

Give about equal weight to testing positively and testing negatively. The system should perform correctly with good data—while rejecting bad data. Try numerous combinations of tests. However, do not try all possible scenarios if they are too numerous. No one can completely test a complex system. The number of possible tests increases exponentially with the number of system parts.

Identify the risks of system failures. Concentrate the tests on those failures that are disastrous, but do not ignore the others. Prepare some test data randomly. Often, when tests are too methodical, they just confirm the team's *own* understanding of the system.

After the test plan is developed, check that it is accurate and complete. Then, ask a peer for a further independent review. Remember that more errors are eliminated through prevention and inspection than through testing.

Produce Modules

Following the application structure, write the module in the chosen language or development-tool format. Strive for reusability and independence from the application distribution. Rather than writing code for specific environments, write to a middleware API (application-program interface) that bridges the application to specific environments.

A method to support version control should also be in place. Include a means to identify the module version, so that the compatibility of all software and hardware versions is ensured. This is particularly important when pieces of the application reside in different locations and are supplied by different manufacturers. If possible, compatibility should be downward, so that previous versions are still supported.

Write code to handle the requirements for database security and integrity that are not performed in the database itself. Coordinate with the transition team to ensure that their bridge procedures can support integrity requirements for structures not handled by the database server.

In addition to writing the code to perform the business requirements, routines that control access and check for viruses should be developed. Routines should also be written to ensure that users have the correct version of both the application and the database definitions.

Unit Test Modules

Review the unit test plan to ensure its validity. The tests should include all the business rules. Consider the following questions:

- Are the functions identified for the module complete?
- Are the interfaces complete?

- Will the test data exercise each function and interface?
- Will the tests exercise each path through the module?

The team may now need to prepare some stubs to test the interface from a module. This is done either because the CALLed module does not yet exist or because testing is simpler this way.

Select the appropriate approach to testing. Do not forget to test modules that are being reused. (Each of these modules should come with its own reusable script.) A test may require components from the presentation and data layers and may need both client and server facilities.

Now, follow the plan and execute the unit test on the module. Be sure the results check with those predicted by the plan and that every piece of code has indeed been checked. However, if the code has considerable branching, many permutations will exist in the available paths. In that case, not all paths can be tested.

Where tests have failed, try to complete the testing cycle and collect all the errors. Then, correct the errors and rerun the entire test cycle. This rerun should be assigned to another test cycle, so that the project can continue to move forward based on the parts that work. Generally, if too many errors are found in the initial testing of a module, many undiscovered errors remain. Conversely, if initial tests show few errors, the module will likely be relatively free of errors.

The completed tests and their results should be reported. Keep the metrics on the number and types of errors found. Review the results of the test program and then submit them to a peer review.

Assemble Integration Groups

Assemble the modules into lower-level integration groups, as defined in the construction test plan. A lower-level integration group contains the modules (or methods) that apply to a single major object. After testing a lower-level integration group, assemble higher-level integration groups to test the interaction between the major objects.

Test Integration Groups

Review the integration tests devised in the earlier Devise Unit and Integration Tests subtask to assure that they still apply. Test for the integration of the modules and determine that each individual module still works. Include tests that prove that outer layers have successfully inherited rules from inner layers. Also, test that the rules implemented in more than one layer are consistent. Make sure there are tests to check that all client and server versions are compatible.

CONSTRUCT NETWORKS

The Construct Networks task (illustrated in Fig. 36.4) ensures that the network is made available to users and to the system while adjusting network parameters to meet the system's performance requirements. This includes checking that the network packet size is

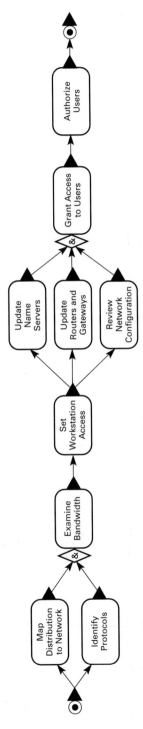

Figure 36.4 A method to Construct Networks.

appropriate for the type of communication traffic that the system will generate. It also establishes network addresses for the databases and external connections as well as addresses and access privileges for users.

To help make the network available, establish the mechanics of running the network. This would include:

- Specifying how and when to back up the network.
- How to handle adding and dropping nodes (both clients and servers).
- Determining which nodes must be active.
- Upgrading the network with new releases of the network software.

Some of these policies and procedures may already be in place. Others may have to be established or modified to meet the needs of the new system.

Map Distribution to Network

This subtask should begin as soon as the design team has determined the distribution of data and process and should occur parallel with the system design stage. In this subtask, determine the network load that the distribution design imposes and what this means for the network capacity, capability, and disaster-recovery plans.

The design team must factor into the distribution design the recovery requirements and acceptable data delay that are caused by lags in propagation and limitations in network capacity. Before starting the design, the design team has already checked the critical elements and has considered performance in arriving at the distribution design. However, the design team may still change the distribution design because of issues discovered in performing this subtask.

Examine the volume of network traffic implied by the distribution design and compare it to the network capacity. Look for potential bottlenecks to performance during average or peak processing periods. Check any unusual or unique events that could materially affect performance.

Review both the data distribution and data requirements of the (distributed) processes. Then, determine the volume of information that must be accessed from each server, workstation, and network segment. Assess whether the resulting performance will be acceptable to the end user. The network construction team should work closely with the database-construction team (or database administrator) to understand the database-distribution design and the reasons for the design decisions.

Evaluate the contingency plans for network capacity in terms of disaster recovery. Factor in the specific software products, databases, and database-management systems (database servers) that the system will use. Each of these items has potentially unique requirements that affect performance and availability of the application to support the business requirement.

Prepare the network-configuration plan for the system. Incorporate any changes to the network-capacity plan and the technical architecture. As a result of the findings in this task, plan to acquire additional capability and capacity.

Identify Protocols

Review the proposed products for the system to determine the communication protocols that must be supported. Identify the servers and databases that the system will access to determine what existing equipment and network access are available.

Map the protocols to the servers, hardware, and software. Include the specific version and release of each element so that network compatibility (i.e., interoperability and coexistence end to end from the workstation) can be ensured. Such compatibility must be determined by examining each segment of the network that supports the system. Create maps for both development and production environments and for each element note whether it already exists in the environment or is planned.

Include such products as database-management systems (DBMS), transaction-processing (TP) monitors, enterprise networks, wide-area networks (WAN), metropolitan-area networks (MAN), local-area networks (LAN), specialty hardware, and local and remote access.

Consider both the short- and long-term impact of each component on the enterprise network. Add the protocol requirements to the network configuration plan. Incorporate any changes to both the network and technical architecture. Based on the findings in this task, plan to acquire additional capability and capacity.

Examine Bandwidth

The preparation for acquiring network capacity or capability should be done long before an individual system requires it. This ensures that the team has adequate lead times for its acquisition and implementation. In this subtask, examine bandwidth requirements to ensure that the network plans have the latest and best information available.

Check the bandwidth of any network component that the business system may affect, such as bridges, routers, gateways, hubs, access to the services of third-party communications, and so on. Compare the network capacity to the aggregate volume the system will use, adjusting for the expected growth over the enterprise's planning period for the network.

Compare existing bandwidth and capacity to the proposed requirements of this system and all other proposed projects that fall into the planning horizon. Map existing, planned, growth, and peak requirements for each system or application area against the distribution matrix and existing network-configuration diagrams.

For large or complex networks, undertake a detailed study to evaluate available capacity, bottlenecks, and potential business impact associated with the network. If benchmark and stress testing have not yet been done as part of the test of critical environment elements, they can now be performed. Additionally, site visits can be made to other organizations running software products similar to those proposed. This will validate vendor claims of performance and capacity requirements.

Incorporate the bandwidth requirements into the network-configuration plan. Also, incorporate any revisions to both the network and technical architecture and to the acquisition-planning documents. Prepare the necessary documents to acquire both the network components and infrastructure, including the cabling plant.

Set Workstation Access

Use the network configuration plan to determine configuration requirements that allow the workstations to access the network services. Prepare set-up instructions for the entire suite of required products, software, and hardware. Assemble the products and have the installers test the set-up instructions.

Determine and test all network-access requirements now. They will be implemented as specified in the transition plan. Grant developers and end users access to the network with the necessary privileges and authorities as specified in the security and integrity design.

Update Name Servers

A name server provides the addresses of resources on the network, such as database servers, routers, gateways, printers, faxes, and modems. The domain specifies the region for which the name is unique. Ensure that all domains and servers are integrated into the network and named consistently within the enterprise guidelines. Update the corresponding network documents with the new names. Maintain detailed audit logs of the changes to minimize conflicts and violations of security or access.

Update Routers and Gateways

Routers provide access across networks, choose the most efficient path, and can also serve as fire walls to isolate portions of the network. Gateways provide access to the host in a three-level architecture, to WANs, and to networks outside the enterprise. Update the routers and gateways with the network addresses to provide developers and end users the appropriate access to the servers, processors, and services. Maintain detailed audit logs of all changes that were made and update the corresponding documents for network configuration.

Review Network Configuration

Review the entire network configuration that the system requires before granting access to the services. Make sure that each document and its change log is incorporated into the enterprise-network documentation.

Identify the skill requirements for developers and end users. Convey this information to the transition team, so that they can incorporate network training in the training plan.

Grant Access to Users

The appropriate network administrators execute the updates, as necessary. These will permit access to users, providing each user with the appropriate grants and security specified in the security and integrity design.

The network administrators notify the developers when the network configuration is complete and services are available to support the project. The network administrator also provides the documentors and transition team with escalation procedures, network help, and trouble reporting procedures which can be incorporated into training and documentation.

Authorize Users

The developers and end users should be granted access to all required network services and facilities. Schedule any necessary training for the developers. End-user training will be carried out according to the transition plan.

CREATE TEST DATA AND DOCUMENTS

This task (illustrated in Fig. 36.5) develops the necessary test data that will verify the system operation and those supporting documents that aid system operation. The data will be used during the system and acceptance tests to check that the system operates correctly. The documents will be tested with the system to ensure that their contents are correct. This task develops:

- Test cases and conditions as well as the data used during testing.
- User guides that will be tested with the application.
- Necessary instructions for computer-operations personnel to ensure the successful system operation.

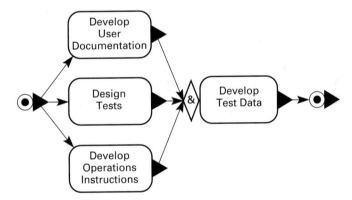

Figure 36.5   A method to Create Test Data and Documents.

Develop User Documentation

User documentation describes how to use the system. The documentation should be brief, employing simple sentences and nontechnical language. The best documentation writers are those who can write, not those who know the system best.

Develop the documentation in time for the users to test the documentation while they test the system. Clarify which version of the system the documentation describes. Include provisions for notifying the users of changes to the documentation that result from changes to the system or errors in the documentation.

Define what documents are required—typically, user guides, quick reference cards, installation guides, and tutorials. Determine the scope and objectives of each user document and the form in which it will appear. Examples include online help, computer-based training modules, paper manuals, plastic-coated cards, instructions on a disk label or disk holder, and so on.

Provide online help. The user often does not have access to paper documents, which tend to get separated from the system and the user.

In a GUI environment, a user can frequently choose from many paths to complete an operation. The user guide should describe at least one path for the novice user plus shortcuts and customization for those more experienced.

Include a guide to the manual procedures needed for system operation. The manual instructions may be repeated in the online help. However, the manual instructions must be available to the user when the system is not operating. Describe:

- How to start the system and to exit gracefully.
- Who performs backups of what, how frequently, and what the user must do. (For example, the procedure may include that backups are controlled from a central site and the client computer must be on, but not in use, between 2 A.M. and 3 A.M. local time.)
- How to recognize an error and what to do about it.
- Fallback procedures for use when the system is inoperable.
- How to provide feedback on the system and documentation, and who should receive the feedback.

Design Tests

The construction team designs the systems tests, and the appropriate user groups design their acceptance tests. Review the test conditions required for the test plans. For each condition, develop test cases, specifying the initial conditions, actions, and expected results. In a GUI environment, specifying the initial conditions is done most easily by marking up a screen image. The following should be included:

- Initial and final state of the relevant databases.
- Initial and final display states.
- Initial and final contents of any associated reports and files.

Develop Operations Instructions

A portion of the system operation is not under the user's control. Operations personnel, such as the LAN manager or database administrator, need instructions to perform their system responsibilities, which include:

- System start-up and shut-down.
- Routine system data backup.
- Disk space allocation.
- Communications management.

- Coordination with other systems.
- Error response, including restart/recovery after system failure.
- Security/access control.

Develop and document instructions for these procedures, using existing procedures wherever possible. The documents become part of the operations staff manuals.

Develop Test Data

Generate data to load the test databases. Wherever possible, automated testing tools should be used to create input data. Save the test scripts and database backups in order to speed the testing of new versions. Generating test data can be minimized if the team can use the results from one test cycle as input into another. However, avoid taking this approach to the extreme. By keeping groups of test cycles independent, testing can be continued in one area while others are awaiting correction.

VERIFY SYSTEM CONSTRUCTION

This task (illustrated in Fig. 36.6) ensures that the complete system and each of its components performs according to the user requirements. The goals include:

- Confirming that the system's objectives and requirements have, as a whole, been met.
- Confirming that the individual modules or transactions are free of errors and conform to user requirements.
- Verifying that the system performance is acceptable for the transaction volumes expected in production.
- Verifying that the system can continue to operate under conditions of stress (i.e., the system is operated at or above its maximum processing rate).
- Verifying that the system is usable.
- Verifying that the user and operator documents are complete and accurate.
- Confirming that the end users are willing to use the system in production mode.

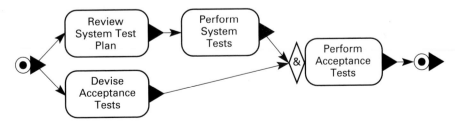

Figure 36.6   A method to Verify System Construction.

Review System Test Plan

Review the system test plan in light of the system that has been built. Determine if the test cycles still apply and if any new test cycles are needed. Check to see that the testing facilities and personnel will be available and, if not, revise the schedule.

Perform System Tests

Perform the system tests according to the test cycles specified in the system test plan. In each test case, compare the output to the expected results. If there are any discrepancies, the construction team should determine which portions of the system require changes. These changes will be made by the database builder, the database administrator, the network builder, the LAN manager, the application builders, or the documentors. In some cases, the team must develop workarounds—particularly if components have been purchased from outside suppliers.

Regenerate the changed portions of the system and repeat the failed test cycle. A failed test case may be assigned to a subsequent test cycle. This process should be repeated until the actual test output for the system corresponds with the expected output or until the users understand and approve any remaining discrepancies. Fully document all test results, including all iterations and their causes.

Devise Acceptance Tests

The users devise their own acceptance tests, based on the acceptance criteria to which they agreed during the system design. The acceptance test plan identified the groups who must perform the acceptance tests. They now develop test cases and specify the initial and expected conditions. The construction team may generate test data for the acceptance tests—possibly reusing the test data developed for the systems tests.

Perform Acceptance Tests

In addition to the user-devised acceptance tests, the users should participate in usability testing, to make sure that the system meets their usability criteria. Perform acceptance testing and check actual results against those expected. Record:

- Errors.
- Whether the user completed cycle or test.
- The difference between the actual versus expected time required to complete the test or cycle.
- Frequency of user problems.
- Number and length of Help references.
- Number of times human help was required.
- Quality of screen wording, layout, or interactions.
- Degradation of service when volume testing.
- Quality and timeliness of data.

- Ease of recovery.
- Enhancements for future releases.

If the system has problems, the users must decide whether to accept the system or request changes. Determine if changes are feasible in this project or whether changes can be deferred until the next release. Remember that when the system is changed, it should be retested to ensure that the correction process did not break other things. Just testing the corrections is *not* sufficient.

BUILD INSTALL AND REMOVE ROUTINES

Building *install* and *remove* routines is necessary. This task (illustrated in Fig. 36.7) recognizes that an application is useless unless installed and may be useless afterwards. The task prepares for both conditions: for installing the application where needed and removing it where no longer useful.

Removal routines restore the user's computer hardware and configuration software to their state before the application's installation. This may involve removing data files and databases, as well as deleting application files and restoring configuration files. A removal routine must check that the information being removed is not, at the same time, being used by another application or database.

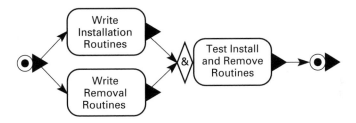

Figure 36.7   A method to Build Install and Remove Routines.

Write Installation Routines

Develop software both to install the system and upgrade the system installation at all server/client sites. Remember that the equipment at the client site is controlled by the users—not the construction team. The software should be able to detect:

- A previous version of the system components.
- Duplicate components.
- The same components that have been installed by another system that this system also uses.
- Components with the same name, but not the same contents, that may be used by another system.

The installation routine should tag any files it creates with the name of the system that created it. Similarly, it should tag any section of existing configuration files that it changes. Thus, the installation routine can more easily determine what it can upgrade. For removal routines, this makes it easier to detect what should be cleaned up when the system must be removed, in whole or in part, from the client or server site.

If some components are optional, the installation routine should let the user specify what portions to install (or omit) from the installation. A commercial installation routine may be used for which an installation script is developed. Follow organization standards for the installation look and feel as you would for any other part of the system.

Write Removal Routines

Removal routines delete all or part of the installed system along with the files created by the system. Removal routines may also be written to clean databases. Some files used by the system may also be used by other systems. Therefore, the removal routine should first determine if it is safe to remove files or portions of configuration files. One way is to identify the files or sections that are candidates for removal. Then, the list can be presented, giving the operator the option to select (or deselect) before removing the items.

Test Install and Remove Routines

Both installation and removal routines must be tested in a variety of client configurations. In testing the mechanism, two aspects are important. First, check that the correct versions of the system are installed. Second, check that the partial installation and removal routines are working correctly.

PREPARE TRANSITION PROCEDURES

This task (illustrated in Fig. 36.8) has three goals. These goals are to ensure that the system has everything it needs in order to work, to ensure that the users know how to use the system, and to recover from system failure so that the users can continue their

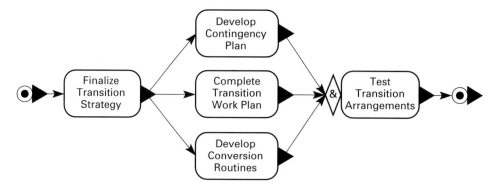

Figure 36.8 A method to Prepare Transition Procedures.

work. Training is covered in another task. This task ensures that the system will work by:

- Completing all plans for the system's transition into production, including both a detailed work plan for transition activities and a contingency plan to cover a failure of the new system.

- Developing procedures to convert data from existing formats to the formats required by the new application and upgrading previous releases of the system, writing bridging and conversion modules, and, where needed, programs.

- Testing and rehearsing all transition arrangements prior to their actual use.

Transition is on the critical path of the project plan, because the bridges and conversion routines can be complex. This is especially true when the data must be converted from one database-management system to one or more different systems residing on different platforms. Do not wait until the system design stage is completed before preparing transition procedures. Otherwise, the transition procedures will not be ready when the rest of the system is ready to implement.

Finalize Transition Strategy

Review the transition strategy once more with users before proceeding further with transition planning. Discuss any new considerations based on the system construction. Update the list of tasks that need to be carried out during transition, breaking these down by system and location. Include items such as:

- Machines to be installed or moved.
- Software to be installed or updated.
- Communications equipment and software to be installed.
- Data to be prepared.
- Operational procedures to be prepared and presented.

Hold review meetings with all the parties involved to develop the list of tasks. Visualize how the transition will take place. Look at how the system will operate through the day, week, and month. Is there enough time to do everything? Do additional procedures need to be developed? Does additional equipment need to be purchased?

Develop Contingency Plan

All critical applications should have a plan for recovering from any failures of the new application. This recovery usually involves restoring the previous systems and procedures back to their status before the transition started.

The need for a contingency plan and the level of detail required for it depend greatly on the circumstances surrounding the new application. If the application is simple and its operation not critical to the organization, a contingency plan is probably unnecessary. If the application is complex, has a significant probability of failure, or is essential to the day-to-day functioning of the organization, a contingency plan is mandatory.

Develop the appropriate contingency procedures to cover each step of the transition process. Then, make sure these procedures are correct by carrying out a structured walk-through. Finally, assess the risk of failure (and its associated loss) and establish whether the risk is acceptable. If the risk is unacceptable, modify the contingency plan.

Complete Transition Work Plan

Complete a detailed plan for performing the transition. This plan lists the specific steps necessary to move the application into production. The plan reflects the general transition strategy defined previously.

Define and document the steps that users will perform. Many of these procedures involve data preparation tasks that must be performed manually. Other procedures cover operational tasks, such as reconfiguration or relocation of equipment and people. They also establish communications' arrangements (both through the network and human interface) and the backup of critical data. In addition, procedures must be developed to implement the contingency plan. This plan should address restoring old systems and procedures after the new application has failed. Include in the work plan a provision that explains these steps to the users who will perform them.

The resources required to complete each step on the work plan should be listed. This list should include the dates planned for starting and completing each work step, as well as the milestone events in the transition. The schedule should be confirmed with the stakeholders.

Develop Conversion Routines

The data transition and bridging routines were designed in the transition plan. Build or set up the programs or utilities identified to convert existing data. Build new programs or interface modules to construct bridges to and from new databases. Where possible, make the bridging process automatic, so that it will not require ongoing attention from an operator or programmer.

To eliminate errors for the conversion and bridging programs, use the same approach as was used to build the main system. This includes:

- Designing the unit test first.
- Developing the program or module.
- Inspecting the product and having a second, independent person inspect it also.
- Reviewing the test plan and ensuring its validity.
- Testing the program or module with data.

If the existing systems require updating, work with a maintenance programmer from the existing system to review the test plan. Test the migration to ensure that the data can be moved from the old environment to the new. Since conversion always takes place at a hectic time, the team will want to avoid any unnecessary, last-minute glitches.

Test each conversion and bridging program. Manual procedures generally involve collecting and converting data by hand—a time-intensive task. Test manual procedure migration plans and start executing them.

Test Transition Arrangements

The transition plan should be tested before you start the System Transition stage. In this test, all the plan's steps should be executed, following the same sequence as the actual transition. Those users who will be performing the transition tasks should participate in the test. This will help train them in the process and clear up any of their misunderstandings. All computer routines should be executed to verify that they operate correctly. By noting the time required to perform each transition task, you will be able to verify the planned schedule for the transition.

DEVELOP TRAINING

This task (illustrated in Fig. 36.9) identifies the points at which the system users require training and determines how to meet their training needs. This project may reveal new skill requirements and responsibilities for users that were previously not required. Such situations are common when an organization moves computing from the computer room to the desktop or from isolated desktop computers to the shared environment of client/server systems.

One stated reason for moving to a graphic user interface (GUI) environment is that it is easier to learn. What that really means is that the *second* GUI system is easier to learn, because users already know the basics of using a GUI. There is still a learning curve, especially when the users must learn how to use new equipment, new approaches to doing the job, and a new interface. Training should not be neglected just because GUI interfaces are reputed to be intuitive.

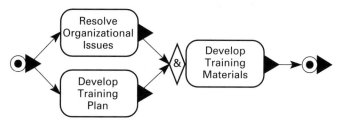

Figure 36.9   A method to Develop Training.

Resolve Organizational Issues

The transition plan identifies issues of cultural change that emerge from the new system and must be addressed. Any additional issues that arise from design changes or transaction arrangements should now be identified. These include new or modified roles, responsibilities, skill requirements, and the readiness for change. Role assignments should be filled and incentives developed to ready the organization for change.

Develop Training Plan

The training plan identifies the type of training to provide and the criteria for selecting the people who will be trained. Update the training requirements matrix developed for the transition plan with any new skill requirements and role assignments.

Prepare a training curriculum that outlines the courses and the topics to be covered in the training sessions. Describe the training materials and instructor qualifications for each topic. Determine how many copies of the training material and sessions will be needed, based on the number of users, optimum class size, and the time span in which the training must be delivered.

Develop Training Materials

Determine the training methods and whether the materials must be acquired from outside sources, developed in-house, or both. Materials to support each curriculum should be developed and include:

- Presentation slides and wall charts.
- Computer-based training.
- Videotapes and interactive videos.
- Examples and exercises.
- Instruction manuals and instructor notes, student workbooks.
- Relevant documents, such as sections of the user documentation.
- Course assessment forms.

In developing the training materials, remember that people learn through repetition and example. Some guidelines include beginning with a summary of what is to follow. Material should be organized into modules of no more than one hour in length. Mix the lecture with exercises and examples and provide reviews that question the learner's comprehension. Work with the computer-operations group and the construction team to identify the equipment and location to use for demonstrations and exercises.

Chapter 37

System Construction: Management Tasks

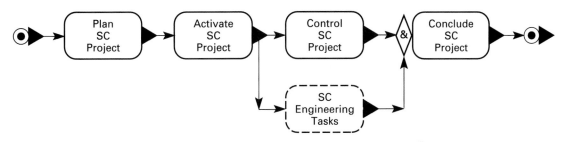

A method for the management tasks of system construction.

PLAN SYSTEM CONSTRUCTION PROJECT

Planning the system construction (SC) project (illustrated in Fig. 37.1) establishes the work plan for the project. The work plan provides the blueprint for the project manager. In this task, the scope and objectives for the work plan are set. The construction aims to produce a system free of defects and acceptable to users.

Define Project

Each of the three teams producing the system develops its own plan in the system design (SD) stage. The builders of the databases, networks, and programs build the *construction*

Figure 37.1   A method to Plan System Construction Project.

plan. The builders of the bridges and conversion requirements build the *transition design,* while the producers of the tests and documentation build the *test plan.* These three plans have already defined the basic structure of this project. In this step, fill in the details of the project objectives, scope, constraints and assumptions, deliverables to be produced, and standards for the deliverables and procedures for carrying out the project.

The primary *objectives* of a system construction project are to build a defect-free system, to integrate it with existing systems, to prepare the system for the users, and to prepare the users for the system. The specific goals are to:

- Build the databases, networks, and programs.
- Build the bridges and the conversion routines and procedures.
- Ensure that the system performs acceptably.
- Prepare for user training.

The *scope* lists the databases, networks, application areas, organizational units or roles, and locations involved. It includes the current systems that this system will replace or interface.

Detail any *constraints,* such as the budget or time limits, the availability of skills, knowledge, and equipment. List the *assumptions* that will be employed in developing the schedule for the system construction project.

There are two types of *deliverables:* those that build the system and those that plan for its deployment. See the tasks and deliverables in Chapter 36 for details of these deliverables and their components.

Establish the documentation and diagramming standards for deliverables. Standards for the deliverable reviews and procedures for revising the project plan were established in the strategy planning project (in Chapter 30). The same standards and procedures are applicable to this project. The strategy plan itself includes the standards for the overall look and feel of the systems being developed under the plan's direction.

Make Project Plan

Identify the tasks, effort, and resources needed to produce the deliverables, establish a schedule and budget, estimate the risk, check the plan against the constraints and assumptions identified earlier, and verify the plan's feasibility.

Identify Tasks, Effort, and Resources

Use the previous chapter to identify the tasks. For each task, determine the amount of time, the resources, and the scheduling requirements. Choose the most appropriate technique for each task.

Do not underestimate the burden of project management and the clean-up tasks. Schedule adequate testing and make sure that the deadlines are reasonable. Identify and include the milestone reviews. Major milestones for an sc project occur at the end of this task, at the end of the Verify System Construction task, and at the project's conclusion. Schedule other milestone reviews, depending upon the project's complexity and scope.

Estimate the size and composition of the teams for construction, transition, and test writing. Keep the core teams small—ideally three to six people. At least one member of each team should be a holdover from the SD project team. Use outside experts and reference groups for specific tasks, rather than enlarging the team. Strongly consider establishing a team of end-user alpha testers who will perform unit and integration testing alongside the construction team.

Establish the Project Schedule

Use estimates of the resource requirements and availability, task dependencies, and effort. Consider timeboxes when developing the schedule, particularly for testing. The schedule will likely be adjusted after the specific team has been established.

Develop a Budget

The project budget should take into account the project schedule and resource usage, equipment and facilities, and, if needed, other expenses, such as travel, office support, and rental of test facilities.

Document Project Risk

Identify the areas of risk in the schedule. In addition to the risks that apply to all projects, look for the following:

- Inexperience with new technology.
- Untested technology.
- Nonstandard "standards."
- Inadequate facilities.
- Design changes.

Build risk reduction into the project plan. If there is high risk, treat the project as if it were much bigger. Manage expectations from the start.

Check Plan Against Assumptions

The constraints and assumptions may require adjusting to produce a feasible schedule. In particular, check the project scope, team composition, and construction facilities.

Obtain Project Approval

Present the project plan to the project sponsor and to the other people required for plan approval. There may be a task force that has been established to oversee the fulfillment of the strategy plan.

Reconfirming support for development is always a good idea, particularly if the project meets resistance. Identify the other stakeholders whose unofficial approval will help ensure the project's success:

- The ultimate *customers* of information and processes within the project scope. Some of them may be alpha testers or acceptance testers.

- Potential *adversaries* of the project. Determine who will lose power or influence if this project succeeds and identify how to gain their confidence and support.

- *Process facilitators.* Determine who supplies information or otherwise supports the processes and clarify how the process will affect them.

ACTIVATE SYSTEM CONSTRUCTION PROJECT

The purpose of activating the system construction project (illustrated in Fig. 37.2) is to launch the project. Install the additional facilities for system development, making sure each system construction team has the right resources to meet their specialized needs. The five SC teams include: the database builders, the network builders, the application builders, the documenters and test data producers, and the system transition team. Use the project kickoff to establish good working relationships between the teams.

Figure 37.2   A method to Activate System Construction Project.

Establish Project Environment

Set up the equipment and facilities for the project. Each of the subteams will need specialized computer facilities. Do not stint on access to the right equipment. The specific hardware, software, and network access will depend on the technical architecture selected. At the start of the project, space and equipment will be needed for team training and team meetings.

Train Team

Train the individual team members in the techniques that they will be using. Combining the project kickoff with a session directed at the whole team is a good idea. Here, you should identify the areas in which the subteams will have to coordinate their work with other subteams. Make sure that each team member knows how to use the software to help produce project deliverables and work products.

CONTROL SYSTEM CONSTRUCTION PROJECT

This next task (illustrated in Fig. 37.3) completes the project by controlling its progress—taking corrective actions within the scope of the plan. It also identifies the need to change the critical project elements: the objectives, the scope, the budget, or the time span in a timely manner. In addition, the project may have to coordinate with the results of prior projects and with concurrent events outside the project. The Control System Construction Project task manages this coordination.

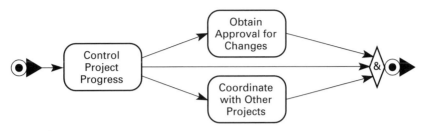

Figure 37.3   A method to Control System Construction Project.

In an SC project, the main emphasis is to maintain the construction team's momentum and to ensure that everything comes together for a smooth transition. In addition, this task allows for coordinating changes that may be required because of the testing that takes place during the SC project.

Control Project Progress

Project control is vital to the success of the project. Project control involves assigning project tasks, monitoring task and deliverable status, checking progress against the plan, and periodically reporting progress to the project sponsor and other stakeholders.

The project manager must keep the project moving forward, motivate the team, and keep the support of the project stakeholders. Project control should minimize bureaucracy. The team should devote most of the time to performing the project, not filling out project-control reports.

This project should have a finite time and expense budget. Do not let excessive requests for "small" increases in scope derail the project. Record requests that are not recommended for inclusion as *enhancement requests*.

Assign Project Tasks

The project plan typically includes initial task assignments. During the course of the project, these are often adjusted and amended as the plan confronts reality. Circulating a weekly assignment sheet should be done either before or during the *short* weekly staff meeting. Items to discuss at a status meeting include the following:

- Major events.
- Action items.
- Recap of expected deliverables.
- Actual achievements and variances.
- Overall project assessment.
- Next week's deliverables.
- Action items for next meeting.

Monitor Tasks and Deliverables

The project's progress and management issues are visible. Post schedules, reports, and issues, and assign all issues a due date. Review whether an answer to an issue is overdue.

Check Progress Against Plan

Compare the resources used and the time spent to the planned resources and time. Identify progress that is ahead of schedule, as well as tasks that are behind schedule or likely to fall behind. Determine any delays that are externally imposed and identify any unproductive work.

Report to Sponsor

Give periodic progress reports to the project sponsor and keep influential stakeholders informed as well. Reports to the sponsor should include the time spent by each team member for each task, the deliverables produced, and a completion estimate for each task.

Obtain Change Approval

The project plan is a contract between the SC team and the project sponsor. Make minor corrections, such as changing meeting times, trying alternative techniques, or getting users more involved—within the original plan. However, the difference between planned and actual performance may be too great to overcome by working smarter. Corrective actions that change the schedule, the cost, the scope, or the deliverables require a formal change approval.

Look for early warning signs that the project will not meet the plan. For example, the team might not be completing deliverables by the milestone dates, or the quality may be low. The cause could be inadequate resources, poor productivity, an unreasonable schedule, or an inappropriate scope. Identifying the root cause is important in order to come up with the right solution.

Examine each proposed solution for its impact on the project's objectives, scope, benefits, schedule, quality, and resources. Changes to scope, timing, and resource use may affect other projects. Therefore, the development-coordination group should also review the proposal. In reviewing its impact, remember to repeat tasks that were thought to be complete.

Decide which actions to recommend to the project sponsor. Justify the proposed change in business terms. Make the sponsor and steering committee aware of the alternatives and the consequences of not making the change.

When the project sponsor, steering committee, project manager, and development-coordination group agree to the changes, publicize the new plan to everyone on the project. Notify the SC project team, reference groups, stakeholders, and any business users and technical specialists whose schedules may change as a result of the plan change. Work closely with the project sponsor.

Coordinate with Other Projects

A project does not happen in isolation. The project manager is the liaison between this SC project and other developments that might affect the direction, contents, and schedule of the project. Maintain close contact with concurrent SC projects whose scope may overlap this project—as well as those system design projects whose contents may be affected by what is learned in this SC project. Be aware of other work that will affect the availability of resources, especially access to computer and network resources and testers.

CONCLUDE SYSTEM CONSTRUCTION PROJECT

Concluding the system construction project (illustrated in Fig. 37.4) creates an orderly finish to the project, frees project resources for other activities, and ensures that its participants are recognized for their participation. While most projects reach completion, occasionally a project will have to be stopped before its objectives are achieved. For example, this could occur if a mid-project review indicates that a project should be suspended or canceled. The environment must be such that the project manager can recommend such an action, if justified.

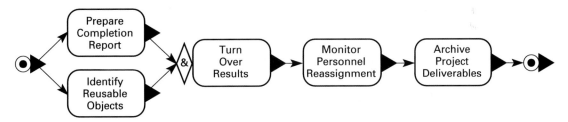

Figure 37.4   A method to Conclude System Construction Project.

Prepare Completion Report

The *project completion report* contains sections for management summaries, deliverables for subsequent projects, evaluation of resource performance, the project analysis, and project metrics. Prepare these according to the organization's requirements and conventions. The management summary section should include an overview, summaries of analysis findings, project metrics, and recommendations.

The deliverables section describes the system that was produced and the organization and environment changes needed to deploy the system: project background, scope, objectives, conclusions reached, and outline of the plan for transition and training. Summary descriptions of the major deliverables should be placed in an appendix containing the databases, applications, networks, and the results of systems and acceptance testing. Include the transition and training plans and note where the system documentation can be found.

The project analysis section recaps the project performance. Include the business accomplishments, lessons learned, a summary of metrics, and any unusual or interesting project aspects.

The project is not complete until the steering committee and executive owner accept its results. An executive presentation of the report prior to final sign-off may also be required.

Identify Reusable Objects

Everything produced during this project has the potential for reuse. Review the project deliverables with an eye to reusability. Make sure that they are cataloged and stored in a form in which they can be accessed for reuse.

Turn Over Results

In addition to deploying the system, there will most likely be follow-up projects to maintain the system and incorporate enhancements that were previously planned or suggested by the team and users during system testing. Determine what these projects will require using the deliverables, work products, open issues (noting compromise decisions), lessons learned, and any other applicable documentation.

Monitor Personnel Reassignment

Take care of project members. This increases the chance of success for other projects. More importantly, it is the right thing to do. Personnel actions to consider include performance reviews, recognition and rewards, and the placement of team members at project's conclusion.

Archive Project Deliverables

If it was important to do, it probably is important to keep. Identify how and where to archive project deliverables and work products within the organization. Work with a development-coordination unit to ensure that the correct versions of shared objects are passed to other teams and that they know how to access and update these objects.

Chapter **38**

System Transition: Engineering Tasks

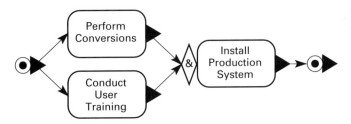

A method for the engineering tasks of system transition.

PERFORM CONVERSIONS

Conversions must be performed (illustrated in Fig. 38.1) to:

- Load the databases with the data required for system operation.
- Avoid errors or inconsistencies in the converted data.
- Allow for recovery from failure of the conversion or the new system.
- Minimize disruption of normal business activities.

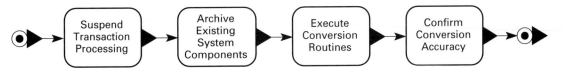

Figure 38.1 A method to Perform Conversions.

A distributed-database, client/server architecture may not be able to accomplish this task in one shot. The transition plan identifies how frequently and at what locations this task should be repeated. It also indicates the temporary bridges that may be required to support the gradual conversion.

Suspend Transaction Processing

During the transition from an existing to a replacement system, all activities associated with the existing system must usually be suspended in order to convert the data for the new application. However, suspending operations often causes major business disruptions. For this reason the suspension must be carefully planned and its length minimized. Inform users well in advance and instruct operations staff when to disable the existing application.

In certain circumstances, suspending all processing activity associated with an application may not be possible. However, the transition plan should have identified these circumstances and developed an appropriate strategy. Usually this strategy involves some type of phased transition, in which a particular grouping of either users or functionality is converted first, followed by another grouping, and so on.

A phased conversion implies that the old and new applications must be operated in parallel for a period of time. Such a phased conversion is difficult to execute, generally requires more resources to complete, and must be carefully planned and managed. This is particularly difficult when the new client/server system accesses distributed data, only some of which is converted at a time. Substantial problems of data integrity will need to be resolved when the system's next phase goes online.

Archive Existing System Components

The old system's components of developed software, purchased software, files, and hardware should remain easily accessible. If the new business system fails, it can be reinstalled. Even after the new system is in place and return to the old system is impossible, the documentation, files, and software should still be kept. In either case, procedures to implement archiving or storage should be in place and the following guidelines considered:

- All file names should be changed during the period between conversion to the new system and the point of no return. This change prevents an inadvertent use of the old system.

- Key transactions that are in the old system, but not the new, should direct the user to the new system. Make this change during conversion.

- Keep data files along with enough supporting documentation and software to decipher them as required for audits, government reporting, or management requests for trend analysis. Keep the data well past the point of no return.

Execute Conversion Routines

Convert data for the new system, using the conversion routines and procedures developed by the transition team. Plans for recovering from failures of conversion routines should be in place before the actual execution begins.

Automated conversion efforts may require extensive use of computer resources on a one-time basis. Make arrangements well in advance to obtain the required resources.

Manual conversion tasks may require many people and take substantial time. Often, manual conversion tasks can start independently of the existing system backup. Prepare a schedule for completing large manual conversions, making sure that the personnel are available. Detailed instructions and, if necessary, training should be provided to assist manual conversion. The schedule for manual conversion should allow enough time to minimize the gap between turning off the old and turning on the new system. Track the progress against the schedule.

Confirm Conversion Accuracy

Carefully review the result of the conversion, step by step, before committing to production. The conversion procedures should specify the methods to check that the conversion is accurate and complete. Assign enough staff to conduct the review.

CONDUCT USER TRAINING

Future users of the new system must be trained in its operation, as illustrated in Fig. 38.2. In addition, system-support personnel, such as help-desk staff, must be trained in both the system operation and the activities related to its installation, removal, adjustment, and interaction with other systems. The number and frequency of the training sessions should be based on the need to meet the skill requirements and shortages identified in the training plan.

Figure 38.2　　A method to Conduct User Training.

Schedule Training Sessions

Based on the requirements determined in the training plan, identify the individuals who will receive the training. Contact each person to explain the purpose of the training and to determine the most convenient time and place for their attendance.

Determine the number and location of each type of training session, based on the number of trainees, capacity of each session, and availability of equipment and instructors. User supervisors will coordinate attendance at training sessions and be involved in determining the most convenient training schedule.

All organizational issues should be resolved before training starts. Morale problems could occur if someone does not receive training because of a planned, but unannounced, organizational change.

Conduct Training

Training sessions should be carried out using the training materials prepared in the construction stage and following the outline described in the training curriculum. Participant feedback will identify needed revisions to curriculum, materials, training facilities, and trainers.

Develop Permanent Training

Establish permanent arrangements for training future users of the system. Usually, permanent training materials for new users are merely copies of the training materials used in the transition stage. If future training requirements are significant, it may pay to modify the materials to incorporate feedback gathered in the initial training. References to the prior system should be deleted from the materials, since they are irrelevant to a new user.

INSTALL PRODUCTION SYSTEM

The production system must be installed. This task (illustrated in Fig. 38.3) prepares for system production. The application itself is first distributed only to the beta-test sites. Any distributed databases necessary for the beta operation of the system are distributed to the appropriate sites. Since client/server applications typically run on systems with different configurations, it is good practice to check out the system at selected sites before distributing the application to all user sites. The beta-test cycles follow the schedule of the beta-test plan.

Once the beta tests are completed, the application and databases are distributed to the users—possibly in a phased implementation. At this time, responsibility for system maintenance passes from the development group to operations support.

Configure System Environment

Install the new technical architecture components to support the system. Operation of the system may require changes in the systems environment. Typical hardware changes include the installation of additional workstations or upgrading the capabilities of existing workstations, additional disk storage or new storage devices, replacement of current computers, and the addition of new communications equipment.

System software modifications usually involve changes to the client and server operating system files. These modifications are caused by new developments in hardware, software, and network configuration, the installation of new database servers, middleware, and new or modified communications software. Record the configuration requirements for each category of client and server computer.

Activate Help Support

Tasks that are usually performed by operations staff in host-based environments are often performed by the users themselves in client/server environments. The help support provides

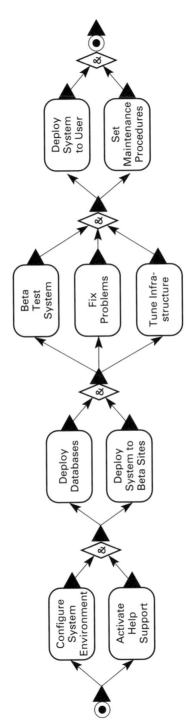

Figure 38.3 A method to Install the Production System.

technical expertise and assists the users as needed. Brief the help-support staff on the new system operation. In addition to receiving the same training that the system users receive, the help-support staff should also have:

- User documentation.
- Operations documentation.
- Configuration requirements.
- Backup schedule.

Help support must be operational before the system is distributed to the beta sites.

Deploy Databases

Databases must be installed at *all* locations necessary for beta testing the system, because these sites must be able to verify that the distributed databases work with their equipment. As a result, the databases may be installed at sites where there are no testers.

Deploy System to Beta Sites

The beta sites were identified when the test plan was developed. Contact the sites to make sure that the people are still available for beta testing and that their equipment configuration still meets the testing needs. Finding replacements for some sites might be necessary. Distribute the installation package to the beta sites. Include the following:

- Installation routine that the beta tester will use to install the application.
- Removal routine that the tester will use to remove some or all of the application from the user's equipment.
- User guides.
- Beta test schedule, highlighting the cutoff dates for each beta cycle.
- Instructions for reporting errors.
- How to contact help support.

Emphasize that enhancements go on the wish list, not the problem report.

Beta Test System

The system should have been thoroughly tested for system-related bugs. In beta testing, the beta sites check for environmental bugs. Some beta sites may have already helped to debug the system in the unit and integration testing, and some may have participated in the systems and acceptance tests.

The beta testers now check the system for installation, removal, workstation configuration, for access to the databases, and for compatible operation with the other software on their workstation.

Fix Problems

The construction teams fix the problems that the beta testers report. The database team corrects problems with the databases. They may work with the transition team if the problem is related to conversion or bridging routines. The application builders correct problems with other processing, including the user interface. The documenters correct errors in the user guide and online help.

Tune Infrastructure

Some problems may be related to the network connections, configurations, or hardware capacity. The network builders modify the network and network-related configurations. The central operations staff (e.g., LAN manager and database administrator) may need to resolve some performance problems. Equipment problems may be solved by purchasing additional memory, disk space, and so on—though such purchases may require approval from the steering committee.

Deploy System to Users

After the beta-test cycle, the executive owner of the system will decide whether to deploy the system. A positive decision means that the remaining servers and user sites will receive the system components, according to the schedule in the system-deployment plan.

Install and configure any additional servers. Install the necessary hardware, networks, and databases at the user sites specified by the system-deployment plan. Check that these components work properly before installing the application at the user sites.

Distribute the system installation package to the user sites. Depending upon the organization, either an installation team or the users themselves will install the application. The package should include:

- Installation files.
- Removal routines.
- User guide.
- Instructions for reporting errors.
- How to contact help support.

Set Maintenance Procedures

Prepare to turn over system maintenance to the maintenance staff. Place the components of the new system in protected libraries, including the source files, installation files, and all supporting material. These source files should not receive any further changes. Maintenance personnel should make any corrections or modifications by creating new versions of the files. This change should occur regardless of plans for a subsequent system deployment at another site.

Once in production, no executable file should be directly changed. A new version, perhaps created from a copy of the old version, is the only acceptable way to get a new or different functionality from application software that is already in production.

Establish procedures and responsibilities for reporting and evaluating change requests. Requests include fixes and enhancements. The maintenance staff should review the strategy plan and the design-area development plan to determine whether the enhancement requests and fixes are best handled by iterative development projects already on the schedule or whether new initiatives are necessary.

Chapter 39

System Transition: Management Tasks

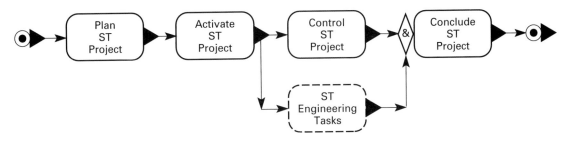

A method for the management tasks of system transition.

PLAN SYSTEM TRANSITION PROJECT

This first task (illustrated in Fig. 39.1) puts the finishing touches on the system transition (ST) plan. The transition strategy was first established during strategy planning (in Chapter 30) and provided the starting point for the transition plan produced during the system design (SD) project (in Chapter 34). Now the details of the transition work plan will provide the blueprint for the ST project manager.

Much of the plan should be completed by the time this task begins. By this point, actual people, real resources, and definite dates should be assigned. The risks too should

Figure 39.1   A method to Plan System Transition Project.

already be calculated. By anticipating the unexpected, you can ensure that the plan's acceptance is a mere formality.

Define Project

The transition work and training plans developed in the system construction (SC) stage have defined this project's outlines. In this subtask, fill in the last minute details. The primary *objective* of a system transition project is deploying the system successfully, which includes:

- Training the users in new skills and responsibilities.
- Converting existing systems and data stores to the new requirements.
- Installing the new system at user sites at a rate compatible with the organization's ability to manage the change.

The *scope* lists the databases, networks, application areas, equipment, facilities, organizational units or roles, locations involved, and the current systems that will be replaced by this system.

Detail any *constraints,* such as the budget or time limits and the availability of skills, knowledge, or equipment. List the *assumptions* that will be employed in developing the schedule for the system transition project.

The deliverables and their components are indicated in Chapter 38. Establish the *standards* for deliverables. *Procedures* for revising the project plan were established in the strategy planning project (see Chapter 30). The same procedures apply to this project.

Make Project Plan

Identify the tasks, effort, and resources needed to produce the deliverables, establish a schedule and budget, estimate the risk, check the plan against the constraints and assumptions identified earlier, and verify that the project plan is feasible.

Identify Tasks, Effort, and Resources

Use Chapter 38 to identify the tasks. For each task, determine the effort, the resources, and the scheduling requirements. Choose the most appropriate technique for each task.

Do not underestimate the time and effort required for project management and cleanup tasks. Make sure that the beta-test deadlines are firm and reasonable. Identify and include the milestone reviews. Major milestones for an ST project occur at the completion of user training, at the end of system installation, and at the project's conclusion. Other milestone reviews may be scheduled, depending upon the project's complexity and scope.

Verify the composition of both the transition and beta test teams. The transition team should be comprised of holdovers from the system construction stage, and the beta testers should already be identified.

Establish the Schedule

Check the transition work-plan schedule using estimates of resource requirements and availability, task dependencies, and effort. Consider timeboxes when developing the schedule—particularly for testing.

Develop a Budget

The budget should take into account the project schedule and resource usage, the equipment and facilities, and, if needed, other expenses, such as travel, office support, and test-facility rental.

Document the Project Risk

Identify the areas of risk in the schedule. In addition to the risks that apply to all projects, look for the following:

- Inexperience with new technology.
- Untested technology.
- Inadequate testing facilities.
- Insufficient user involvement.
- Inadequate conversion quality.

Build risk reduction into the project plan. If risk is high, treat the project as if it were much bigger. Manage expectations from the start.

Check the Plan Against the Assumptions

The constraints and assumptions may require adjusting to produce a feasible schedule. In particular, check the rate of system deployment to users, conversion expectations, and availability of test facilities.

Obtain Project Approval

Present the ST project plan to the project sponsor and to the other people required for plan approval. A task force may be established to oversee the fulfillment of the strategy plan.

ACTIVATE SYSTEM TRANSITION PROJECT

The activation task (see Fig. 39.2) starts to move the system into production. In this task, training facilities are set up and the production environment is put in place. A major objective is smoothing the way for changes to user roles and user interaction.

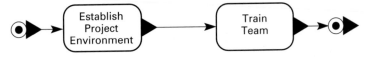

Figure 39.2   A method to Activate System Transition Project.

Establish Project Environment

Set up the equipment and facilities for the project. Check that the production facilities and the space and equipment for training are in place at training locations. The project team's productivity will be increased if each team member has easy access to the following software:

- Word processor.
- Spreadsheet.
- Diagrammer.
- Presentation.
- Project management.
- The methodology.

Train Team

Train the team members in the system and its equipment. Combining the project kickoff with a training session is a good idea. Each team member should know how to use the new system.

CONTROL SYSTEM TRANSITION PROJECT

This next task (illustrated in Fig. 39.3) gets the ST project done by controlling the project's progress, taking corrective actions within the ST plan's scope, and identifying the need to change the critical project elements in a timely manner. These include the objectives, the scope, the budget, or the time span. In addition, the project may have to coordinate with the results of prior or concurrent projects. The Control System Transition Project task manages this coordination.

The main emphasis of this task is to maintain the transition team's momentum and to ensure that everything comes together when the system is installed in the user environment.

Control Project Progress

Project control is vital to the success of the project. Project control involves assigning project tasks, monitoring task and deliverable status, checking progress against the plan, and periodically reporting progress to the project sponsor and other stakeholders.

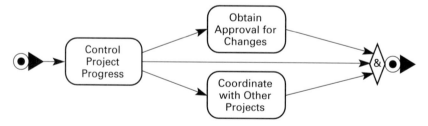

Figure 39.3   A method to Control System Transition Project.

The project manager must keep the project moving forward, motivate the team, and retain support of the project stakeholders. Project control should minimize bureaucracy. The team should devote most of the time to performing the project, not filling out project-control reports.

This project should have a finite time and expense budget. Do not let excessive requests for "small" scope increases derail the project. Record the requests that are not recommended for inclusion as *enhancement requests*.

Assign Project Tasks

The project plan typically includes the initial task assignments. During the project, these are often adjusted and amended as the plan confronts reality. A good practice is to circulate a weekly assignment sheet, either before or during the *short* weekly staff meeting. Items to discuss at a status meeting include the following:

- Major events.
- Action items.
- Recap of expected deliverables.
- Actual achievements and variances.
- Overall project assessment.
- Next week's deliverables.
- Action items for next meeting.

Monitor the Tasks and Deliverables

Keep the project's progress and management issues visible. Post schedules, reports, and issues. Assign all issues a due date. Review whether an answer to an issue is overdue.

Check the Progress Against the Plan

Compare the resources used and the time spent against the planned resources and time. Identify progress that is ahead of schedule, as well as tasks that are behind schedule or likely to fall behind. Identify any externally imposed delays or unproductive work.

Report to the Sponsor

Give periodic progress reports to the project sponsor and keep influential stakeholders informed as well. Reports to the sponsor should include the time spent by each team member for each task, the deliverables produced, and an estimate of time required to complete each task.

Obtain Approval for Changes

The ST project plan is a contract between the team and the project sponsor. Make minor corrections, such as changing meeting times, trying alternative techniques, or getting users more involved, within the original plan. However, the difference between planned and actual performance may be too great to overcome by working smarter. Corrective actions that change the schedule, the cost, the scope, or the deliverables require formal approval.

Look for early warning signs that the project will not meet the plan. For example, the team might not be completing deliverables by the milestone dates, or the quality may be low. The cause could be inadequate resources, poor productivity, an unreasonable schedule, or an inappropriate scope. The root cause should be identified, so that the right solution can be developed.

Examine each proposed solution for its impact on the project's objectives, scope, benefits, schedule, quality, and resources. Because changes to scope, timing, and resource use may affect other projects, the development-coordination group should also review the proposal. In reviewing the impact, do not forget to repeat tasks that were thought complete.

Decide which actions to recommend to the project sponsor, justifying proposed changes in business terms. Make the sponsor and steering committee aware of both the alternatives to and consequences of not making the change.

When the project sponsor, steering committee, project manager, and development-coordination group agree to the changes, publicize the new plan to everyone on the project. Notify the project team, reference groups, stakeholders, and any business users and technical specialists whose schedules may change as a result of the plan change. Work closely with the project sponsor.

Coordinate with Other Projects

A project does not happen in isolation. The project manager is the liaison between the transition project and other developments that may affect the direction, contents, and schedule of the transition project. In particular, be aware of other work that will affect the availability of resources. This is especially true of the people who must be trained, the equipment on which the system will be installed, and the number of people available to handle support calls.

CONCLUDE SYSTEM TRANSITION PROJECT

Concluding the system transition project is the final task of the development cycle. After this, the system belongs to the users. This task (illustrated in Fig. 39.4) creates an orderly finish to the project, frees project resources for other activities, and ensures that the people

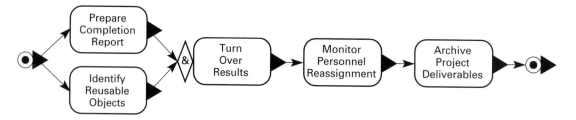

Figure 39.4   A method to Conclude System Transition Project.

who have worked on the project are recognized for their participation. Finally, it turns over responsibility for system operation to the users and for maintenance to the production crew.

Prepare Completion Report

The *project completion report* contains the sections for management summaries, the deliverables for subsequent projects, the evaluation of resource performance, the project analysis, and the project metrics. Prepare these according to the organization's requirements and conventions. The management summary section should include an overview, summaries of analysis findings, project metrics, and recommendations.

The deliverables section describes the system installation: the project background, the scope, the objectives, and the conclusions. The major deliverables should be included in an appendix containing an evaluation of the training presented, the results of the data and systems conversion, and a record of where the system has been deployed.

The project analysis section recaps the project performance. Include the business accomplishments, the lessons learned, a summary of metrics, and any unusual or interesting aspects of the project.

The ST project is not complete until the steering committee and executive owner accept its results. The organization may require an executive presentation of the report prior to final sign-off.

Identify Reusable Objects

Everything produced in the course of this project has the potential for reuse. Review the project deliverables with an eye to reusability. They should be cataloged and stored in a form in which they can be accessed for reuse.

Turn Over Results

The system is now the responsibility of the people who will operate and maintain the system. In addition to the training and documentation they have already received, determine what additional information they may find useful, using the deliverables, work products, open issues (documenting compromise decisions), lessons learned, and any other applicable documentation.

Monitor Personnel Reassignment

Take care of project members. This increases the chance of success for other projects. More importantly, it is the right thing to do. Personnel actions to consider include performance reviews, recognition and rewards, and the placement of team members at project's conclusion.

Archive Project Deliverables

If it was important to do, it probably is important to keep. Identify how and where to archive project deliverables and work products within the organization. Work with a development coordination unit to ensure that the correct versions of shared objects are passed to other teams and that they know how to access and update these objects.

Index

A

Abstract data types (ADTs), 133
Accessor operations, 152–53, 154, 155, 156, 157, 166, 170, 175
ACID test, 479
Acquisition strategy, 468
Activities:
  definition of, 113
  leveling of, 117–19
  paired with products, 115–16
  persistence of, 113–14
  primary versus supporting, 117–19, 121–22
  subtypes of, 119–22
  value added by, 114–15
Activity-directed object-flow analysis method, 125, 127–28
Activity-driven methods, 8
Actors, represented in context diagrams, 32
Ada, 133, 143
ADALINE, 209
Adapter (wrapper), 373
Adaptive resonance theory (ART), 210
Adaptive systems, 205
Add state change, 59
Ad hoc reuse, 340
Advanced Automation System (AAS) project (FAA), 302
Agenda, for end user workshops, 256, 260, 278, 286–87
Aggregation, definition of, 51
Air-traffic control system, U.S., 302
Alexander, Christopher, 341
Algol 60, 132
Algol 68, 133
Algorithms, in neural networks, 209
Alternate advance technique, 268
Analysis. *See also* System analysis
  of behavior, 53–54
  of business direction, 403–5

of domains, 338–39, 350, 438–40
of interviews, 294
Analysis paralysis, 19, 461
ANSI C++, 370
Application frameworks, reuse of, 342
Application generators, 342–43
Application Objects (AO), 354, 359, 365, 373
Application package prototypes, 315
Application software development, 15–17
Application views, 307
Architect tool (James Martin & Company), 11
Artificial intelligence (AI), 197, 199, 204, 379
Artificial neural systems, 205
Assembly language, 225
Association objects, 155–56
Associations:
  creation and termination of, 60–61, 62
  definition of, 41
  design templates for, 152–58
  identification of, 55, 442
  mapping of, 41, 43–44
  reconnection of, 62
  relationship types (relations) of, 41–43, 55
  representation of, 41
Asynchronous message passing, 186
At-most-once execution, 370
Attribute type, 55, 158
Authorization, 480–81, 517
Automated Methods Environment (AME) tool (Ernst & Young), 11
Automated programmers, 342

B

Back office, 315
Back-propagation (back prop) network, 209–11

Balancing, 401
Bandwidth, 515
Batch processing, 312, 389
Behavior:
  analysis of, 53–54
  definition of, 39
Behavioral method, 100, 303–4
Behavioral view of business, 436, 437, 443–46, 472–73, 474
Behavior management, 276
Ben Franklin close (modified T-chart), 277–78
Best effort execution, 370
Beta testing, 400, 484–87, 538, 540–41
Bidirectional associative memory (BAM), 210
Blackboard system, 236
Black-box components:
  activities as, 113–14
  operations as, 71
  reuse of, 341, 352, 401
Boltzman and Cauchy machines, 210
Boomerang technique, 268
Brain State in a Box (BSB), 210
Brainstorming, 268–69, 316
Bridges, 488, 524–25
Budgets:
  for strategy planning projects, 427
  for system analysis projects, 459
  for system construction projects, 529
  for system design projects, 497
  for system transition projects, 545
Business:
  behavioral view of, 436, 437, 443–46, 472–73, 474
  conceptual view of, 436–37, 440–43, 472, 473–74
  desired structure of, 419–20
  development strategies of, 420–22
  direction of, 403–5
  environment of, 417–20, 467
  locations and roles in, 451–52